FAMINE INQUIRY COMMISSION

REPORT ON BENGAL

Famine Inquiry Commission

Report on Bengal

MANOHAR
2026

First published 1945
Reprinted 2026

ISBN 978-81-944962-1-2

Published by
Ajay Kumar Jain *for*
Manohar Publishers & Distributors
4753/23 Ansari Road, Daryaganj
New Delhi 110 002

Printed and bound in India

THE FAMINE INQUIRY COMMISSION

CHAIRMAN

Sir John Woodhrad, K.C.S.I., C.I.E.

MEMBERS

Mr. S.V. Ramamurty, C.I.E., I.C.S.
Sir Manilal B. Nanavati, Kt.
Mr. M. Afzal Husain.
Dr. W.R. Aykroyd, M.D., Sc.D. C.B.E.

SECRETARY

Mr. R.A. Gopalaswami, O.B.E., I.C.S.

CONTENTS

CONTENTS

APPENDICES

INTRODUCTION

The Famine Inquiry Commission was appointed under Ordinance No. XXVIII of 1944, with the following terms of reference:—

To investigate and report to the Central Government upon the causes of the food shortage and subsequent epidemics in India, and in particular in Bengal, in the year 1943, and to make recommendations as to the prevention of their recurrence, with special reference to—

(a) the possibility of improving the diet of the people and the quality and yield of food crops, and

(b) the possibility of improving the system of administration in respect of the supply and distribution of food, the provision of emergent medical relief and the emergent arrangements for the control of epidemics in famine conditions in those areas and in those aspects in which the present system may be found to have been unsatisfactory.

Section 4(1) of the Ordinance, in pursuance of which this report is submitted, provides that "the Commission shall, in the first instance, direct its attention to the Province of Bengal, and......shall make a report and formulate recommendations in relation to that Province in advance of the final report......"

We met for the first time on July 18th, 1944, in New Delhi. After spending some weeks in Delhi, where numerous official witnesses were heard, we went to Bengal on August 11th, and remained there for about 6 weeks. During this period we heard 130 witnesses in Calcutta, 45 official and 85 non-official. We took the opportunity, when in Bengal, of visiting various districts to observe the situation as it existed at that time and to obtain further evidence from witnesses. Chittagong, Tipperah, Dacca, Khulna, and Midnapore were visited by different members of the Commission and 33 official and 55 non-official witnesses were heard in rural Bengal.

A wealth of information about the causes of the famine and other questions included in our terms of reference was obtained in Bengal. But in order to view the past and present situation in Bengal in its proper perspective we felt it necessary to make inquiries in other parts of India. We wished to study procurement, rationing, and food administration in various provinces and states. Further, we are concerned with broad developments in food and agricultural policy in the country as a whole in connection with the prevention of famine in the future. Accordingly, on leaving Bengal on September 26th, we visited in succession Bombay City, Walchandnagar, Bijapur (where famine occurred in 1942-3), Madras City, Calicut, Cochin, Travancore, Tanjore, Bezwada and Nagpur. In all these places we interviewed numerous official and non-official witnesses, studied the existing food situation and food administration, and made inquiries about immediate and long term prospects of producing more food and improving the diet of the people. We returned to Delhi on November 2nd to prepare our report.

At the beginning of the inquiry we decided to hear witnesses *in camera*. The reasons for this decision were given as follows by the Chairman at a press conference on July 31st, 1944:—

"As you know, our terms of reference are wide and I think you will agree with us that our inquiry is of first class importance to the welfare of the people of this country. We have a definite and responsible task to perform and we feel that nothing must be allowed to prejudice its success. You would wish us, therefore, to obtain the best possible evidence of what occurred and why it occurred, so that we may be able to apply our minds to cause and effect and to make recommendations for the prevention of those events which were such an unhappy feature of the year 1943. It is to that task that we are dedicated. We must be allowed to undertake it in the best possible conditions for success. Above all, we must be able to hear, weigh and judge the evidence in a calm and dispassionate atmosphere. I need not remind you of the strong feelings which have been aroused by past events. There has, perhaps unavoidably, been acute controversy and indeed bitterness and recrimination. We want those who give evidence before us to be free to speak their minds fully and without any reserve. It would be most unfortunate if evidence given before us should lead to an atmosphere of controversy, prejudicial to our work and to the manner in which other witnesses give their evidence before us. It would, indeed, be disastrous if the day to day labours of the Commission were to give rise to political or communal controversy or disturb the co-operation of all the different units in carrying out the all-India food plan.

It would be equally unfortunate if things were said and written which would have the effect of retarding the growth of public confidence. In short, our aim and object must be to do our work in a manner best calculated to ensure a report of the highest practical value in the shortest possible time. It is for these reasons that, after careful consideration, I and my colleagues have unanimously decided that our proceedings should be *in camera*. We are confident that the Press will appreciate these reasons and the spirit in which we are approaching our task and assist us by their support and confidence."

We feel that our decision to sit *in camera* was fully justified by results. Witnesses expressed themselves, both in giving oral evidence and in the memoranda prepared for our perusal, with a freedom that might have been restricted had our proceedings been open to the press. Our witnesses included officials, experts in various fields, and representatives of political parties and relief organizations. A great variety of views were put forward about the causes of the famine and the prevention of famine in the future. We are grateful to the many witnesses, official and non-official, who assisted us in our efforts to arrive at the truth.

This report is concerned largely with the past, with the story of the Bengal famine and the causes of that famine. We have also considered the immediate future and made certain immediate recommendations. We propose to deal in a later report with the second part of our terms of reference—the development of agriculture and the raising of standards of nutrition so as to make recurrence of famine impossible. But in order to lay plans for the future it is necessary to understand the past, and hence we feel that our analysis of the causes of the famine should not be regarded solely as a "post-mortem". Numerous lessons which should be of value in the future can be drawn from the sequence of events which led to the tragedy of 1943.

We are grateful to the Governments of the provinces and states visited by us for hospitality, and we wish to thank these and other governments for the readiness with which they have supplied us with information o the wide range of subjects covered by our inquiry.

Acknowledgement to the staff of the Commission may suitably be made when our work is over. We feel, however, that we cannot submit the present report without expressing our appreciation of the services of our Secretary, Mr. R. A. Gopalaswami, O.B.E., I.C.S. Throughout our inquiry and in the preparation of the report he has worked untiringly at every stage and has given us invaluable assistance.

PART I

FAMINE IN BENGAL

CHAPTER I.—THE FAMINE

1. The Bengal famine of 1943 stands out as a great calamity even in an age all too familiar with human suffering and death on a tragic scale. Between one and two million people died as a result of the famine and the outbreaks of epidemic disease associated with it. Many more who escaped death went hungry for many months, fell sick of disease, and suffered in other ways from the disintegration of normal life which the famine occasioned. Famine has, of course, been a common event in the ancient and modern history of India. As far as history stretches back, the country has been a prey to recurrent famines and during the nineteenth century a number of serious famines occurred. The terrible famine of 1769-70, in which it was estimated that 10 millions died out of a population of 30 millions, seriously affected the whole of Bengal, except the districts of Bakarganj and Chittagong in the south-eastern corner, but during the nineteenth century and the twentieth century up to 1943, Bengal was almost entirely free from famine.[1] The Famine Commission of 1880 included the eastern districts of the province, which suffered so severely in 1943, among the parts of the country which "enjoy so ample and regular a rainfall and such abundant river inundation as to ensure the safety of the crops in the driest years". The western districts are liable to scarcity but the only area which has been prone to famine from time to time is the district of Bankura on the western boundary of the province.

2. The most recent famines accompanied by high mortality took place in 1896-7 and 1899-1900. Thus, for over 40 years previous to 1943, India had been free from great famines. The relatively small famines of the last few decades occurred for the most part in rural areas remote from cities, were controlled by effective measures, and hence did not attract much public notice. Famine on a catastrophic scale had indeed faded from memory and was regarded by many as a thing of the past. In 1943 an enemy generally thought to have been finally vanquished reappeared in full strength and its victims thronged in their thousands the streets of the greatest city in India, Calcutta. The horrors of famine at its worst were clearly exposed to the public view. All this came as a great shock to the public in India.

3. The famine affected only the province of Bengal and, to a much less serious extent, the neighbouring province of Orissa. Its general course was as follows: during the early months of 1943, there were reports of distress from various parts in Bengal and apprehension on the part of District Officers that famine was imminent. In May and June it became clearly evident in the districts of Chittagong and Noakhali, situated on the eastern border of the province, and a steep rise in mortality occurred in these districts. By July most of rural Bengal was involved, the death rate in almost all districts being in excess of the normal. From this point onwards the number of deaths rose rapidly and the peak was reached in December, 1943. With the reaping of the *aman* crop in December and the arrival and distribution of supplies from outside the province during the closing months of the year, the famine was relieved, but the death rate remained high throughout the greater part of 1944. Severe epidemics of malaria, small-pox and cholera accompanied the famine. Of these diseases, malaria caused the greatest number of deaths.

[1] We refer here to Bengal according to its present boundaries.

4. In 1943 the mortality rate in certain districts in which starvation was most acute and widespread was higher than in the rest of Bengal, but nearly all parts of the province were affected in greater or lesser degree. While there were variations in the extent of local scarcity, the phenomenal rise in the price of rice which placed it beyond the means of the poor occurred everywhere in Bengal and the poor were nowhere immune from starvation. During the first half of 1944 there was little difference between various parts of Bengal in respect of disease and mortality. Disease associated with the famine became prevalent throughout the province. The famine therefore affected the whole of Bengal and was not confined to certain districts.

5. Only one section of the community suffered from starvation—the poorer classes in the rural areas. Well-to-do people, and industrial workers in Greater Calcutta and elsewhere did not go short of food in 1943. We have estimated in our report that perhaps one-tenth of the population—6 million people—were seriously affected by the famine. As the price of rice rose during the first half of 1943, the poor in the villages without sufficient stocks of grain in their possession found themselves unable to buy food. After an interval during which they attempted to live on their scanty reserves of food, or to obtain money to buy rice at steadily rising prices by selling their scanty possessions, they starved. The majority remained in their homes and of these many died. Others wandered away from their villages in search of food, and the mass migration of starving and sick destitute people was one of the most distressing features of the famine. Thousands flocked into towns and cities; the number in Calcutta in October 1943 was estimated to be at least 100,000. The migration of disorganized masses often occurred in the great famines of bygone ages, but during more recent famines it has been prevented or greatly limited. Its appearance during a famine shows that the famine is out of control.

6. The wandering famine victims readily fell a prey to disease and spread disease in their wanderings. Families were broken up and moral sense lost. In their distress they often sank to sub-human levels and became helpless and hopeless automata guided only by an instinctive craving for food. We shall refer in our report to the problems to which the large scale migration of destitutes gave rise.[1] Here we are simply outlining the general features of the famine and it is sufficient to say that, by degrees, after the height of the famine was passed, the destitutes throughout the province returned to their villages and homes. By the end of November 1943 Calcutta was more or less free from famished wanderers. A residue of homeless and indigent famine victims remained to be cared for in relief institutions in Calcutta and the districts.

7. The turning point of the famine was reached in the closing months of 1943. In November His Excellency the Viceroy, Lord Wavell, brought in the Army to the rescue of the province and in December a bumper crop was harvested. During 1944 recovery took place slowly. But so serious a famine must necessarily have its after-effects on the life of the community. Even when food became available much remained, and still remains, to be done to heal the wounds which it inflicted on Bengal.

8. Such, briefly and barely described, is the tragedy which we are called upon to investigate. We shall fill in the details of the picture in our report and give our views as to the causes of the famine. It is as regards the latter that our responsibilities differ from those of previous Famine Commissions in India, which had the comparatively simple task of reporting on famines due to drought with consequent failure of crops over wide areas, and the straightforward measures necessary to relieve such famines. The causes of the Bengal

[1] The word "destitute" was generally used in Bengal as a noun to describe famine victims. However objectionable as English, the word is convenient and its use has not been avoided in this report.

famine, and the measures taken to relieve it, have given rise to much bitter controversy, centering round the question whether responsibility for the calamity should be ascribed to God or man. We have had to unravel a complicated story, to give due weight to a multiplicity of causes and apportion blame where blame is due.

9. **Scope of the report.**—Our report is designed as follows: first, to provide a background, a brief account is given of the geography, population, and social organization of Bengal. Next, the supply and distribution of rice in Bengal, and the supply position in recent years including 1943, are considered. Since the all-India food situation obviously influenced the situation in Bengal, we describe, in Chapter IV, the development of the former from the outbreak of war up to the end of 1942. In the following 3 chapters an objective account is given of the course of events in Bengal leading up to and culminating in the famine. A chapter on relief follows: here we describe the effect of the famine on the life of the people and the measures taken to relieve distress in Calcutta and the districts.

10. In the following chapter "Looking Back" we review in a critical vein the history of the famine and point out the mistakes made by the governments concerned. The chapter includes sections on "high prices and failure of distribution", "control measures during 1942", "the people and the government", "the situation in January 1943", "the situation in March 1943", "external assistance", "free trade", "distribution of supplies" and "famine relief". All these subjects are critically discussed. In a final chapter we state and sum up our conclusions on the course and causes of the famine.

11. Part II deals with the health aspects of the famine. An estimate of total excess mortality during the famine is made. The subjects considered are "mortality", "causes of disease and mortality", "medical relief and public health work", "the failure to prevent high mortality" and "health in other parts of India". Certain recommendations about the health services in Bengal are made. The health chapters are for the most part written in non-technical language for the benefit of the general reader and certain medical aspects of the famine of interest to the medical profession, notably the treatment of disease associated with famine, have not been fully dealt with. We consider it important that all useful medical and public health experience gained during the famine should be placed on record to add to existing knowledge about the relation between nutrition and disease. At an early stage we drew the attention of the Government of India to this point, and at our request a medical officer with experience of medical relief work during the famine was given the task of preparing a technical report on certain of its medical aspects.

12. In Part III we consider the immediate future. Procurement, rehabilitation and the supply of protective and supplementary foods are discussed and a number of recommendations are made on matters of immediate importance to Bengal. Finally there are a number of appendices which explain and expand certain passages in the main body of the report. These include analyses of production and consumption in 1943 and preceding years, a chronological account of events during 1943 supplied by the Government of Bengal, and a list of witnesses appearing before the Commission.

13. While we have summarized our general conclusions on the famine at the end of Part I, we have not prepared a summary of the report chapter by chapter. The detailed story which has to be told and our critical reviews do not lend themselves readily to summarization. We may add that matter which is not essential to the main theme of the report has been as far as possible excluded.

CHAPTER II.—GENERAL DESCRIPTION OF BENGAL.

1. **Area and Population.**—Bengal is pre-eminent among the provinces of India in two respects; it has the largest number of mouths to feed and produces the largest amount of cereals. The area of the province is 77,442 square miles, rather more than the area of England, Wales, and one-half of Scotland. The population is a little over 60 millions, which is well in excess of that of the United Kingdom, and not much less than the aggregate population of France, Belgium, Holland, and Denmark.

2. **Natural Divisions.**—The province naturally divides itself into four parts, namely, North, West, Central, and East Bengal. North Bengal extends from the Himalayas to the Ganges and, with the exception of the Darjeeling district and an elevated tract on the south-west, consists of a large area of alluvial land which has been subject to great fluvial action. West Bengal falls into two zones, of which the eastern is a low alluvial tract, while the western zone is higher and rocky and becomes more and more undulating the nearer it approaches the uplands of Chota Nagpur. Central Bengal was formerly the Ganges delta; in this area new land formation has almost entirely ceased and the greater part is no longer subject to inundation. It is a land of dead and dying rivers; a land which no longer receives the fertilizing silt from the large rivers which formerly flowed through it. East Bengal is the present delta of the Ganges as well as the Brahmaputra, and it is here that land formation is still proceeding. This is a country of innumerable rivers, large and small, the waters of which overflow the country-side during the rainy season and enrich the soil with their fertilizing silt.

3. **Soils and Rainfall.**—The soils of Bengal are almost entirely of alluvial origin and fall into two well defined types. The more important is known as the "new alluvium" and this is generally easily cultivable. The other type, the "older alluvium", occurs mainly in the west and consists of laterite formations of varying grades of sand and clay, with nodules of haematite. Cultivation of this "older alluvium" in a dry state presents great difficulty; for the most part, therefore, crops are sown on it only during the summer rains, whereas on the "new alluvium", crops are also grown during the winter. The province receives its rainfall from the south west monsoon current and by far the greater part of it falls between the months of June and October. Rainfall ranges from 50 to 60 inches westward of Calcutta and from 60 to 120 inches further east and north.

4. **Communities.**—According to the Census Report of 1941, over 54 per cent. of the people of Bengal are Muslims, about 42 per cent. Hindus, and approximately 4 per cent. members of other communities. The distribution of the population by communities in the four natural divisions of Bengal is shown below:

	Muslims	Hindus	Others
North Bengal	61·3	32·1	6·6
East Bengal	71·9	26·2	1·9
Central Bengal	44·6	53·7	1·7
West Bengal	13·9	79·0	7·1

5. **Rural and Urban Population.**—According to the census figures, the population of the province increased from 42·1 millions in 1901 to 60·3 millions in 1941. While the population of India increased by 37 per cent between the years 1901 and 1941, that of Bengal increased by 43 per cent. Nine-tenths of the people of Bengal live in about 84,000 villages. Of these nearly 70,000 are small

villages, with less than a thousand inhabitants. The urban population numbers about 6 millions. About two-thirds of this number live in Greater Calcutta which includes Calcutta, Howrah, and the industrial areas to the north and south of these cities along the banks of the river Hooghly. Greater Calcutta, moreover, is one of the most important industrial areas in India and includes within its boundaries a very large proportion of India's war factories. Except for Greater Calcutta and the area covered by the coal-fields in the west, the province is predominantly—indeed almost entirely—agricultural; and the vast majority of its enormous population are dependent upon agriculture for their livelihood: In spite of the expansion of industry in the province, the percentage of total population depending on industrial employment for its livelihood is decreasing.

6. **Area under different crops.**—The total extent of the cultivated land in Bengal is nearly 29 million acres. Some of this is cropped more than once, and the total area sown under various crops is normally 35 million acres[1]. The principal crop is rice which accounts for a little less than 26 million acres[2]. In fact, Bengal may be described as a land of rice growers and rice eaters. The area under other staple foodgrains is small; that under wheat, for instance, is less than 200,000 acres, and the total area under food crops of all kinds other than rice is somewhat over 4 million acres. This includes land devoted to the cultivation of fruits and vegetables. The most important non-food crop is jute, which accounts normally for between 2 million and 2·5 million acres.

7. **The Permanent Settlement**[3].—The land revenue payable in respect of the greater part of the land in Bengal was fixed in perpetuity in 1793 and hence the term "Permanent Settlement". The settlement was concluded not with the cultivators but with the *zamindars*, through whom the State's share of the produce of the land was collected. It fixed the revenue at ten-elevenths of the assets, *i.e.*, annual gross rental, and left to the *zamindar* the remaining one-eleventh. In addition, the *zamindars* were given the benefit of any future increase in the assets of their estates resulting from the extension of cultivation or other causes, and the State promised not to make any demand "for the augmentation of the public assessment in consequence of the improvement of their respective estates". The *zamindars* were declared to be the proprietors of their estates subject to the prescriptive or customary rights of the tenants. These rights were not defined in the Regulation but the State reserved the right to legislate for the benefit and protection of the tenants. Finally, the estates became liable to be sold for arrears of revenue if the revenue was not paid by sunset of the latest date fixed for payment; and no excuses, such as drought or famine, were to be accepted for non-payment.

The fixation of the revenue in perpetuity, followed as it was by an increase in the *zamindar's'* profits, encouraged sub-infeudation and brought into existence a large body of tenure holders. In some estates the number of such intermediate interests is extraordinarily large and in some districts 15 to 20 grades of tenure holders are not uncommon. The report of the Simon Commissions pointed out that in some cases as many as 50 or more intermediate interests have been created between the *zamindar* at the top and the actual cultivator at the bottom. The number of rent receivers continues to increase and of recent years there has been a further process of sub-infeudation below the statutory ryot.

Under the t nure holders are the ryots. Formerly the ryots were the actual cultivators but owing to sub-letting and the right of transfer the actual cultivators are to an increasing extent men who are either paying a cash rent corresponding to a full economic rent, or are cultivating under the *barga* system and

[1]Report of the Bengal Land Revenue Commission, 1940, Vol. II p. 88.
[2]*ibid* p. 105.
[3]Based upon the Report of the Land Revenue Commission, Bengal.

paying as rent one half of the produce. The ryots to-day possess a large measure of proprietary rights; the provisions of successive tenancy acts have endowed them with the practical ownership of their land. Under the ryots are the under-ryots, that is, the persons to whom ryots have sub-let. Under-ryots are not tenants at will and are protected by tenancy legislation.

The number of *bargadars* is increasing rapidly and in consequence a large and increasing proportion of the actual cultivators possess no security of tenure.

8. **Cultivation and their holdings.**—The cultivator in Bengal is a small producer. This fact is well known, but it is so important for the purposes of our inquiry that it is necessary to have some idea of the number of families which depend mainly on agriculture for their livelihood but either do not hold any land at all or hold only very small areas. Precise information on this point, however, is somewhat difficult to obtain. In 1939, at the instance of the Land Revenue Commission, Bengal, the Settlement Department investigated the economic position of nearly 20,000 families in typical villages of each district of the province. After studying the results of these investigations, together with certain further information subsequently collected during the 1941 census, we have arrived at the following estimates[1]:—

(i) The number of families in Bengal wholly or mainly dependent upon the cultivation of land for their livelihood is approximately 7·5 millions.

(ii) Less than 2 million families hold more than 5 acres each; about a third of this number hold more than 10 acres each.

(iii) About 2 million families hold between 2 and 5 acres each.

(iv) All the others, constituting about one half of all the families depending wholly or mainly on the cultivation of land, either hold less than 2 acres each or are landless.

(v) The cultivating families of Bengal include roughly about one million families living mainly or entirely as *bargadars*, *i.e.*, crop sharing tenants.

(vi) The number of families living mainly or entirely on agricultural wages is approximately 2 millions.

9. **Poverty.**—These estimates are important, for they afford a clear picture of the classes of cultivators who live, even in normal times, on the margin of subsistence, as well as the probable numbers of these classes. The general consensus of opinion among witnesses who appeared before the Land Revenue Commission, Bengal, was that "5 acres would be the minimum area required to keep the average family in reasonable comfort; but if the land is capable of growing nothing but *aman* paddy, the area required would be about 8 acres". The Commission considered these figures to be substantially correct.

The Land Revenue Commission also observed that "about half of the holdings in Bengal are barely sufficient for the maintenance of the families which own them". This, we have no doubt, applies to all those whose holdings are less than 2 acres, but the same would also apply to some among the 2 million families which cultivate between 2 and 5 acres each. As the Land Revenue Commission more than once observed in their report, "there is not enough land (in Bengal) to go round". We endorse this view.

In later chapters we shall deal with the immediate causes of the famine. It is necessary, however, to draw attention at the outset to the condition of the people in normal times. The standard of living was in general low. Population was growing rapidly, leading to increased pressure on available land suitable for cultivation. How far agricultural production was keeping pace with the increase in the number of mouths to be fed, it is difficult to say. At the

[1]Appendix I.

best of times, however, a section of the poorer classes, both in villages and towns, did not get enough to eat and their diet, largely composed of rice, was of poor nutritive quality. Sir John Megaw, Director General, Indian Medical Service, carried out in 1933 an inquiry into the physical condition of villagers in different parts of India, by means of questionnaires sent to local doctors. Dispensary doctors in Bengal reported that only 22 per cent. of the population were well nourished, while 31 per cent. were very badly nourished. The corresponding figures for India as a whole were 39 and 20 per cent. respectively. Since the assessment of the state of nutrition depended on the subjective impressions of doctors in different provinces, it is difficult to accept these figures as showing conclusively that nutritional conditions in Bengal were worse than elsewhere in India. Nevertheless, the results of the investigation may be quoted as indicating in a general way the unsatisfactory state of nutrition of the people of rural Bengal 10 years previous to the famine.

Poverty and malnutrition left a section of the population with few reserves, material or physical, to meet superimposed calamity. For them there was no "margin of safety" and little possibility of "tightening the belt". The fact that such conditions are common to most other provinces of India, which escaped the famine, does not detract from their fundamental importance. They provide a background against which the events which led to widespread starvation in 1943 must be viewed.

10. **The Administrative Organization in the Districts of Bengal.**—We have been struck by the weakness of the administrative organization in the districts of Bengal owing to the absence of a subordinate revenue establishment comparable with that maintained in those provinces in which the land revenue has been temporarily settled—not permanently settled as in Bengal—and in particular in those provinces in which the *ryotwari* system of land revenue prevails. In the *ryotwari* areas the land revenue, which is liable to periodic resettlement, is paid by the peasant proprietor and not, as in Bengal, by the proprietor of an estate. In these areas it is, therefore, necessary for Government to maintain detailed village records showing *inter alia* the land held and the revenue payable by each ryot, all changes in possession and ownership and the crops grown in each field. This involves the maintenance in such areas of a revenue staff in every large village or group of small villages, as well as an adequate subordinate revenue establishment to supervise and control the work of the village establishments. In Bombay, for instance, each sub-division of a district is divided into *talukas*, the number depending upon the area and population of the sub-division and each *taluka* is divided into circles consisting of 30 to 50 villages. The *talukas* are in charge of officers called *mamlatdars* and a Circle Inspector is attached to each Circle. Finally, each village has a *patel*, an accountant (the accountant is sometimes for a group of villages) and a number of village servants who work under them. Although the primary object of this organization is the assessment and collection of revenue, it is available, and is in fact used, for assisting almost all branches of the district administration in rural areas. In Bengal, as we have indicated, there is no such organization effectively linking the District Officer and the Sub-divisional Officer to the villages in their charge. The only functionary in the Bengal village is the village *chowkidar* who carries out police duties. He is poorly paid, usually illiterate, and in no way comparable with the village officers of the *ryotwari* areas who are persons of established standing with considerable local influence. It is true that there are Circle Officers in Bengal each in charge of an area of about 400 square miles, *i.e.*, two or three to a sub-division. These officers, who were appointed primarily for the purpose of assisting and supervising Union Boards—the smallest unit of local self-government in the province—certainly form a link between the District and Sub-divisional Officers and the villages. The area of their jurisdiction is, however, large, and they have not the assistance of officers corresponding to the Circle Inspectors, *patels*, and accountants in

Rombay. We have drawn attention in some detail to this difference between the subordinate revenue establishment in Bengal and elsewhere for three reasons. First, an organization such as exists in the *ryotwari* areas keeps the Collector of the district in almost day to day contact with life in the villages; secondly, it provides machinery for the collection of reasonably accurate and recent information about crop conditions, and the conditions in the villages generally, and thirdly, it provides a foundation on which to build and expand in an emergency. The existence of such an organization would have been of the greatest value to the Government of Bengal in dealing with the situation as it developed in 1943.

11. **Union Boards.**—Union Boards, the smallest unit of local self-government in the Province, came into existence on the passing of the Bengal Village Self-Government Act of 1919 and combine the functions of the *Chowkidari Panchayats* under the Village Chowkidari Act of 1870 and the Union Committees under the Local Self-Government Act of 1885. At the end of 1939-40 there were 5,120 Union Boards with a gross annual income of Rs. 1·16 crores and an expenditure of Rs. 1·03 crores.

The number of members of a Union Board is normally nine, of whom six are elected and the remainder nominated by the District Magistrate. The duties of a Board are generally speaking, first, the control of *daffadars* and *chowkidars* (village police servants) of the Union, secondly, the carrying out of measures for the sanitation and conservancy of the Union and the improvement of public health within the Union, and thirdly, the construction and maintenance of local roads and water-ways. A Board can also undertake other duties, such as the provision of a water supply, the management of pounds under the Cattle Tresspass Act, the registration of births and deaths, the development of cottage industries, etc. The income of the Boards is derived from rates imposed on owners and occupiers of buildings and from grants made by District Boards and the Government.

Two or more members of a Union Board may be appointed to be a Union Bench or a Union Court for the trial of certain classes of criminal cases and civil suits respectively. Such Benches and Courts have been established in many Unions.

The administration of a Union Board is subject to the superintendence of the District Board, except in matters relating to *daffadars* and *chowkidars*. In regard to the latter, control is exercised by the District Magistrate through the Superintendent of Police or the Sub-Divisional Magistrate. Union Boards are organized in circles and each circle is in charge of a Sub-Deputy Magistrate and Collector. This Officer, known as the Circle Officer, is charged with the duty of supervising and assisting the Union Boards in the discharge of their functions. He forms the connecting link between the Boards on the one hand and the District Magistrate and the Sub-Divisional Magistrate on the other.

12. **Communications.**—Our description of Bengal would be incomplete without reference to one other factor which distinguishes it from most parts of India. We refer to transport and communication in the province. The outstanding features of the transport system are the important country boat traffic on its water-ways and the meagreness of road communications. The nature of the terrain is such that the making and maintenance of roads are extremely difficult. Throughout the greater part of the province roads have to be raised above flood level, frequently to the height of several feet, and have to be provided with a large number of bridges over the smaller rivers and *khals*. Moreover, the larger rivers present an insurmountable obstacle to any system of through communication by road; the largest of them are too wide to be bridged and others are unbridgeable except at a prohibitive cost. In many districts, therefore, the chief means of communications are by country boats supplemented by a limited number of river steamer services.

This is particularly the case in the southern districts which consist of a vast network of rivers and *khals*. Another difficulty is that throughout nearly the whole of the province road metal is not available locally. It has to be transported long distances and this makes the construction and maintenance of metalled roads especially expensive. The province is, therefore, ill provided with roads, and in many parts the transport of goods to and from railway and steamer head is by country boats, a slow but cheap means of communication. Bengal, while it lacks roads, is rich in water-ways.

CHAPTER III.—SUPPLY AND DISTRIBUTION OF RICE IN BENGAL

A.—The process of supply and distribution described

1. In Bengal, as elsewhere in India, about 80 to 90 per cent of the food of the people consists of cereals. The staple cereal of Bengal is rice. Some wheat is also consumed, particularly by the population of Greater Calcutta, but in the province as a whole, wheat accounts for less than 4 per cent of the total cereal consumption. Only a portion of this wheat is grown within the province, the greater part being imported from other provinces or from overseas. The production and consumption of millets are negligible.

2. Bengal, we are told, used to be called the "granary of India". This picturesque description, though misleading in some respects, is certainly justified by the size of the Bengal rice crop. It is believed that the production of rice in India is almost equal to the aggregate production of all other countries in the world, excluding China, and Bengal produces about one-third of the Indian rice supply.[1] During the course of the year, three rice crops are grown in Bengal. Winter rice, which is known as the *aman* crop, is by far the most important. It consists mainly of lowland rices which are sown in May and June, and mature in November and December. The autumn crop, which is known as the *aus* crop, ranks next in importance. It comprises highland types sown in April or thereabouts, and harvested in August and September. Another crop of minor importance is also grown between the *aman* and the *aus*. This is called the *boro* and is sown in November and harvested in February or March. As in other areas with a relatively high rainfall, irrigation plays a small part in the agriculture of Bengal. Only about 7 per cent. of the total area under rice is irrigated; the remainder is dependent entirely on rain.

3. The supply of rice in the province at the beginning of a calendar year consists of almost the whole of the *aman* crop reaped at the end of the preceding year and "old rice", that is, the balance of earlier grown and imported rice carried over from the previous year. During the year this initial supply is augmented by the *boro* and *aus* crops and imports. Apart from the small portion used as seed, the greater part of the year's supply is consumed by the people, and what remains is carried forward as "old rice" to the following year. The proportion of *aman* rice consumed within the year in which it is harvested is normally negligible. In exceptionally bad years, however, it is consumed to some extent. Thus, the annual rice supply position of the province may be visualized in the form of a balance-sheet as shown below.

1. Balance of "old rice" carried over from the previous year.	1. Seed.
2. Yield of the *aman* crop.	2. Exports.
3. Yield of the *boro* and *aus* crops.	3. Consumption.
4. Imports.	4. Balance of "old rice" carried forward to the succeeding year.

4. Consumers of rice may be broadly divided into three classes. First, there are those who buy their supplies from the market all the year round. This class comprises practically the whole of the non-agricultural population, both in urban and rural areas, as well as a large proportion of the agricultural labourers. In Bengal, labour is generally hired on a cash payment basis. The second class consists of all those who do not buy any supplies from the market, that is, that section of the agricultural population whose holdings are large enough to provide their annual rice requirements in addition to seed and a margin

[1]Report on the Marketing of Rice in India and Burma (1941) page 482.

for meeting the expenses of cultivation, the payment of rent, and other essential cash needs. Lastly, there are groups who buy their supplies from the market only during certain parts of the year and not at others. These include numerous small holders who do not grow sufficient rice for their own needs as well as agricultural labourers who receive wages in kind.

5. How much of the rice crop is retained by the grower and how much comes on the market depends upon various factors and varies from district to district, from village to village, from one holding to another, and from year to year. Primarily, it depends upon how much the cultivator retains for his domestic consumption and seed, and it may be taken as a general rule that the proportion retained varies inversely with the size of the holding. Small growers, however, often sell a proportion of their crop immediately after the harvest for the payment of rent, repayment of debt, and for meeting other pressing cash obligations even though the produce in their possession may not be sufficient for their needs throughout the year. Again, in those districts in which jute is the principal cash crop, the proportion retained is higher than in districts where rice is the main cash crop. Taking the province as a whole, it has been estimated that normally 54 per cent. of the total rice crop is retained by the producer; that is, the proportion which comes on the market is 46 per cent.[1]

6. The season of marketing is determined by the time of harvest. In Bengal, as we have seen, the *aman* crop, which is the most important, is harvested by the end of December. An indication of the rate at which paddy and rice move into the markets of Bengal during different months of the year is given by the following account of movements into the Calcutta market:—"Fifty per cent of the total annual arrivals of paddy as well as rice were received in the four months, January to April. Incomings of paddy were heaviest in January and February, amounting to 28 per cent of the annual total arrivals in the market, while receipts of rice were highest in February and March, being also 28 per cent. of the total yearly imports. After March, arrivals diminish gradually, the months of least activity being July and August in the case of paddy, and from September to November in respect of rice".[2]

7. Paddy, after it is harvested, has to be de-husked before it can be consumed. Roughly one half of the market supply is de-husked by manual labour in the villages, while the other half passes through rice mills. The high proportion of the market supply which is de-husked by villagers and professional de-huskers as a cottage industry is of some importance in the rural economy of the province. The number of rice mills in Bengal is relatively small in comparison with the size of the crop and with the numbers in certain other provinces, particularly in Madras, Bombay, the Punjab, and Sind. The cultivator generally sells his paddy and hand-pounded rice to village merchants or to itinerant traders known as *paikars*, *beparis*, and *farias*. These sales sometimes take place in the villages themselves, but more often in the rural markets of which there are nearly 7,000 in Bengal. This represents the first stage of the movement of paddy and rice into the market. Part of the grain thus collected passes into distribution locally through retail shops, and a part, probably the greater part, passes to the larger markets where it is sold to the bigger merchants, known as *aratdars*, or to local rice mills. Cultivators, particularly the larger cultivators, also bring their grain for sale to these markets. This is the second stage in the marketing process. Once more, part of the grain assembled at this stage passes into local consumption. In fact, the whole of it may be absorbed locally if the market is situated in or near to an urban or deficit rural area. The next stage in the marketing of the grain is reached when the paddy and rice move from these assembling centres. Part is despatched to consuming centres in different parts of the province. and part

---

[1] **Report on the Marketing of Rice in India and Burma (1941), pages 27 and 492.**
[2] ***Ibid.***

travels to the final wholesale market in and around Calcutta, where a large amount of paddy is converted into rice. That is a brief, and in many respects an over-simplified, account of the extremely complicated process by which food in Bengal is collected in small lots from millions of growers, transported stored, de-husked, transported and stored again, and finally distributed through tens of thousands of retail shops to millions of households. The number of persons engaged in this business, so vitally important to the life of the community, must run into several hundreds of thousands.

B.—The supply and distribution aspects of food shortage

8. In normal times, the intricate processes of supply and distribution, described in the last section, took place of their own accord. Householders who did not produce their own food went to the shops to which they were accustomed to go and bought the supplies they needed. The shopkeepers, in their turn, bought their supplies from larger traders, and so on back to the growers in the villages. It was no one's responsibility, either in the trade or outside, to ensure that the supplies necessary for every one were actually produced and distributed. The free activities of producers, traders, and consumers, largely sufficed to secure this result. In the main, the necessary supplies were always available; and the bulk of the population found that they had either the food, or the money necessary to buy the food, which they needed. Even in normal times, however, considerable numbers among the poorer classes live on the margin of subsistence because they do not grow enough food, and do not earn enough money to buy the amount of food which they need. Food shortage in this sense may, and does, exist even when crops are good and prices low, and stocks are abundant, and are exported. It is the result, not of a shortage in the total supply of food, but of lack of purchasing power in the hands of the poorer classes, that is, of their poverty.

9. "Food shortage" of this kind becomes more pronounced in years in which seasonal conditions are unfavourable and the yield of crops is seriously diminished in consequence. The immediate effects of a total or partial failure of crops in any area are twofold: on the one hand, it reduces the supply which would have been otherwise available, and, on the other, it increases the number of people who are without enough food of their own, and who have to buy their requirements from the market, and lack the purchasing power necessary for that purpose. It is in such circumstances that relief measures are undertaken by Government. The essential feature of these measures is, not the direct provision of supplies, but the provision of purchasing power to the affected population, mainly in the form of wages paid to labourers employed on relief works, and to a lesser extent in the form of loans and gratuitous payments. It is assumed that, once the purchasing power has been provided, the necessary supplies will become available for purchase. According to experience in Bengal, as well as in other parts of India, throughout this century, this expectation has been fulfilled, and the normal operations of the trade have sufficed to bring the necessary supplies to the markets. This is possible because the total supply available for consumption, in any area during any particular year, does not consist merely of the yield of crops during that year; it includes the stocks carried over from the previous year and the net imports into that area. When the yield of crops is reduced, the price rises and this helps, first, in bringing local stocks into the market more quickly and in larger quantities than usual: secondly, in making it more profitable to import larger quantities than usual from outside the area; thirdly, in making it less profitable to export; and lastly, the rise in price leads to a reduction of consumption which in the aggregate, is by no means inconsiderable. The rise of prices thus automatically adjusts the normal trade machinery to the abnormal situation, and enables it to maintain the distribution of supplies. Inevitably, the rise of prices makes it difficult

for the distressed classes to buy their food, rendering relief measures all the more necessary; but it is not the cause of distress occassioned by crop failure. The provision of purchasing power through relief measures is useless, unless supplies are available for purchase, and the rise of prices helps to ensure their availablity.

10. It is therefore clear that sufficiency of food for everyone can be ensured only when total supplies are sufficient to meet requirements and purchasing power is adequate in relation to the prevailing level of prices. Two aspects of food shortage may thus be distinguished, one of which may be called the supply aspect, and the other the distribution aspect. Food shortage of the most serious degree—famine—occurred in Bengal in 1943, and it is essential to our inquiry to study the famine from both these angles.

Some estimate of the supply position in 1943 is therefore necessary. We shall attempt this in the next section. Here we may draw attention to certain facts relating to food shortage in past years which are relevant and important. It has already been pointed out that in normal years a section of the population suffers from insufficiency of food, and it has been suggested that this is due to lack of purchasing power rather than an over-all shortage of supplies. In the course of the 15 years preceding 1943, there were 3 years (1928, 1936 and 1941) in which the supply obtained from the *aman* crop reaped in the previous year, was seriously short because of the partial failure of that crop from natural causes. During these years, distress prevailed in many parts of the province and relief measures on a considerable scale had to be organized. When, however, purchasing power was provided by these measures, the necessary supplies became available for purchase, and no deaths from starvation occurred. This suggests that in these years sources of supply other than the *aman* crop were important, that there was little or no overall deficiency in supplies in relation to requirements, and that the distress which occurred, not very serious in degree, was due primarily to lack of purchasing power. In 1943, the shortage in the previously reaped *aman* crop was comparable to that which occurred in the 3 years referred to above. Actually, it was less serious than in 1941. A phenomenal rise in the price of rice, however, occurred which was of a very different order from the small rise which took place in the earlier years of shortage. This suggests at first sight that the famine of 1943 was due to a breakdown in distribution rather than to insufficiency of supplies. In order, however to reach a satisfactory conclusion on this question, we must attempt to compare in greater detail the supply position in 1943 and in previous years. This is one of the most difficult parts of our inquiry because the available information is both incomplete and defective.

C.—Review of supply in relation to requirements

11. The sources of rice supplies in any given year have been described in paragraph 8 of this Chapter. To assess the supply position, some estimate must be made of the yield of the different crops from year to year, the quantities imported and exported, the amounts required for seed and for consumption; and information about the amount of stocks carried over from year to year is also necessary. The defects in the relevant statistics are familiar. They have been commented upon by various Commissions and Committees from time to time and need not be recapitulated here. We must, however, make the best use we can of available information and attempt to reach conclusions which approximate to the truth. We append to this Report a note containing an analysis of supply and requirements during 1943 as well as during fifteen preceding years. The conclusions given below are based on this note.[1]

[1]Appendix II.

12. **Current supply (1928 to 1937).**—We use the term current supply, in relation to a calendar year, to mean the yield of the *aman* crop reaped at the end of the previous year, the yield of the *boro* and *aus* crops reaped during the year, *plus* imports into, and *minus* exports out of, the province during the year.

On the average of the ten years 1928 to 1937, the yield of the *aman* crop was sufficient, after meeting seed requirements, to provide the rice required for about 42 weeks in the year. The yield of the *boro* and *aus* crops was sufficient for about 12 weeks. Thus, the yield of crops in the province was more than sufficient for requirements. The balance of imports and exports was negligible; in the first half of the ten year period, net exports amounted to less than one week's requirements per annum, and, in the second half, net imports were of the same order.

The current supply varied from one year to another, mainly because of variations in the principal source of supply, namely the yield of the *aman* crop. In eight years out of ten, current supply was equal to or in excess of annual requirements. In two years namely 1928 and 1936, it was materially short. In these years, current supply was sufficient for the requirements of about 45 and 44 weeks respectively.

13. **Current supply (1938 to 1942).**—On the average of the 5 years 1938 to 1942, the yield of the *aman* crop was sufficient for about 38 weeks, as against 42 weeks in the previous decade. The yield of the *boro* and *aus* crops was sufficient for about 10 weeks as against 12 weeks in the previous decade. The supply derived from external sources, namely the balance of imports over exports, provided over one week's supply, as against *nil* in the previous decade. Thus, the current supply was, on the average, sufficient for only 49 weeks in the year as against 54 in the former period.

The supply position had deteriorated for two reasons. First, population was increasing faster than the acreage under rice. Secondly, seasonal conditions were less favourable in the later period than in the earlier period. This is borne out by the figures in the following table:—

Period	Average acreage under rice (millions of acres)	Percentage increase from one quinquennium to another	Average rate of yield (in tons) per acre
1928 to 1932	23·71	...	0·39
1933 to 1937	24·53	3·5%	0·40
1938 to 1942	25·53	4·1%	0·37

While, on the average, current supply was short of annual requirements by 3 weeks, it was sufficient or more than sufficient in two years out of the five. In one year, 1941, it was seriously short, as it amounted only to about 39 weeks' requirements.

14. **Current supply (1943).**—The yield of the *aman* crop reaped at the end of 1942, which came into supply during 1943, was sufficient for about 29 weeks. The yield of the *boro* and *aus* crops was sufficient for nearly 13 weeks. External supply provided rather more than one week's requirements. Thus, current supply was sufficient for about 43 weeks. As compared with the average of the previous quinquennium, current supply was short by an amount equivalent to 6 weeks' requirements.

The year 1943 was, therefore, comparable as regards current supply with the three lean years in the preceding 15 years, as shown in the following table:—

Year	Current supply (in terms of weekly requirements)
1943	about 43
1941	„ 39
1936	„ 44
1928	„ 45

15. **Carry-over and total supply.**—It is very unlikely that the stock of all rice physically in existence in the province on the first day of any year is smaller than the yield of the *aman* crop reaped at the end of the previous year. We use the term "carry-over" to mean the difference between the two. The supply available for meeting the requirements of any year consists of the carry-over and the current supply; the two together may be called "total supply". An absolute deficiency of supply in relation to requirements exists only when total supply is less than sufficient for the requirements of the year. We have no information about the actual size of the carry-over in any year, apart from such indications as are afforded by the difference between current supply and requirements from year to year. It is thus inevitable that conclusions reached about the carry-over (and, consequently also, total supply) must be subject to more uncertainty than those put forward about the sources of supply in the previous paragraphs. With this proviso, we believe that the following conclusions are consistent with the available evidence:—

(i) In relation to the requirements of the year, the carry-over was largest in 1936, and considerable in 1941. It was probably not so large in 1928, and still smaller in 1943.

(ii) It is probable that total supply was appreciably in excess of annual requirements, both in 1936 and 1941. It is unlikely to have been much in excess of annual requirements in 1928 and was probably not sufficient for such requirements in 1943.

(iii) The carry-over at the beginning of 1943 was probably sufficient for about 6 weeks' requirements. As the current supply was sufficient for 43 weeks, total supply during the year was probably sufficient for 49 weeks. Thus, during 1943, there was an absolute deficiency of supply in relation to requirements, of the order of about 3 weeks' requirements.

16. If these conclusions are accepted, it follows that the total supply position was worse in 1943 than in 1941, 1936, and 1928. Under any circumstances there would have been distress in 1943 and relief measures on a considerable scale would have been necessary. The supply position was not, however, such as to make starvation on a wide scale inevitable, provided the trade was capable of maintaining the distribution of available supplies subject only to a moderate rise in the price level. Towards the end of 1942, however, a situation, developed, not only in Bengal but also in other parts of India, in which the normal trade machinery began to fail to maintain and distribute supplies at moderate prices.

One of us, Mr. M. Afzal Husain, holds that the shortage of supply in the beginning of 1943 was even larger than is indicated in the foregoing paragraph. His views on the subject are contained in a separate minute.

CHAPTER IV.—DEVELOPMENT OF THE FOOD SITUATION IN INDIA

A.—The situation in 1942

1. When the war broke out, the supply and distribution of foodgrains over the whole of India depended entirely on the normal trade machinery. The nature of this machinery was much the same as we have described in the last Chapter as operating in Bengal. Today, this is no longer the case. Throughout India the grain trade is under government control of varying degrees of intensity. No grain moves from within the boundary of one province or state to another except in accordance with a plan framed by the Government of India. Within every province and most of the states, the movement of grain from surplus areas to deficit areas is similarly planned by the Provincial and State Governments. In large sections of the wholesale trade government agency has replaced private traders and other sections operate under close control and supervision. It is not merely the trader who comes under such control. The consumer in all the cities and most of the larger towns, and also in extensive areas of the country-side, is rationed. In many parts of the country the producer is no longer free to retain his surplus grain at his discretion. In such areas the surplus of each cultivator is regularly assessed, and millions are required to sell the quantities prescribed to Government at a fixed price.

2. This is a tremendous change in the life of the country and in its economic and administrative organization, which took time to come about. The change began early in 1942 and is still proceeding. A critical and potentially most dangerous stage in the process of transition occurred in the summer of 1942, with the springing up all over the country of "barriers" preventing the movement of grain from one province to another and often from one district to another, except under the specific permission of local authorities.

3. There is one view which attributes the disaster that befell Bengal in 1943 to these barriers as a primary cause. An exponent of this view has expressed it before us in these terms: "Until Japan declared war, India had no serious food problem beyond the fundamental truth that two-thirds of its population normally existed at a level little above the starvation line, and, by western standards, well below it. That in itself is an important fact, the effect of which is to be fully grasped before the true significance of the situation which ultimately developed can be understood. Its effect was that a slight disturbance of the economic practices of the country, and a small diminution of the over-all available supply, had consequences altogether out of proportion to their intrinsic gravity. So delicate was the balance between actual starvation and bare subsistence, that the slightest tilting of the scale in the value and supply of food was enough to put it out of the reach of many and to bring large classes within the range of famine ..... On the 29th November, 1941, immediately before the beginning of the war with Japan, the Central Government gave the provinces concurrent powers under the Defence of India Rules to exercise the power of prohibition of movement, and of requisition, over foodgrains and other goods. .... It was a mistake .... Practically every province and every state placed a fence round itself ... A death blow was given to the traditional conception of India, and in particular, the Eastern Region, as one economic entity for food, without restriction on flow and movement, built up to form the delicate machine which the people understood and by which they lived. Even districts followed suit. It was each one for itself.

. . . . Every province, every district, every taluk in the east of India had become a food republic unto itself. The trade machinery for the distribution of food throughout the east of India was slowly strangled, and by the spring of 1943 was dead".

4. We shall point out elsewhere that the erection of inter-provincial and inter-district barriers was a necessary step in the assumption by government of control over the trade. It was a mistake only in so far as it preceded the planned and controlled movement of supplies across such barriers. What is important is to note that conditions had arisen by the summer of 1942 which imperatively dictated the adoption by almost all Provincial and State Governments and their officers of a whole series of measures in restraint of the normal operation of the machinery of trade. These were adopted independently and largely without reference to one another, as a result of local initiative in dealing with local emergencies which had arisen more or less simultaneously in widely separated areas. There was a scramble for supplies which occurred simultaneously in many parts of the country. Unusual quantities were being purchased at unusual prices and being moved out of areas which needed them. The price level was rising too rapidly and tending to pass beyond the limit at which large classes of the population could afford to buy their food. We now proceed to describe the course of events which led to this situation and the nature of the measures followed in the attempt to bring it under control.

B.—TREND OF SUPPLIES

5. Rice is the cereal most widely consumed in India and wheat and millets come next in importance. As we have already mentioned India produces about as much rice as all the other countries of the world excluding China. Though the Indian production of wheat is considerably less than that of rice it is larger than that of Australia or the Argentine.[1] The average figures of production of rice and wheat have during recent years fluctuated round 25 million tons and 10 million tons respectively. That of the two most important millets, *jowar* and *bajra*, is approximately 10 million tons.

6. The trend of production, imports, and exports of rice during the 10 years ending 1942-3 can be seen from the figures in Table 1 of Appendix III. One fact which clearly emerges is that seasonal conditions were less favourable for rice cultivation during the five years ending 1942-3 than in the preceding quinquennium. The average production for the five years ending 1937-8 was 25·84 million tons, whereas that for the succeeding period of five years ending 1942-3 was only 24·42 million tons.

7. The harvest of the year 1940-1, was a very poor one. We have seen already how the winter rice crop of 1940 in Bengal, that is, the crop which came into supply during 1941, was the worst in 15 years. There was also a shortage, though less serious, in Bihar, the United Provinces and the Central Provinces. Madras alone among the more important rice producing areas had a normal crop. By this time the decline in imports had also commenced as a result of a shortage of shipping towards the end of the year 1940-1. There can be little doubt that stocks were heavily drawn upon during 1941.

8. The yield in 1941-2, although much better than in the previous year, was less than the average for the five years ending 1937-8 and only slightly larger than the average for the 10 years ending 1942-3. Bengal had an outstandingly good crop but Bihar which had suffered during the previous year had a subnormal crop this year also; while in the United Provinces and the Central Provinces crops were poorer even than those of the previous year. Imports also were shrinking rapidly; the net imports during 1941-2 were less than 0·75 million tons, as against an average of 1·72 million tons during the quinquennium ending 1937-8.

[1] Page 77 of the Report on the Marketing of Wheat in India, 1937.

9. The rice crop of 1942-3 was not as good as that of the previous year and was about one million tons less than the average for the quinquennium ending 1937-8. Bengal had another bad crop and the harvest in Madras was below the average. Bihar, on the other hand, had a good crop and so also the Central Provinces. But this year imports ceased altogether while exports continued at about the same level as in previous years. The amount available for consumption was less than the average during the 5 years ending 1937-8 by 3 million tons. Stocks must once again have been drawn on to a considerable extent.

10. There is a striking difference between the average amount available for consumption (production *plus* net imports) during the five years ending 1937-8 (27·56 million tons) and the immediately succeeding period of 5 years ending 1942-3 (25·41 million tons). It is impossible to estimate consumption with accuracy, but bearing in mind that the population was increasing rapidly, there can, we think, be little doubt that, during the 5 years ending 1942-3, stocks were heavily depleted and that towards the close of that period the market was being subjected to considerable strain.

11. The figures for wheat are given in Table II of Appendix III. In contrast with that of rice, the average production of wheat during the 5 years ending 1942-3, was higher than during the 5 years ending 1937-8, the average production during the former period being 10·37 million tons as against an average of 9·81 million tons during the latter. Production, however, was not evenly distributed and the increase in the average production during the five years ending 1942-3 was largely due to the good crop in 1939-40, which came into consumption in 1940, and a super-abundant crop in 1942-3, which came into consumption in 1943. On the other hand, the crops of the years 1940-1 and 1941-2 were not much larger than the average crop reaped during the quinquennium ending with the year 1937-8. In the meantime population had increased, and having regard to the amount available for consumption in these years, that is, production less net exports, it is reasonable to assume that in the years 1941 and 1942 consumption slightly exceeded current supply.

12. There was also another factor affecting the wheat situation, namely, the increased purchases for the Army. In 1940-1, these purchases amounted to 88,000 tons; they had increased by 1941-2 to 238,000 tons, and by 1942-3 to 312,000 tons. It is true that a large proportion of these purchases did not represent a net addition to consumption; for the Indian soldier would eat foodgrains even if he remained in his village. They did however, constitute an additional demand on market supply, and it is the pressure of demand on such supply which affects price levels. Army purchases of rice were much less important, as the following figures show:—

Year	Purchases for the Army ('000 tons.)
1940-1	22
1941-2	47
1942-3	115

C. The Movement of Prices and Price Control.

13. With the outbreak of war in September 1939, there was an immediate rise in the prices of many commodities throughout India. We have included in Appendix III a table showing the index numbers of average monthly wholesale prices of rice and wheat from September 1939 onwards at quarterly intervals. For purposes of comparison, the index numbers showing the movement in price of all primary commodities, all manufactured articles, as well as of cotton manufactures, have also been included. The base period for these index numbers is the week ending 19th August, 1939.

14. By December 1939 prices had risen considerably and the position in that month was as follows:—

Commodities	Index number
Wheat	156
Rice	114
All manufactured articles	144·5
Cotton manufactures	126
All primary commodities	135·9

The rise was sudden and led to public agitation against profiteering and a demand for action by the Government. On the 8th September 1939, the Central Government delegated to the Provincial Governments powers under the Defence of India Rules to control the prices of certain necessaries of life. These powers were actually exercised in some areas and remained as a threat in the background in others. The general result was to check the initial panic and to slow down, if not stop altogether, the rise in prices. The Government of India were, at that stage, not convinced of the necessity for price control. It was expected that prices would soon stabilize themselves at a reasonable level as supply and communications were normal. They were, however, impressed by the views expressed by various Provincial Governments that the powers delegated under the Defence of India Rules were necessary in order to keep under control a situation which might otherwise lead to disturbances of the public peace. But the results of experience in the use of these powers had to be reviewed and future policy settled; and for this purpose the Government of India summoned a conference of the representatives of the Provincial and State Governments. This was the first of a series of six Price Control Conferences which met at different times during the next three years to discuss the prices of foodgrains and other commodities.

15. The consensus of opinion at the two Price Control Conferences held in October 1939 and January 1940 was clear in respect of foodgrains. It was opposed to any interference with the course of foodgrain prices; the rise in prices was welcomed. It was recognised that the agricultural classes had suffered from unremunerative prices over a long period preceding the outbreak of war. The sharp fall in prices which had occurred in the early thirties as a result of the world economic depression had greatly diminished agricultural incomes, increased the burden of debt, and generally weakened the economic condition of the agriculturists. This in turn led to the contraction of revenues with a consequent restriction of the resources available for economic development and social services. Some recovery had indeed taken place and agricultural prices had risen during the years immediately preceding the war. But the recovery was not complete. The rise in prices which took place after the outbreak of war was, up to a point, calculated to produce entirely beneficial results.

16. The price of wheat rose rapidly during the three months following the outbreak of war but by January 1940, when the Second Price Control Conference met, the rise had been checked and the price was falling. While the level actually reached was not disturbing, the rate of increase caused some uneasiness and the possibility of its reaching an unduly high level could not be disregarded. This led to a discussion of the functions which would have to be assumed by the Central and Provincial Governments if and when price control became necessary. The conclusion reached was that the control of primary wholesale prices and the regulation of the primary wholesale markets should vest in the Central Government, and that the control of the retail markets should vest in the Provincial and State Governments. It was also agreed that in exercising control in the wholesale markets, the Central Government should consult the Governments of the provinces and the states mainly concerned with the commodity to be controlled.

17. The course of prices during 1940 was not unsatisfactory and the position in September 1940, after the first year of war, is illustrated by the following figures:—

Commodities	Index number
Wheat	133
Rice	133
All manufactured articles	111·6
Cotton manufactures	110
All primary commodities	110·3

18. The situation changed in 1941. There was a sharp upward trend between June and September. At this time the war was taking a grave turn. On the 22nd June Germany invaded Russia; on the 25th July the Japanese assets in the British Empire were frozen; on the 28th July the Japanese landed in Indo-China; and on the 25th September the Germans were in the Crimea. The war was coming nearer to India. The scale of the war effort in the country was increasing. We have referred already to the increase in the Army purchases of wheat which was at the same time an index of the increase in recruiting. The sharp increase by nearly 50 points in the index numbers for the prices of wheat and cotton goods, which took place between June and September, was the reaction of the markets not so much to any existing shortage as to anticipation of coming events and an inevitable increase in the pressure of demand on available supply. Thus, the end of the second year of war marked the beginning of the "food situation" in India. The following figures indicate the position reached in September 1941:—

Commodities	Index number
Wheat	193
Rice	169
All manufactured articles	166·3
Cotton manufactures	190
All primary commodities	138·3

19. When the Third Price Control Conference met on the 16th and 17th October 1941, the attitude of satisfaction with price levels in general had disappeared. The attention of the Conference was mainly directed to the steep rise which had occurred in the price of yarn and cloth, but there was also a good deal of concern about the trend of wheat prices. The need for distinguishing between the interests of the wheat producer and those of the speculator was strongly emphasized at this Conference. The representative from the United Provinces pointed out that normally the price of wheat rose only in January or February and never in July or August. But in 1941 the price of wheat in the Hapur market had risen by about 11 annas per maund in the month of July. The reason, he said, was that "speculators were forcing up prices since producers had disposed of 80 to 90 per cent of their produce and during July and August no exports from the province were observed". The representative of the Punjab, the most important wheat exporting province, "saw no reason why profiteering on the part of the middlemen should not be stopped", and agreed to control being instituted after the grower had parted with his produce to the dealer. The result of the deliberations of the Conference was recorded as follows:—

"On the whole there does not seem to be very grave apprehension at the moment regarding the rise in the price of agricultural products, but the question of wheat prices has to be carefully watched. It may be possible, or it might even be necessary, for the Central Government to intervene at any stage if there is a tendency for a rise in the price of wheat". This stage was reached within a few weeks after the Conference.

20. We have already seen that the rice harvest reaped in the winter of 1940-1, in many provinces was a poor one. Nevertheless, the price of rice had not risen to the same extent as that of wheat. This was due, in part, probably to the smaller demands made on the market by the Defence Services but mainly to the fact that imports from Burma, although on a reduced scale, were still available. Discussion about rice at the Third Price Control Conference was, therefore, mainly concerned with the conversations then proceeding between the Government of India and the Government of Burma in regard to the export of rice from Burma and the endeavours which were being made, with some success, to secure sufficient shipping for importing that rice. Nevertheless, references were made at this Conference to the occurrence, here and there, of those difficulties in the internal distribution of supplies of the kind which subsequently became so serious in the summer of 1942. The representative of the Central Provinces referred to the "scramble for supplies" occurring in that province. The representative of Assam suggested that steps should be taken not merely to control prices but "also for regulating the movement of rice to the competing consuming provinces". The conclusions reached at the Conference were that although rice prices had risen, they had not reached such a high level as to cause serious concern, and that, subject to a satisfactory solution of the question of imports of rice from Burma, rice, generally speaking, was a problem for which a solution would have to be found by the provincial authorities.

21. Towards the end of November 1941, the price of wheat was more than twice the pre-war level. The Government of India, therefore, decided that intervention was necessary and, after a preliminary warning, issued an Order on the 5th December fixing the maximum wholesale price of wheat at Rs. 4/6/- a maund[1] in the markets of Lyallpur in the Punjab and Hapur in the United Provinces, and authorising the Provincial Governments to determine the maximum prices in other markets having regard to the normal parities. This was the first step taken by the Central Government towards the assumption of control over the operation of the normal trade machinery and it provoked an immediate reaction in the wheat markets. This reaction and the consequences are important and must be described in detail.

D.—Control of supply and distribution

22. Statutory control of wheat prices was notified by the Central Government on the 5th December 1941. From about the middle of January 1942, acute local scarcity was suddenly and simultaneously experienced in many important wheat consuming areas. The places specially affected were urban and particularly industrial centres of major importance, such as Bombay, Calcutta, Cawnpore, and Delhi. Shortage was acute even in Lahore and Amritsar. There can be no doubt that this was an artificial shortage and the direct result of the refusal of the trade to operate within the limits of the maximum price prescribed. Evidence of the causal connection between the imposition of control and the disappearance of supplies from the markets, is afforded by observations made by the representative of the Punjab Government at the Fourth Price Control Conference, held early in February 1942. He said: "If there had been no control there would not have arisen any difficulties. The only result of this control has been to drive all the stocks of wheat underground. You lift the control and tomorrow you will have any amount of wheat from so many corners of the Punjab and from other parts of India also. I do not think there is really such a shortage of wheat as is indicated at present, but this control has brought about many difficulties in its train".

23. The disappearance of supplies from the principal urban centres of the Punjab immediately affected the poorer classes of the population and the Punjab Government, in order to conserve supplies, placed an embargo on the export of wheat, except under permit. This further aggravated the difficulties in

consuming centres outside the province. The position, as the Punjab Government saw it at the time[1], was described by their representative in the following terms: "We have been placing an embargo on the export of wheat off and on, and each time that we have tried to impose a ban on the export of wheat we have been asked to lift it and we had to lift it.........After all, the first care of a Provincial Government is the supply of food to those who live within its jurisdiction. What we are prepared to do is, that anything that is needed for consumption in the province itself may be left with us, and the rest we are prepared to place at the disposal of the Government of India. The Government of India may take what steps they like to distribute the surplus produce of the Punjab. At present we are supplying about 1,500 tons a day to the Army alone. And there are at least three more months to go before the next harvest produce comes in.........After the Army, comes the claim of the provinces which adjoin the Punjab, for example, Delhi.........Then our neighbour, the North-West Frontier Province, depends practically entirely on such surplus as it can get from the Punjab. After having met the demands of the Army, the North-West Frontier Province, and Delhi, I think we also receive a large number of demands from the United Provinces and Bengal......We have certainly received very insistent demands from Bengal. Therefore, it is a practical impossibility to meet all these demands and, at the same time, to feed our own population. The best exporting districts in the Punjab are Lyallpur, Montgomery, and Ferozepore; and yet within the last two or three days we have been receiving very alarming reports as to the depletion of stocks in those districts. In view of these alarming reports, I am afraid it would be necessary to impose some sort of a ban on free exports to every part of India."

24. It was thus evident that some authority had to determine the quantity of wheat which could be taken off the Punjab market from time to time and how it should be distributed between the Army and the various consuming areas. This was, however, not the only problem. There was the further question as to how the exportable surplus was to be secured if traders and cultivators refused to sell except at ever-increasing prices. The steps taken by the Government of India towards solving these problems were as follows: At the end of December 1941 a Wheat Commissioner for India was appointed, whose functions, generally speaking, were to advise the Provincial Price Control authorities, to regulate the distribution of wheat, and to acquire wheat, if necessary, for sale through provincial agencies. But before the Wheat Commissioner could prepare the ground for the introduction of central control over distribution, he was faced with the acute local shortages which we have already described, and his energies were fully occupied in securing *ad hoc* supplies to relieve the situation. It was not till the end of April 1942, that the Wheat Control Order was issued regulating the rail-borne movement of wheat from producing provinces to consuming areas. On the basis of this Order, an all-India distribution plan was prepared and put into operation through a system of permits issued by the Wheat Commissioner. At the beginning of March 1942, the stocks of wheat pledged with the banks in Northern India were requisitioned. The results of this expedient were meagre, but it helped to secure some stocks which were urgently needed. In the same month the Government of India raised the maximum wholesale price of wheat to Rs. 5 per maund. Some improvement followed, and during May and June, the price of wheat remained, for the most part, below the new maximum. By August, however, it had reached and passed it and a flourishing black market had come into existence. The distribution of supplies steadily deteriorated, and towards the end of the year 1942, shortages in the large industrial centres had again become acute. As we shall see later, the shortage of wheat in Calcutta towards the

[1] February 1942

end of this year, and the early months of the following year, was one of the links in the chain of events which ended in famine.

25. By the beginning of 1942, the war in the East had taken a dangerous turn for India. War with Japan had broken out on the 8th December 1941. The first air raids on Rangoon took place on the 23rd January 1942. On the 15th February Singapore fell. On the 7th March Rangoon was evacuated. On the 23rd of that month the Japanese occupied the Andamans, and on the 5th and 6th April the first enemy bombs fell in Ceylon and on the east coast of India. The military situation was transformed overnight with profound repercussions on civil life. Among the most important was the effect on railway transport.

26. Before the entry of Japan into the war, Indian railways had been called upon to provide engines and rolling stock for operational theatres in the Middle East and Indian Engineer Companies for operating, building and maintaining railways overseas, had been raised from amongst Indian railwaymen. The railways had also provided track and other equipment. These demands had been met out of their own resources and by the dismantling of uneconomic branch lines. By the end of 1941, the railways were working with depleted stock and personnel. In view of the shortage of shipping, a large volume of essential heavy materials such as coal, which had previously moved by sea, was being carried by rail. The Japanese war enormously increased the strain on the railways. The direction of army operations completely changed and railway traffic which had hitherto centred on India's western outlets had to be oriented to meet the new situation. Rigid control of goods traffic had to be introduced. None but essential traffic could move, and even if supply conditions had not deteriorated, the transport situation alone necessitated rigid control over the movement of foodgrains.

27. But supply conditions could not, and did not, remain unaffected. There was an imminent possibility of invasion and air raids, and a general feeling of uncertainty about supplies prevailed over large areas. In many parts of the country, cultivators were becoming cautious in parting with their produce, and the supplies arriving in the markets were dwindling. At the same time, the pressure of demand on the market supply was increasing; larger and larger numbers were being employed in industry and on constructional projects, and consumers anxious to ensure their supplies were increasing their purchases.

28. Conditions in the rice markets had remained on the whole healthier than in the wheat markets, in spite of growing difficulties of supply, as long as the possibility of imports from Burma existed. With the fall of Burma, the situation in the rice markets also deteriorated. Provincial Governments in most of the important rice producing areas were faced with problems similar to those which had developed in the Punjab earlier in the year, namely, a scramble for supplies, rising prices, competitive buying, reluctance to sell, and speculation. In the Central Provinces, which is normally a surplus province but which had had a succession of poor crops, the scramble appears to have occurred earlier than elsewhere, and in March 1942, in order to conserve the resources of the province, the Provincial Government prohibited the export by rail of foodgrains to places outside the province except under permit.

29. Madras differed from the Central Provinces in two respects. It was a deficit province but it had had two fairly normal crops in succession. Here, during the hot weather of 1942, merchants from Travancore and Ceylon bought rice for export and competitive buying led to a steep rise in prices. Merchants were bidding against one another and buying not only in surplus but also in deficit districts, thereby creating local scarcities. A series of measures were taken in order to deal with the situation. In May, the Provincial Government introduced a scheme for the distribution of rice through the

allocation of supplies from specified surplus areas to specified deficit areas, and also for export, determining the quantities to be moved and the railway routes to be followed. On the 1st June 1942, exports of paddy and rice to places outside the province were prohibited except under permit, and in September 1942 an official purchasing agency was set up to undertake all buying for export.

30. The Government of Bihar had, in the course of two years, developed an organized system of price control, assisted by a Market Intelligence Service. This control sufficed to maintain internal prices in parity with prices prevailing in the principal rice markets outside the province, particularly Calcutta, but as long as inter-provincial movements were free, it could not prevent prices within the province following upward movements of prices outside its boundaries. In the beginning of 1942, prices of rice began to rise in Calcutta and, as we shall see later, the Government of Bengal decided to fix maximum prices with effect from the 1st July 1942. The Bihar Government accepted those prices and decided to adjust their own maximum prices in parity with them Prices, however, suddenly rose in the United Provinces and unusually large quantities of rice began to be exported from Bihar to that province. This upset the markets of North Bihar and prices rose. Bihar is normally a deficit province and these abnormal exports to the United Provinces caused alarm. Again, the high prices in the United Provinces made it impossible for the Bihar Government to maintain prices throughout Bihar in parity with those fixed in Bengal. The Bihar Government therefore decided to prohibit the exports of rice to any market outside the province by rail, road or river, except under permit. This prohibition took effect from the 1st July 1942.

31. In the same month, the Orissa Government also imposed an embargo on the movement of foodgrains to places outside the province. They were compelled to do so because of a shortage in the Orissa market, attributed mainly to an increase in the exports to Bengal, and also because of difficulties in the movement of foodgrains in the coastal areas arising out of the "Denial Policy" to which we shall refer later. At about the same time, the Government of Bengal also took similar action as regards exports from Bengal.

32. We have now described the sequence of events leading to the situation which we described in paragraph 4 of this chapter. The transition from a system of supply and distribution of foodgrains through normal trade channels to a system supervised, controlled, and in part, operated by agencies established by Government, had begun. We have described the first step taken in this transition as a critical and potentially dangerous stage in the process. The possibilities of danger were twofold. First, it was essential that, once the process had begun, the machinery of control should get into working order as quickly as possible; otherwise, with the normal machinery of trade temporarily paralysed, and with nothing to take its place, any serious or sudden deterioration in internal supply, arising out of natural causes, was liable to lead to disaster. Secondly, the provinces and states of India are not self-sufficient economic entities. It was, therefore, not enough that a system of controlled supply and distribution should be instituted within each province; it was necessary that a machinery should be created, capable of ensuring that the necessary flow of supplies, from surplus provinces and states to deficit provinces and states, was maintained.

CHAPTER V.—EVENTS IN BENGAL DURING 1942.

A.—The threat of invasion

1. The outstanding feature of the situation in Bengal in the early months of 1942, was the rapid approach of the enemy to the borders of the province, and the universal expectation of an invasion of the province itself. One of the witnesses who appeared before us gave the following vivid account of the prevailing atmosphere:

"There was a feeling of tenseness and expectancy in Calcutta. Calcutta was largely empty. Houses were vacant. Shopkeepers had very largely moved off and a great deal of the population had gone out. The families of Government servants were ordered out of the coastal and exposed districts. . . Valuable records were removed from the southern districts of the province to safer districts in the north. In general, the impression was that nobody knew whether by the next cold weather Calcutta would be in the possession of the Japanese . . . There was little panic in the districts, but there was a great deal of confusion. Transport was unpunctual and very crowded and the districts of Chittagong, Noakhali. and Tipperah were just like an active theatre of war behind the front . . . A continuous stream of refugees was arriving from Burma. They were finding their way through Assam, after the initial influx into Chittagong, and were moving into the country. They were arriving diseased, bringing in a virulent type of malaria, and bringing hair-raising stories of atrocities and sufferings. . The natural effect of all that on the people of Bengal was to make them feel that the times were extremely uncertain and that terrible things might happen."

By about August, however, Calcutta returned to a feeling of security. The monsoon had set in, rendering Japanese movement by sea unlikely. Troops had been arriving and there was a large number visible in Calcutta.

2. The danger of a Japanese invasion compelled the military authorities to put into operation early in 1942, a "denial" policy involving two important measures. One was the removal from the coastal districts of Midnapore, Bakarganj, and Khulna of the rice and paddy estimated to be in excess of local requirements until the end of the crop year, and the other was the removal of all boats, capable of carrying 10 passengers or more, from those parts of the delta considered vulnerable to invasion.

3. **Denial of Rice.**—The preliminary arrangements for the purchase and removal of stocks of rice and paddy were completed by the middle of April 1942, and the agents appointed by Government commenced their purchases. Initially the maximum price to be paid was fixed at the market price then prevailing *plus* 10 per cent, but subsequently, early in May, the ceiling price was fixed definitely at Rs. 6 a maund for rice; later on, it was raised to Rs. 6/4/-. Market prices were, however, rising and by the end of May were above the ceiling prices, with the result that large scale purchases practically ceased by the end of that month. Purchases on a small scale continued for some time longer and finally ceased in July when directions to this effect were issued. The quantity bought was not large—it did not exceed 40,000 tons—and even allowing for errors in the estimated surplus formed a relatively small proportion of the surplus supplies available in the districts concerned.

4. It is difficult to estimate the effect of these purchases on prices, but in view of the relatively small amount bought it was probably not great. But the purchases synchronised with a sharp upward movement in the price level

and a general disturbance in market conditions which was occurring at about the same time in other parts of India. We shall refer to this rise in prices later. There is no evidence to show that the purchases led anywhere to physical scarcity. But, on the other hand, they brought home to the people, in the most emphatic manner, the danger of invasion; they increased local nervousness and probably encouraged cultivators to hold on to their grain as an insurance against invasion and isolation.

5. **Denial of Boats.**—The area to which the "Boat Denial" policy should be applied was the subject of discussions between the Bengal Government and the Military Authorities, and it was agreed that it should be limited to the area lying south of a line running from Chandpur on the east, through Barisal, Khulna, Basir Hat, and Diamond Harbour, to Kharagpur on the west. A considerably larger area had originally been proposed by the Military Authorities. Orders were accordingly issued on the 1st May 1942 for the removal from the area, of boats capable of carrying more than 10 passengers. It was always recognized that the removal of a large number of boats from the delta, in which communications are almost entirely by river and not by rail and road, would cause considerable hardship and inconvenience. Relaxations of the measure were accordingly introduced, as circumstances allowed, from time to time. In June 1942 the line was adjusted so as not to interfere with the free movement of boats from East Bengal to Calcutta by the "inner boat route". Instructions were also issued at about this time for the issue of temporary permits for boats entering the area for the specific purpose of trade or distant cultivation. Again, it was decided that it would be necessary to leave large boats permanently among the *chars* in the Bakarganj district, roughly on the scale of one boat per mile of the river bank for the purpose of cultivation. Further, in November 1942, special sanction was given for an increase in the number of boats in the area during the reaping of the rice harvest.

In January 1943, an additional relaxation was introduced. This gave practically unrestricted passage, subject to passes being obtained and renewed, to rent collectors, rice traders who agreed not to purchase rice at prices exceeding those fixed by Government for their purchasing agents, and other traders. Finally, in June 1943 all restrictions were removed.

6. The following figures show the effect of the boat denial policy at the end of November 1942:—

(*a*) Total number of boats capable of carrying 10 or more people registered within the denial area.	66,563
(*b*) Total number :—	
(*i*) requisitioned for military use	1,613
(*ii*) destroyed	3,373
(*iii*) sunk but recoverable	4,143
(*iv*) taken to " reception " stations	17,546
(*v*) left the area to find work elsewhere	19,471
(*vi*) remaining in the area	20,417
	66,563

(NOTE.—Owners of boats were free either to take them into reception areas or to remove them to a place north of the "denial" line. Those deprived of their boats were granted compensation).

7. The measures were necessarily unpopular. From the reports of local officers it appears unlikely that the area under cultivation was reduced. As regards the extent to which the movement of rice was impeded, it is impossible

to frame an estimate. Obviously, the removal of so large a number of boats—there were still 16,655 boats in the "reception" areas on the 1st April 1943—must have had a considerable restricting effect on the movements of foodgrains from the denial area.

The Bengal Government have informed us that it was not a practical proposition to maintain in repair the thousands of boats brought to the reception stations. We are, however, not convinced that it was not possible to make better arrangements. In the area to which the "denial" policy was applied boats form the chief means of communication, and if the boats taken to the reception stations in 1942 had been maintained in a serviceable condition they would have been available for the movement of foodgrains from the denial area during the difficult times of 1943. Again, the fishermen who had been deprived of their boats suffered severely during the famine. If it had been possible to provide them with boats from the reception stations they would have been less affected by the famine and the number of deaths amongst them would have been smaller.

8. Considerable areas of land were requisitioned for military purposes during 1942, and 1943. We have not complete particulars of the number of persons affected but from the information available, it appears that more than 30,000 families were required to evacuate their homes and land. Compensation was of course paid but there is little doubt that the members of many of these families became famine victims in 1943.

B. The rise of prices and price control.

9. We have seen already how, with the loss of Burma, unusual demands were made on the rice supplies in the principal rice growing provinces of India. Bengal was the most important of these provinces and nearest to the advancing enemy; and it is therefore not surprising that the rice markets in the province were also disturbed. Prices began to rise even while the crop reaped in the winter of 1941-2 was moving into the markets and reached an unprecedented level by the end of the year.

10. The rise which took place in 1943 was so much more spectacular than that in 1942, that the unprecedented rise in the former year is apt to be overlooked. The Bengal Government have furnished us with a chart[1] which shows the movement of the wholesale price of coarse rice in Calcutta at quarterly intervals from April 1931 to January 1943. The price was lowest between October 1932 and April 1933, when it reached Rs. 3 per maund, a level which it touched again in January 1934. It then rose gradually and was as high as Rs. 4/8/0 per maund during 1936, which, it will be recalled, was a year of poor harvest in Bengal. After this it fell and touched Rs. 3/4/0 per maund in April 1938. During the next two years it moved slowly upwards. A sharp rise took place after April 1941, and the price was somewhat above Rs. 7 per maund in July of that year. This, however, was not surprising, for the winter rice crop of 1940-1 was the smallest in Bengal during the 15 years preceding 1943. The peak was reached shortly before the arrival of the *aus* crop, after which the price fell.

11. The *aman* crop at the end of 1941 was an excellent one, promising adequate supplies for 1942, and there was, therefore, every reason to expect that the price would remain well below the level of the previous year. By April 1942, however, the price had reached the same level as in April 1941. A sharp rise occurred towards the end of May and in July the price was Rs. 8. Between July and September the market was very unsettled, but by the middle of

---

[1]Appendix IV.

September the price had steadied itself and in October stood at Rs. 8/8/0. The middle of November was, however, marked by another violent movement which carried the price to Rs. 12/8/0 a maund early in January 1943. The level thus reached was without precedent. It had not been so high even during the boom period after the end of the last war.

12. The unusual character of the rise in price from May 1942 onwards was not a phenomenon peculiar to Bengal, but was a feature of the markets in other important rice producing areas of the country. Burma had fallen and it was to be expected that a keen and pressing demand should arise from places like Ceylon and Western India, which were dependent to a large extent on supplies from Burma. There can be no doubt that purchases were being made in order to meet these demands in a market where the progress of the war made sellers who could afford to wait reluctant to sell. An officer of the Government of India who was in close touch with the rice markets in Bengal at this time described the situation in these terms: "Cultivators on the one hand were becoming very cautious and unwilling sellers, and speculators on the other hand, were operating on a larger scale than in normal times and circumstances, with only one consequence, a steady rise in prices".

13. We give below figures of imports and exports of rice into and from Bengal during the first seven months of the years 1941 and 1942.

(in thousands of tons)

Month	1941		Net imports+ Net exports—	1942		Net imports+ Net exports—
	Imports	Exports		Imports	Exports	
January	42	15	+27	29	45	—16
February . . .	62	22	+40	28	60	—32
March	60	31	+29	41	61	—20
April	66	22	+44	8	66	—58
May	51	20	+31	12	32	—20
June	83	15	+68	9	30	—21
July	68	11	+57	8	26	—18
	432	136	+296	135	320	—185

It will be noticed that while imports during the first seven months of 1942 were less than during the corresponding period of 1941 by nearly 300,000 tons, exports during the same period increased from 136,000 tons in 1941 to 319,000 tons in 1942. The result of this decrease in imports and increase in exports was that a net import figure of 296,000 tons in 1941 was changed into a net export figure of 185,000 tons in 1942.

During the last five months of the year 1942, exports decreased and were only 30,000 tons. It will be recalled that exports, except under permit, were prohibited by the Bengal Government in July, the exact date being the 16th July 1942. Imports during these months were also small, amounting to 27,000 tons.

The increase in the exports during the first seven months of 1942, as compared with the corresponding period of 1941, affords a clue to the increase in the price of rice which took place in Bengal in April-June, 1942. This was no doubt due to the increased demand from those areas which had suffered more severely than Bengal by the loss of the imports of rice from Burma. It is true that the imports into Bengal during the first seven months of 1941 were higher than normal owing to the poor *aman* crop reaped in December 1940. But even if allowance is made for this it seems clear that external demand had increased as compared with available supply, and it was this increase in the export demand which caused prices to rise in Bengal.

14. The markets were in this condition when, in June, the Government of Bengal decided to intervene and issued an order fixing, with effect from 1st July, maximum prices for medium and coarse rice in the Calcutta market. The wholesale price of coarse rice was fixed at Rs. 5/12/- per maund. This had been agreed upon as a suitable price in the course of discussions which had taken place several weeks earlier, but prices had risen rapidly, particularly between May and June, with the effect that the rates fixed under the order proved to be well below the market prices prevailing on the 1st July. The immediate effect of the price control order was that supplies disappeared from the Calcutta market. A similar position arose in the districts. It was reported that, in Howrah, the effect had been to drive underground all the available stocks of the controlled qualities and that food riots were apprehended. The District Magistrate had been compelled to seize stocks which were not being sold. Again, it was reported from the Burdwan Division that price control had completely broken down. The Divisional Commissioners protested against the system, and the rates, and pressed for the stoppage of uncontrolled exports from Bengal to areas outside the province. On the 16th July the Government prohibited all exports of rice and paddy from the province except under permit. As we have noticed, a similar step was taken in other provinces at about the same time. On the 21st July, the Government of Bengal revised the price control order and increased the statutory maximum prices by one rupee. It will be recalled that in March 1942 the Government of India, faced with similar difficulties, had raised the statutory maximum price of wheat. In Bengal the increase in the statutory maximum price produced no result except that the price actually prevailing in the province "advanced by almost exactly a rupee"

15. At this point the stocks of "denial" rice proved most useful. A portion of these stocks was moved into Calcutta and distributed, partly through controlled shops to the general public, partly through issues to employers of industrial labour who had organized their own purchasing schemes, and partly through the Calcutta Corporation. To some extent this eased the situation, but the result was not sufficient to make the maximum statutory price effective. The Government then considered the abrogation of price control. Opinion, however, differed and the final decision was that, although it would be inadvisable to withdraw the notification by which statutory maximum prices had been fixed, District Officers should be instructed not to enforce the control prices except in cases of gross profiteering. This decision was made known to the trade informally. The flow of supplies recommenced and prices steadied themselves. Four factors helped towards this temporary improvement: First, a large decrease in exports as a result of the embargo; secondly, the judicious use of denial stocks; thirdly, good rain in September and October which promised, deceptively as it turned out, that the *aman* crop would be good; and, fourthly, the decision not to enforce price control. Supplies and prices appeared to have again reached something like a state of equilibrium.

16. We shall describe later how this equilibrium was again upset in the last few weeks of 1942 and the stage was set for the tragedy of 1943. We now

proceed to give a brief account of certain other developments which were taking place at this time in Calcutta and which had a bearing on the course of events during 1943.

C.—Distributive organizations in Calcutta.

17. Early in the year 1942, when the war position in the Far East had deteriorated, an exodus from Calcutta took place. Among the people who left were a large number of dealers engaged in the wholesale and retail supply of foodstuffs. The disappearance of these shopkeepers and the consequent difficulty in buying supplies added to the nervousness of labour in the city and the surrounding industrial area. It was important that the morale of the labour force should be maintained and regular attendance at the factories ensured. The Provincial Government, therefore, advised large industrialists to undertake the supply of foodstuffs for their own employees. It was in this way that employers' grain shops came into existence. In July and August 1942, when rice was in short supply in Calcutta, it was apparent that something more was necessary than a chain of employers grain shops, each purchasing its own requirements in a highly competitive and speculative market. At this stage "the Bengal Chamber of Commerce Foodstuffs Scheme" was brought into being with the approval of the Government of Bengal. Though the scheme was administered by the Bengal Chamber of Commerce, its purpose was, and still is, the supply of essential items of food to the grain shops of industrial concerns which are members of or connected with the Chamber. In August 1942 the scheme catered for approximately 500,000 employees, exclusive of dependants, while by December 1942 the number had risen to 620,000, and the total number of persons served, including dependants, to approximately one million.

18. In August 1942, in a letter addressed to the Chamber, the Government of Bengal described their attitude to the scheme in the following terms:

"Government agree that the maintenance of essential food supplies to the industrial area of Calcutta must be ranked on a very high priority among their war-time obligations, and welcome the decision of the Chamber to set up its own organization for the purchase and distribution of essential supplies for the industrial labour of its constituents. Government, for its part, will do all in their power to create the conditions under which essential supplies may be obtainable in adequate quantities and at reasonable prices. Direct provision of stocks from Government sources must, however, be regarded as an abnormal procedure, and the extent to which Government may be able to make such provision must depend upon circumstances". The letter also stated that the Indian Chamber of Commerce and the Bengal National Chamber of Commerce had been informed that comparable facilities would be afforded to them.

19. Towards the end of 1942, organized industry was faced with the problem of how the steadily increasing cost of living of workers should be met—whether by increasing dearness allowances or by the subsidized provision of foodstuffs. Employers connected with the Bengal Chamber of Commerce, in consultation with the Government of Bengal, came to the conclusion that it was in the interests of their employees, and in conformity with Government's price control and anti-inflationary policy, to compensate for further increases in the cost of living by supplying at least a portion of the essential food requirements of their employees at subsidized rates, rather than to give progressively larger dearness allowances. This policy was adopted. The Chamber and the Industrial Associations recommended that employers should, as far as possible, keep cash dearness allowances at the then existing levels, that compensation for further rises in prices should be in the form of the sale of foodstuffs at the controlled retail prices of August 1942, and that employers should meet the difference

between these controlled prices and the actual cost. This policy has been continued ever since and is still in operation.

20. This was the process by which an organization came into being for the purpose of protecting a considerable proportion of the population of Greater Calcutta from the effects of high prices and the short supply of food. The price of food consumed by this section of the population of Greater Calcutta was henceforth subsidized.

21. An arrangement on somewhat similar lines to that of the Bengal Chamber of Commerce was also subsequently undertaken jointly by the Bengal National Chamber, the Marwari Chamber, the Indian Chamber, and the Muslim Chamber of Commerce. The labour force provided for was about 170,000. The Central and Provincial Governments, the Railways, the Port Trust, the Calcutta Corporation, and other employers of labour also arranged for the provision of supplies, at subsidized prices, to their employees. These numbered about 300,000.

22. The nucleus of another type of distributive organization also made its appearance during this year. We have described already how during August-September, 1942, when supplies disappeared from the market in Calcutta, stocks of "denial" rice were moved in and distributed. It was at this time that the first "controlled shops" were started. These were shops approved by Government and through which stocks held by Government were issued to the general public in limited quantities, at controlled prices. One hundred such shops were opened, but with the improvement in supply towards the end of September and the beginning of October, the demand on these shops was not heavy, and it was not found necessary at that time to increase their number. Earlier in the year a scheme had also been prepared for the distribution of food in the event of an emergency caused by air-raids. This scheme provided for the utilization of certain selected shops in the main markets, described as "approved markets", for the sale of foodgrains from Government stocks, and was put into operation early in 1943.

D.—Shortage of wheat

23. The population of Greater Calcutta and other industrial areas in Bengal is not composed entirely of persons whose staple diet is rice. A considerable proportion of the industrial population consists of people drawn from other provinces whose staple foodgrain is wheat. Bengal produces very little wheat, and during the five years ending 1941-2, imported from outside the province on an average 21,000 tons a month. Of this, about 18,000 tons were required to meet the needs of Greater Calcutta. During the closing months of 1942, the supply steadily decreased, and this continued during the early months of 1943. The following table shows the quantities of wheat imported into Bengal from other provinces and from overseas during the last five months of 1942 and the first six months of 1943:—

Month	Tons
August, 1942	13,259
September ,,	14,911
October ,,	11,814
November ,,	7,996
December ,,	9,397
January 1943	2.584
February ,,	1,620
March ,,	21,376
April ,,	20,735
May ,,	8,842
June	8,177

The Government of Bengal made repeated representations to the Government of India as regards the supplies of wheat, and in November 1942, the Wheat Commissioner was informed that, if supplies could not be secured, the Government of Bengal could not accept responsibility for any consequence to the industrial areas of Calcutta and any damage to the war effort that might ensue. As we have already seen, difficulties had arisen in the principal wheat markets of Northern India, and adequate supplies were not forthcoming. Statutory price control had failed and purchases could not be made except in violation of the law. The significance of this shortage of wheat in Greater Calcutta was that it increased the consumption of rice at a time when it was becoming clear that the *aman* crop had failed and an acute shortage of rice was imminent. It also undoubtedly increased the general feeling of uncertainty as regards food supplies.

E.—The failure of the aman crop

24. The season of the *aman* crop of 1942, that is the crop which would provide the main supply of rice for the year 1943, did not open propitiously. In June rain was needed in most parts of the province, the monsoon having been late in establishing itself; and, although rain was more plentiful in July, still more was needed. Cultivation had been delayed and the *aman* seedlings were suffering from drought in many places. The prospects, however, improved in August, and in September rain benefited the crops throughout the province. Taking the season as a whole the weather was not favourable, particularly in West Bengal—the most important rice producing area in the province.

25. It was at this stage that West Bengal was visited by a great natural calamity, a calamity which took a heavy toll of life and brought acute distress to thousands of homes. On the morning of October 16, 1942, a cyclone of great intensity accompanied by torrential rains, and followed later in the day by three tidal waves, struck the western districts of the province. The tidal waves laid waste a strip of land about 7 miles wide along the coast in the districts of Midnapore, and the 24-Parganas, and caused similar damage to an area 3 miles wide along the banks of the Hooghly, the Rupnarayan, the Haldi, and the Rasulpur rivers. Another effect of the tidal waves, reinforced by heavy rain, was to push up the water level in the northern reaches of the rivers, thereby causing extensive floods. The effects of the cyclone itself and the torrential rains which accompanied it were felt over a very wide area though in different degrees of intensity. The severest loss of life and damage to property occurred in the southern parts of the two districts already mentioned, that is, in the areas nearest to the sea. In areas more distant from the coast, there was little or no loss of life but crops and property were damaged and communications interrupted. It is estimated that the total area affected was 3,200 square miles, of which 450 square miles were swept by the tidal waves, and 400 square miles affected by floods. Throughout this large area the standing *aman* crop, which was then flowering, was in large measure damaged. In the worst affected areas it was not only the standing crops which were destroyed; reserve stocks of the previous crop in the hands of cultivators, consumers, and dealers were also lost.

26. After the cyclone came crop disease. We have been told by several witnesses about the damage caused by fungus and "root-rot". The Government of Bengal have stated that their effects were even more serious to the outturn than the damage caused by the cyclone. The *aman* crop reaped at the end of 1942 was thus seriously short. As we have seen in an earlier chapter the crop was sufficient, on an average of the five years preceding 1943, to provide

about 38 weeks' supply for the province. During this year the crop was sufficient for only about 29 weeks.

F.—Market conditions at the end of 1942

27. Shortly after the occurrence of the cyclone became known to the public, the trade in Bengal realized that a short crop was certain. The immediate result was a resumption of the upward movement in prices which, starting in February, 1942, had gained momentum in May, and had been temporarily arrested during September and October. A report written at the time describes this rise in the following terms: "The price of rice and paddy rose abruptly throughout Central and Western Bengal (except for Contai subdivision, Midnapore) and to a lesser extent in the districts of Southern Bengal, and was between Rs. 12 and Rs. 16 per maund according to quality, with isolated transactions at higher rates. The rise appears to have been due principally to heavy buying, entirely unco-ordinated and to a large extent manifestly speculative, which began about the middle of November, and seems to have reached its peak in the first week of this month (December 1942)". A fortnight later, the following was reported: "Prices of agricultural produce appear to have declined in the Burdwan and Presidency Divisions, though they are still very high. They have reached alarming figures in Rajashahi, Dacca and Chittagong divisions. The gravity of the situation is emphasized in Commissioners' reports, and it is pointed out that, unless some improvement takes place, there is a danger of resort to violence as a result of shortage and high prices". The swiftness with which the rise of prices was taking place may be seen from the following table which shows the course of prices in one of the markets of the Burdwan district:—

Date	Market price per maund of medium rice		
	Rs.	A.	P.
18th November 1942	7	8	0
25th „ „	10	8	0
2nd December „	11	8	0
7th „ „	14	0	0

28. A review of the conditions prevailing in the markets of Bengal early in December 1942 is contained in a note prepared at that time by the Civil Supplies Department of the Government of Bengal, which runs as follows:—

"*Present situation.*—High prices are running from Howrah to places across Western Bengal, with local high spots at places like Dinajpur which have easy means of transport to Calcutta and so can be quickly drawn upon.

There are high priced areas in one or two districts where high prices are probably due to poor crop.

Causes—I. *Psychological.*—(i) Depressing reports regarding crop forecast. (ii) Fears as to the result of the Midnapore cyclone and exaggerated statements as to its effects on the supply position of the province as a whole. (iii) Propaganda, sometimes perhaps interested, in certain trade circles, making out that the coming crop was going to be 'worst for the last 20 years' (iv) Exaggerated reports of exports from Bengal. (v) Fear of Foodgrains Control Order.

* * * * * *

III. *Supply position.*—(i) Restriction on export from Midnapore. (ii) Obstruction to transport in the Kulti Canal. (iii) Comparative difficulty of transport from south of Calcutta and comparative ease of transport from north of Calcutta. (iv) Late transplantation and consequent late arrival of new crop in Western

In the result, both rural population generally in surplus areas and large sections of the population in urban areas were being supplied from their existing stocks, *e.g.*, labour of industrial area, employees of commercial firms and khas holders who had bought stocks previously. The actual ruling prices were therefore chiefly affecting that portion of the population which had to buy from hand to mouth but they were suffering great hardships. This was probably the reason why despite higher prices there was by no means universal distress".

29. The evidence presented by these contemporary documents leaves no room for doubt that the upheaval in the Bengal markets towards the end of 1942, was due to the fact that in November and December of that year, that is, before the bulk of the *aman* crop had been reaped, unusual purchases were being made by persons who were convinced, quite correctly, that the yield of the *aman* crop would be so short and stocks in hand so low, that a crisis in supply was inevitable and was fast approaching. There is also evidence that such purchases were not confined to Bengal, but extended to the adjoining areas of Bihar and Orissa. Reports received at the time by the Bihar Government showed that a large number of buyers from Bengal were advancing money on standing crops at the end of November in the bordering districts of Bihar, and officers in these districts reported great uneasiness and impending trouble in consequence. In a letter addressed to the Government of India shortly after these events, the Government of Bihar reported that "there was a rush to corner supplies and withhold them from the provincial markets in order to smuggle them, in defiance of the provincial embargo, to the more attractive markets across the border." The Government of Orissa have told us that this was happening at the same time in Orissa also.

30. It was at this stage, when all the elements of the crisis which finally overwhelmed Bengal had gathered, that the enemy took a hand. The first air-raid on Calcutta took place on the 20th December and was followed by raids on the 22nd, 23rd, 24th and 28th. There were further raids in January. The military value of the raids proved to be negligible. Their effect on civilian morale was not considerable and proved to be temporary. But one of the important effects of the air-raids was the closing down of a large number of food-grain shops. On the 27th December, the Government of Bengal, in order to maintain the distribution of supplies in Calcutta, were reluctantly compelled to requisition stocks from wholesale dealers and from that moment the ordinary trade machinery could not be relied upon to feed Calcutta. The crisis had begun.

CHAPTER VI.—THE DEVELOPMENT OF THE CRISIS IN BENGAL

A.—Nature of the crisis

1. It is necessary before proceeding further with our narrative to take stock of the situation prevailing in Bengal at the beginning of 1943. The primary element in that situation was the failure of the *aman* crop. This, however, was not necessarily in itself an unmanageable problem. An even more serious failure had occurred only two years before in 1941, and had led to nothing more serious than a state of scarcity which was successfully alleviated by the usual relief measures. The necessary flow of supplies to the areas affected by the shortage was maintained, and supplies were available at prices which the bulk of the poorest classes of the population could afford to pay. This did not happen in 1943. Wherein lay the difference between 1941 and 1943? The answer is twofold: first, a serious diminution occurred in the sources from which a shortage in production was normally met; and secondly, the normal machinery for the distribution of supplies was out of order.

2. It was not only the yield of the *aman* crop which was short; the carry-over was also short. Thus, the stock of all rice in Bengal at the beginning of 1943, was considerably smaller than in 1941. This was primarily the consequence of the heavy drain on stocks during 1941, and to some extent also to a decrease of imports and an increase of exports which occurred during 1942. It was, therefore, clear that, from the supply aspect alone, 1943, promised to be a more difficult year than 1941. In an earlier chapter we came to the conclusion that the total supply of rice in Bengal during 1943, was probably sufficient for about 49 weeks, which meant an absolute deficiency of supply of about three weeks' requirements. A deficiency of this order involves a more serious difficulty in distribution than appears at first sight. Broadly speaking, there are three classes of consumers. First, the non-producers; secondly, the producers who do not grow sufficient for their own needs; and, thirdly, the producers who grow quantities which are more than sufficient for their own needs. The third class of consumers would not themselves go short because even in a year of shortage they would retain sufficient for their own needs throughout the year and probably in addition a reserve which they are accustomed to keep. In these circumstances an over-all shortage does not correctly indicate the degree of shortage in the supply available to the first two categories. A hypothetical example will illustrate this point. Suppose 50 per cent. of the population consists of producer-consumers who are self-sufficient in rice, and that the remaining 50 per cent. are non-producer-consumers. Also suppose that the weekly consumption of the entire population is Y, tons and the total supply available for the year is $49 \times Y$ tons instead of $52 \times Y$, tons. If the producer-consumers retain an amount equal to their consumption for 52 weeks the amount available for the non-producer-consumers is $49 \times Y$ tons *minus* $52 \times \frac{Y}{2}$ tons, that is $46 \times \frac{Y}{2}$ tons. The supply therefore available for non-producer-consumers is sufficient for 46 weeks and not for 52 weeks, that is, a shortage of 6 weeks' supply. Moreover, the shortage would be greater than this if the producer-consumer, who grows more rice than he needs for his own consumption, kept a reserve. Thus, it follows that even if all producers sold their entire stocks without retaining a reserve for consumption after the next harvest and even if stocks so placed on the market were evenly distributed to all consumers, the latter would not have secured their normal requirements in full.

3. The state of supply was such that, even if market conditions were normal, prices were bound to rise and difficulties were bound to be experienced in maintaining an adequate flow of supplies to the consumer. Market conditions were, however, not normal. The most obvious symptom of the unhealthy conditions which had arisen was the movement of prices during 1942, and the level reached at the end of that year. In January 1941, the wholesale price of coarse rice at Calcutta was Rs. 5/8/- per maund, and it rose to Rs. 7/1/- by July 1941. In January 1942, the price was Rs. 5/10/- per maund, and it rose to Rs. 8 per maund by July 1942, even though there was no question at that time of the province being short of rice. In January 1943, the price was Rs. 12/8/- per maund. What would it be in July 1943?

4. This was not a problem to be solved by any simple rule of three. It was a question of the psychology of millions of producers, traders, and consumers. The life of the community depended on the producer, who had a surplus, placing on the market, more quickly than in normal times, all his produce in excess of what he required for seed and the maintenance of his family, without retaining for himself even the usual carry-over beyond the next harvest. But with conditions as they were, his natural instinct was to assure his own safety by retaining an even larger carry-over than usual. And what was safe was also likely to prove profitable, for prices were rising. He had sold his surplus at the usual time in the previous year and had found that the trader who bought from him, had made a larger profit than usual, which he could have secured for himself if he had waited. He probably argued that he would not make the same mistake again. The traders no doubt argued likewise. The petty merchant was tempted to wait for a better price from the big merchant, and the big merchant from the bigger merchant. The fact that prices had risen abnormally and were still rising was sufficient to diminish both the volume and the rate of flow of supplies through the market. In such a situation, prices must rise even more sharply than before in order to overcome these "resistances".

5. It was imperative that the flow of supplies from the producer to the consumer should be maintained; and it was equally imperative that prices should not be allowed to rise much further. Failure in either respect would entail widespread starvation. A situation had already arisen in which it seemed certain that the normal operation of the trade machinery would fail to secure one or other of these results, if not both. Hence the crisis.

B.—Controlled procurement

6. The abnormal rise in prices in the latter half of November and December caused concern and the Bengal Government decided that steps must be taken to reduce the price level. The key to the situation was the Calcutta market, because prices in that market govern prices throughout the province. They, therefore, visualized the remedy in the first instance, as one of checking speculation and restoring healthy conditions in the Calcutta market. The process was later described as "breaking the Calcutta market". The question was the method by which this was to be brought about. Statutory price control had been tried and had failed. A simple order to the trade not to buy or to sell above a prescribed price, would only make conditions in the market worse, but experience had shown that the use of the "denial" stocks had helped to check the rise in prices. The Government proceeded to build on the results of this experience. They therefore undertook their first procurement scheme.

7. The area selected for the procurement operations was the Rajshahi Division in Northern Bengal—an area which was normally surplus and which had not been affected by the cyclone. Exports of rice and paddy from the Division were prohibited except under permit, with effect from the 22nd December,

and District Officers were directed to commence buying operations through local traders. The total quantity to be purchased was fixed at 2 lakhs of maunds (about 7,400 tons) and each district was given a quota out of this amount. Ceiling prices were fixed within which purchases should be made and District Officers were informed that, if necessary, requisitioning was to be resorted to till the quota fixed for the district had been procured. The scope of the scheme was naturally limited by the purpose for which it was framed. District Officers were told that the operations were not intended to enable them to build stocks for their own districts, and they would not be permitted to immobilize stocks for local purposes, except with previous sanction. All rice and paddy acquired were to be sent to Calcutta, with the exception of a limited quantity intended for Darjeeling. This scheme was abandoned on the 9th January, because the situation following the air-raids on Calcutta demanded a more comprehensive measure. By that time District Officers had purchased about 2,800 tons against the target of 7,400 tons.

8. Air-raids on Calcutta took place on the 20th, 22nd, 23rd, 24th, and 28th December 1942. The first raid had comparatively little disturbing effect, but evacuation began on a small scale on the 22nd and increased in volume until the 24th and 25th, after which there was little further exodus. The most important effect, however, of the raids was the closing down of a considerable number of foodgrain shops and the consequent interruption to the city's food supplies. At first immediate needs were met from air-raid reserves. The opening of closed shops in the markets was also tried, but this yielded little result as the shopkeepers had either removed or sold their stocks before leaving. Finally, on the 27th December, it was decided to requisition stocks in the city and to distribute them through controlled shops and "approved" markets.

9. Having been compelled to requisition stocks in Calcutta, the Bengal Government came to the conclusion that urgent steps would have to be taken to maintain supplies; and they therefore proceeded to undertake procurement operations on a more extensive scale than had been contemplated in December. The second scheme came into operation on the 9th January, and the monthly requirements were assessed at 3 lakh maunds of rice (11,021 tons) and 4·5 lakh maunds of paddy (16,532 tons). Purchases on this scale, the Bengal Government thought, could not be made by District Officers. They therefore selected seven agents from the trade and allotted to them areas in which to make their purchases. The maximum prices at which purchases were to be made were prescribed and District Officers were directed to warn all dealers in the buying areas that their licences would be cancelled and their stocks requisitioned if they bought above the Government buying rates. This direction, it may be incidentally noted, was inconsistent with the policy already adopted, namely that a legally prescribed maximum was not to be enforced on the transactions of private trade. A dealer who could not buy above the maximum rates fixed for Government purchases, except at the risk of the cancellation of his licence and the requisitioning of his stocks, was just as effectively subject to price control as if he had been liable to prosecution for a breach of a statutory order fixing maximum prices. But this inconsistency was unavoidable. As a letter sent out to District Officers on the 9th January said, the agents appointed by Government were unlikely to obtain the quantities of grain which Government required, unless competitive buying was prevented as far as possible. It was soon found that the warning did not suffice to protect the agents against competitive buying. Embargoes were, therefore, placed round the buying areas, prohibiting export except under permit. Similar embargoes were also placed round the non-buying areas in order to protect these areas against speculative buying. All these measures proved of no avail. The agents were not successful in purchasing the quantities required and the system was abandoned on the 17th February. The quantity purchased between the 10th January and the 17th February was only about 2,200 tons.

10. Early in January the Bengal Government appointed a Foodgrains Purchasing Officer. His functions generally were to supervise and control the activities of the buying agents and regulate the issue of export permits from districts from which exports were restricted. On the abandonment of the system of buying through trade agents, the procurement system consisted solely of the Foodgrains Purchasing Officer taking offers direct from the trade. The embargoes round the buying areas were maintained so as to enable the Purchasing Officer to combat competitive buying by control over exports from these areas. The non-buying areas also continued to be protected by locally administered embargoes on exports. The pace of purchases by the Foodgrains Purchasing Officer was, however, too slow. He bought only about 3,000 tons between the 18th February and the 11th March.

C.—"De-control"

11. The failure of successive schemes of procurement was accompanied by a steady rise in the price of rice, a diminution, week by week, in visible stocks, and signs of increasing panic in Calcutta. On the 4th January 1943, the price of coarse rice had dropped to Rs. 11/4/- a maund following sales by shopkeepers who left the city after the air-raids. On the 20th January, the price had moved up to Rs. 12/8/-, on the 3rd February to Rs. 13/2/-, on the 17th February to Rs. 13/12/-, and it reached Rs. 15 per maund on the 3rd March.

12. We have made a detailed study of the relevant trade statistics and the information supplied by the Government of Bengal about the movement of supplies throughout 1943 into Bengal from outside the province as well as in and out of Calcutta. We append to this report a note showing the results of our analysis.[1] These show that the net receipts into Calcutta during January and February 1943 were approximately 7,000 tons in each of these two months. This was only a fraction of the normal monthly requirements. Wheat also was in short supply and this added to the demand for rice. There is no doubt that the stocks in Calcutta at the beginning of the year were much smaller than in previous years, and that these were being consumed far more rapidly than they were being replaced. By the beginning of March, stocks were down to such a low level that it looked as if the city must starve within a fortnight, unless large supplies arrived quickly. Thus by early March the crisis had become acute in Calcutta.

13. As we have explained, it was imperative, at the beginning of 1943, that the flow of supplies to the consumer should be maintained and that prices should not be allowed to rise still further. Up to this point the Bengal Government were attempting to achieve both these objects. But they had failed. A breakdown in the supplies for Calcutta appeared imminent. A vital decision on policy had to be reached, and reached quickly. Was it practicable to hold prices and to maintain the flow of supplies? If it were not,—and the state of Calcutta appeared to show that it was not—what was to be done? Two courses were open. One was to intensify the policy of controlled procurement, hold prices rigidly, and pass over from reliance on voluntary sales to coercion, to whatever extent was necessary, to secure supplies at a price determined by Government. This meant seeking out stocks wherever they were held whether by traders or producers, and requisitioning those stocks not sold voluntarily. The other course was to allow prices to rise and to secure stocks by purchase in the market and by imports from other provinces, in the hope that it would be possible by the use of such stocks to moderate prices as had been done by the use of the "denial" stocks in the previous year. The Bengal Government carefully considered the *pros* and *cons* of both these courses. Risks were inherent in both. The former involved widespread and highly organized coercion. Were the administrative resources of the Government equal to

[1] Appendix V.

the task? If coercion failed, it would drive stocks even deeper underground, lead to disorders in the districts, and a complete break-down in Calcutta. On the other hand, the latter, *viz.*, de-control, particularly if it were not possible to acquire stocks sufficient to enable a moderating effect to be produced on prices, might result in prices rising to a level at which widespread famine would be inevitable. The probable consequences of both courses were recognized. Before a conclusion was reached, Commissioners and District Officers were consulted on the issue of coercion. With one exception, they were of opinion that measures which would probably involve the use of force were not practicable and would not produce sufficient supplies.

14. The Government of Bengal then made their choice. The decision was taken to abrogate any vestige of price control, and it was announced publicly on the 11th March in the following terms:—

"No Price Control in Wholesale Rice and Paddy Markets"

"To clear up misapprehensions which are still impeding the flow of paddy and rice into the markets, the Bengal Government declare categorically that there is and will be no statutory maximum price for wholesale transactions in paddy and rice. Both cultivators and traders are free to bring their grain to the market without fear of having it taken from them at a price to which they do not agree. No trader who has declared his stock under the Foodgrains Control Order will be compelled to part with it below the prevailing market price.

"(ii) The Bengal Government, in full accord with the Government of India, adhere to the policy of buying as much rice and paddy as possible by free market operations in order to secure the best use of the resources of the province and their most equitable distribution.

"(iii) The clear abrogation of any vestige of price control in the primary wholesale market does not imply unrestricted profiteering. Government's own operations as buyer and seller coupled with the removal of the black market are in their opinion most likely to be successful in moderating prices at a reasonable level; but to prevent buying at reckless prices by wealthy areas the embargoes prohibiting the movement of paddy and rice from one area in the province to another will remain in force. The Government itself takes the responsibility for the movement of paddy or rice to deficit areas."

15. Earlier in the year, the Central Government made a similar decision as regards the control of wheat prices. Arrangements had been made for the shipment of substantial quantities of wheat to India and at the end of January 1943, the statutory maximum prices for wheat which had been imposed in December 1941, were withdrawn. At this time the Government of India were of the opinion that prices should not be regulated by statutory control but by other methods. The decision reached by the Government of Bengal was, therefore, in accord with the policy of the Government of India at the time, and was indeed taken with their approval.

16. Simultaneously with the announcement of de-control, District Officers were directed to explain the policy to grain dealers in their districts and inform them that Government's object was to buy considerable quantities of rice and paddy. District Officers were also told to purchase without limit of price any rice and paddy offered to them in the first three days, up to a limit of 20,000 maunds; and after that, to report all offers to the Foodgrains Purchasing Officer for his orders. They were further directed to explain the measures which Government were taking to the public at large, through influential persons throughout the districts.

17. The immediate effect of de-control was an increase in the volume of supplies purchased by Government. Between the 12th and the 31st March, the total purchases made by the Foodgrains Purchasing Officer, direct or through

District Officers, exceeded 17,000 tons. This was much more than what had been purchased between the 22nd December 1942 and the 17th February 1943 under three different systems of procurement. The effect was, however, temporary and the rate of purchase subsequently slowed down. Purchases made from 1st April to the end of August amounted to only about 18,000 tons.

18. Prices, as had been expected, rose sharply. The following table shows how the price of coarse rice rose in Calcutta from Rs. 15 on the 3rd March to Rs. 30/10/- on the 17th May:—

Date	Price per maund
3rd March 1943	15 0 0
17th " "	19 6 0
22nd " "	21 4 0
29th " "	22 0 0
5th April "	21 3 0
12th " "	20 7 0
19th " "	19 5 0
26th " "	21 0 0
3rd May "	21 1 0
10th " "	25 0 0
17th " "	30 10 0

Prices in all the markets in Bengal were rising similarly. The following table gives the minimum price per maund of rice rulling in the last week of each month in five districts:

Month	Khulna	Burdwan	Rajshahi	Faridpur	Tipperah (Brahmanbaria)
1	2	3	4	5	6
	Rs. a. p.	Rs. a. p.	Rs. a. p.	Rs. a. p.	Rs. a. p.
1943					
January	10 6 0	11 12 0	13 4 0	12 4 0	9 8 0
February	12 8 0	13 8 0	13 8 0	13 2 0	12 0 0
March	18 12 0	20 6 0	18 0 0	25 0 0	20 0 0
April	22 8 0	23 8 0	20 0 0	24 0 0	31 0 0
May	30 0 0	29 12 0	26 5 0	31 0 0	25 0 0

19. The prices mentioned in the foregoing table are the minimum ruling prices. Actual prices were often higher and supplies were not always available for purchase even at these high prices. The effects of the high prices were felt throughout Bengal. On the 13th of May, the Commissioner of Burdwan Division reported: "Economic conditions approaching a crisis. Rice out of reach of the poor. Rice should be imported if the people are not to starve". A picture of the conditions developing in the Chittagong Division is given by the report from local officers, some of which we extract below.

11th May 1943.—Price of rice rose to Rs. 43 per maund in Noakhali but has come down again. Famine conditions prevailing among certain percentage of the population in Chittagong district. High prices keeping people on one meal.

29th May 1943.—Many people starving in Chittagong district owing to high prices. First gruel kitchen started in Chittagong.

11th June 1943.—No fall of prices in Chittagong or Noakhali. Definite cases of deaths from starvation throughout Chittagong and number of living skeletons increasing. Soup kitchens have already been started in acute starvation areas. 15 kitchens are feeding 1,500 persons daily. Scarcity should be declared. Gruel kitchens start working in Noakhali.

28th June 1943.—Number of destitutes in town increased. Eleven deaths in streets.

Thus, towards the end of the second quarter of 1943, famine had begun in parts of Bengal.

CHAPTER VII—SUPPLIES FROM OUTSIDE BENGAL

A.—NATURE OF THE PROBLEM

1. Bengal, always a net importer of wheat, was in the course of the decade preceding 1943, also becoming a net importer of rice. During the closing months of 1942 and in January and February 1943, arrivals of wheat into Bengal were much below requirements and were causing great anxiety. The consumers of wheat are largely concentrated in Greater Calcutta where the shortage of rice became acute early in March 1943. There was therefore, urgent need for imports of both rice and wheat. They were needed not merely for making good the shortage which had arisen. What was even more important, they were urgently needed in order to increase the stocks under the control of the Bengal Government, without which they were unable to check the dangerous rise of prices occurring in Bengal.

2. Imports from outside India had, however, ceased and the movement of supplies within India across the frontiers of provinces and states had been interrupted. We have described in Chapter IV the sequence of events which led to that situation. We saw that conditions had arisen in which the movement of supplies by the trade in accordance with effective market demand had become disorganized. The need for planning these movements had arisen. The capacity of surplus areas to export and the need of deficit areas to import had to be carefully assessed. The technique and organization required for this purpose were being evolved, in so far as the movement of supplies across provincial and state frontiers was concerned, by the Central Government. But their arrangements were not complete by March, 1943, when the need for imports became acute in Bengal. We must, therefore, describe briefly the nature of the problem with which the Government of India were faced and the arrangements they were making for solving the problem.

3. The following table shows the figures of net exports of rice from, and net imports of rice into, different areas in India on an average of 5 years ending 1941-42:—

RICE

In tens of thousands of tons

Net exports		Net imports	
Orissa (and Certain Eastern States)	18	Madras (and Travancore and Cochin)	50
Central Provinces (and Certain Eastern States)	15	Bombay (and States)	44
Sind	17	Bihar	19
Assam	2	United Provinces	17
Punjab (and States)	1	Bengal	14
		Hyderabad	6
		Mysore	4
		Rajputana States	3
		Central India States	1
		North-West Frontier Province	1
		Delhi	1
	53		160

The figures in this table are not complete because they take no account of the movements by road and country-boat across provincial and state frontiers, and they also exclude imports from Nepal and by sea through certain maritime States. But they are adequate for our present purpose, which is to indicate the areas which were normally surplus and those which were normally deficit in rice, and the approximate magnitude of those surpluses and deficits.

4. The experience of the previous five years suggested that the quantity of rice available from the surplus areas was between 500,000 and 600,000 tons, while the quantities required by the deficit areas amounted to 1·6 million tons. There was thus a gap of more than one million tons, which was normally covered by net imports but could not be so covered during 1943. Purchases on behalf of the Defence Services were increasing. During 1942-3 they exceeded 100,000 tons and in 1943-4 were nearly 200,000 tons. To that extent, the pressure of the demand on supplies available for export was increasing. A system of planned movement of supplies, therefore, first of all involved a decision as to how much should be exported from each area, and how the total of the exportable supplies was to be allocated between deficit areas and the Defence Services. Decisions on these points were not a matter of mere arithmetic, because the outturn of crops varied from season to season; the carry-over was a significant factor moderating the effects of seasonal variations in production and this factor also varied; and lastly, the proportion of the supplies arriving in the markets had become uncertain owing to abnormal disturbances in marketing conditions. Under these conditions it was extremely difficult to reach agreed decisions.

5. The following table furnishes, in respect of wheat, figures corresponding to those for rice:—

WHEAT

In tens of thousands of tons

Net exports		Net imports	
Punjab and States	68	Bengal	25
Sind	15	Bombay (and States)	22
Central India States	10	Madras (and States)	8
United Provinces	8	Rajputana States	8
Central Provinces	2	Bihar	7
		Delhi	4
		North-West Frontier Province	2
		Mysore	2
		Assam	2
		Orissa	1
		Hyderabad	1
	103		82

On the basis of the experience of the five years preceding 1942-3, the surplus areas were able to provide one million tons, while the deficit areas required 820,000 tons. The demand of the Defence Services was, however, greater for wheat than for rice. This had risen to 300,000 tons during 1942-3 and nearly 400,000 tons in 1943-4.

6. Though the production and consumption of millets in India are about the same as those of wheat, they do not enter into the long distance trade of India to anything like the same extent, as will be seen from the following table:—

MILLETS

In tens of thousands of tons

Net exports		Net imports	
Central India States	6	Bombay (and States)	8
United Provinces	5	Rajputana States	3
Sind	1	Madras	1
Punjab (and States)	1	Delhi	1
Hyderabad	1	Bihar	1
Mysore	1		
	15		14

It was necessary, however, that the flow of these supplies should be maintained and, in view of the rice shortage, increased as much as possible.

7. The determination of the quantities to be exported from surplus areas and their allocation to deficit areas and to the Defence Services was only the first step towards a planned movement of supplies. Arrangements had to be made for these quantities to be purchased and distributed. The functions to be undertaken by the Central Government and by the Governments of the importing and exporting areas had to be agreed upon. The agencies to be employed and the mode of their operation had to be settled. It was not until these agencies were established and were in proper working order that the movement of supplies could proceed according to plan. We shall now describe the successive stages in the evolution of the system of planned movement of supplies and the position reached by March 1943.

B.—The evolution of the basic plan

8. At the end of December 1941, a Wheat Commissioner for India was appointed, and on the 30th April 1942, the Wheat Control Order was notified. In July 1942, a Civil Supplies Commissioner for rice and other commodities was appointed. Before these officers could proceed to plan, their energies were occupied in making *ad hoc* arrangements for meeting the immediate pressing difficulties of deficit areas. The first scheme for centralized purchase of foodgrains emerged in September 1942, and was considered at the Sixth Price Control Conference which met in that month. The plan of action approved by this Conference was as follows:—

"(i) That in order to eliminate competitive buying, exports of wheat from the surplus provinces and states should be prohibited except by a Central Government organization which should purchase the requirements of the military, labour, and the deficit provinces and states up to a pre-determined figure for each surplus province or state in consultation with the Provincial or the State Government concerned and arrange for transport;

"(ii) That the Central organization should make its purchases in the surplus provinces or states through agencies selected in consultation with the Provincial or the State Governments concerned;

"(iii) That the Central organization should conduct its purchase operations in close collaboration with the price control authorities in the surplus provinces and states and that the latter authorities should give the Central organization all possible assistance in obtaining supplies at controlled rates;

"(iv) That in allocating the supplies available for civil distribution, the Central organisation, in consultation with the Provincial Governments and

States should give priority to the requirements of fair price shops, consumers' co-operative societies, industrial areas, big cities, public utilities, and places where large military works are under construction;

"(v) That the supplies allocated to a deficit province or state should be despatched only to consignees approved by the Director of Civil Supplies or the Director himself in that province or state;

"(vi) That in calculating the export quotas from the producing areas and the import quotas for the consuming areas, the principle of 'equality of sacrifice' should be borne in mind; in other words, the consumption in each area as revealed by the available data regarding normal production, receipts, and despatches, should generally be subjected to the same percentage reduction (subject to variations in the case of particular areas in view of changes in population and other special circumstances) as that which the consumption in the country as a whole is likely to suffer owing to inadequacy of supplies....."

9. The system thus described, it will be noticed, applied specifically to wheat. The Conference also recommended the adoption of a similar scheme for the "staple competitive foodgrains, namely, rice, jowar, bajra, ragi, barley, gram, and maize". But whereas in the case of wheat the whole of India was regarded as one unit, and the responsibility was laid on the Centre for purchasing supplies from surplus and allocating them to deficit areas and to the Defence Services, the Conference favoured the division of India into different regions, and the treatment of each region as a unit for the control of inter-provincial movements of staple foodgrains other than wheat. It was proposed that the "primary responsibility for distribution within each region" should be vested in the Regional Price and Supply Board, operating "either through its own machinery or through the machinery of the Provincial Governments subject to the general direction of the Central Government". It was, however, realised that it would be necessary to make purchases within one region for export to another, and the Conference recommended that such purchases should be made by the Central Government, or by the Provincial Government acting on behalf of the Central Government. These Regional Prices and Supply Boards had been constituted only shortly before; and, though they performed some useful co-ordinating functions, they did not in fact undertake the "primary responsibility" for inter-provincial movements within the region as visualized at this Conference.

10. On the 7th October 1942, the Government of India addressed a letter to the provinces outlining a scheme of co-ordinated purchases of foodgrains in surplus provinces in order to meet the requirements of the Defence Services and deficit provinces. The scheme followed, with certain modifications, the general outline of the recommendations of the Sixth Price Control Conference.

11. On the 21st November the Government of India informed the Provincial Governments that they had decided to initiate a scheme whereby wheat would be purchased by a Central organization through selected agents, and the produce assigned to importing centres. The grain would be consigned to the Provincial Director of Civil Supplies or his nominee. The Provincial Governments were told that they should keep the Wheat Commissioner informed of their requirements, and he would meet their demands to the extent that supply was available.

12. A separate Food Department was established at the Centre on the 2nd December 1942, and on the 14th of that month the first Food Conference met. The first item on its agenda was "to frame agreed estimates of the foodgrain requirements and resources of the main administrative areas of the country, and to draw up a programme for the utilization of such stocks as may be available on the lines best calculated to meet the most essential needs of the country; in other words, to frame a quota programme for supplying the deficit areas".

13. When the Conference met, the winter rice crop was being harvested in some provinces and was still on the ground in others. The wheat crop had only recently been sown, and nothing could yet be predicted about its outturn. A rough calculation of the requirements of deficit areas and the surpluses of surplus areas was made, and the result, which was as follows, caused some dismay: "The shortage in rice alone is 19 lakhs of tons, assuming that Bengal gets no rice from outside. If Bengal has to get rice, the deficit is increased by the quantity that Bengal requires. The shortage in wheat is 4 lakhs of tons. But that only covers the next five months. This is the position based on the statements that have been made this morning".

14. The reference to the possibility of Bengal requiring imports of rice, it will be noticed, was couched in terms which indicated uncertainty. From what we have said about conditions in Bengal, this might appear surprising, but it correctly reflected the assessment which those present at the Conference, including the representatives of Bengal, made of the relative urgency of the need for imports of the several deficit areas. This fact is so important that we must explain the situation at the time in provinces other than Bengal.

15. Bombay produced on the average of the five years ending 1941-2, 760,000 tons of rice and consumed 1·05 million tons. If it received no imports, it would have to manage with, less than three-fourths of its normal supply. The dependence of Travancore and Cochin on imports was even greater. Madras was no less deficit than Bengal and had had a poor rice crop at the end of 1942. Bengal had experienced poor crops before and yet had imported relatively small quantities. Could it not manage this time without any imports? That was the general attitude.

16. The case of Bengal for imports of wheat was quite clear; not so the need for imports of rice, in a situation which was apparently so much more serious for other deficit areas. The representatives of Bengal pressed their claim for wheat, made it clear that exports of rice were out of the question, and left open the possibility of the province requiring imports of rice to a later date. The Director of Civil Supplies, Bengal, said, "We do not require rice in the next few months, but statistically we are heavily in deficit for the coming year". When a doubt was expressed about the correctness of the crop forecast, he added, "I should say at once that this is the first forecast, and the indications are that the final forecast is likely to be worse."[1]

17 The Conference also discussed the question whether purchases for export and for the Defence Services should be made in the provinces by an organization under Central control or by agencies set up by the Provincial Governments. Divergent views were expressed, and a conclusion was not reached on this important point. On the 2nd January 1943, the Provincial Governments were addressed by the Government of India on the subject. Pending a decision as to whether the buying organization should be Central or Provincial, the provinces were directed to prohibit, except under permit, the export of all major foodgrains and to limit permits to purchases made by, or on behalf of, importing Governments.

18. On the 27th January, the Government of India informed the Provincial Governments that they had decided that purchases for export should be made by Provincial Governments and not by a Central organization, and the Provinces were requested to set up procurement machinery immediately, so that

---

[1]In the light of subsequent events, the attitude of the representatives of the Government of Bengal at this Conference evoked considerable public interest and has been the subject of much misunderstanding. Our attention has been drawn to the following passage occurring in a publication entitled "Food Rationing and Supply, 1943-44" issued in 1944 by the Office of the League of Nations, Geneva: "Bengal alone among the principal Provincial Governments confident that it could manage to subsist on its own rice crop, declined to join in the collective scheme drawn up at the December 1942 Food Conference. when the main anxiety was about wheat." This is not a correct description of the attitude of the Government of Bengal.

purchase operations could begin in advance of the settlement of the target figures for surplus and deficits. No target figures were given in this letter. A formula for the fixation of target figures was sent to the Provincial Governments on the 16th February. The Second Food Conference met in the third week of February. Agreement was reached between the Provinces and the Centre on the operative details forming part of the general scheme of the Basic Plan arrangements, but the question of the quantities to be supplied by surplus to deficit areas was left undecided.

19. The conclusions reached at the Second Food Conference were announced by the Government of India to the provinces and the states in a letter dated the 12th March which indicated the action required on the part of local administrations and stressed the urgency of setting up purchasing organizations. This was followed about a month later by a letter giving preliminary figures under the plan. This letter also recalled that over three months had been spent in reaching the greatest common measure of agreement in respect of the plan and the methods to be adopted, and reminded the provinces and states that the figures put forward were "targets" at which all Governments must aim. Early in May, a monthly movement plan was forwarded, showing the quantities to be despatched month by month with sources and destinations.

20. The total quantity of foodgrains which it was planned to distribute was over 4 million tons, including 1·5 million tons of wheat, 1·1 million tons of rice, the same quantity of millets, and nearly 400,000 tons of gram. The figures for rice and millets represented the quantities to be moved between the 1st December 1942 and the 30th November 1943, while the corresponding period for wheat and gram was the 1st April 1943 to the 31st March 1944. The total quota allotted to Bengal was 350,000 tons of rice, 224,000 tons of wheat, 200,000 tons of millets, and 19,000 tons of gram. The sources from which these supplies were to be moved were as follows:

	Tons
RICE—	
Assam	63,000
Orissa	37,000
Eastern States	50,000
Bihar	185,000
United Provinces	15,000
	350,000
WHEAT—	
Punjab	160,000
United Provinces	20,000
Bihar	24,000
Overseas	20,000
	224,000
MILLETS—	
United Provinces	195,000
Punjab	5,000
	200,000

C. The "Rescue" Plan and Free Trade.

21. We have described at the end of Chapter VI the emergency which arose in Calcutta early in March 1943, when the Government of Bengal decided on "de-control" in order to increase the flow of supplies within Bengal. The position was serious, and the Government of India decided that an emergency mobilization of supplies should be made from the areas adjoining Bengal in the

Eastern Region, in order to assist the Bengal Government in checking the rise in prices. The subject was discussed at a meeting held in Calcutta on the 10th March 1943 and subsequent days, attended by the representatives of Bengal, Bihar, Orissa, Assam, and the Eastern States. The specific measure of assistance which it was proposed to give to Bengal, was the supply of 60,000 tons of rice within a period of from three weeks to a month. It was hoped that, if this quantity were obtained in a short period, it would be possible to "break" the Calcutta market, start supplies moving again, and cause prices to fall to more reasonable levels. It was proposed that this quantity of 60,000 tons should be obtained in equal proportions from the provinces of Orissa, Bihar, and Assam, and from the Eastern States.

22. The plan failed because, with the exception of supplies from Orissa, the quotas were not forthcoming. The Bihar Government maintained that market conditions in Bihar had rapidly deteriorated since the beginning of March, and that, until confidence had been restored in the province, it would be impossible to make purchases even for their own deficit areas, let alone for Bengal. Their final conclusion was that, provided they were able to satisfy the monthly demand of 8,000 tons for the industrial areas in their own province, they would allow the export to Bengal of two tons for every one ton they were able to supply to their own deficit areas. Eventually Bihar provided something less than 1,000 tons to the Darjeeling district in Bengal. Orissa agreed to help and supplied about 25,000 tons. The Eastern States had a large surplus but no purchasing organization was in existence and communications were difficult. A purchasing agency was appointed, but the quantity procured was small—less than 5,000 tons. Assam promised assistance but the quantity supplied at the time was only 2,350 tons of paddy.

23. We have seen that the immediate effect of de-control was an improvement in the flow of supplies within the province. This, together with arrivals from Orissa, eased the position in Calcutta but the supplies were not sufficient to achieve the primary object of "breaking" the Calcutta market. Prices kept on rising. The Provincial Government despatched some of the stocks which they had acquired, to deficit districts, and this effected a temporary improvement. The situation in Chittagong was described as easier. The arrival of larger supplies of wheat also helped, and there was a marked decline in the prices of wheat and wheat-products. But the improvement was only temporary. By the end of April, stocks of rice in Calcutta were again running low, and there was reason to fear that, by the middle of May when the supplies from Orissa would cease, Calcutta would be back again in the same state as it was in March. Meanwhile, reports from the districts clearly indicated the approach of famine. The crisis had not been overcome.

24. By the beginning of April the Bengal Government were reaching the conclusion that the Basic Plan could not help them. In a letter addressed to the Central Government early in April 1943, the Provincial Government, while expressing their great appreciation of the measures taken by the Government of India to enable them to meet the situation which had developed in Bengal, felt it their duty to inform the Central Government that "the attempt to treat the provinces of Assam, Bengal, Bihar, and Orissa as separate units for the procurement of, and movement of trade in, rice and paddy was fast leading to disaster. If not quickly abandoned, it will result not only in frustration of the Government of India's purchase plan, starvation in deficit areas, and disorder, but also in grave shortage of the future crop owing to interruption in the flow of seed supplies". The Government of Bengal did not challenge the merits of the Basic Plan in regard to wheat. The argument was that as wheat had to be moved long distances by rail to deficit provinces, a Government agency could canalize the trade as effectively as a private agency. But the case of rice in the Eastern Region, they argued, was different. "Obstructions to the movement of paddy and paddy products, in an area so

closely interlinked as the north-eastern region, are fraught with the gravest consequences. They are grave in the case of rice; they are more grave in the case of paddy since they not only interrupt the supply of paddy to the mills but also interrupt the hundreds of cross streams of paddy flowing by multifarious channels across the provincial boundaries from the producing rural areas to other rural areas where paddy can be hand milled and distributed". The Bengal Government realized that the fact that events had compelled them to impose an embargo round the province as well as round certain districts within the province was inconsistent with their contention. The answer to this apparent inconsistency, they said, was "that the Bengal Government was trying to achieve some measure of internal price and supply equilibrium before completely breaking down these barriers; but if the desired equilibrium cannot soon be obtained, the barriers will have to be broken despite the risk from the pent up forces that will thus be let loose. They are of opinion that the logic of events will compel the Central Government to adopt the same course in respect of this region".

25. Towards the end of April 1943, the Government of India were also beginning to doubt whether the Basic Plan would solve the Bengal problem. The Plan had come into operation from the middle of April and from that date surplus provinces were to begin deliveries in accordance with the programme prepared by the Government of India. But the "target" figures had caused dismay among the provinces. The Government of Bihar, which had been assessed to supply 200,000 tons of rice and 50,000 tons of wheat, lost no time in pointing out that Bihar was a deficit and not a surplus province and that they could not undertake the responsibility for the disastrous effects which would, in their considered opinion, follow from the attempt to give effect to the Central Government's proposals. Again, procurement machinery had not been established in the majority of provinces and until such machinery was in operation deliveries according to the programme could not begin. The emergency arrangements made in March had failed. Something had to be done to get more supplies into Bengal.

26. The situation was discussed during the last few days of April in Calcutta at a meeting between the representatives of the Government of India and the Bengal Government. The attitude of the Government of Bengal was that if the Government of India could not give a guarantee that the entire supply of rice provided for in the Basic Plan would be delivered within the next few months, they must press for the immediate abolition of the trade barriers between the provinces of the Eastern Region. After careful consideration the Government of India came to the conclusion that the arrangements for procurement were so far behind in the provinces of the Eastern Region, that the supplies to Bengal under the Basic Plan would not be forthcoming in time. It was also impossible to make good the deficiency by draining other areas; the urgent needs of Bombay, Travancore, and Cochin had to be met from those areas. An attempt to maintain the Basic Plan in the Eastern Region and divert to Bengal supplies of rice from outside the Eastern Region was, therefore, likely to destroy the all-India Basic Plan.

27. Two proposals were considered. One was unrestricted free trade and the other was a scheme described as "modified free trade". Both the proposals involved the withdrawal of powers from the provincial Governments, but "modified free trade" involved the retention of powers of control and their exercise by a single authority, the Regional Food Commissioner. Inter-provincial exports were to be controlled by a system of licences to private traders, issued on the recommendation of the importing Government, and it was contemplated that those recommendations would be made on the basis of each trader undertaking to bring the imports to a specific point for sale at that point. To that extent the Bengal Government would be in a position to

control the distribution of supplies. It was also the intention that the licences granted in any month should conform to the figures of the Basic Plan as regards the quantity to be moved into Bengal. By this means the arrangements already made for railway movements would be maintained and the accuracy of the Basic Plan figures would be given a reasonable test. It was argued that the system, being under full Central control, could if necessary be developed into complete free-trade, or, if the necessary organization in the provinces could be rapidly established on an efficient basis, reversion to the Basic Plan could follow. In a letter dated the 6th May the Government of India communicated to the Provincial Governments of the Eastern Region their decision to introduce "modified free trade" on this basis, and fixed the 10th May at Calcutta for consultations on administrative and operational details. It was also explained that the gravity of the emergency had made it impossible to consult the Provincial Governments concerned.

28. This scheme never came into effect. During the further discussions between the representatives of the Government of India and the Bengal Government, the Provincial Government maintained their preference for unrestricted free trade. At the meeting held on the 10th May with the representatives of other Provinces of the Eastern Region the two schemes were discussed. Opinion was not unanimous. The Assam representative preferred "modified free trade" while the Orissa representative preferred complete free trade on the assumption that it would enable Orissa to obtain supplies from the adjoining States. The Bihar representative considered both equally objectionable. He pointed out "that a probable result of free trade would be that the scramble for supplies by Bengal buyers, with the resulting movement of enormous stocks from Bihar to Bengal, would make it impossible for the Bihar Government to guarantee food for its own labouring population at a reasonable price". The Government of India decided that some form of free trade was essential, and in view of the insistence of Bengal on unrestricted free trade abandoned their initial preference for modified free trade. Once again, the urgent need for a decision did not allow of the provinces being consulted. The representatives of the provinces who attended the conference on the 10th May, had no opportunity of consulting their Governments as regards the relative merits of unrestricted free trade and modified free trade.

29. The introduction of free trade led immediately to the invasion of the provinces of Bihar, Orissa, and Assam by a large army of purchasers from Bengal; in fact, it began a week before. The Bihar Government have described the position as follows:—

"The new policy resulted in large scale incursion of speculators, agents of big business, hoarders and small buyers from Bengal into all the markets...... Prices flared up almost immediately. Merchants, who had previously sold their stocks to Government tried to evade delivery by any means in their power because they received higher offers from Bengal buyers. The Bengal merchants or their agents went into the interior villages and offered fantastic prices, as a result of which the arrivals of supplies in local markets were extremely poor. Prices fluctuated almost from hour to hour due to wild speculation, and ownership of goods passed through various hands before they actually moved".

But it was not only private dealers who were buying. The Provincial Governments were also in the market. The Bengal Government through their agent were making extensive purchases. Directly free trade was established, the Government of Bihar ordered their Trade Adviser and District Officers to buy all available foodgrains; stocks in the mills were also bought or requisitioned. Purchases, however, had ceased by the end of June, as by that time prices in Bihar were above the maximum limits laid down by the Provincial Government. The Government of Orissa improvised purchasing agencies in every district. In addition they obtained stocks by the rigorous enforcement of the Foodgrains Control Order. Merchants from outside Orissa who, without obtaining licences from the Orissa Government, had made purchases were prosecuted and their stocks requisitioned. By these means and by active purchases in the local markets the Orissa Government were able within a fortnight to acquire several thousand tons of rice at reasonable prices.

In Bihar, the food situation deteriorated rapidly on the introduction of free trade, and in order to prevent widespread distress and panic, the Provincial Government opened departmental shops for the supply of foodgrains at concessional rates to low-paid Government servants and the essential services, and "poor" shops for relief to the poorer sections of the community. The Government of Orissa have described the effect of free trade as follows:—"It was undoubtedly the greatest factor in causing high prices, hoarding, and the unavailability of foodgrains to consumers in the latter part of 1943. . . . It caused the disappearance of rice from the local markets and led to serious mal-distribution and economic maladjustments.".

30. Free trade led to serious disputes between the Bengal Government, their agent, and other Bengal traders on the one hand and the Governments of Bihar and Orissa on the other. Bengal traders were loud in their complaints of the treatment they were receiving both in Bihar and Orissa, and the agent of the Bengal Government complained that his staff was subject to many forms of obstruction in both the provinces. It was asserted that in Orissa stocks had been requisitioned in order to prevent them leaving the province. The Bengal Government joined in these complaints and asserted that other Provincial Governments were doing their best to prevent rice leaving their provinces. In short, the allegations were that free trade was not being allowed to operate. These did not go unchallenged. The Bihar Government in a letter to the Central Government dated the 4th June 1943, denied emphatically that they had placed any obstruction whatsoever in the way of free trade; nor were they aware of any obstruction on the part of their officers. They added that should any specific case of obstruction be brought to their notice they would of course take necessary action and rectify the mistake, and in conclusion drew the attention of the Government of India to "the probability of such charges being made by merchants and speculators from outside the province who, in collusion with the sellers whose stocks had already been bought by the Provincial Government's purchasing organization, are anxious to get control of such stocks by any means". The Orissa Government maintained that the requisitioning undertaken in the province was confined to stocks bought by unlicensed dealers. Fortunately the dispute between the Government of Bengal and the Orissa Government in regard to requisitioning was settled amicably in September 1943.

D.—Restoration of the basic plan

31. The free trade policy succeeded in procuring some supplies for Bengal. This apparent initial success and the continued slowness of deliveries under the Basic Plan to other deficit areas, which was causing concern, led the Government of India to a further change of policy. They decided to introduce with effect from the 15th June free trading conditions throughout India with the exception of the region comprising the Punjab and Sind, and certain other areas in North-West India. This decision, which was also taken without consultation with the provinces and states, aroused immediately a storm of protest from the deficit as well as from the surplus areas. In view of the strength and unanimity of the opposition the Government of India postponed the introduction of free trade in other parts of India and called the Third All-India Food Conference. That conference met on the 7th July, emphatically rejected free trade, and recommended that the Basic Plan should be continued with such adjustments of quotas as might be necessary. The

Government of India accepted its views and rejected free trade "as a policy which was not to be considered except as an objective for the return to normal conditions". At the same time, a Food Grains Policy Committee was set up, consisting of non-officials, and officials representing the Central Government as well as Provincial and State Governments. The recommendations of this Committee, which covered the whole range of the problems of supply and distribution of foodgrains, were accepted almost in entirety by all the Governments concerned. The fundamental principles of policy and administration were firmly laid down and the country as a whole proceeded to build up the system of food administration which is functioning today.

32. Free trade in the Eastern Region continued a little longer. On the 9th July 1943, the Government of India issued instructions to the effect that first, Bengal should not be isolated by the re-imposition of provincial barriers until the revised Basic Plan based on the reassessed figures had been drawn up and had come into effective operation, and, secondly, the Governments of the Eastern Region must be prepared for the continuance of the existing conditions, that is free trade, until the Government of India decided that supplies to Bengal had begun to move in accordance with the programme laid down in the revised Basic Plan. On the 15th July these instructions were modified and it was laid down that first, free trade contracts for export from one province to another would be valid provided the date of such contracts was not later than the 8th July 1943, and secondly, no free trade contracts requiring export from one province to another, which had been executed between the 9th July and 31st July, would be valid unless approved by the appropriate authority in the province in which the purchase had been made. The Government of Bengal protested strongly against these modifications, and urged that their effect would be to deprive Bengal of all supplies from the other provinces in the Region with effect from the 9th July, although the allotments under the revised Basic Plan had not begun to move.

33. Although, as a result of an agreement with the Bihar Government in regard to the movement of foodgrains contracted for export during the free trade period, the embargo round Bihar was re-imposed with effect from the 31st July 1943, formal orders restoring to the Governments of Assam, Bengal, Bihar, and Orissa, powers under sub-rule 2 of rule 81 of the Defence of India Rules were not issued till August. The restoration took effect from the 16th of that month and from that date free trade in the Eastern Region formally came to an end. In practice, it had ceased to operate from the middle of July. In restoring the powers under the Defence of India Rules to the Provincial Governments the Government of India laid it down that valid contracts for export from one unit to another made under free trade conditions should be fully honoured, with no attempt to avoid them in any way, and that the movement of foodgrains in the fulfilment of these contracts should not be hampered.

34. The net effect of free trade on supplies and prices of rice can now be described.

(i) It has been estimated that during the free trade period 91,000 tons of foodgrains moved into Bengal from other parts of the Eastern Region. Of these 38,000 tons represented despatches out of purchases made by the Government of Bengal through their agent.

(ii) The effect on prices in Bengal was negligible. The price of coarse rice in Calcutta had risen from Rs. 21/1/- per maund on 3rd May 1943 to Rs. 30/10/- per maund on the 17th of that month—the day before the introduction of free trade. A considerable drop in prices on the first day of free trade was reported but it proved to be momentary. The following table shows that, apart from a slight drop in the week immediately after the introduction of free trade, the price continued to remain above Rs. 30 a maund throughout the free trade period:

Date	Price Rs. A. P.
24th May 1943	29 2 0
31st „ „	30 6 0
7th June 1943	31 8 0
14th „ „	31 10 0
21st „ „	31 0 0
28th „ „	31 0 0
7th July 1943	30 8 0
14th „ „	30 8 0
21st „ „	30 11 0
28th „ „	31 3 0
2nd August 1943	31 5 0

Prices in some of the districts of Bengal were higher than in Calcutta and in a few cases touched Rs. 40 a maund.

(iii) While prices in Bengal did not fall, prices in the other provinces of the Eastern Region rose steeply. For instance, the price of rice in Bihar during the week ending 12th May varied between Rs. 8/12/- to Rs. 9/4/- a maund, whereas during the week ending July 12th, it rose to Rs. 23 and Rs. 25 a maund.

Again, in Orissa, in the Balasore District, the price rose to Rs. 24 a maund within a few weeks of the introduction of free trade.

35. The Third All-India Food Conference had recommended that the Basic Plan should continue with such adjustments of quotas as might be necessary. The revised Plan was announced by the Government of India on the 27th July 1943. The original Plan provided for the delivery of the following quantities of rice to Bengal between July 1943 and November 1943:—

	Tons
July	43,300
August	43,200
September	39,300
October	44,200
November	46,900
Total	216,900

In place of this total of 216,900 tons, the revised Basic Plan gave Bengal 15,000 tons of rice. In addition, Bengal was given 340,000 tons of wheat and wheat products, 46,000 tons of gram, and 40,000 tons of millets. The reaction in Bengal to this meagre allotment of rice was one of utter consternation. But, as the Government of India pointed out, the total surplus of rice declared by the administrations of the surplus areas was only 79,000 tons, and of this, Bengal had been given 15,000 tons. This allotment was, however, considerably exceeded by the end of the year.

36. The result of all the measures taken during the course of the year 1943 was as follows:—

(a) The total quantity of rice despatched during 1943, on private as well as on Government account from other parts of India was 294,000 tons. Despatches from Orissa amounted to nearly 110,000 tons, from Bihar 52,000 tons, from the Punjab 39,000 tons, from the Eastern States 32,000 tons, from Sind 24,000 tons, from the Central Provinces 17,000 tons, from Assam 12,000 tons, and the balance was made up of smaller quantities from other areas.

(b) The Bengal Government have told us that the despatches during 1943 from outside Bengal according to railway receipts held by them amounted to 177,000 tons. This includes purchases made during the free trade period by their agent but does not, of course, include arrivals in Bengal on private account.

(c) According to "trade" statistics the total arrivals of rice in Bengal during 1943, exclusive of rice in transit through Bengal, amounted to 264,000 tons.[1] The net arrivals during each of the four quarters of the year are shown separately in the table below.

	(In thousands of tons)
1st quarter	17
2nd ,,	78
3rd ,,	69
4th ,,	100
Total	264

37. (i) The total quantity of wheat and wheat products despatched to Bengal during the year 1943 amounted to 373,000 tons, of which 222,000 tons were sent from the Punjab, 35,000 tons from the United Provinces, and 10,000 tons from Sind. The imports from overseas amounted to 93,000 tons.

(ii) The total arrivals in Bengal during the year amounted to 339,000 tons, thus—

	(In thousands of tons)
1st quarter	26
2nd ,,	38
3rd ,,	99
4th ,,	176
Total	339

(iii) In addition to wheat, about 55,000 tons of millets were received from other provinces during the year. The greater part came from the United Provinces.

[1] Figures compiled by the Department of Commercial Intelligence and Statistics. The amount of net arrivals is smaller than that mentioned in Sub-para. (a). The difference is presumably due to goods in transit.

CHAPTER VIII—SUPPLY AND DISTRIBUTION IN BENGAL

A.—The "food drive"

1. We have seen that on the 11th March, the Government of Bengal, having decided on de-control, made a public announcement declaring "that there is and will be no statutory maximum price for wholesale transactions in paddy and rice. Both cultivators and traders are free to bring their grain to the market without fear of having it taken from them at a price to which they do not agree. No trader who has declared his stock under the Foodgrains Control Order will be compelled to part with it below the prevailing market price". It is clear that if the cultivator or the trader were free to bring his grain to the market, he was also free to withhold it from the market; in other words, hoarding was permissible. If grain was withheld from the market to any appreciable extent, prices were bound to go up, and it would be legitimate for the cultivator or the trader who had withheld his stocks to get the benefit of the higher price; in other words, he could profiteer. The Government of Bengal feared that this might happen, but they did not intend that it should, and hence they announced that "the clear abrogation of any vestige of price control in the primary wholesale market does not imply unrestricted profiteering. Government's own operations as buyer and seller coupled with the removal of the blackmarket are, in their opinion, most likely to be successful in moderating prices at a reasonable level; but to prevent buying at reckless prices by wealthy areas, the embargoes prohibiting the movement of paddy and rice from one area in the province to another will remain in force." Again, early in April, District Officers were instructed to impress upon stockholders, cultivators, and the public generally that peace-time stocks cannot be maintained under the stress of war, and that "the maintenance of what might ordinarily be regarded as a normal peace-time stock will not necessarily absolve the individual from the offence of hoarding." Most of the embargoes referred to in the announcement of the 11th March were removed within a few weeks and experience proved that the operations of Government as buyer and seller were on too limited a scale to reduce prices to a reasonable level. The first major attempt to "break" the Calcutta market by imports from other provinces had also failed. Prices had risen; the price of rice was higher than what the poorer sections of the population could afford to pay and they were beginning to starve.

2. This was the situation when, at the end of April and early in May, the representatives of the Government of India and the Government of Bengal conferred in Calcutta and the decision was taken to introduce free trade in the Eastern Region. Another decision taken during these consultations was to launch a propaganda drive for the purpose of convincing the people that the supply position did not justify the high prices prevailing. It was hoped that this propaganda, coinciding with the arrival of imports, would induce a freer flow of stocks into the market and bring down prices. These objects were not achieved, and the propaganda failed.

3. In the first week of June, 1943 the Government of Bengal launched a province-wide "food drive" the objects of which were defined as follows:—

'To ascertain the actual statistical position, to locate hoards, to stimulate the flow of grain from agriculturists to the markets, and to organise distribution of local surpluses as loans or by sales to those who were in need of foodgrains."

In March 1943 something of a similar nature had been considered as an alternative to de-control. It was not undertaken at the time, partly because it was believed that rural opinion would have regarded it essentially as an operation to drive food out of the rural areas into Calcutta and the towns, at a time when there was strong and in many cases violent opposition to the movement of grain from local areas. In June it was considered that conditions were more propitious because of the introduction of free trade in the Eastern Region. The feeling of isolation had lessened, Calcutta was in a position to draw on external markets, and a large *aus* crop was on the ground. The problem in the villages was the effective distribution of local resources, and for this purpose it was expected that the co-operation of influential villagers could be relied upon.

In carrying out the drive the entire province, with the exception of Calcutta and the municipalities of Howrah and Bally, was divided into units consisting of two unions in the case of rural areas and a municipal ward or block comprising 3,500 or 4,000 houses in the case of urban areas. Each unit was further sub-divided into sub-units consisting of a village or a group of villages. In urban areas a sub-unit consisted approximately of 100 houses. Each unit was put in charge of a squad consisting of one officer, 4 official subordinates, and 4 non-officials. They were given instructions to organize sub-unit committees, each committee to consist of 12 members who were elected, as far as possible, by the residents in the sub-unit concerned. Under the supervision of the squad in charge, the committee of each sub-unit was made responsible for undertaking a systematic house to house inquiry to discover the quantities of rice, paddy, and other foodgrains held by each family, as well as the requirements of that family, according to a prescribed scale, for the period from the 16th June to the 31st December 1943. The intention was that a complete balance sheet for each sub-unit should be prepared showing the food stocks in hand, the amounts likely to be received from the *aus* harvest, the actual requirements of each family, and the balance available on the 16th June. The committees were then to use their influence to prevail upon persons holding surplus stocks to sell or lend, directly or through the committee, to those who either had nothing or did not have enough.

4. It was also laid down that the stocks of traders who had not taken out licences under the Foodgrains Control Order, or who had not declared, or had mis-declared, their stocks were to be requisitioned. Further, traders who had declared their stocks correctly but were either withholding them from the market, or refraining from importing stocks into deficit areas, with the intention of keeping local prices high, were to be severely warned that if they did not release substantial quantities for sale at reasonable intervals, or persisted in refraining from importing supplies in reasonable quantities, their licences would be cancelled, and their stocks requisitioned. Again, 25 per cent of all stocks in excess of 300 maunds found with any individual owner, whether a trader or agriculturist, was to be requisitioned. Further, District Officers were given discretion to requisition from agricultural stocks whatever quantities they considered necessary, provided the unit was left self-sufficient in food. The stocks obtained by requisitioning were 23,000 tons of rice and 18,000 tons of paddy.

5. The Government of Bengal have informed us that the real value of the drive was that it succeeded in securing a considerable dissemination of local resources, in demonstrating that the sum total of all stocks that could be traced was insufficient to keep the province going without large scale help from other parts of India and in putting the administration into touch with village committees. It was hoped that this contact would enable the administration to secure the help of village leaders in matters relating to food.

6. The statistical results of the food drive show that the enquiries covered stocks held by nearly 10 million families consisting of 56 million members. The stocks held by them were estimated at one million tons. But there was a consensus of opinion that stocks had been under-estimated and that this under-estimation was partly due to concealment. The extent of the under-estimation cannot be reliably ascertained. The Bengal Government assumed that it was about 25 per cent. If this assumption is correct, the stocks on the 16th June 1943, together with the estimated yield of the *aus* crop then on the ground, fell short of the requirements of the population up to the end of the year, by about one million tons. It may be that the stocks which were under-stated or concealed were larger than 25 per cent. of the ascertained stocks; but unless they were considerably larger than the ascertained stocks it is evident that there must have been some deficiency. We are inclined therefore to regard the results of the food drive as consistent generally with the opinion we have formed about the supply position during 1943.

7. A feature of the drive which evoked considerable criticism at the time was the exclusion of Calcutta and Howrah. The substance of the criticism was that, as ample warning had of necessity to be given of the drive, large stocks were transferred to Calcutta from the districts and that the Government had thereby played into the hands of, and extended protection to, big hoarders and profiteers. The Bengal Government have explained that the exclusion of Calcutta and Howrah was due to the fact that the administrative resources of the province were inadequate to cope with simultaneous operations in the districts as well as in Calcutta and Howrah. The suggestion that large stocks were removed from the districts to Calcutta is not supported by the record of quantities of rice which arrived in Calcutta by rail or river steamer from Bengal districts during the months March to July, 1943. The figures are as follows:—

MONTH	TONS
March	13,383
April	13,824
May	14,267
June	13,483
July	7,914

These figures do not, of course, include imports into Calcutta by country boat but in view of the difficulties which were experienced in boat transport, it is hardly likely that large quantities were despatched in that way.

8. In the first week of July it was decided that a food drive in Calcutta and Howrah should be undertaken. The scope of the operations in these two cities was somewhat different from that of the rural food drive and was more in the nature of a food census. The object was to ascertain the actual statistical position and, incidentally, to locate any hoards or stocks held in contravention of the Foodgrains Control Order. It was no part of this plan to stimulate distribution. For the purpose of the census, the population was divided into three main categories, namely, (i) big merchants and traders with stocks known or likely to be over 2,000 maunds; (ii) medium merchants and traders with stocks between 200 and 2,000 maunds; (iii) all others, including house-holders, small retailers, and shops, with stocks generally expected to be under 200 maunds. In the case of the third category, the census was carried out through the agency of a staff of about 2,000, recruited partly from non-officials and partly from officers drawn from Government Departments. Enquiries in respect of the second category were made by the local police, and in the case of the first by the intelligence staff of the Civil Supplies

Department. The result of the census showed that the total stocks held in Calcutta and Howrah were:—

	Tons
Rice	30,226
Paddy	2,980
Wheat	8,678
Dhal	18,650

With regard to this result the Bengal Government stated that "as anticipated, there was no large-scale hoarding by consumers and that the stocks held by traders are in close accord with the figures they had declared"

B: Restoration of controls and the procurement of the Aus crop.

9. On the 11th March 1943, the crisis had developed so far that it forced the Bengal Government to decide on de-control. This meant a withdrawal from the course which Bengal, in common with many other areas in the country, had been following from about the middle of 1942. De-control, within Bengal, failed to resolve the crisis and this led to free trade in the Eastern Region. This was another step away from control. Free trade also did not resolve the crisis in Bengal and caused prices to rise steeply over wider areas. Finally, the original policy was restored, and the country as a whole moved forward to the system of controlled supply and distribution which is functioning today.

10. In Bengal the food drive in June, providing as it did for the requisitioning of stocks in excess of 300 maunds, was the first step towards the reversal of the policy of de-control. The next step was taken in August. In that month the Bengal Government announced their decision to fix statutory maximum prices for rice and paddy on a descending scale. The rates fixed were Rs. 30 a maund for rice and Rs. 15 a maund for paddy between the 28th August and 9th September; Rs. 24 a maund for rice and Rs. 12/8/- a maund for paddy between the 10th September and 20th September; and Rs. 20 a maund for rice and Rs. 10 a maund for paddy with effect from the 25th September onwards.[1] At the same time, the Government announced their decision to buy all rice and paddy offered to them by agriculturists or traders at local market rates or at the statutory maximum prices, whichever were lower. In addition Government decided to embark on active purchasing operations with a view to procuring as much as possible of the stocks coming on the market. For this purpose nine purchasing agents were selected from among the rice traders in Calcutta and each agent was allotted one or more of the 20 districts selected for the purchase operations. Exports were permitted from six of these districts, purchases in the remaining 14 districts being reserved principally for the relief of deficit pockets within those districts. The aim was to purchase about 213,000 tons in the six surplus districts, and to export 174,000 tons out of this amount to deficit districts.

11. The scheme was not a success, the total amount procured being only 23,900 tons of rice and about 38,600 tons of paddy. Prices did not come down appreciably and black-markets prevailed. The Government of Bengal attributed the failure principally to three causes. The most serious was the widespread reluctance on the part of agriculturists to place their stocks on the market, coupled with the disinclination of the trade to operate under control. Another reason was the unexpected delay of about a week in putting the scheme into operation, at a time when every day counted, pending the conclusion of financial arrangements with the Imperial Bank. This meant that the agents who should

[1]The generous margin between the price of paddy and rice was intended to put a premium on rice. *Aus* paddy is difficult to handle, its outturn is low and it was considered that there was advantage in encouraging the production and sale of hand-pounded rice.

have been operating in the districts on the 28th August when the statutory price first came into force, did not reach the districts till the 8th of September, that is, only two days before the drop in the statutory price of rice from Rs. 30 to Rs. 24 a maund, and of paddy from Rs. 15 to Rs. 12/8/- a maund. Large quantities of rice and paddy changed hands during the interval preceding this fall in price and Government's agents could only collect a fraction of the crop which had already been sold. Finally, there were delays in the districts in keeping the agents supplied with funds.

C. Distribution of Supplies

12. In Section C of Chapter V we described the growth of the arrangements in Greater Calcutta for the distribution of supplies through private employers' shops to a large section of the population at subsidized rates, and how similar arrangements had been made by the Central and Provincial Governments, Railways, etc. We also referred to the emergence of "controlled shops" through which supplies purchased by Government were distributed at controlled prices in limited quantities to the general population. At first there were 50 of these shops; they were later increased to 100. Early in January 1943, after the air raids, a scheme for the distribution of supplies through "approved markets" was brought into operation. At the outset their number was 25. It was later increased to 37 and the number of shops in these markets selected for the distribution of Government supplies was ultimately 257. The difference between shops in approved markets and controlled shops—the latter were outside the markets—was that the limit of individual sales was 5 seers in the case of the former and 2 seers, in the case of the latter.[1] Both classes of shops were under an obligation to sell at retail prices fixed by Government. Anybody could purchase from a controlled shop if he was prepared to stand in a queue and wait, perhaps for hours. Great difficulty was experienced in supervising these shops and controlling the queues, which grew longer and longer, and towards the end of June 1943 it was decided that all articles, the supply of which was under Government control, should be distributed through centres directly controlled by Government, and not through private shops. This decision, however, did not come into effect as progress in opening these centres was slow, and by the beginning of September only 25 had been started.

13. The retail price of rice sold from controlled shops was originally fixed at 6 annas per seer but was raised to 8 annas towards the end of August 1943. As regards supplies of rice for distribution through employers' shops, in April 1943 the price charged to the employer was fixed at Rs. 20 a maund. After the introduction of free trade, the price charged was the price at which the Government agent was buying in the Calcutta market. This was again changed in August, when statutory maximum prices were fixed, in relation to the statutory maximum wholesale price in force on the day of transfer. As regards wheat, the procedure was different. Wheat was sold outright to the mills which were under an obligation not to dispose of flour and *atta* except to persons approved by Government. The prices at which the mills sold their products were fixed on the basis of the price charged by Government for the wheat, and retail prices were determined with reference to the ex-mill prices.

14. During 1943 the population of Calcutta drew its supplies from three categories of shops, first the ordinary retail shops, secondly, the "controlled shops", including in this category the shops in the "approved markets" and Government distribution centres, and thirdly, the shops maintained by the employers of those large sections of the population of Greater Calcutta which came to be known as the "essential services and industrial priorities", or for short, "the priority classes". The ordinary shopkeepers purchased their supplies in the open market and sold their stocks at the market prices prevailing from time to time. They were uncontrolled and received no supplies

[1] One Seer=2·06 lb.

from Government. The "controlled shops" received their supplies from Government, and the supplies for the employers' shops were obtained in part by purchases in the open market and in part from Government. Government obtained their supplies partly by purchases within the province, partly from outside Bengal under the Rescue and Basic Plan arrangements and through their purchasing agent during the free trade period, and to a small extent by purchases from the trade in Calcutta. A certain amount was also obtained by requisitioning. The supplies which passed through the hands of Government in Calcutta were distributed in three ways: by despatches to deficit districts, by deliveries to controlled shops, and by issue to employers' organizations.

15. There is no reliable information about the quantities of rice and paddy held in stock in Calcutta at the beginning of the year 1943. The Foodgrains Control Order had been brought into force on the 15th December 1942, but it was not efficiently enforced. We know, however, from the statistics of rail-borne and sea-borne trade that the net imports into the Calcutta Trade Block were 304,000 tons during 1941, and only 115,000 tons during 1942. The area served by supplies received into the Calcutta Trade Block does not correspond exactly with the area of Greater Calcutta which is now under rationing. It is not, therefore, possible to estimate accurately the annual rice requirements of the area served by the imports into the Calcutta Trade Block, but it may be safely assumed that they are between 200,000 and 250,000 tons. On this assumption the net imports into the Calcutta Trade Block during 1942 were much below actual requirements. The stocks held on the 1st January 1943 must therefore have been considerably smaller than those held on the 1st January 1942.

16. The following table shows the net imports into the Calcutta Trade Block from outside Bengal, imports from Bengal districts, exports to Bengal districts and the net quantities retained in Calcutta of rice and paddy in terms of rice during 1943:—

(Thousands of tons)

Period	Net imports from outside Bengal	Imports to from Bengal districts	Expot to Bengal districts	Net retention in the Calcutta Trade Block
1st quarter	7	32	7	32
2nd "	51	47	9	89
3rd "	52	22	13	61
4th "	86	21	15	92
	196	122	44	274

The figures for the first quarter clearly indicate the severity of the crisis through which Calcutta was passing during the first three months of 1943. Net arrivals during the two months of January and February amounted in all only to about 14,000 tons and those for the whole quarter were equivalent only to about six weeks' supply. During this period stocks were being consumed and not replaced. Hence the pressure on the supply position which led to the decision to de-control prices of rice early in March. In the second quarter supplies improved considerably. This was due to the assistance given by Orissa; the increase in the flow of supplies from Bengal itself owing to de-control, and the introduction of free trade in the Eastern Region. During the third quarter, supplies decreased in comparison with the previous quarter;

this was due to smaller supplies from the districts of Bengal. The increase in the last quarter is accounted for by the larger supplies reaching Bengal under the Basic Plan.

17. The following figures show the arrivals on Government account of rice in Calcutta and the manner in which the Provincial Government disposed of these supplies:—

(Thousands of tons)

	1st quarter	2nd quarter	3rd quarter	4th quarter
Arrivals on Government account .	23	50	36	87
Despatches to the districts[1] . .	2	15	19	28
Deliveries to employers' organizations and for essential services .	17	36	18	20
Deliveries to controlled shops and approved markets . . .	7	18	14	11
Total despatches and deliveries .	26	69	51	59

During the first three quarters, the total amount distributed by Government exceeded the total arrivals on Government account. The difference was made up of private stocks which were either requisitioned or purchased. It was only in the fourth quarter that arrivals exceeded the amounts distributed.

18. Paragraph 16 of Appendix V shows the quantities of rice, wheat, wheat-products, and millets despatched to the different districts from Government stocks in Calcutta. In addition to these supplies the districts also received consignments of rice direct from other provinces, and District Officers supplemented their resources by local purchases and requisitioning. It will be recalled that 41,000 tons of rice and paddy were obtained by requisitioning during the 'food drive'. We calculate that about 60,000 to 70,000 tons of rice were received in the districts direct from other provinces but we do not know what proportion of this quantity was received on Government account. The stocks which passed through the hands of the District Officers were used to meet the requirements of the essential services, and for distribution to the general public. Distribution to the general public was done partly by wholesale and retail dealers who sold at prices fixed by Government, and partly through cheap grain shops, of which a large number was opened for the sale of grain at subsidized rates to the public.

19. From August onwards, large supplies of grain, despatched on Government account from outside the province, began to arrive in Calcutta. During the last quarter of the year, the quantity of rice received was more than twice that received during the preceding quarter, and during the same period 176,000 tons of wheat arrived, a quantity approximately equivalent to total arrivals during the preceding 9 months. In addition, considerable quantities of millets were despatched to Calcutta. The arrivals of these supplies found the Bengal Government completely unprepared as regards the supervisory staff, transport vehicles, and storage accommodation necessary for the reception of the grain and its despatch to places where it was needed. Towards the end of the year, grain was stocked in the open, covered by tarpaulins in the Royal Botanical Gardens owing to lack of more satisfactory arrangements. In some districts there was a similar failure in organization. A number of witnesses referred to stocks of *aus* paddy which lay for a long time undistributed in Jessore. The

[1]These figures are not comparable with the figures under column 4 of the statement in para. 17 above, for reasons mentioned in paragraph 13 of Appendix V.

Bengal Government have provided us with accounts of the storage of grain in the Royal Botanical Gardens and Jessore, of which resumés will be found in annexures II and III respectively to Appendix V. Extracts from a report of the Bengal Government regarding storage and distribution generally, are given in Annexure I to Appendix V. In a later section of the report, we have ourselves commented critically on storage and transport arrangements during the famine.

D. The Army comes to the aid of the civil authorities

20. The general course of the famine and the mortality rate have been described in other sections of our report. During the months August to October, the number of deaths was 100 per cent. or more in excess of the average. Numerous deaths from starvation occurred and epidemic diseases were widely prevalent. Famine victims left their villages in thousands and wandered into towns and cities, particularly into Calcutta. Relief measures failed to supply and distribute food and prevent starvation, and the medical and public health situation was out of hand.

His Excellency the Viceroy, Lord Wavell, visited Bengal at the end of October 1943, when the famine was at its height, and as a result of his visit, military assistance was given to the civil authorities in Bengal. The help provided by the Army was in three forms: first, officers were loaned to assist the headquarters staff of the Department of Civil Supplies in organizing and controlling the movement of foodstuffs from Calcutta to distribution points within the province; secondly, troops were allotted to assist the civil authorities in moving and distributing supplies in the districts; thirdly, military medical officers were seconded to organize medical and public health relief, and military hospital units and mobile medical units were placed at the disposal of the province and located where the need was greatest. The co-operation of the Army in medical and public health work will be described in Part II.

21. Advance parties of the troops reached the famine areas by 11th November and the main bodies—their strength amounted to several thousands—arrived between the 19th and 27th of that month. The arrival of the troops effected an immediate improvement. By the third week of November, 8,000 tons had been distributed with military assistance and by the middle of December, 24,000 tons had been handled by the troops. The main tasks on which the military units were employed were the provision of motor transport vehicles for the carriage of bulk supplies to district distribution centres and the transport of supplies from those centres to the villages, the loading and unloading of foodstuffs at transhipment and distribution points, the provision of personnel to assist the civil authorities at distribution points, the escort of convoys, and the guarding of dumps of foodstuffs. One of the first tasks undertaken by the Army on arrival was to assist the civil authorities in Calcutta in the distribution of food. The troops willingly turned themselves into temporary coolies for the loading and unloading of thousands of maunds of rice. Military guards and escorts were placed on trains and river steamers in order to help the Director of Movements in ascertaining where delays and "bottlenecks" were occurring. In districts best served by water-ways, travelling shops were placed on boats, and supplies thus taken to villages situated far from the usual routes. Unarmed patrols were also organized to visit distant villages and to report upon their economic condition, so that adequate measures could be taken to meet their requirements. The extent of the work carried out by the military units can be gauged by the fact that the total quantity of foodgrains handled between the arrival of the troops in November 1943 and their withdrawal in March—April 1944 amounted to over 70,000 tons and the mileage covered by motor transport to 836,000 miles.

22. The Army also carried out demonstrations with the object of popularising alternative foods to rice. Small parties of troops were despatched to the districts to show the people the correct way to prepare millets for consumption, and in certain areas some success was achieved in the popularization of *bajra* as a food. The Royal Engineers improved communications for motor transport by the construction of pile bridges, the reconstruction of ferries, the improvement of river crossings, and the strengthening of existing bridges and culverts. Again, salvage operations were undertaken for the recovery and repair of boats collected at reception centres under the Denial Scheme of 1942. Over 2,000 boats were re-conditioned and made available for the distribution of foodgrains. With the onset of the cold weather many among the poorer sections of the population were in dire need of blankets and warm clothing. This was also a matter in which the Army rendered great assistance. By the middle of December 600 tons of warm clothing had been despatched to the worst affected areas. Out of this total, 100 tons were flown to East Bengal by the United States Army Air Force.

E. CALCUTTA RATIONING

23. From the description we have given of the arrangements in force for the distribution of supplies in Calcutta, it will be obvious that the city was not rationed. The ordinary retail shops were entirely uncontrolled. The supplies available for distribution through the controlled shops were limited and attempts to supervise the working of these shops were not successful. The provision of supplies by Government to employers' organizations and by the latter to individual concerns was regulated in the manner which we now proceed to describe.

24. In the earlier stages of the Bengal Chamber of Commerce Foodstuffs Scheme, the requirements of each participating employer were assessed by the employer himself and supplies were made by the Chamber accordingly. This continued till early in 1943, when, because of the increasing difficulty in obtaining supplies, a greater degree of uniformity was brought about. The arrangement finally adopted was to supply employers' grain shops with 5 seers of rice per week per head of the average daily labour force. An exception was made in the case of engineering works, including dockyards, and public utility concerns, where the supply was assessed at the rate of 7 seers per week per employee. This was considered necessary as the employers concerned were bound by an arrangement whereby each employee should be given, at controlled prices, the estimated requirements of each adult worker, one adult dependant and two children; and it was thought undesirable, in the interests of industrial peace, to reduce this below 7 seers except under conditions of extreme necessity. A further factor which justified the additional quantity was that the concerns which were supplied at the rate of 5 seers per week per employee, included in their labour force a percentage of women entitled to draw their rations from the employers' shops. When this rice ration was decided upon no *atta* was available and it was not until early in May 1943 that *atta* became available in sufficient quantity to allow a cut of 50 per cent in the rice ration. There were also many occasions when, owing to the shortage of *atta* and rice, reduced issues had to be made by the Chamber to the participating employers' shops, and by the latter to their employees with consequent discontent and hardship.

25. During 1943 the total of all foodstuffs, excluding purchases by the individual firms, handled by the Chamber amounted to about 129,000 tons at a cost of approximately Rs. 7 crores. Out of this, rice amounted to about 55,000 tons and wheat and wheat products to approximately 47,000 tons. Of the total of 55,000 tons of rice, roughly one half was purchased from the Foodgrains Purchasing Officer of the Bengal Government, and the other half in the

open market. From January to May 1943 the total stocks of rice held by the Chamber and the employers' organizations connected with the Chamber exceeded two weeks' supply only once and that was in the month of March. During the remainder of the year, the stocks were at a higher level but they never exceeded more than six weeks' supply.

26. We have described in some detail the Bengal Chamber of Commerce Scheme because it catered for the largest number of employees. But as we pointed out in paragraph 20 of Chapter V, similar arrangements were in operation for the benefit of employees of other Chambers of Commerce, the Central and Provincial Governments, Railways, etc. While the ration scales adopted by the priority employers varied and were in some cases on the high side, the actual supplies from Government stocks were insufficient to allow them to implement the adopted scales. The scale adopted by the Directorate of Civil Supplies was 3½ seers of grain a week for each adult employee, and the objective was to make supplies at this level available on the one hand to the priority employers for their employees, and on the other to controlled shops and approved markets for the rest of the population.

27. We shall explain later in the report our view that, if effective preparations had been made in 1943 for the introduction of rationing in Calcutta, the crisis would not have begun as early as it did, nor would it then have developed as quickly as it did. The failure to introduce rationing at any time during 1943 added greatly to the difficulties encountered by the Government in coping with the emergency throughout that year. We now proceed to give an account of the endeavours to introduce rationing during 1943.

28. In October 1942 the Central Government addressed a letter to Provincial Governments and asked them to examine the practicability of working a system of individual rationing in respect of rice. By the beginning of the year 1943, however, the general food position had deteriorated and the need for rationing of all important foodgrains (not only rice) in the larger cities and towns was becoming more and more obvious. The Government of India, thereupon again addressed the Provincial Governments advising them to prepare for the rationing of all the main foodgrains in important urban areas. At that time, although most of the provinces were examining the matter, little actual progress had been made except in Bombay, where, in view of the precarious position of the food supply for Bombay city and other towns, the Government had already taken preparatory steps towards the introduction of urban rationing. Full rationing was introduced in Bombay city early in May 1943.

29. At the beginning of February 1943, the Government of Bengal placed an officer on special duty to prepare a scheme for the organization of food and fuel distribution in Calcutta and its adjoining industrial area. The draft scheme, the report on which was completed by the middle of March, provided for the full rationing in Calcutta and the surrounding industrial area, of foodgrains, pulses, sugar, kerosene oil, salt, and mustard oil, on the basis of ration cards, issued to individual messing units. In April and May a considerable amount of preparatory work was accomplished. The Bengal Food and Fuel Distribution Inquiries Order, the Bengal Food and Fuel Retail Trade Returns Order and the Bengal Residential and Catering Establishments Food and Fuel Inquiry Order, were passed. The Controller and the Food Executive Officers were appointed and the enumeration of messing units was completed by the end of May.

30. At this stage further administrative preparations were interrupted by a change of plan. The scheme under preparation provided for over-all rationing irrespective of income. Towards the end of June, however, it was decided in regard to rice to adopt what may be described as a low income preferential scheme. Under this scheme, instead of over-all rationing, the rice ration was limited to the supply of one seer of rice per head per week at subsidized rates

to persons with an income of Rs. 20 or less a month. We have been informed that the reason for this change was that the Government were not in a position to ensure that supplies for over-all rationing would be available. At the same time it was decided that the distribution of all articles the supply of which was controlled by Government should be through Government distribution centres and not through private shops. Progress in the opening of these centres was, however, slow and by 3rd September only 25 had been started. Another change in policy was made in the middle of August. On the recommendation of the Rationing Adviser to the Government of India, it was decided to abandon the "preferential" rationing scheme and to introduce, as quickly as possible, a comprehensive scheme for the rationing of Greater Calcutta on the basis of ration cards for individuals as opposed to messing units. It was not, however, until the 31st January 1944, that rationing came into force in the city of Calcutta and certain neighbouring municipalities, and not until the 1st May 1944 that it was extended to the whole of Greater Calcutta.

One of the reasons for this delay was the insistence of the Bengal Government on the exclusion of the ordinary retail trader from the distribution arrangements. On the 21st December 1943, the Government of India directed the Bengal Government, under Section 126-A of the Government of India Act, that the number of retail shops under the direct control and management of the Provincial Government should be not more than 450, and that the remainder should be licensed retail shops, owned and managed by selected private traders.

The Government of Bengal were also directed that there shall be set up and operating not later than the 31st January 1944 at least 1,000 retail centres for the distribution of rationed foodstuffs in addition to shops operated by industrial concerns for their employees.

CHAPTER IX.—RELIEF

1. In this chapter we propose to consider the impact of the famine on the life of the population of Bengal and the relief measures taken to reduce its violence. Medical relief will be described in Part II. There is, however, no clear-cut line of distinction between medical and non-medical relief. In a famine such as that which afflicted Bengal, any steps taken to provide food or the means to purchase food, or to restore social and economic life to normal, affect the health situation, and, on the other hand, health measures are equally necessary to mitigate the effects of famine and hasten social and economic recovery. The present chapter and the chapters dealing with health measures should, therefore, be regarded as complementary.

A.—THE CYCLONE

2. The Midnapore cyclone, which took place some 8 months previous to the famine, produced severe distress in the affected areas, which had not recovered from the first disaster when stricken by the second. In this part of the province famine conditions and economic disorganization preceded their appearance elsewhere. Relief measures had to be taken in Midnapore from the time of the cyclone onwards, and these merged into the broader measures of famine relief initiated at a later stage. The Midnapore cyclone and its effects were an integral part of the general calamity and it is unnecessary for present purposes to draw a distinction between cyclone relief and famine relief.

3. The cyclone did very serious damage, which has been referred to in another section of our report. Some 14,500 people and 190,000 cattle were killed and dwellings, food-stores, and crops destroyed over a wide area. Corpses and ruins littered the countryside. Military units in the area, who themselves suffered some loss of life, took the initiative in the clearance of debris and the removal of the dead. Immediate measures to succour the survivors were called for. Relief parties bringing food, water, and medical supplies were despatched from Calcutta and a special medical staff was appointed under the Director of Public Health. On November 11th the Revenue Secretary was appointed as Additional Commissioner of the Division concerned, to direct and co-ordinate relief.

4. Between November 1942 and the end of May 1943, over two crores of rupees (Rs. 2,00,00,000) were spent on relief in the affected areas. About one-quarter of this sum was distributed as gratuitous relief while the remainder was used in the granting of agricultural loans, and in test relief.[1] Expenditure on relief was increased in the subsequent period when the effects of the general famine reinforced those of the cyclone. Homes for children and infants were opened. Fishermen in the coastal areas were helped with free grants of money for boats, nets, etc., and with loans the total amount of which amounted to Rs. 1,29,000. Officers in the Departments of Irrigation, Agriculture, and Education visited the devastated areas to report on the damage caused and the measures needed for reconstruction.

5. The Midnapore cyclone was in fact a very serious catastrophe, if overshadowed by the greater one which followed. While the measures undertaken afforded considerable relief, recovery was far from complete by the middle of 1943. Operations in the affected areas provided some experience of famine relief

[1]Test relief means relief in the form of payment for work. The distinction maintained in some other provinces between Test Works and Famine Relief Works is not observed in practice in Bengal.

and its difficulties, but there is little evidence that this was made use of at a later stage. Reports of voluntary workers on the cyclone-damaged areas contain many complaints of confusion, lack of co-ordination, and unnecessary delays in relief work, of a very similar nature to those made during the major famine.

6. One point must be emphasized in connection with the Midnapore cyclone and the widespread destruction which resulted. An additional burden of worry and responsibility was thrown on the administration by a natural calamity at a time when all its energies were needed to deal with the darkening food situation throughout the province.

B.—Conditions produced by the famine

7. We must now turn to the great famine of 1943. In previous chapters we have described the shortage of rice supplies and the rise in prices which prevented a considerable section of the population from obtaining its staple food. Before discussing relief measures it is necessary to give the reader some idea of the effect of famine on the life of the community and the extent of the task to be faced in the provision of relief and the subsequent rehabilitation of the affected population.

8. In chapter II a brief account has been given of the economy of rural Bengal in which it is shown that about half the families in the rural areas, depending wholly or mainly on the cultivation of land, hold less than 2 acres or are landless. Of these, some 2 million families—about 10 million people—are dependent mainly or entirely on agricultural wages. In addition, there are artisans such as potters, carpenters, basket-makers, weavers, etc., who depend mainly upon their trade for their livelihood and generally speaking are not themselves producers of food. And lastly, there are in each village indigent people who, for various reasons, depend wholly or partially on charity. A considerable proportion of the rural population lives on the margin of subsistence, with few or no reserves of grain, money or other assets. As prices rose in the early part of 1943, non-producers were the first to suffer. Village charity, customarily in the form of gifts of rice, dried up not only because rice was in short supply but also because it had become such an expensive commodity. Those dependent on charity were thus soon reduced to starvation. Village labourers and artisans, at a somewhat higher economic level, sold their domestic utensils, ornaments, parts of their dwellings such as doors, windows and corrugated iron sheets, trade implements, clothes and domestic animals if they had any—sold indeed anything on which money could be raised—to more fortunate neighbours at cut-throat prices. They reduced their food intake by degrees to make their dwindling reserves of money and food last as long as possible. As the famine developed, numerous small holders were reduced to the same straits. With the rise of prices early in the year, many were tempted to sell their stocks at prices which seemed at the time prodigious, but were in fact low in comparison with prices prevailing in subsequent months. They hoped to re-purchase rice later for their own needs at lower prices, but actually prices soon soared far beyond their reach. Faced with starvation, many sold their land and other possessions to obtain money to buy rice, but with continually rising prices the proceeds of the sale could ward off hunger for only a brief period.

9. Larger landholders benefited from the situation, since they could sell most of their rice at an enormous profit and keep sufficient for themselves and their families. But the cultivator of a holding below a certain size was not in this happy position. It has been said that small holders who possessed less than 5 *bighas* of land (1·7 acres) were vulnerable and usually forced to sell house and land and look for food elsewhere. This we consider to be on over statement, but there can be no doubt that many small holders were compelled to sell their land.

10. The famine thus principally affected one section of the community—the poorer classes in rural areas. It is impossible to estimate the percentage of the rural population that suffered; possibly it was about one-tenth. The amount of distress differed, of course, from district to district. Well-to-do people in country areas were not short of food and rice dealers and merchants prospered. The industrial population of Greater Calcutta was assured of its food supply throughout the famine, and while some of the urban lower middle classes found it difficult to obtain an adequate diet, there was no starvation amongst them. It should be clearly understood that the greater part of the population of Bengal did not suffer from lack of food in 1943.

11. Those who found themselves unable to buy food reacted to the situation in various ways. Some remained in their villages and starved there. Many men left home in search of work, particularly on military projects, leaving their families behind. As things worsened, many thousands of people left their homes and wandered across the countryside in the direction of towns or cities where they hoped to obtain food. The existence in various urban centres of controlled food shops, at which rice was available at lower prices, and later of relief kitchens providing free food encouraged the migration. The greatest flow was towards Calcutta. The Calcutta destitutes came mainly from the 24-Parganas, while nearly all the rest belonged to Midnapore and other districts not far removed from the capital. Many travelled by train without tickets and stations on railway lines south of Calcutta were thronged by starving crowds waiting for transport. Some destitutes living in villages near Calcutta came daily by train to the city to obtain food at relief kitchens and returned home by night. Migration of destitutes towards other centres in Bengal also occurred, though on a smaller scale. No figures are available as to what proportion of the population affected left home. While many thousands migrated, it is probable that the majority of famine victims remained in their villages.

12. Famine and migration led to much family disintegration. Husbands deserted wives and wives husbands; elderly dependants were left behind in the villages; babies and young children were sometimes abandoned. According to a sample survey carried out in Calcutta during the latter half of 1943, some breaking up of the family had occurred in about half the destitute population which reached the city.

13. The famine stricken population made little attempt to loot food shops and stores, and there was no organized rioting. The lack of violence can be explained in various ways. In general, famine victims belonged to the poorer classes and were accustomed to accept misfortune passively. The migrating crowds came from different villages and there was no corporate spirit amongst them to initiate any concerted move to obtain food by violent means. Lastly, and most important, the famine victims were soon reduced to a state of debility which prevented vigorous action. There was a very serious rise in the number of dacoities reported in Bengal in 1943. Thefts of rice, particularly from boats, were very common and in certain areas its transport was attended by considerable risk. It appears, however, that the dacoits were not in general famine victims, but usually ordinary thieves taking advantage of the prevailing situation. Rice had become a very valuable commodity, selling at a high price, and hence well worth stealing. Violence and looting on the part of famine victims was thus not one of the problems with which the authorities had to deal.

14. The situation was further complicated by the fact that famine victims rapidly became physically weak and a prey to epidemic and other disease, by the difficulty of obtaining and transporting the necessary food supplies, and by the lack of sufficient and satisfactory staff for employment on relief work.

C.—Relief measures

I. General:

15. During the early part of 1943 the bulk of relief expenditure was devoted to relief in the cyclone-affected areas, which was further extended later in the year. Reports of growing distress were received from Commissioners and Collectors in many parts of the province during the first 6 months of 1943. Relief operations, however, were undertaken only on a limited scale. How distress grew during the period, and how widespread it was, can be seen from the summary of reports from Commissioners and Collectors given in **Appendix VI.** At the beginning of June a confidential circular was issued to Collectors indicating that famine might have to be declared and requesting them to report to Government on the position in their districts. This was followed towards the end of the month by a letter in which Collectors were asked to forward detailed demands for funds for relief. The object of these enquiries was to obtain information on which the relief policy of Government could be based. Replies, received about the middle of July, showed the situation to be grave.

In the same month District Officers in Chittagong and Noakhali, where the famine had already started, were authorised to employ whatever relief staff was necessary and an allotment for gratuitous relief was sanctioned. Food kitchens were opened in these districts at about this time. In June 1943, the Government of India were approached for financial help to meet the obligations of relief. In February 1944, the Government of India gave the Government of Bengal Rs. 3,00,00,000 for "Famine and Rehabilitation".[1]

16. During the first quarter of the year relief was given mainly in the form of agricultural loans. Expenditure under this head during the second quarter, in districts other than the cyclone-affected districts, was quadrupled and a considerable sum was spent on test relief. Gratuitous relief was on a small scale at this stage. During July the amount of money allotted for relief in general was reduced, since it was reported that the agricultural operations were proceeding on a large scale in all parts of the province and that the demand for labour had increased. From August onwards, however, large allotments were made for all forms of relief, with the emphasis on gratuitous relief. The total sum sanctioned for the latter during the second half of the year was in the neighbourhood of Rs. 1,80,00,000.

17. In August it became abundantly clear that Bengal was in the grip of a great famine and that relief on a very wide scale was necessary. Commissioners and Collectors were called to a conference in Calcutta on August 14th, 15th and 16th, and were given instructions by the Government. On August 18th Government issued a memorandum on the relief of distress in which the necessity for "speedy and resolute action" was emphasized. District Officers were instructed to set up food kitchens at once and funds were made available for this purpose. It was pointed out that "relief work was of such paramount importance that it must take precedence over the ordinary duties of the administration". A circular issued by the Revenue Department on August 20th described in detail the relief measures to be taken and the administrative procedure to be adopted. Relief could be given in any of the following ways:—

(a) Gratuitous relief in the form of gruel, uncooked foodgrains and cash.
(b) Wages for test relief in kind or cash.
(c) Agricultural loans for—
  (i) maintenance—in kind or cash.
  (ii) purchase of cattle—in cash.
  (iii) agricultural operations in kind or cash.
(d) Sale of foodgrains at cheap rates to the poor.

---

[1]This has been since increased to half the direct cost of the famine, subject to a maximum of Rs. 10,00.00,000.

Union relief committees were to be established, the unit of relief being the Union. Collectors were instructed to forward requisition lists for food and other essentials, but they were urged to use local resources as far as possible. As regards staff, the circular pointed out that the Government could not arrange for the deputation of extra staff for relief work and that District Officers would consequently have to find the necessary workers from amongst the staff employed in their respective districts. The duties of those employed on relief work were defined in detail. The circular also laid down the prices to be charged by the Civil Supplies Department for rice and other food sent to districts. In practice, however, the issue of these instructions was not accompanied by the adequate provision of food and funds, with the result that the relief measures taken failed to prevent distress and death on a large scale.

18. At the end of September a senior I.C.S. officer was appointed Relief Commissioner. He was not given the plenary powers of a Famine Commissioner but was an inspecting and reporting officer only, ranking as an additional member of the Board of Revenue. In practice the Relief Commissioner had to issue local orders in much the same way as prescribed in the Famine Code in the case of a Famine Commissioner. He had, however, no control over food supplies, which was vested in the Civil Supplies Department. In January 1944 he was given the powers of a Secretary to Government.

From October 1942 to March 1944, Rs. 7,42,00,000 was allotted for various forms of relief. Of this about Rs. 2,94,00,000 was used for agricultural loans, Rs. 3,03,00,000 for gratuitous relief and Rs. 1,45,00,000 for test relief.

II. Food Kitchens:

19. The provision of cooked food to starving people was the most important relief measure during the acute stages of the famine. In November 1943 the total number of food kitchens reached 6,625. Of these, 551 were financed and run by private relief organizations, 4,469 by Government, while the remainder were subsidized by government but run by other agencies. Most of the kitchens were opened after the issue in August of the circulars giving instructions about relief measures. From December 1943 onwards the food kitchens were gradually closed down and homeless and indigent people were housed and fed in workhouses, destitute homes, and orphanages.

III. Clothing:

20. Some of the destitutes were clothed in rags. Others had no clothes at all. The majority of destitute children were naked. During the sultry months of summer and autumn, this state of affairs did not perhaps occasion much additional suffering. It was clear, however, that supplies of clothes and coverings were needed not only for protection against the colder weather which begins in November, but also to restore decency and self-respect. Clothes totalling 1,600,000 pieces and some 600,000 blankets were distributed by Government through official and non-official relief agencies. The latter were supplied with clothes or blankets free or at half price.

IV. Relief in Calcutta:

21. Calcutta presented a special problem of relief. The migration of destitutes to the Capital, from July and August onwards, has already been described. It was reckoned that in the middle of October the number in Calcutta rose to nearly 100,000. In the early weeks of the famine, there was some individual distribution of food by the charitable Destitutes in Calcutta begged for food and sought for scraps even in refuse bins. They flocked round military and hotel kitchens to get such food as they could. They lay on pavements even in the busiest parts of the city, and corpses became a familiar sight. Complaints of delay and inefficiency were made against the authorities responsible for the removal and disposal of corpses. It was at this stage that most of

the gruesome photographs of famine victims were taken, which, when published in the "Statesman" and subsequently in newspapers and journals in England and America, familiarised the world with the horrors of the Bengal famine. In publishing such photographs for the first time the "Statesman", we consider, rendered a valuable public service.

22. The opening of free kitchens, and famine hospitals and wards, had some visible effect on the situation. In September a small daily ration of cooked food became available to all destitutes for the asking. Meals were given at the same time of the day in all kitchens, to prevent destitutes from getting more than one meal. The destitutes tended to gather in the neighbourhood of kitchens, sitting or lying on the pavements throughout most of the day and night. The influx of famine victims created a serious sanitary problem in the city.

23. The relief authorities were impressed by the necessity of getting the destitutes out of Calcutta and back to their villages. A special officer was placed in charge of relief work in Calcutta (the Relief Co-ordination Officer) and plans were formulated along the following lines. The first necessary step was to collect destitutes from the streets and put them in poor-houses or destitute homes in the city, those requiring medical attention being sent to hospitals. This involved the establishment of suitable homes and the development of hospital services. Next, it was proposed to create a ring of famine camps round Calcutta to which destitutes could be sent in the first stage of their homeward journey; these would also serve the purpose of diverting fresh swarms of destitutes *en route* to the city. Since people could not be sent back to their villages unless food was available for them there; the scheme included the provision of poor-houses and kitchens in the rural areas concerned, to prevent the starvation of the people on return to their villages.

24. In practice the scheme did not work altogether smoothly. There was at first difficulty in finding suitable accommodation in Calcutta, which was partially solved when a *bustee* area capable of accommodating several thousand people was placed at the disposal of the relief authorities by the Calcutta Improvement Trust. Camps constructed for evacuation in the event of air raids were available outside Calcutta, but these lay mostly to the north, whereas the great majority of destitutes came from the south. New camps had, therefore, to be established and the usual obstacles imposed by lack of transport and shortage of materials circumvented. Operations in Calcutta were hindered by the weak and diseased state of the famine-stricken population and their reluctance to enter Government institutions. Malicious rumours were spread about the motives of Government in collecting the destitutes. Further, the destitutes had acquired a "wandering habit" and resented confinement in camps. Many, placed under control, absconded if opportunity occurred. The peculiar mental condition induced by lack of food, to which reference is made in Chapter II of Part II, reduced their amenability to restraint. The following passage from the evidence of a witness concerned in famine relief illustrates some of the difficulties encountered in dealing with the destitute population:

"Sickness of the population very much complicated the arrangements. There was mental demoralization which followed and it made our problem very difficult. The wandering habit amongst the children was difficult to stop. Famine orphanages had to have prison rooms. Children—skin and bone—had got into the habit of feeding like dogs. You tried to give them a decent meal but they would break away and start wandering about and eat filth. You had to lock them up in a special room. They would come to normal after they had been fed and kept for a fortnight in a decent manner. They would not wander then. They developed the mentality of wandering."

Some force was used in collecting destitutes from the streets and unpleasant scenes occurred. In the early stages the task of removal was entrusted to the police and the arrival of a police lorry in a street crowded with destitutes would be a signal for their rapid and noisy dispersal. Towards the middle of October, some 15 lorries were made available to the relief authorities, and responsible Government officers, accompanied whenever possible by non-official volunteers, toured the streets and collected destitutes by more persuasive and gentle means.

25. Reference has already been made to the disruption of family ties which occurred when the destitutes left their homes and wandered into towns and cities. In the confusion prevailing in the Capital, further family separations took place. When people were picked up on the streets and taken to hospitals and homes, members of the family left behind would usually have no idea where to look for them and the latter would be equally at a loss. A special officer was appointed to undertake the re-uniting of separated families. The nature of his task, and the steps taken, are illustrated in the following account given by a witness:

"In Calcutta people were very often picked up from the food kitchen centres and brought to the poor-houses. There some woman would complain that she had lost her child and that her husband had gone away. When we picked up people under compulsion it very often happened that some persons were separated from their relations. What we did in the end was to set apart one poorhouse in Calcutta to which we sent all the people who were separated from their relatives. Such persons were sent to that particular poor house and when they were there picked out their lost relatives. Besides if anybody in the street said that his daughter or wife was lost he was told to go to that particular poor-house and find her."

26 By the end of November 1943, the majority of destitutes had left Calcutta and had returned to their villages. It was estimated that during the relief operations, over 55,000 people were received in destitute homes and camps. The relief organization employed a paid staff of nearly 1,500. Actually a very considerable proportion of the destitute population did not leave the city *via* the Government organization. When it became known that a good *aman* crop was on the ground numerous destitutes found their way home on their own account. A few thousands remained in relief institutions in Calcutta and throughout 1944 there was a steady influx of small numbers of vagrants and beggars, including people reduced to penury by the famine, who required institutional relief. But in general Calcutta had returned to normal by December 1943.

V. Relief in the districts:

27. It is not easy to give a general account of famine relief work in rural Bengal, since the urgency of the famine situation, and the extent and efficiency of relief measures, differed from district to district. The availability of supplies, the size of the district, the personality of the District Magistrate—all these affected in various ways the provision of relief and the degree of success attained. Comprehensive relief measures were first undertaken in the Chittagong district, in which a serious situation was reported as early as January 1943. Distress first became evident in the town of Chittagong and was temporarily relieved, during the early months of the year, by requisitioning supplies of rice from big cultivators in the southern parts of the district. Some 15,000 to 20,000 maunds were requisitioned. In April a scheme for supplying a ration of rice to the poor in Chittagong town was instituted.

In rural Chittagong famine became imminent in February and March. Test relief works were opened in April and were attended by large numbers of women. Thousands of men left their families to work on military projects. It became evident, however, that work and wages alone could not prevent famine. Food was required. Free kitchens were opened in Chittagong in May, the first in Bengal. Credit for initiating this system of relief, later to be extended to most of the province, is due to the Circle Officer of Rouzan. Supplies of food for relief of various kinds were obtained with great difficulty. Some were secured by local purchase and requisitioning and in July, during the free trade period, 50,000 maunds were purchased in Assam. During the later months of the year supplies received through the Department of Civil Supplies relieved the situation. It has been estimated that about 100,000 people, out of a population of 2 millions, received a small ration of cooked food at the free kitchens.

28. Mortality in Chittagong was high during the early months of the famine, reaching its peak in July and August. During the remaining months of 1943 it declined and by June 1944 had returned to the normal level. In Tipperah, on the other hand, where the famine began a few weeks later than in Chittagong, the peak in mortality was not reached until December, when the number of deaths was 272 per cent in excess of the quinquennial average. Throughout the first six months of 1944 mortality remained high in Tipperah. In this district relief operations compared unfavourably with those in Chittagong, chiefly owing to lack of supplies. In October 1943 it was reported that food could not be provided for kitchens, that relief was intermittent and scanty, and that cases of emaciation and deaths from starvation were numerous. The contrasting mortality trends in Tipperah and Chittagong can unquestionably be related to the adequacy of relief.

29. In Faridpur, where famine was severe, great difficulty was experienced in the running of food kitchens owing to scarcity of supplies, lack of transport, and corruption on the part of local officials in charge. Workhouses providing food and shelter were established at an early stage to replace the kitchens, and this measure proved a success. Another step was the rationing of towns and of a number of villages.

A Co-operative Community Scheme, embracing some 20 villages, was initiated by the District Magistrate. This involved the pooling of the food resources of each village. Each family in the villages participated and was given a ration card ensuring its own supplies. No food was allowed to be sent out of the villages until their own needs were satisfied.

In Dacca city a local rationing scheme was organized by a public-spirited Judge. This helped to eke out the limited supplies of rice available and assisted not only the poor, but also middle class families, to obtain food during the famine.

30. Each district had in fact its own difficulties to contend with. In some districts the situation was got under control fairly rapidly; in others confusion, inefficiency, and lack of transport and supplies hindered the provision of relief. Medical and public health measures were an essential part of relief and here again there were different degrees of achievement. The general course of relief was approximately as follows: As the famine developed, ineffective attempts were made to relieve distress by agricultural loans, test relief, and gratuitous relief as money on a small scale. Test works, which were mainly under the administration of District Boards, were unsatisfactory in many areas. No measured task was exacted, supervision was lax, and there was great waste of public money. When the famine reached its height, the main problem was to obtain supplies of food, either locally or through the Government, and distribute them to the needy through free kitchens. Relatively small amounts of dry grain were issued. At this stage destitutes flocked into towns in the districts, as into Calcutta, and similar scenes were enacted, though on a smaller scale. By degrees food was provided and acute starvation diminished, relief in many areas being hastened in November and December by the help of the military transport organization. With the arrival of the harvest, and the increase in, and accelerated transport of, provincial supplies, food and work became available for the survivors. Free kitchens were replaced by workhouses and orphanages which provided food and shelter for famine victims who remained destitute and homeless. Complete recovery did not, however, follow

the relief of starvation. The death rate from epidemic disease remained high for many months and the satisfactory rehabilitation of the classes in the population most affected by the famine is an extensive problem which will be discussed in a later chapter.

VI. Work of non-official relief organisations:

31. Many non-official bodies participated in relief work. In Calcutta, 40 food kitchens were run by such bodies, and several hundreds were opened in districts. Numerous cheap canteens and centres for the issue of free doles of uncooked food were also established by voluntary organizations. The latter were allowed to buy food for distribution through the Department of Civil Supplies at controlled prices. Most of the gruel issued in Calcutta was cooked in Government kitchens, 7 in number, and distributed to Government and voluntary kitchens. Some of the voluntary organizations made their own arrangements about food supplies. Charitable organizations assisted in the distribution of milk and cloth, and at a later stage of the famine some of them played a useful part in establishing and running homes and orphanages.

32. At the end of September a Relief Co-ordinating Committee was set up by Government, including representatives of voluntary relief agencies and some representatives of the press. The Relief Co-ordination Officer had the task of co-ordinating the work of non-official agencies in Calcutta, where there was some overlapping of charitable activities. Some voluntary organizations were reluctant to combine in relief work. The fact that some had political affiliations did not facilitate co-operation but all communities benefited equally from the distribution of voluntary relief. The criticism has been made that non-official relief was concentrated in Calcutta to the exclusion of the districts. It was, however, natural that organizations centered in Calcutta should prefer to work in the city where voluntary workers and suitable premises were easily available. There was plenty of visible distress in Calcutta for charity to relieve. Actually valuable work was done in the districts by old-established non-official bodies with experience of work in villages and with a trained staff at their disposal. While it is invidious to draw distinctions, it may be said that the Commission heard from many quarters of the excellent work carried out by the Ramkrishna Mission in various rural areas.

33. Complaints have been made, by various voluntary organizations, of lack of assistance and co-operation on the part of the Government. In particular it has been said that difficulties arose with regard to supplies of food for voluntary relief work. Unquestionably there were delays and some friction, inevitable in the circumstances. But on the whole co-operation between the Government relief organization and the voluntary agencies seems to have been reasonably satisfactory.

Hard things have been said about the reluctance of the well-to-do to share surplus food with poorer neighbours. Many witnesses appearing before the Commission expressed bitter views on this subject. There was unquestionably much callousness and indifference to suffering on the part of people who were themselves in no danger of starvation. On the other hand, the appeal for gifts of money to support voluntary relief met with a generous response from the public in general in Bengal. Mention must also be made of contributions for famine relief received from other parts of India and also from abroad.

The extent of distress was so great that relief on a wide scale could be provided only by Government action. The contribution made by voluntary effort could only be relatively small. It must, however, be said that the voluntary organizations very materially assisted in the mitigation of suffering.

VII. Transport:

34. The difficulties of transporting food supplies to and within Bengal have been referred to in another chapter. Lack of transport, and defects in the organization of whatever transport was available, were serious obstacles to relief work in rural areas in the early stage of the famine. Until the arrival of the military in November 1943, it was, as put by one witness, "a case of making the best of a bad job with the limited transport available". When the army organization undertook the transport of food and medical and other supplies to the districts, the problem of relief was immediately simplified.

VIII. Military assistance in relief:

35. An account has already been given in chapter VIII, of the part played by the military in the relief of the famine. In another chapter military co-operation in medical and public health work will be described. Here we shall refer to the effect of military assistance in two spheres of relief.

Officers and men were encouraged to visit and report on food kitchens, to see that food was satisfactorily prepared and that adequate accounts were maintained. This acted as a check on corruption. Assistance given in another branch of relief—the distribution of clothing—is illustrated in the following passage from a report:

"Civil arrangements were extremely slow in maturing and in many places much of the cold weather had passed before adequate supplies were made available. The army did everything in its power to speed up the distribution of clothing and to ensure that as far as possible it was distributed to the most deserving cases. The utmost vigilance had to be maintained in the early stages when there was mal-administration and it was not uncommon for District Board officials to distribute clothing to their relations and friends who were in a position to obtain them for themselves. Army supervision helped to rectify this state of affairs".

The relations between military and civil authorities in the application of relief measures, after some friction in the early stages, were on the whole satisfactory. The public appreciated the rescue work of the army and friendly relations were established. In general military participation was invaluable in restoring public confidence, shattered by the extent of the catastrophe, and in stimulating and improving famine relief work in all its aspects.

CHAPTER X—LOOKING BACK.

A.—Preliminary remarks.

1. The Famine Inquiry Commission Ordinance has given us the task of determining the causes of the food shortage in India generally, and particularly in Bengal. In the discharge of this duty, it is not enough merely to explain why there was a food shortage in Bengal as a whole; we must also explain why such a large number of the people of the province were deprived of their share of the supplies available—how in fact, the over-all shortage was converted into famine. As we look back on the events in Bengal during 1943, the high prices of that year clearly stand out as unprecedented, much more so, indeed, than the failure of the crop. Men, women, and children died, as much because they could not pay for the food they needed, as because food was not available. Why did this happen? Were the high prices an inevitable result of the underlying scarcity? Or were they the result of an avoidable failure in price control and in the distribution of available supplies according to needs? We must attempt to furnish answers to these questions.

2. Such questions obviously cannot be answered merely by an arithmetical computation of supplies and requirements. We must examine the working of the machinery of the trade as it existed in Bengal before the shortage occurred, and determine whether it was capable of distributing supplies equitably in the circumstances which arose during 1943. If it was not, what were the measures which were necessary and feasible for ensuring proper distribution? We must review the measures which were actually taken and assess their effectiveness. If we conclude that, at the various stages in the crisis, the measures taken were inadequate or inappropriate, we must suggest what, in our opinion, would have been the correct action in the circumstances.

3. With these objectives in mind, we shall now proceed to review critically the course of events described in earlier chapters. We fully realise that we are in a very different position from the men who in various spheres of authority had the responsibility for dealing with the crisis at it developed from day to day. As a result of our inquiries, we are in possession of information about the situation which was not available at the time. We have also had the advantage of being able to "look back" and survey the effects of the policies adopted and the measures taken on the course of events. We are not unmindful of the saying "it is easy to be wise after the event" We would add that we have not always found it easy, in spite of the advantages of our position, to reach conclusions as to what would have been the most effective means of dealing with various crucial problems which arose during the famine. This has given us an understanding of the difficulties which confronted those who had to take immediate decisions and give effect to them in the midst of the crisis. We should be sorry if, in any part of our critical review, we have conveyed the impression of not being fully aware of these difficulties.

B.—The causes of the Bengal famine.

4. The crisis in Bengal which culminated in the famine began by the end of December 1942. The shortage of supplies developed rapidly in Greater Calcutta and became acute in March 1943. The measures taken by the Government of Bengal and the Government of India succeeded in averting a catastrophe in Greater Calcutta. At the same time distress was developing more slowly but steadily in other parts of Bengal, and successive efforts to avoid a

disaster failed. Famine raged over large areas in the province and came to an end only with the reaping of the *aman* crop in December 1943.

5. On a review of all the facts which we have set out in earlier chapters, we are led to the following conclusions about the causes of the Bengal famine:—

I. During 1943, there was a serious shortage in the total supply of rice available for consumption in Bengal as compared with the total supply normally available. This was due to

(A) a shortage in the yield of the winter rice crop (*aman*) of 1942, combined with

(B) a shortage in the stock of old rice carried forward from 1942 to 1943.

II. Out of the total supply available for consumption in Bengal, the proportionate requirements of large sections of the population who normally buy their supplies from the market, either all the year round or during a part of the year, were not distributed to them at a price which they could afford to pay. This was due to

(A) the incapacity of the trade operating freely in response to supply and demand, to effect such a distribution in the conditions prevailing; and

(B) the absence of that measure of control, by the Bengal Government, over producers, traders, and consumers in Bengal necessary for ensuring such a distribution.

III. The supply of rice and wheat which, under normal conditions, would have been available to Bengal from sources external to the province, was not available during the closing months of 1942 and the early part of 1943. This was due to

(A) the loss of imports of rice from Burma; and

(B) the delay in the establishment of a system of planned movement of supplies from surplus provinces and states to deficit provinces and states.

The supply position during 1943 has been discussed in Chapter III and in section A of chapter VI, and recapitulation is unnecessary. There is no doubt that shortage of supplies was a basic cause of the famine. We can put this in another way by saying that, if the *aman* crop had been a good one, the famine would not have occurred. With regard to the conclusions stated above about external supplies of rice and wheat, the non-availability of such imports during the period in question was a much less important factor in the causation of the total shortage than the failure of the *aman* crop and the depletion of reserve supplies. It was, however, an important factor in creating and maintaining a tendency to a rise in prices.

The causes of the rise in the price of rice which, in combination with shortage, led to famine on a wide scale will be discussed in the sections which follow.

C.—High prices and failure of distribution

6. In theory, it should have been possible to distribute the total supply, even if it fell short of normal requirements, in such a way that everyone got an equal share of it and none need have starved merely as a result of foregoing a small fraction of his normal food requirements. In theory, again, it should not have been impossible during 1943 to effect this distribution at a price not much in excess of that at which consumers obtained their supplies during the latter half of 1942. The cost of production and distribution had undergone no striking change in the meantime. It is true that the failure of the crop meant a diminution in the purchasing power of large sections of the rural population as compared with the preceding year. But this could have been met in the same

way as it had been met during 1941, namely, by the provision of relief to the affected classes through loans, wages on relief works, and gratuitous relief. Actually, the normal distribution of supplies did not take place, and in many parts of the province consumers could not obtain even a fraction of their requirements. Prices rose fantastically placing food above the reach of large numbers of people and rendering the usual form of relief largely ineffective.

7. What were the conditions prevailing in Bengal at the end of 1942 which prevented the distribution of supplies at reasonable prices by normal unrestricted trade? They cannot be described in a single sentence for they include a series of inter-connected events which occurred during 1942, and the reactions of those events on the minds of sellers, (producers and traders) and buyers (traders and consumers). The events to which we refer have been described first in section D of chapter IV, where we have dealt with the disturbances occurring in the rice markets of different parts of the country almost simultaneously within a short time after the fall of Burma, secondly, in section B of chapter V, where we have described the course of events in the rice markets of Bengal at about the same time and before the failure of the *aman* crop, and thirdly, in section F of the same chapter in which a description has been given of the swift developments in Bengal which followed the failure of the *aman* crop.

8. The initial phase of the disturbances in the rice markets in India was the direct result of the fall of Burma. Until then, the movement of rice prices had been more subdued than that of wheat prices, even though the relation between total supply and total demand was more unfavourable in the case of rice than in the case of wheat. As long as the possibility of imports from Burma remained, there was little speculative activity in the rice markets. When Burma fell and it became plain that the areas which were largely dependent on imports from Burma, must obtain their supplies in India and nowhere else, prices of rice rose suddenly and alarmingly. This was mainly due to purchases in the rice producing areas for export to Western India, Travancore, Cochin, and Ceylon. A reference to the figures in paragraph 3 of Chapter VII shows that Western India, Travancore, and Cochin were the areas in India which were most severely hit by the loss of imports from Burma. The figures also indicate the weight of the additional demand which the fall of Burma threw on markets in India, most of which were themselves somewhat short of supplies because of the loss of imports from Burma. Unquestionably, the main factor in the disturbances in the rice markets in the summer of 1942 was the demand from areas which depended largely on imports from Burma.

9. Prices rose in the rice markets of India in the first instance because the need of the buyers from the areas to which we have referred was urgent and sellers in the principal markets could demand a higher price. The latter in their turn had to secure supplies from the secondary markets more quickly and in larger quantities than usual, in order to meet further demands from the outside buyers. The merchants in the secondary markets were then in a position to demand and obtain higher prices for their stocks. The rise in prices which was thus spreading could not be confined to the stocks which were purchased for export; it affected all transactions in the principal and secondary markets. It is necessary at this stage to emphasize the sharply contradictory character of the reaction of the markets to rising prices in different conditions. A rise of prices which is believed to be likely to continue influences the minds of producers, traders. and consumers very differently from a rise of prices which is generally expected to be temporary. In the latter case, sellers—both producers and traders—are anxious to sell before prices fall; and buyers—both traders and consumers—reduce, so far as possible, the quantities they buy. Such a reaction automatically corrects the temporary mal-adjustment between

the available market supply and the demand which caused the upward movement in prices. If the mal-adjustment is corrected by an increase in supply in the market and a reduction in demand, prices fall again. This does not, however, happen when the rise in prices is sharp and unusual, and is also expected to continue. In these circumstances, it produces an exactly opposite reaction in the minds of buyers and sellers. Buyers are anxious to buy before a further rise occurs and therefore increase their purchases, while sellers are reluctant to sell because they wait for still better prices. This further decreases the supply available in the markets and increases the demand on the diminishing supply. Prices move up still further in consequence. This reinforces the fears of buyers and the greed of sellers and intensifies the market disturbances. Given sufficient time for the psychology of greed and fear generated in this manner to penetrate, on the one hand, to the primary markets and the producers—the ultimate source of supply—and, on the other hand, to the retail shops and the consumers—the ultimate source of demand—prices may rise to such an extent that large sections of the population find themselves unable to buy.

10. There is, therefore, no quantitative relation between the movement of prices and the volume of the additional demand which initiated the movement. Unquestionably, the volume of imports which was lost as a result of the fall of Burma and had to be met from the principal rice producing areas of India was only a very small proportion of the total supply in these areas. Nevertheless, it was the diversion of the demand formerly met from Burma to the Indian markets which started the increase of prices in the summer of 1942. The extent of the rise was out of all proportion to the disturbing cause because of its repercussions on the local markets which we have described. There were also certain other factors during 1942 favourable to a steady rise in prices. The rise which had occurred during the war period had enabled the cultivators to meet their cash obligations by selling a smaller quantity of their produce than formerly. This meant that they were, in general, better able than before to wait for better prices by withholding supplies from the market. At the same time, the demand from a large class of consumers had become more effective. In many parts of the country, the assuring of supplies for labour engaged in industry, transport, and the essential services, became of primary importance for the prosecution of the war. Purchases were therefore being made by employers on their behalf. Also, in areas which were exposed to invasion or air raids, there was a sense of insecurity which reinforced the effect of the rise in prices and the uncertainty about supplies. Consumers became alarmed and, as far as their purses permitted, purchased and stocked more than they would have done in normal conditions.

11. This, we believe, is in broad outline the picture of what happened in 1942, after the fall of Burma, in many provinces and states, including Bengal. The pressure of demand which arose in consequence of the loss of rice imports from Burma was only the first of the factors leading to disturbances in the markets and the rise in the price level. The disturbances developed in successive phases until all the local markets were affected and not merely those in which purchases were being made for export. The various phases of the market disturbances were reached in different places at different times, and were of varying degrees of intensity, depending on various factors, such as the conditions of local supply and transport, the extent to which different areas were affected by war conditions—the threat of invasion or air raids or the speeding up of defence preparations—and they no doubt also varied to some extent with the general psychology.

12. Looking back, we have no doubt that in such conditions normal unrestricted trade operations could not ensure distribution at reasonable prices.

A breakdown in distribution could be averted only by an intervention of Government, which would have the effect of restoring public confidence and of demonstrating to producers and traders the determination and the ability of Government to prevent a further rise in prices, and of assuring traders and consumers that the flow of supplies would be maintained. We have also no doubt that it was this compelling necessity which led a number of Provincial and State Governments to undertake at about the same time a series of measures in restraint of trade. The measures which they adopted differed in several respects, but one measure was taken by all. Unusual exports were the original cause of the trouble. Control of exports was, therefore, the necessary first step in the attempt to control prices and ensure a satisfactory distribution of supplies. It was, however, only the first step. Other measures were necessary in order, first, to deal with questions of price control and distribution within the province or state, and secondly, to ensure a flow of supplies from surplus provinces and states to deficit provinces and states.

13. We must now turn to Bengal and consider the course of events within the province in the latter half of 1942. Prices in Bengal rose sharply in May and June 1942, and the Provincial Government issued an Order fixing maximum prices with effect from the 1st July. This Order failed in its purpose but by the middle of September prices had steadied. It will be recalled that four factors helped in producing this improvement. First, a decrease in exports, secondly, the judicious use of "denial" stocks, thirdly, good rain in September and October, and fourthly, the decision not to enforce price control. All the markets in Bengal, however, had been affected and prices were well above the maxima prescribed by Government in July. The inability of Government to enforce price control had become manifest. Would prices begin moving up again or not? No one knew for certain—neither those who feared that prices would rise nor those who hoped that they would. Exports, though on a much reduced scale, were taking place. Perhaps the needs of other areas might compel Government to allow larger exports, and in that case surely prices must rise. Markets in the province generally, and Calcutta markets in particular, were in a state of suspense about the future when the cyclone struck the province and within a few weeks it became generally known that the *aman* crop would be a poor one.

14. The suspense was ended. It was clear that prices must rise again and no one believed that Government could control them. The events that followed have been described in section F of chapter V. Prices rose rapidly and by January 1943 had reached levels never before known in Bengal. This rise in prices continued unchecked and converted a shortage of supply into a famine. The rise of prices, which we hold to be the second basic cause of the famine, was something more than the natural result of the shortage of supply which had occurred. It was the result of the belief of the producers, traders, and consumers in Bengal at the end of 1942 and the beginning of 1943 that an ever-increasing rise in prices was inevitable and could not be prevented. This belief had been created, not only by the failure of the *aman* crop but by the entire course of events during 1942.

D.—Control measures during 1942

15. In this section we propose to consider whether any measures could have been taken by the Bengal Government during 1942 to restore confidence, and to prevent the steep rise in prices which took place at the end of the year.

Statutory price control was a failure. At the time the Order was issued Government had no control over supplies and the only means of enforcing the Order was through the ordinary staff employed for the maintenance of law and order. It was not till August that the Director of Civil Supplies with a small staff was appointed. There was little information about the stocks held by traders, for the Foodgrains Control Order was not brought into force till December. In these circumstances, an attempt to control prices by the prescription of statutory maxima aggravated the situation by driving stocks underground. The subsequent decision not to enforce the Order, while alleviating the difficulties which the Order created, advertized the inability of Government to control the markets.

16. The control of exports and the use of "denial" stocks were measures which had helped to ease the situation. Was it possible in the light of this experience to have taken further measures which would have prevented conditions deteriorating so rapidly in the latter half of November and in December? In considering this question, it is useful to compare the course of events in Bengal and Madras during the months following the fall of Burma. Conditions in Madras were at this time somewhat similar to those in Bengal. Both were important rice producing areas and the over-all supply position was fairly satisfactory in both provinces; market conditions had been disturbed in substantially the same way by similar causes; and control of exports was introduced at about the same time. The Government of Madras did not impose statutory price control. They proceeded instead to develop the control of exports into a Government monopoly of exports, and in September an official organization was set up in the principal surplus areas to undertake all buying for export outside the province. At the same time private buying for such export was stopped. Later the organization was used for the purchase of supplies in the surplus areas for export to deficit areas within the province. This enabled the Government to maintain better control over the markets in the surplus areas and to introduce control over imports into deficit areas. Early in the following year, monthly quotas were fixed by Government for all deficit areas of the province. These quotas could be purchased only by traders operating under official control, and purchases could be made only through the official purchasing agency.

17. The advantages of developing control on these lines were clearly indicated by conditions in Bengal during 1942. Markets in Bengal were dominated by conditions in Calcutta. Experience during the months of July and August had shown, first, that reliance could not be placed on the trade to bring supplies to Calcutta at prices considered reasonable by Government; secondly, that the use of "denial" stocks had helped; and thirdly, that the absence of adequate supplies had made it impossible to enforce maximum prices. There was also the circumstance that organized industry, in the effort to assure supplies for its large labour force, was seeking the help of Government. Finally, there was the danger that air raids on Calcutta might seriously interfere with the flow of supplies to the city. We think that at this stage, that is, in September, Government should have organized an adequate procurement machinery with the object of maintaining supplies for Calcutta, the heaviest deficit area in the province, and should have undertaken, certainly in Calcutta, rigorous and drastic enforcement of the Foodgrains Control Order. The purchasing organization could also have undertaken the purchases of the limited amounts which were then being exported under permit and by this means another disturbing element in the situation would have been removed. Larger supplies in the hands of Government would have enabled the system of controlled shops, which came into existence in September, to be expanded, and this might have paved the way for the introduction of rationing at a later date. It would also have been possible to make larger allocations to employers organizations, and thereby to have reduced the pressure on the market by wealthy buyers. Further, the enforcement of the Foodgrains Control Order would have provided accurate information about stocks, and would have enabled Government to watch and if necessary exercise control over the distribution of those stocks. If these measures had been adopted

by September and their scope and purpose clearly explained to the people, public confidence would have improved; the scope for speculative buying would have been curtailed, and competitive buying for the provision of supplies for Calcutta would have been greatly reduced. Indeed, in view of what followed, it is now clear that September was a critical month in the development of the famine. The failure of price control had caused a loss of confidence in the ability of Government to control the markets, and it was important that Government should demonstrate without delay their determination to prevent a further rise in price, and to assure traders and consumers that the flow of supplies would be maintained.

18. We do not wish to suggest that the Bengal Government were oblivious to the need of obtaining control over supplies. They were not. At this time, however, ideas had not crystallized as to the form foodgrain procurement organizations in India should take, whether they should be under central or provincial control, or whether for rice they should be on a regional basis. The Provinces, with one or two exceptions, had not established purchasing organizations. The Government of Bengal favoured central control and in September 1942 were considering a scheme for "making the whole of Assam, Bengal, Bihar, and Orissa into one producing region", within which there should be "no restriction on the movement of rice except in gravest emergency or when possibilities of centralized control have broken down". The scheme also contemplated the establishment of a "Rice Commission, a small body of integrity and commercial experience, whose duty it would be to carry out the general instructions of the Central Government but who would be as completely free from Government influence in their actual business operations as is a statutory body such as the Port Commissioners or the Calcutta Improvement Trust". The Government of India also at this time favoured the control of rice on a regional basis, and the Sixth Price Control Conference held in Delhi in September 1942 recommended that the primary responsibility for distribution within each region should be vested in the Regional Price and Control Board, operating either through its own machinery or through the machinery of the Provincial Governments, subject to the direction of the Central Government. The idea of the regional control of rice was not proceeded with, but it was finally decided that the procurement organizations should be under provincial and not under central control.

19. There was also another reason which, no doubt, influenced the Government of Bengal at the time. By September and October 1942, prices had steadied themselves, and supplies and prices appeared to have reached a state of equilibrium. The anxiety about the lack of rain had been relieved in August, and by the end of September and the beginning of October an average *aman* crop seemed assured. The *aman* crop would be coming on the market within a few months, and that would be the most favourable time for making purchases. Subsequent events unfortunately proved how quickly crop prospects can change owing to the vagaries of the weather, and how dangerous it is to delay taking action in regard to such a vital matter as food. There was, however, a real danger of air raids upsetting the Calcutta market, as actually happened towards the end of December 1942. The province was also still in the "front line" and the feeling of insecurity which was so pronounced in the early months of 1942, owing to the rapid approach of the Japanese to the borders of the province, had not entirely disappeared. It could not be said with certainty that all danger had passed, and that Government might not once again find themselves unable to maintain supplies at prices which they considered reasonable. The only way of preventing such a situation developing was by control over supplies, and that could only be assured by the operations of an efficient procurement organization.

20. We are confident that if an efficient procurement organization had been developed about September 1942, the crisis which began towards the end of 1942, would not have taken such a grave form. We have also said that we think Government should have taken steps to establish such an organization. We believe we are right in that view. It is true that prices had steadied themselves about the middle of September, but it was impossible to say that all danger of disturbances in the markets had passed. The events of 1942 had shown how necessary it was for the Bengal Government to secure control of supplies. In these circumstances, we think that the wise course would have been for Government to have recognized that it was inadvisable to wait for a decision whether the control of rice should be a central, provincial or regional responsibility, and that the proper course was to establish as quickly as possible their own procurement machinery.

E.—THE PEOPLE AND THE GOVERNMENT

21. We now come to the beginning of 1943, and in the course of the following sections we shall consider what was done and should have been done to prevent or mitigate the famine which began in June and reached its height in the second half of the year. For this purpose we must first make clear our conception of the actual process of events, and thereby indicate the state of affairs which had to be remedied. What happened was that producers sold their rice as they thought fit at the best price they could obtain, or held it in the hope of still higher prices. Traders bought, held and sold with the object of obtaining maximum profits, and consumers who could afford it bought as much as they could and not as much as they needed. The results were on the one hand unprecedented profiteering and the enrichment of those on the right side of the fence; on the other, the rise of prices to fantastic heights and the death of perhaps one and a half million people. It has been reckoned that the amount of unusual profits made on the buying and selling of rice during 1943, was 150 crores.[1] We cannot vouch for the accuracy of this figure, but beyond question huge profits were made. Very naturally, in the circumstances, there was great indignation against "profiteers, speculators, and hoarders", to whose greed the famine was ascribed; while equally naturally the Government were blamed for their failure to deal drastically with such enemies of society. Popular views about large profiteers who speculated and hoarded amid growing distress, and the inability of Government to control them, were indeed not without foundation. There were such profiteers, but they were not the only culprits.

22. Many witnesses appearing before us laid great stress on profiteering on the part of traders, particularly large traders, and attached much less importance to the attitude and actions of the producer. They pointed to the negative results of the "Food Drive" in June 1943 as evidence against the view that withholding of stocks by the producer played a part in causing the famine. Representatives of the trade, on the other hand, maintained that stocks in the hands of traders were generally much lower during 1943 than in normal years, and referred to the results of the food census in Calcutta and Howrah in support of this contention. They emphasized the reluctance of cultivators, large and small, to part with their produce. The fact is that a large section of the com-

[1] The details of this gruesome calculation are as follows :—

Normally, about 4·5 million tons of rice and paddy in terms of rice pass through the markets and are bought by consumers in the course of the year. At least 5/6th of this quantity, or 3·75 million tons, must have been bought during 1943. Judging from the differences in the prices which prevailed during 1942, and those which prevailed during 1943, as well as the available statistics about prices which actually were paid during 1943, the average difference was not less than Rs. 15 per maund or Rs. 400 per ton in round figures. Hence the figure of Rs. 150 crores as the excess price charged for 3·75 million tons during 1943. Thus every death in the famine was balanced by roughly a thousand rupees of excess profit.

munity, including producers, traders, and consumers, contributed in varying degrees to the tragic outcome. The movement of prices which started in 1942 did not originate in the villages but by the end of the year producers as well as traders were infected by the unhealthy atmosphere of fear, greed, and speculation. At this point the upward movement of prices was resumed. The rise reflected the prevailing mood of producers as well as of traders and consumers. Thereafter every producer who retained his surplus grain or sold it at prices much higher than those prevailing in the autumn of 1942, every trader who held back stocks in the hope of further gain or made a big profit on his sales, every consumer who held larger supplies than usual, helped in accelerating the rise in prices and in precipitating the final catastrophe.

23. It is, therefore, clear that further deterioration in the situation as it existed at the beginning of 1943 would have been prevented only by strict measures of control, affecting not only traders and urban consumers but large numbers of producers in every part of the province. Further, such measures depended for their complete success on full popular co-operation and support. Unfortunately all this was lacking and co-operation was not obtained. We have no desire to enter current political controversies and shall confine ourselves to a brief discussion of the reasons for the lack of full co-operation between the Government and the people.

24. Except for a few days in 1943, the legislature was functioning in Bengal and Ministers responsible to that legislature were in office. At no time, however, was the Government so constituted as to command the support of all principal parties in the legislature. We have had the benefit of discussions with leading representatives of several of these parties, and all have told us that the emergency required an "all-party" Government. This we have no doubt is correct. In a situation such as that arose in Bengal in 1942 and 1943, endangering the food supply and hence the very life of the people, it was clearly necessary that the measures taken by Government should receive the full support of public opinion. This was difficult when counsels were divided, and food administration was the subject of public controversy conducted on party lines. It was necessary that the leaders of the principal parties should all speak with one voice. We are convinced that political strife in Bengal was a serious obstacle to an effective attack on the problems created by high prices and food shortage.. Ministries which were subjected to bitter assaults by their political opponents must have been hampered in their endeavour to take decisive action. The opposition parties, on the other hand, would no doubt claim that their assaults were justified, and that they themselves would have handled the food situation more efficiently than the Government in office. We cannot pass judgment on these matters and confine ourselves to emphasizing the lack of unity in the political sphere.

We have been informed that a series of attempts were made to form an "all-party Government" before and after the change of Ministry in March—April 1943. They all failed. We understand that the main reasons for the failure were, first, the refusal of the Muslim League party in accordance with its all-India political policy, to join a government which included any Muslim who did not belong to the party, and secondly, the refusal of other principal parties either to join or support a government from which Muslim leaders, who did not belong to the Muslim League party, were excluded.

25. The formation of an all-party Government was not, however, the only possible means of securing public confidence. The alternative would have been to establish an *ad hoc* advisory body consisting of representatives (including members of the legislature) of producers, traders, and consumers, to promote co-operation between the administration and the public. Such bodies have been set up in several other provinces, and have helped governments to reach satisfactory decisions on food policy and obtain popular support in executing

them. If a body on similar lines had been established in Bengal, it would, we think, have enabled questions arising out of high prices and food shortage to be considered in an atmosphere less charged with political controversy. We understand that a proposal to set up such a body was considered but that Government and the Opposition could not agree on its functions. As a result, food administration continued to be involved in party politics.

26. While there was little co-operation between members of Government on the one hand and the opposition leaders on the other, matters were not improved by the friction and misunderstanding which appear to have prevailed towards the end of 1942 and in the early months of 1943, between the Governor and his Ministers. We have been told by certain of those who held the office of Minister at the time that decisions on food policy were taken by the Governor on the advice of permanent officials, and that Ministers were not "allowed a free hand to deal with the situation in the light of the experience and knowledge they undoubtedly possessed, of the situation in the country". We are unable to endorse this contention. We are satisfied from the material which has been placed before us that important issues of food policy and administration were referred to the Cabinet and decisions taken in the normal way. The statements referred to, do however, indicate differences at the seat of Government which cannot have facilitated the handling of such extremely difficult issues.

27. Finally, reference must be made to the political disturbances which started in August 1942. Apart from the fact that they claimed the attention of Government at a time when the development of the food situation required all their special attention, they added to the difficulties of securing public co-operation and maintaining public confidence. The fact that the disturbances took place in the district of Midnapore where the cyclone had caused such serious damage to life and property was a most unfortunate combination of events in a part of the province which suffered seriously in 1943.

28. We have shown that by the end of 1942 all the signals were set at danger and that great efforts were needed to avoid catastrophe. We do not however, wish to imply that famine, in the form in which it finally appeared, had become inevitable. The lack of political unity was a handicap, but the possibility of effective leadership of the people, and effective action stimulated by such leadership, had by no means disappeared. It may be that when this stage was reached, distress and starvation, in some degree, could not have been entirely averted. But opportunities for mitigating the famine and its lethal results still remained open.

F. The Situation in January 1943

29. In Section B of Chapter VI we described the purchasing schemes undertaken by the Bengal Government towards the end of December 1942 and in January-February 1943. The object of the first scheme was to secure from the districts in the Rajshahi Division a limited quantity of rice and paddy (7,400 tons) to be used for the purpose of moderating prices in the Calcutta market. This objective, it will be noticed, bore no relation to the situation in Bengal as we have described it. On the 9th January, this scheme was replaced by a more extensive one. If the second scheme had been a success, the supplies obtained would have been almost sufficient to feed Calcutta, and imports into that city on private account would have been practically unnecessary. The scheme failed, primarily because purchases could not be made on a voluntary basis within the price limit fixed by Government. It was abandoned on the 17th February. The quantity procured under the second and more ambitious scheme was smaller than that under the first, in spite of the fact that purchases were made in a wider area and for a longer period. Whereas under the earlier scheme, purchases were made by District Officers, agents chosen from the trade were employed for this purpose under the later scheme. Had this change anything to do with the result?

30. This brings us to an important question, namely, the type of organization which is most suitable for undertaking procurement on behalf of Government. At first sight it might appear that a commercial firm with experience in the buying and selling of foodgrains would be a more suitable agency than a purchasing organization manned by officials. This, however, has not been the experience of the large majority of the provinces. Madras, Bombay, Orissa, Bihar, United Provinces, the Central Provinces, and the Punjab have all preferred an official agency, and even more significant is the fact that when a change has been made it has been the substitution of an official for a trade agency. The result of this experience, in our opinion, shows conclusively that in the conditions prevailing in India the procurement of foodgrains on behalf of Government should be carried out by responsible officers in the public service and not by firms chosen from the trade. We shall refer to this matter again in a later chapter, but it is convenient at this stage to indicate the reasons for our view.

31. To begin with, the establishment of a non-official agency raises a problem of selection. The selection of the few gives rise to jealousies and friction which may often lead to difficulties for the agents actually chosen, and this in its turn hinders the co-operation between Government and the trade which is so important for the success of control measures. Again, selection may be influenced by political considerations, and there is the danger that political animosities may lead to allegations against the firms selected. Further, the employment of agents chosen from the trade has been found to impair the confidence of the public generally in the intentions of Government and their ability to carry them out. The public does not readily believe that private firms can be imbued with a spirit of public service; it tends rather to assume that their objective in the circumstances is gain at the public expense. Thus it was alleged at the time, and has been repeated before us, that some of the agents chosen by the Bengal Government under the "denial" scheme, took unfair advantage of their position as agents of Government to make purchases on their own account. It has also been said that some of those employed in January and February 1943 made large private purchases and large profits on such purchases after Government decided on de-control. In fairness to those agents we should state that these allegations were not substantiated by evidence and that the witnesses who appeared before us, did not claim that they possessed such evidence. Nevertheless, the fact remains that such accusations were made, were believed, and did harm in undermining public confidence in the measures undertaken by Government

32. Another reason why an "official" procurement agency is preferable to a "trade" agency is that there is a fundamental difference between normal trading and the procurement of supplies on behalf of Government. Normal trading rests entirely on voluntary contracts; there is no obligation on the seller to sell. A procurement organization established by Government must, however, in the last resort depend on coercion. Any attempt by traders or producers to combine and withhold supplies with the object of forcing up prices must be broken by requisitioning. Requisitioning involves the use of legal powers which must be entrusted only to responsible state officials and not to private individuals. It can be undertaken more effectively, and with less risk of misunderstanding as to its necessity in the public interest, by officers who are part of an official purchasing agency than by officers who are normally outside the procurement organization and are only occasionally called in to support the operations of the trade agents.

33. We can understand why the Government of Bengal in January 1943, at a time when little experience of the technique of procurement was available, decided to entrust the purchasing operations to agents chosen from

the trade. But we have no doubt that they were on right lines when, at the end of December 1942, they started making purchases through District Officers We believe that if after deciding in January 1943 to increase the scale of these purchases, they had strengthened the official purchasing agency by the substitution of special procurement officers for District Officers, fixed ceiling prices within which purchases would be made, and made it clear that they would not hesitate to requisition from large producers as well as from traders, better results would have been obtained.

34. Procurement, as we have already remarked, must in the last resort depend on coercion. If supplies are held back by traders or large producers, requisitioning is essential. At the beginning of 1943 the Government of Bengal did not take this view. They regarded requisitioning from the cultivator as "quite unthinkable" and feared that if it were done otherwise than occasionally in a local emergency it would end in widespread violence and disorder. But by January 1943 the danger of famine was already imminent. It was of the utmost importance that Government should obtain control of supplies, and if they were not brought to the market voluntarily, there was, in our view, no alternative to the use of coercion in the form of requisitioning from the hoarder, whether he were a trader or a large producer. Clearly, the longer such action was postponed, the more difficult and dangerous it would become. In January 1943 the *aman* crop had just been reaped. The crop was a poor one but was not equally bad all over the province; it was in the western districts that the crop had suffered most. Requisitioning at this time was least likely to arouse opposition, particularly in the areas where the crop had been fairly good. We recognize, of course, that procurement, if it is to be successful in times of shortage, must have the support of public opinion. This applies with special force to requisitioning. The "hoarder" must not be in a position to rely upon public sympathy; public opinion must make him realize that hoarding grain is an anti-social act. As we have already pointed out, there is in Bengal no establishment linking the District and Sub-divisional Officers with the villagers, corresponding to the subordinate revenue establishment in the *ryotwari* provinces.[1] If there had been such an establishment in Bengal, the fears that coercive measures would fail might not have been so pronounced, for Government would have had ready at hand a staff which could have been used not only for obtaining information about the large producers who were holding up supplies, but also for explaining to the villagers the necessity that producers who had a surplus should not withhold it from the market. Its absence was a serious handicap at this time. The question, therefore, which we have to ask ourselves is this: was it possible, at the beginning of January 1943, in the conditions then existing in Bengal, for the Government to undertake a scheme of procurement as outlined in the previous paragraph, without precipitating a breakdown of the administration? We think this would have been possible provided:

(i) procurement was undertaken by Government to assure supplies, not merely for Calcutta but also for other deficit areas in the province;

(ii) a "propaganda drive" was undertaken simultaneously to explain the danger threatening the province, and the reasons for the measures Government were taking; and

(iii) local food committees were set up for the purpose of mobilizing public opinion in the villages in support of the administration.

35. We realize that local opinion in the districts, particularly in those in which the *aman* crop had suffered most, was likely to be opposed to purchases

---

[1]Paragraph 9 of Chapter II.

being made by Government for supplying other deficit areas, particularly Calcutta. It would be inclined to favour local self-sufficiency. We doubt, however, whether in January this opposition was very pronounced, and we think it would not have been impossible to have reconciled rural public opinion to the need for an equitable distribution of available supplies to urban as well as rural consumers. The announcement that the procurement operations were being undertaken not merely for supplying Calcutta but also for meeting the needs of rural deficit areas would have helped in overcoming any such opposition.

36. In view of what we have said in paragraph 34, the need for the "propaganda drive" referred to therein is, we think, obvious. Such a campaign was undertaken later towards the end of April and during May 1943. It failed and has been severely criticized. We have been told that Government advised people that there was no shortage at a time when everybody knew that there was a shortage, and that this increased the prevailing lack of confidence. At that time the original Basic Plan had just been drawn up, and it will be recalled that under the Plan Bengal was to receive, in monthly quotas, a total quantity of 350,000 tons of rice, in addition to large quantities of wheat and millets. It was calculated that, taking into account these supplies, there would be no shortage in Bengal, and so far as we can gather it was on the result of this calculation that the propaganda was based. Certainly this was the line taken by the spokesman of the Government of India about the middle of May in Calcutta. The impression created in the public mind, however, was that Government were maintaining that there was no shortage in Bengal irrespective of the supplies to be received under the Basic Plan. Conditions actually prevailing in Bengal at the time were far too serious for anyone to believe anything of the kind. We consider that this propaganda of sufficiency was quite ill-advised. We think that it would have been wiser to have told the people the truth, that is, that there was a shortage, and that although it was hoped to obtain supplies from other provinces it was essential, if famine was to be averted, that everybody who had stocks should dispose of them without waiting for higher prices. It was considered at the time that it was inadvisable to alarm the public by referring to the possibility of famine, and that it was undesirable that the enemy in Burma should be acquainted with the serious position in regard to food supplies in Bengal. We are not impressed by these arguments. The emergency was such—famine started in Chittagong by the beginning of June—that it could not be hidden, and in the circumstances it was essential that the people should be truthfully informed about the real position.

37. We now turn to the proposal for the formation of local food committees. We do not over-estimate the capacity of village committees for sustained effort; nor do we minimize the usual difficulties arising out of personal, communal, and political factions which, in rural areas no less than in urban areas, often tend to impair the usefulness of such committees. Nevertheless it seems plain that the problems which had arisen at the beginning of 1943, were such that the district administration in Bengal could not cope with them without the support of an emergency organization of local committees. We believe that the organization which was subsequently created in June, (which we described in paragraph 3 of Chapter VIII) served a valuable purpose and must have helped to save some lives. If local committees had been set up earlier, they could have been used as a medium for explaining Government's policy and the need for the stringent measures which were being taken. They could also have helped in the prevention of hoarding in their own villages. We recognize that all would not have been efficient, and that some might even have hampered rather than assisted the carrying out of Government's policy. But we take the view that on the

whole these committees would have been of considerable assistance in the circumstances.

G.—The situation in March 1943

38. As we have explained in Section C of Chapter VI and Section C of Chapter VII, two inter-related measures—"De-control" and a "Rescue Plan"—were undertaken in March, 1943, in an endeavour to increase the flow of supplies and to moderate prices. Early in March the developing crisis came to a head in Calcutta. During the two previous months, the Government of Bengal had tried to keep supplies moving without allowing prices to rise, and had failed. They were faced with this dilemma. If they continued their policy, Calcutta would starve with the certainty of serious disorder among the large labour force employed in war industries. If, on the other hand, they attempted to secure supplies by coercion in the rural areas, it was feared that widespread violence and disorder would occur. They decided to concentrate on the purchase of supplies and to abandon "any vestige of price control", in the hope that prices, after an initial flare-up, would settle down near the level at which they originally stood. The "rescue plan" aimed at obtaining 60,000 tons of rice from neighbouring provinces and the Eastern States within three or four weeks for the purpose of "breaking" the Calcutta market.

39. The hope that under de-control prices, after a preliminary rise, would fall was not realized. On the 3rd March 1943, the price of coarse rice in Calcutta was Rs. 15 a maund; by the 20th of the month it had risen to Rs. 21 a maund. The supply position was for a time easier but by the end of April the stocks of rice in Calcutta were running low again. The "rescue plan" contemplated the despatch to Bengal of 60,000 tons of rice but only about half that quantity was obtained. It has been urged that if the 60,000 tons had been obtained within three or four weeks as originally intended—the quantity actually received was spread over about 6 weeks—de-control would have proved successful. We doubt it, for in the conditions prevailing in Bengal producers and traders would have held on to their stocks in the knowledge that the 60,000 tons would be quickly consumed.

40. In the absence of internal control, the only method by which control could be exercised was by securing large imports from outside the province, and thereby convincing the producer and the trader that nothing would be gained by holding on to stocks in the expectation of higher prices. This, however, would have required the import not of a few thousand tons but of hundreds of thousands of tons. Indeed in the conditions of scarcity, fear, and greed prevailing in Bengal by the middle of March 1943, it would have been necessary to "flood" the markets not for a week or two but for a considerable period; without this it was impossible to spread among producers, traders, and consumers the idea that a fall in price was imminent. The immediate import of so large a quantity from the other provinces and states was not a practical proposition. An export surplus of this magnitude did not exist and it was quite unreasonable to expect the rest of India to feed Bengal while the trader and producer were being convinced that the game was up.

41. The dumping of relatively small quantities of rice thus gave no hope of reducing prices and huge imports were out of the question. In the circumstances, was there any course left open which offered a prospect of retaining control? We recognize the risk involved in requisitioning from the large producer at that time, particularly if the stocks requisitioned were to be used mainly for supplying Calcutta. Was there any way by which requisitioning could be made less risky? We suggest there was. It seems to us that the position by March had so deteriorated that some measure of external assistance had become indispensable if a disaster was to be avoided. A heavy burden was placed upon the resources of the province in 1943 by the demands of Greater Calcutta. The population of this important industrial area, over 4

millions, includes a large number of persons employed by the Provincial and Central Governments, local Bodies, the railways, utility companies, and firms engaged on war work. It was essential that they should remain at work, for the life of the community and the prosecution of the war depended upon their being at their posts. The extent to which external assistance could be given was limited, and moreover its value depended on the intensification of controls and not on their relaxation. We think, therefore, that the correct course in March was for the Government of India to have *announced* that they would provide, *month by month*, first, the full quantity of wheat required by Greater Calcutta and secondly, a certain quantity of rice. We do not suggest that it would have been possible to supply the full quantity of rice required by Greater Calcutta, but the assurance that a specified amount would be forthcoming regularly would have had a good psychological effect and would have eased the situation in the city. It should then have been possible for the Government of Bengal to undertake requisitioning. It is true that the scheme we have outlined would have involved the risk of a full supply not reaching Calcutta. In the circumstances, it was justifiable that Calcutta should have some share in the risk of short supplies which faced the province as a whole.

42. The question then arises whether the Government of India could have ensured these supplies. We think there would have been no serious difficulty. At the time there was a bumper wheat crop on the ground in the Punjab, price control had been removed, and supplies were moving into the markets. As regards rice, there would have been more difficulty. But supplies were coming in from Orissa and satisfactory arrangements might have been made for procuring the supplies available in the Eastern States. This would have given the Government of India time to explore the feasibility of obtaining supplies from other provinces. We consider that pressure should, if necessary, have been brought to bear upon those Governments to come to the help of Bengal.

43. We have described the dilemma with which the Government of Bengal were faced early in March 1943. They had to decide between two courses of action, both of which involved serious risks. Their decision in favour of decontrol was in accordance with the policy of the Government of India and indeed, was taken with their approval. We appreciate the care with which the Bengal Government weighed the *pros* and *cons* before reaching their decision. But it was, in our opinion, a wrong decision.

H.—External assistance

44. In paragraph 5 of this Chapter, we have stated that one of the causes of the Bengal famine was the delay in the establishment of a system of planned movement of supplies from surplus provinces and states to deficit provinces and states. We shall now consider to what extent external assistance could have influenced the course of events in Bengal, and whether there was any avoidable failure in the provision.

45. In this connection, a clear distinction must be drawn between wheat and rice. The need of Bengal for imports of wheat was never in doubt. We have seen that the supply of wheat received by Bengal during the last five months of 1942 and the first two months of 1943 was seriously inadequate. This shortage unquestionably intensified the demand for rice in Calcutta at a critical time. Was it unavoidable? We do not think so. What happened was that a speculative rise in prices occurred in the wheat producing areas of Northern India. The Government of India attempted to check it by the imposition of statutory maximum prices but failed, and the failure showed the real nature of the problems which had to be solved before control of prices could be made effective. We have explained in paragraph 24 of Chapter IV how it had become evident that an equitable distribution of wheat supplies could not be maintained, unless some authority determined the quantity of wheat to be taken off the Punjab market from time to time, and how it should be distributed

between the Army and the various consuming areas. It had also become clear that the establishment of an adequate procurement organization in the wheat producing areas was necessary to secure the exportable surplus. These problems largely remained unsolved throughout 1942. They could not be solved except by arrangements such as those subsequently made under the Basic Plan of the Government of India. In other words, the Basic Plan should have come into operation very much earlier than it did. Was this possible? We think it would have been if there had been agreement on the matter between the Punjab Government and the Government of India. The key to the situation was held by the Government of the Punjab. The bulk of the exportable supplies of wheat is in the Punjab and the successful procurement of these supplies depended on administrative action by the Punjab Government. The Government of India did not possess the necessary administrative machinery. The situation prevailing throughout the latter half of 1942, when purchases continued to be made by competing private agencies at prices in excess of the statutory limits, should, in our opinion, have been brought to an end sooner than it was. In our opinion an agreement should have been reached at a very early stage between the Government of India and the Government of the Punjab on the price level to be maintained; and price control should have been fortified by the establishment of an adequate procurement organization and consequent control of supplies. If, instead of de-controlling prices, this had been done, and wheat had been procured and distributed under a central plan, Bengal would have secured larger supplies. This would have been beneficial in two ways: first, it would have reduced the pressure on the Calcutta rice market in so far as it arose out of the shortage of wheat, and secondly, in view of the bumper wheat harvest of 1943, it would have been possible to send a large proportion of the supplies which reached Bengal towards the end of the year, at an earlier period when they would have been more useful.

46. The possibilities of help from outside were much more limited in the case of rice. The reasons have been explained in earlier chapters. Here we would merely recall the attitude of the Bengal Government themselves at the Food Conference held in December 1942 as proof of their recognition of this fact. Nevertheless, the Bengal Government maintain the view, which is also shared by many witnesses who appeared before us, that Bengal might have secured larger supplies during the early months of 1943 from the adjoining areas of the Eastern Region. It is urged that this was prevented by the fact that the Central Government had delegated powers to provinces to control exports and the provinces, in their anxiety to conserve their own resources, refused to release sufficient supplies for Bengal. We have already said that in our opinion the system of the control of exports, adopted by the provinces during 1942, was in the conditions created by the fall of Burma a necessary step towards the control by Government over the trade and that free trade could not have continued. The question therefore, to be considered is whether arrangements could have been made quickly enough to provide Bengal at an earlier date with supplies of rice in approximately those quantities which were obtained later in 1943 from other provinces and states. We think that the arrangements under the Basic Plan should have been made earlier in respect of rice also.

47. In retrospect, it now seems clear that the transfer in 1942 of the demand from areas formerly dependent largely on supplies from Burma to the markets in the main rice-producing areas in India was bound to give rise to serious disturbances in those markets. It will be recalled that prices rose sharply soon after the fall of Burma, that is, in the summer of 1942. But we think we are right in saying that it was not realized beforehand how swift and violent the reaction in the rice markets would be. The fall of Burma was also not anticipated until shortly before the event. It is true that difficulties occurred during 1941 which can now be identified as premonitory symptoms of subsequent disturbances in the rice markets during the summer of 1942. We may

refer to the account in paragraph 20 of Chapter IV of the proceedings of the Third Price Control Conference. Difficulties at that time were due largely to the shortage of shipping, and no one then anticipated the loss of imports. The conclusion reached at that conference was that rice, generally speaking, was a problem for which solution should be found by provincial authorities. When the Fourth Price Control Conference met in February 1942, the invasion of Burma had already begun and the dangers were becoming more obvious. The Government of Bihar were concerned about the effect of the possible loss of rice imports from Burma, and at their instance representatives of the Governments of the Eastern Region and of the Government of the Central Provinces met on the day preceding the conference to discuss the regulation of prices and supplies. Various measures, including price control, were discussed at this meeting but complete agreement was not reached. At the conference on the following day, discussion centred round price control and it was generally agreed that prices might have to be controlled in the near future. The distribution of the supplies available in India was not discussed. In April 1942, the Government of India convened a conference for examining the problems of food production, and the question of the arrangements necessary for the maintenance of the distribution of supplies between provinces and states was discussed at this conference. The need for the establishment of a central authority for regulating distribution was recognized, and the dangers inherent in the control of exports by individual provinces and states, with reference only to their own needs and without adequate co-ordination by a central authority, were prominently emphasized. But, even as late as September 1942, when the Sixth Price Control Conference considered the rice situation as it had already developed in several provinces, ideas regarding arrangements for the control of the movement of rice supplies across provincial and state frontiers had not crystallized into a concrete plan. We feel that valuable time was lost during this period when the need for co-ordinating the demands of the deficit areas with supplies from surplus areas was pressing. The rapid imposition of embargoes on export, without provision for meeting the needs of deficit from surplus areas, also indicated the urgency of the problem. Further the time taken for the evolution of the Basic Plan might, in our opinion, have been considerably shortened if the rapidity with which a serious food situation was developing in the country had been realized early in 1942, and a separate department of the Government of India established for dealing with it.

48. In our analysis of the situation in Bengal at the end of 1942 and the beginning of 1943, we have stressed the psychological aspect. One of the causes of the general belief that prices must rise was the sense of isolation. People in Bengal knew that the *aman* crop had failed, that there would be no imports from Burma, and that all the surrounding provinces had closed the door against exports. If at that time the people could have been informed that procurement operations were in progress in other provinces, and that the Central Government would distribute supplies from the surplus areas to provinces in need, the psychological problem would not have been so intractable.

I.—Free trade

49. A turning point in the history of the Bengal famine occurred on the 11th March 1943. Up to that date, the Government of Bengal, as well as the Government of India, had been moving, on the whole, in the direction of increasing control, though the pace of progress proved too slow in the conditions following the failure of the *aman* crop. The situation which developed in January and February 1943, demanded an intensification of control measures. Not only did this not take place, but on the 11th March there was a striking change in the direction of the policy of Government and a retreat from control began. "De-control" was the first step in this retreat. The removal of the

"barriers" within Bengal was the next step. Early in April, as we saw, the Bengal Government told the Government of India that "the barriers will have to be broken despite the risks and the pent up forces that will thus be let loose. They are of opinion that the logic of events will compel the Central Government to adopt the same course in respect of this Region". In the event, free trade was introduced into the Eastern Region.

50. Free trade came into force on 18th May. We have described in Section C of Chapter VII why this policy was adopted, how it worked, and the results it produced. In earlier sections of the present Chapter we have explained why, after the fall of Burma, it was impossible under free trading conditions to ensure the distribution of supplies of rice at reasonable prices in Bengal and the other main rice producing provinces. It is, therefore, clear to us that the decision to introduce free trade into the Eastern Region was a mistake. It could only result, not in the solution of the food problem in Bengal, but in the creation of similar conditions in other areas of the Eastern Region. We have little doubt that if free trade had been continued for a longer period it would have caused widespread distress and starvation among poorer classes in those areas. Indeed, by the middle of July prices had risen very steeply in the Eastern Region outside Bengal, and had reached a level which was placing food beyond the reach of the poorer sections of the population. It has been alleged that the Provincial Governments and their officers took steps to prevent rice being despatched to Bengal. We have ourselves little doubt that there was obstruction to purchases and removal of rice in certain areas. But we do not think that this made any serious difference to the Bengal situation as a whole. As we have said, free trade, while it could not solve the problem in Bengal, was, in the conditions then prevailing, a measure calculated to cause a steep rise in prices and consequent severe distress in buying areas. The attitude, helpful or otherwise, of the provinces concerned was not material to the success or failure of free trade.

51. We must again ask the question: What was the alternative? Two courses were at the time regarded as open. One was "unrestricted free trade" and the other "modified free trade". We have described the difference between these two courses in paragraph 27 of Chapter VII. "Modified free trade" meant the continuance of the Basic Plan, with the important modification of substituting an officer of the Central Government for the Provincial Governments of the Region as the authority responsible for controlling inter-provincial movements. As between the two proposals, the advantages of "Modified free trade" were so obvious that we consider it unfortunate that the Government of India gave up their initial preference for it on the insistence of the Government of Bengal. We appreciate the anxiety of the Bengal Government to secure as large a quantity of supplies as possible, but we feel that they failed to realize the importance of securing control of all the supplies brought into Bengal from outside the province. "Modified free trade" would have enabled such control to be exercised for all purchases would have been made under permits granted by an officer of the Central Government. The Government of Bengal would have been able to control, not only the places to which supplies were sent, but also the prices at which they were sold. Further, the licensed traders could have been allotted different areas in which to make their purchases, and in this way competitive buying would have been avoided. Lastly, the serious disturbances in the markets of the buying areas caused by unregulated purchases during the free trade period would not have occurred. These advantages were lost as a result of the choice of "unrestricted free trade".

52. One of the most unfortunate results of free trade was that it evoked hostility to Bengal in the Eastern Region. We have already described the charges and counter-charges which were made at the time and need not repeat

them. They were the inevitable result of the attempt to extract the maximum amount of rice in the shortest possible time, without regard to its effect on prices and supplies in the areas outside Bengal in which purchases were made. One particular cause of illwill and hostility was the feeling that it was not the Bengal Government or the people in need who reaped the benefit, but the traders themselves. This was true enough as far as private traders were concerned, for prices did not fall in Bengal. The same allegations were, however, made and repeated before us with regard to the purchasing agent of the Bengal Government. At this period the buying of rice on behalf of Government was entrusted to a firm of rice merchants in Calcutta. It was publicly alleged at the time that control over purchases made by this firm was inadequate and that undue profits were made by the firm or its agents at the expense of Government. We have given the matter our most careful consideration but have had no opportunity, within the time at our disposal, of making a detailed inquiry. Accordingly, previous to the submission of this report, we have recommended to the Government of India the investigation of certain accounts and other questions relating to those transactions.[1] We feel that the matter needs to be cleared up in the interests of the Government of Bengal and the public, and in order to promote confidence in food administration in Bengal.

J.—DISTRIBUTION OF SUPPLIES

53. Rationing was not introduced into Calcutta until 1944. During 1943 consumers made their purchases from three kinds of shops, ordinary retail shops, controlled shops, and employers' shops. Retail shopkeepers bought their supplies in the open market and their sales were not controlled as regards quantity or price. Everybody could buy grain in these shops provided he could pay the prevailing high prices. Controlled shops provided a limited supply, at prices subsidized by Government, to consumers who were prepared to undergo the discomfort of waiting in long queues. These shops were supplied from Government stocks. The employers' shops obtained their stocks partly from Government and partly by purchases in the open market. These shops provided a regular supply to about one million consumers at subsidized rates. Throughout the year a large proportion of the supplies arriving in Calcutta were brought in by private traders over whose transactions there was no control. They were free to sell to the highest bidder—and there was no lack of bidders. They were also free to withhold stocks from sale if the prices offered were not according to their expectations. This was the position in regard to the distribution of rice in Calcutta during 1943.

54. Prices in the Calcutta rice market govern rice prices throughout Bengal. In the absence of control by Government over the distribution of the rice supplies reaching the Calcutta market on private account during 1943—and given the shortage of supplies in Bengal—it was inevitable that the pace for the rise of rice prices throughout Bengal should be set by the purchasing power of consumers and employers, including the private and public employers of the "priority" classes in Calcutta. The city was prosperous and the purchasing power was large. Many persons could afford to pay high prices for the supplies required for their own domestic consumption and for that of their servants and employees. The Excess Profits Tax afforded a means whereby a large proportion of the cost of supplying the industrial labour force with food at subsidized rates could be passed on to Government revenues. The cost of feeding other categories of the "priority classes" at subsidized rates fell directly on the revenues of the Central Government, the Provincial Government, or the Railways. It was therefore, possible for Calcutta to pay a price for rice which was beyond the reach of large classes of the population in the rural areas.

[1] One of us Mr. M. Afzal Husain has further recommended that similar inquiries by a similar agency should be conducted into similar allegations regarding food purchases in India.

55. The ordinary consumer in Calcutta was helpless in this state of affairs. He had to buy at the prevailing market prices. The employers of labour had to provide their employees with food at subsidized rates or give ever increasing dearness allowances to enable them to buy it. The individual trader sold at the prevailing market prices, for if he contented himself with a smaller profit than the maximum obtainable, he merely helped another trader to make more profit. The "free market" in Calcutta was in an unnatural condition in which there was no competition among sellers and intense competition among buyers. The only way by which the conditions in the Calcutta market could have been prevented from raising prices throughout Bengal was by Government assuming control of the distribution of supplies in Calcutta, that is, first by controlling the wholesale and retail traders and secondly by the introduction of rationing.

56. Rationing did not come into force in Calcutta until the 31st January 1944. The reasons for this delay, in their order of importance, may be summarized as follows: —

(i) Lack of confidence of the Bengal Government in their ability to undertake the responsibility for supplies which rationing implies.

(ii) The preference by the Government of Bengal for a scheme of distribution under which Government shops replaced entirely private shops.

(iii) Difficulties and delays in securing staff and accommodation.

57. The first of these reasons was the crucial one. By March 1943, as we explained in Section G of this Chapter, the position had so deteriorated that external assistance was necessary. Under the scheme we outlined in that Section it would have been possible, by the combined efforts of the Government of India and the Government of Bengal, to maintain controlled procurement and at the same time provide supplies for Greater Calcutta, though a full supply of rice could not be guaranteed. It would also have been necessary for the Bengal Government to take action, preliminary to the introduction of rationing, to tighten up the control of distribution in Greater Calcutta. This would have involved the strict enforcement of the Foodgrains Control Order and the licensing of retail traders not covered by that Order. In this way full information would have been obtained of stocks and it would also have been possible to ensure that they were not held up or unevenly distributed. Provided this action was taken we do not think that a relatively small deficiency in the rice supply would have caused a catastrophe in Calcutta. In any case some risk had to be run. Preparations for rationing should also have been pushed on as quickly as possible and rationing introduced in two or more stages as in 1944. We recognize that these measures would have thrown a heavy burden on the administration but the danger threatening the province was great. If this scheme had been adopted in March controlled procurement could have continued and at the same time control would have been obtained over supply and distribution in Greater Calcutta. The latter in its turn would have assisted procurement.

58. Under the scheme actually adopted in March, controlled procurement was abandoned and the disturbing influence of conditions in the Calcutta market on prices throughout Bengal continued unchecked. Again when free trade was introduced in May large quantities of rice brought to Calcutta from other areas in the Eastern Region were not under Government control, and the disturbing influence of conditions in the Calcutta market on prices throughout Bengal remained unabated. Controlled procurement was also impossible. In the conditions created by the adoption of a policy of de-control in March and the introduction of free trade in May, it was impossible for the Provincial Government to obtain control of supply and distribution in Greater Calcutta and rationing was impracticable. Free trade was abandoned at the beginning of August but controlled procurement was not undertaken until the end of that month when famine was raging in the province.

59. Large quantities of wheat and rice started arriving in Calcutta on Government account from other parts of India in August and October 1943 respectively and the Provincial Government were assured of adequate supplies of both wheat and rice from the beginning of October. Although the rationing of Greater Calcutta remained a matter of primary importance in the food administration of Bengal, it was not until the 31st January 1944 that rationing was brought into force in the city of Calcutta and certain neighbouring municipalities, and not till May 1944 that it was extended to the whole of Greater Calcutta. The delay was chiefly due to two causes. First, the preference by the Government of Bengal for a scheme of distribution under which Government shops replaced entirely private shops, and secondly, difficulities and delays in securing staff and accommodation. The number of retail shops required to meet the needs of a population of four millions must run perhaps to a couple of thousands. We can understand that it was desirable to have a certain number of Government shops but, clearly, the proposal for the entire exclusion from the distribution system of private retail dealers would have resulted in the introduction of rationing being delayed almost indefinitely. We recognize that the difficulties of recruiting and training the large staff required and of acquiring accommodation were real and great, but we are of opinion that avoidable delay did take place. The delay in the recruitment was accentuated at one stage by an endeavour to maintain communal proportions. We consider this to have been particularly unfortunate. In an emergency, particularly one affecting the food of the people, administrative action should not be delayed by attempts to observe rules fixing communal ratios.

K.—Famine relief

60. In this Section we propose to consider in retrospect the problem of relief and the relief measures taken by the Bengal Government. In a previous chapter we have told how the famine affected the poor in rural areas and how the situation was made more difficult by the migration of large numbers of famine victims. The magnitude of the task of relief should be fully understood. In this connection we may draw attention to the size of the population of Bengal. For administrative purposes the province is divided into five Divisions. Two of these, namely, the Presidency and Burdwan Divisions which include Greater Calcutta, contain a larger population than the province of Bombay, the State of Baroda, and the Gujerat and Deccan States taken together. A third Division, Dacca, has a larger population than the two provinces of Assam and Orissa taken together. A fourth, Rajshahi, is more populous than the Central Provinces and the last, the Chittagong Division has a population equivalent to Travancore and Cochin taken together.

61. There were variations in the seriousness of the famine in different parts of Bengal. According to an estimate made by the Government of Bengal, the intensity of distress was greatest in 29 sub-divisions with a total area of 21,665 square miles and a population of 20 millions. The rise in the price of rice was, however, general throughout the province and involved danger of starvation for the poor everywhere. Hence, while the need of certain areas was particularly urgent, relief operations on a varying scale were required throughout most of the province.

62. The remarkable feature of the Bengal famine was that the rise in the price of rice was one of the principal *causes* of the famine. This, as far as we are aware, makes it unique in the history of famine in India. The great majority of Indian famines have been caused by drought and widespread failure of crops over wide areas. Floods, hail, and cyclones have on rare occasions produced the same effect. War, and civil disorder played a part in some of the great famines of the 18th century and earlier eras. In large famines produced by such calamities the shortage of grain was naturally reflected in a

rise in price, but the latter was a secondary phenomenon, and not a primary cause of the famine.

63. The Famine Code, which took shape during the last quarter of the 19th century, was evolved as a measure against typical "drought famines" (Each province has its own Famine Code, but the principles of all are similar). The course of events in such famines and the way in which the Code operates, are somewhat as follows:—The crops fail because of drought. The people in the affected area are deprived of local supplies of grain, and their reserves of money are reduced because agriculture is their sole means of livelihood. Without help, they would starve. At this point, Government steps in and provides them with money to buy food, the money being provided as loans, gratuitous relief, or as wages for labour on relief works, the last being much the most important. Labourers on famine relief works are paid a wage adjusted to the local price of grain, enabling them to buy enough food to cover their calorie requirements. The system requires that supplies of grain should be available in the famine area at a reasonable price and this again depends on the existence of surplus stocks elsewhere in the country, the free commercial movement of grains, and adequate means of transport into the famine area. In recent famines, apart from the Bengal famine, these conditions have been fulfilled and grain has flowed into the famine area through ordinary commercial channels. In the Hissar famine of 1940, for example, there were abundant supplies of wheat in the affected area throughout the famine, and its price did not rise above the all-India level. Under certain circumstances the Government may intervene to secure supplies of grain for the famine stricken population, but in general the policy of the Code is one of non-interference with private trade.[1] The Code envisages the appointment of a Famine Commissioner, with dictatorial powers, should famine be serious and widespread. In smaller famines a special Famine Commissioner need not be appointed, his functions being exercised by the Collector in the famine area.

64. In the relatively small famines of the last 40 years, the relief procedure embodied in the Code has on the whole proved satisfactory. It has served to mitigate distress and prevent deaths from starvation. Some rise in the death rate might occur in times of famine, due to debility and disease, but mortality on a catastrophic scale was avoided. Experience in the Hissar famine suggested that the Code requires modification in various respects, but in general it has achieved the purpose for which it was designed.

65. It is at once obvious that the Bengal famine, as it had developed by the middle of 1943, and the kind of famine with which the Code is concerned, were two very different things. The Code does not anticipate an enormous rise in the price of grain, to five or six times the normal level. It assumes free trade in foodgrains; free trade no longer existed in India in 1943. It assumes that there are surplus supplies of food in the country and that their transport to the famine area will be unchecked; this was not the case in the Bengal famine. Further, the setting up of relief works on a sufficient scale in the very large area ultimately affected in the 1943 famine would have been, for various

---

[1] Extract from Section 83 of the Bengal Famine Code:—

"(a) Without the previous orders of the local Government no grain shall be imported by the local authorities into any tract or area of relief work. The policy followed should be strictly one of non-interference with private trade.

(b) Every possible facility shall be given for the free action of private trade in time of scarcity or famine"

It is of interest to mention two famines in the second half of the 19th century in which private trade did not bring in supplies. In the Orissa famine of 1866 the threat of famine was not realized until after the monsoon had arrived and the famine area was cut off from supplies by the impossibility of transporting grain during the rains. In the Bihar famine of 1873, Government concluded that private trade could not bring in sufficient supplies and brought large stocks of rice in Burma and distributed them to the affected population through Government depots.

reasons, a formidable if not an impossible task. The organization of relief works in Bengal during the rainy season, when the greater part of the country-side is under water, presents special and almost insuperable difficulties. These considerations would not, however, have hindered the application of relief along the lines of the Code at an earlier stage in the development of the famine.

66. We may now consider certain criticisms of the relief measures taken by the Bengal Government which have been made by numerous witnesses. These can be briefly summarised as follows:—

(i) Failure to declare famine under the Famine Code;

(ii) Failure to make an early start in the organization of relief measures;

(iii) Failure to establish in time an adequate organization for the movement of supplies available to the Government.

67. The declaration of famine is a stage in the procedure prescribed in the Famine Code. The reasons why famine was not declared in Bengal have been explained as follows by the Bengal Government. Up to June 1943 such a declaration would have been inconsistent with the existing propaganda policy by which an attempt was being made to allay fears of shortage and create confidence. After this date, the Government felt it unnecessary to declare famine because "the circumstances envisaged by the Famine Code in administering famine relief did not virtually exist in Bengal at that time." We may quote here from a report presented to us by the Bengal Government:

"The general principles of the Famine Code could not be applied in their entirety: that Code envisages the grant of agricultural loans and the opening of relief works as the basis of operations and postulates that trade will be able to move in supplies (if necessary with help in transport) if loans and money are made available. In the conditions of 1943 the supplies were neither adequate nor free to move. The grant of loans or issue of money would therefore merely aggravate the situation as relief in kind had to be improvised with such supplies as could be got.

"The Revenue Department did actually distribute agricultural loans on a fairly large scale in all areas where it was thought that foodgrains might be had from the small reserves held by various people. The distribution of such loans on a very large scale might have led to greater inflation with a further upward tendency in prices. On the other hand, it was scarcely possible to open large relief works or poor houses on a large scale without a definite possibility of obtaining supplies through the trades or otherwise but this did not exist. Government therefore had to improvise an alternative procedure for the distribution of relief and this mainly took the form of free kitchens for which supplies on a very limited scale could be obtained".

68. We have already expressed the view that the propaganda policy followed during April and May 1943 by the Bengal Government with the support of the Central Government was misguided and that it would have been better to warn the people fully of the danger of famine. As regards the inapplicability of the Famine Code, it is certainly true that the relief measures feasible in the circumstances were very different from those prescribed in the Code. Local Officers would have required guidance in the unusual circumstances and the provisions of the Code would have had to be modified by special orders such as those issued to District Officers in August. Nevertheless, we believe that the declaration of famine would have been attended with certain advantages. It would have led to the appointment of a Famine Commissioner with plenary powers over relief, who would presumably also have assumed control of food supplies allotted to the districts. It would have simplified administrative and financial procedure and removed the uncertainty with regard to such procedure in dealing with problems of relief which we believe existed to some extent in

1943. Under the Code, District Officers are required to make frequent and detailed reports about the situation in their districts; if the Code had come into operation during the premonitory stages of the famine, the Government might have obtained earlier clearer information about the extent of the famine and the number of people in need of relief. Finally the declaration of famine might have quickened public sympathy, both within and without the province, and focussed the attention of other provinces on the plight of Bengal, and her need for assistance, at an earlier date.

69. **Delay in starting relief measures.**—We have already referred to the fact that Commissioners and District Officers reported growing distress in many districts very early in 1943. From March onward the anxieties of local officers increased and they left the Provincial Government in no doubt about the seriousness of the situation. Towards the end of June famine was present in many parts of Bengal. It was not, however, until 11th June that the Government called for detailed information about the areas affected, the numbers involved and the nature of the relief required. Orders for the organization of relief measures were not issued until 20th August, and the Famine Relief Commissioner was not appointed until 26th September. We feel that all this should have been done at least 3 months earlier. When the "food drive" was undertaken famine should have been already declared and the drive should have been linked with arrangements for collecting and distributing supplies for relief purposes. Distribution of food on a large scale was not begun, except in isolated areas as a result of local initiative, until September—several months after the need for it had arisen. With prices of rice soaring to unheard of levels, relief in the form of small payments of money, whether given gratuitously, as agricultural loans, or as test relief in return for work, could do little to relieve distress. Food was required. The delay in organizing relief, and the inadequacy of the quantities later issued as uncooked grain or cooked "gruel", both reflect the disastrous supply situation that had developed.

70. It appears that at one stage in 1943, expenditure on relief was limited on financial grounds.[1] We are of opinion that when the lives of the people are at stake financial considerations must not be allowed to restrict relief operations. If necessary, funds to the fullest extent required should be provided by borrowing in consultation with the Reserve Bank or the Government of India.

71. **Movement and Storage of Supplies.**—We have described the piling up of stocks of grain in Calcutta and in certain procurement areas in the second half of the year. This began in Calcutta in August and continued until the Army took charge of movement in November. The accumulation of stocks urgently needed for the relief of hunger all over Bengal was due to lack of adequate organization for the reception of supplies of foodgrains and their despatch to the districts. The arrival of large supplies from outside Bengal overwhelmed whatever organization already existed in the province. The Government of Bengal stated in July that they were prepared to deal with the arrival of 120 or even 500 wagons of foodgrains daily, and also "to appoint a Transport Officer and a Transport Department who will do the work of receiving goods, handling them here, distributing them to the various districts, and also doing inter-district transport". In the event, they failed to carry out these undertakings. Stocks arriving in Calcutta were not properly located and identified on arrival, the station of despatch and the quantities received were often not noted and arrangements for storage and distribution were unsatisfactory. It has been claimed that the arrival of such large supplies was unforeseen and hence suitable arrangements could not be made to deal with them. In view of what has been said above, this claim appears to be inadmissible. We feel

[1]Extracts from papers relating to certain financial aspects of relief—Appendix VIII.

that an energetic attempt should have been made to secure the necessary personnel and build up the necessary organization; for example, officers could have been obtained from outside the province. According to evidence presented to the Commission, the Government of India offered help in September 1943, but the reply was received that this was not required. In October, two officers from the Department of Supplies, Government of India, were sent to the Government of Bengal to help in supervising the reception and despatch of grain supplies; it appears, however, that their services were not fully utilized. We may add that there were in Calcutta businessmen whose experience of organization qualified them for such work, but according to the Government of Bengal, "all attempts to secure suitable men from the business houses proved abortive". The Bengal Government should, in July or thereabouts, have undertaken the task of setting up the organization needed to deal with the arrival of foodgrains in Calcutta under the Basic Plan and their despatch to the districts, and, if local resources were inadequate, impressed on the Government of India their need for assistance. If they had done so, the latter might have found that suitable help could be obtained only from the Army, which possessed trained personnel with experience of large scale transport problems. We have already described the vigorous steps taken by the Army to organize transport when it came to the rescue in November. If the Army had been called in two months earlier, say in September, famine mortality would have been considerably reduced.

One of the reasons why the arrangements made by the Government of Bengal to deal with transport and other problems arising during the famine were unsatisfactory was that they failed to realize the magnitude of these problems and the scale of the organization required for their successful solution. Associated with this was a reluctance to appeal for outside help even when the organization and personnel available within the province were obviously inadequate. We feel that this attitude was particularly unfortunate in the circumstances.

Reference has been made elsewhere to the inadequate storage accommodation in Calcutta and the fact that during the closing months of 1943, and in 1944, grain was stored in the open in the Royal Botanical Gardens. While we have evidence that only a small percentage of these stocks deteriorated, their storage under such conditions was undesirable for various reasons, including the effect on public opinion. According to non-official witnesses appearing before us suitable storage accommodation could have been found in Calcutta if the trade had been consulted and its co-operation invited.

72. Among other criticisms of relief measures, we may mention the view that the establishment of food kitchens was a mistake—that it would have been better to distribute food as "dry doles" through a reliable method. Unquestionably the food kitchen system led to corruption and there was much mismanagement. It was, however, the only feasible method for the general appeasement of hunger in the situation which developed from July on wards, when many thousands of people left their homes and flocked into towns and cities. The migrating masses could not have been given food in any other way. Further, rice was in short supply and unfamiliar cereals such as bajra, jowar and wheat had to be distributed. The people were unused to these and did not know how to cook them.

73. Lastly, we must refer to the view which attributes the failure to relieve the famine situation in the rural areas to the undue preoccupation of the Government of Bengal with the needs of Greater Calcutta generally, and those of the "priority classes" in particular. It is undeniable that, throughout 1943, the necessary supplies reached Calcutta and a considerable proportion of the population of Greater Calcutta obtained their supplies at subsidized prices from either

employers' shops or the controlled shops. It is also true that a relatively large proportion, about two-thirds, of the supplies of rice reaching Calcutta under the control of Government, much of which was secured from outside the province, was consumed in Greater Calcutta. The quantities sent to the districts were only a small fraction of the requirements of the poorer classes in the rural areas who were unable to buy rice at the prevailing prices. This would have been the case even if all the supplies distributed in Calcutta under Government control, about 141,000 tons, had been sent to the rural area. It seems probable that the rural areas would not have been materially helped by a reduction in the Calcutta allotment, as, in the absence of control, Calcutta would have bought more from the rural areas and raised prices still higher in the province in doing so. This would have further increased the numbers of the people who were unable to buy their supplies. In the opinion of a majority of us, the Government of Bengal is open to criticism not on the ground that Calcutta was provided with the bulk of the supplies reaching that city under Government control, but for their failure to acquire control of supplies and distribution in Bengal.

Sir Manilal Nanavati and Mr. Ramamurty do not agree with the above view regarding the distribution of available foodstuffs in the hands of the Bengal Government, during 1943. Their opinion is as follows:—

"Out of the 206,000 tons that came in the hands of the Bengal Government at Calcutta during 1943, 141,000 tons were retained in Calcutta while only 65,000 tons were sent to the mofussil.

"Prices in many parts of the mofussil were generally higher than in Greater Calcutta; more foodstuffs sent to rural areas might probably have helped to bring down the prices and would certainly have given relief to the needy. Greater Calcutta was all along well supplied with foodstuffs and there was never any serious shortage; the priorities and the Industries carried ample stocks to last them for weeks. Therefore, if more foodstuffs had been sent to the rural areas they would have been materially helped without interference with essential needs in Calcutta".

74. Sir Manilal considers that this question of Calcutta *versus* the rural areas has certain other important aspects which should be stressed. He says:—

"In my opinion, a clear conflict of interest arose early in 1943 between Calcutta, where the maintenance of supplies, especially for the priority services and War Industries, was a primary problem, and the rural areas where the lives of the poorer classes depended on the availability of supplies at reasonable prices. Inflation was raising prices, and wages in the rural areas were not responding. The denial policy in rice, boats, and cycles enforced by the Government of India, the evacuation of villages for military reasons (nearly 35,000 homesteads were affected), the floods, and the cyclone, and the failure of crops had already weakened the economy of rural Bengal. By the end of December 1942 distress had already appeared and by March 1943 widespread famine was anticipated by district officials. Consciously or unconsciously, the Bengal Government allowed the needs of the rural areas to be outweighed by those of Calcutta and particularly its big business interests. If the interests of the rural population had been kept more prominently in mind, the mistaken policies of "de-control" and "unrestricted free trade, the relaxation of the Foodgrains Control Order and other policies which encouraged profiteering and hoarding would not have been adopted. The same policy was adopted in the distribution of available stocks when every ounce was urgently needed to feed the starving, where relief works had to be slowed down at critical moments for lack of food and funds. From the moment the signs of distress appeared, the Government of Bengal should have made it clear to the Government of India as well as to the employers' organisations who had adequate resources and who had great influence, that they could not discharge their primary duty to the population in Bengal as a whole unless they maintained strict contro over prices and that, in the distribution of supplies under their control, Calcutta would not have priority over other deficit areas in the province. At the same time, they should have clearly brought to the notice of the Government of India the seriousness of the situation as it was developing and demanded their immediate attention in the strongest terms as was done by the Bombay Government. If this course had been followed, the need of Bengal for external assistance would have been recognized earlier; supplies would have been procured from outside more expeditiously; earlier attention would have been given to the state of the people in the rural areas and much of the misery would have been avoided. On the contrary when distress appeared, there was a tendency both on the part of the Government of India and of Bengal to minimize the prevalence of famine, with the result that the efforts of the Government of India to secure external supplies were prejudiced even as late as August 1943 by the mistrust and suspicion occasioned by complaints about profiteering which prevailed in Bengal. This atmosphere of mistrust influenced the situation throughout the famine. In the end not a single man died of starvation from the population of Greater Calcutta, while millions in rural areas starved and suffered."

CHAPTER XI.—GENERAL CONCLUSIONS AND OBSERVATIONS.

1. **The Background.**—The economic level of the population previous to the famine was low in Bengal, as in the greater part of India. Agricultural production was not keeping pace with the growth of population. There was increasing pressure on land which was not relieved by compensatory growth in industry. A considerable section of the population was living on the margin of subsistence and was incapable of standing any severe economic stress. Parallel conditions prevailed in the health sphere; standards of nutrition were low and the epidemic diseases which caused high mortality during the famine were prevalent in normal times. There was no "margin of safety" as regards either health or wealth. These underlying conditions, common indeed to many other parts of India, were favourable to the occurrence of famine accompanied by high mortality.

2. **The basic causes of the famine.**—Shortage in the supply of rice in 1943 was one of the basic causes of the famine. The main reason for this was the low yield of the *aman* crop reaped at the close of 1942. Another reason was that the stocks carried over from the previous year (1942) were also short. The *aman* crop reaped at the end of 1940 was exceptionally poor and in consequence stocks were heavily drawn upon during 1941. The *aman* crop reaped in December 1941 was a good one, but not so good as to enable stocks to be replenished materially. After the fall of Burma early in 1942, imports from that country ceased, but exports from Bengal to areas which were more seriously dependent on imports from Burma, increased during the first half of the year. This also contributed to some extent to the smallness of the carry-over from 1942 to 1943. Again, during 1943 the loss of imports from Burma was only partially offset by increased imports from other parts of India. It appears probable that the total supply during 1943 was not sufficient for the requirements of the province and that there was an absolute deficiency of the order of 3 weeks' requirements. This meant that even if all producers sold their entire surplus stocks without retaining the usual reserve for consumption beyond the next harvest, it was unlikely that consumers would have secured their normal requirements in full.

In the summer of 1942, that is, some months before the failure of the *aman* crop in Bengal, a situation had arisen in the rice markets of India, including those in Bengal, in which the normal trade machinery was beginning to fail to distribute supplies at reasonable prices. This was due to the stoppage of imports of rice from Burma and the consequent transfer of the demands of Ceylon, Travancore, Cochin, and Western India, formerly met from Burma, to the markets in the main rice producing areas of India. Other circumstances arising out of the war also accentuated the disturbances to normal trade. In Bengal, owing to its proximity to the fighting zone and its position as a base for military operations in Burma, the material and psychological repercussions of the war on the life of the people were more pronounced in 1942, and also in 1943, than elsewhere in India. The failure of the *aman* crop at the end of 1942, in combination with the whole existing set of circumstances, made it inevitable that, in the absence of control, the price of rice would rise to a level at which the poor would be unable to obtain their needs. It was necessary for the Bengal Government to undertake measures for controlling supplies and ensuring their distribution at prices at which the poor could afford to buy their requirements. It was also necessary for the Government of India to establish a system of planned movement of supplies from surplus to deficit provinces and states.

There was delay in the establishment by the Government of India of a system of planned movement of supplies. The Bengal Government failed to secure control over supply and distribution and widespread famine followed a rise of prices to abnormal levels—to five to six times the prices prevailing in the early months of 1942. This rise in prices was the second basic cause of the famine. Famine, in the form in which it occurred, could have been prevented by resolute action at the right time to ensure the equitable distribution of available supplies.

3. **The Government of Bengal.**—When the price of rice rose steeply in May and June 1942, the Government of Bengal endeavoured to bring the situation under control by the prohibition of exports and by fixing statutory maximum prices. In the absence of control over supplies, price control failed, but by September 1942, supplies and prices appeared to have reached a state of equilibrium. This month was a critical one in the development of the famine. If the Government of Bengal had set up at that time a procurement organization, the crisis, which began about two months later, would not have taken such a grave turn.

With the partial failure of the *aman* crop at the end of 1942, the supply position became serious and prices again rose steeply. If a breakdown in distribution was to be averted, it was essential that Government should obtain control of supplies and prices. The measures taken by the Government of Bengal to achieve control of supplies and prices during 1943 were inadequate and, in some instances wrong in principle. In January and February 1943, the Provincial Government endeavoured unsuccessfully to obtain control of supplies and to regulate prices by means of procurement operations. Better success would have been achieved if procurement had been undertaken by an official agency instead of by agents chosen from the trade, and if Government had made it clear that they would not hesitate to requisition from large producers as well as from traders, in case supplies were held back. The decision in favour of "de-control" in March 1943 was a mistake. In the conditions prevailing in Bengal at the time, it was essential to maintain control; its abandonment meant disaster. We refer to this matter again in the immediately succeeding paragraph. The Government of Bengal erred in pressing strongly for "unrestricted free trade" in the Eastern Region in May 1943 in preference to the alternative of "modified free trade". The introduction of "unrestricted free trade" was a mistake. It could not save Bengal and was bound to lead to severe distress and possibly starvation in the neighbouring areas of the Region.

One result of the policy underlying "de-control" and "unrestricted free trade" was that the greater part of the supplies reaching Calcutta was not under the control of Government. So long as this policy was followed it was not possible to introduce rationing in Greater Calcutta. Even after the policy was reversed, there was considerable delay in the introduction of rationing. The absence of control over the distribution of supplies in Calcutta and the failure to introduce rationing at any time during 1943 contributed largely to the failure of control over supplies and prices in the province as a whole.

The arrangements for the receipt, storage, and distribution of food supplies despatched to Bengal from other parts of India during the autumn of 1943 were thoroughly inadequate and a proportion of the supplies, received during the height of the famine, was not distributed to the needy in the districts, where such food was most required. Better arrangements for the despatch and distribution would have saved many lives.

While reports of distress in various districts were received from Commissioners and Collectors from the early months of 1943, the Provincial Government did not call for a report on the situation in the districts until June, and detailed instructions relating to relief were not issued till August. Famine was not declared. The delay in facing the problem of relief and the non-declaration of famine were bound up with the unfortunate propaganda policy of "No Shortage" which, followed during the months April to June with the support of the Government of India, was unjustified when the danger of famine was plainly apparent. The measures initiated in August were inadequate and failed to prevent further distress, mainly because of the disastrous supply position which had been allowed to develop. A Famine Relief Commissioner was not appointed till late in September. It appears that at one stage in 1943, the expenditure on relief was limited on financial grounds. There is no justification, whatsoever, for cutting down relief in times of famine on the plea of lack of funds. If necessary, funds should be provided by borrowing in consultation with the Reserve Bank or the Government of India. This principle holds even when, as in the Bengal famine, food was more urgently required than money for relief purposes. The medical relief provided during 1943 was also inadequate. Some of the mortality which occurred, could have been prevented by more efficient medical and public health measures.

Between the Government in office and the various political parties, and in the early part of the year, between the Governor and his Ministry, and between the administrative organization of Government and the public there was lack of co-operation which stood in the way of a united and vigorous effort to prevent and relieve famine. The change in the Ministry in March-April 1943, failed to bring about political unity. An "all-party" Government might have created public confidence and led to more effective action, but no such Government came into being. It may be added that during and preceding the famine, there were changes in key officers concerned with food administration. In 1943, there were three changes in the post of Director of Civil Supplies.

Due weight has been given in our report to the great difficulties with which the Bengal Government were faced. The impact of the war was more severe in Bengal than in the rest of India. The "denial" policy had its effect on local trade and transport, and in particular affected certain classes of the population, for instance, the fishermen in the coastal area. The military demands on transport were large. There was a shortage of suitable workers available for recruitment into Government organizations concerned with food administration and famine relief. The cyclone and the partial failure of the *aman* crop were serious and unavoidable natural calamities. But after considering all the circumstances, we cannot avoid the conclusion that it lay in the power of the Government of Bengal, by bold, resolute and well-conceived measures at the right time to have largely prevented the tragedy of the famine as it actually took place. While other Governments in India were admittedly faced with a much less serious situation than the Government of Bengal, their generally successful handling of the food problem, and the spirit in which those problems were approached, and the extent to which public co-operation was secured stand, in contrast to the failure in Bengal.

4. **The Government of India.**—The Government of India failed to recognize at a sufficiently early date, the need for a system of planned movement of foodgrains, including rice as well as wheat, from surplus to deficit provinces and states; in other words, the Basic Plan should have come into operation much earlier than it did. With regard to wheat, an agreement should have been reached at an early stage between the Government of India and the Government of the Punjab about the price level to be maintained and the establishment in that province of an adequate procurement organization. If this had been done, the price of wheat would have remained under control and it should have been possible to send to Bengal a large proportion of the supplies which reached that province towards the close of the year, at an earlier period when they would have been much more useful. In the closing months of 1942, and the first two months of 1943, the supplies of wheat reaching Calcutta were only

a fraction of normal requirements. If adequate supplies had been available in these months, the pressure on the Calcutta rice market, in so far as it arose out of the shortage of wheat, would have been reduced. Again, if the Basic Plan in regard to rice had come into operation in the beginning of 1943, it would have been possible to provide Bengal at an earlier date with supplies of rice in approximately those quantities which were obtained later in the year from other provinces and states.

The Government of India must share with the Bengal Government responsibility for the decision to de-control in March 1943. That decision was taken in agreement with the Government of India and was in accordance with their policy at the time. By March the position had so deteriorated that some measure of external assistance was indispensable if a disaster was to be avoided. The correct course at the time was for the Government of India to have announced that they would provide, month by month, first, the full quantity of wheat required by Greater Calcutta, and secondly, a certain quantity of rice. It would, then have been possible for the Government of Bengal to have maintained controlled procurement, and secured control over supply and distribution in Greater Calcutta. The Government of India erred in deciding to introduce "unrestricted free trade" in the Eastern Region in 1943 in preference to "modified free trade". The subsequent proposal of the Government of India to introduce free trade throughout the greater part of India was quite unjustified and should not have been put forward. Its application, successfully resisted by many of the provinces and states, particularly by the Governments of Bombay and Madras, might have led to serious catastrophe in various parts of India.

By August 1943, it was clear that the Provincial Administration in Bengal was failing to control the famine. Deaths and mass migration on a large scale were occurring. In such circumstances, the Government of India, whatever the constitutional position, must share with the Provincial Government the responsibility for saving lives. The Government of India sent large supplies of wheat and rice to Bengal during the last five months of 1943, but it was not till the end of October, when His Excellency the Viceroy, Lord Wavell, visited Bengal, as his first duty on taking office. that adequate arrangements were made to ensure that these supplies were properly distributed. After his visit, the whole situation took an immediate turn for the better.

We feel it necessary to draw attention to the numerous changes in the individuals in charge of food administration of the Government of India during the crucial year of the famine. Mr. N. R. Sarker, the Food Member, resigned in February 1943, and His Excellency the Viceroy, Lord Linlithgow, held the food portfolio without a Member to assist him until May. The Secretary of the Food Department, Mr. Holdsworth, fell ill during this period and died. His place was taken by the Additional Secretary, Major-General Wood, a Military Officer new to the problems of civil administration. Sir Azizul Haque became Member in charge of the Food Department in May. He was succeeded by Sir J. P. Srivastava in August and a new Secretary of the Department, Mr. Hutchings, was appointed in September.

In Bengal, the new Ministry took office towards the end of April and Sir Thomas Rutherford became Governor in September 1943, replacing the late Sir John Herbert, then suffering from the illness of which he subsequently died.

Thus, during the various critical stages in the famine, heavy responsibility fell on individuals who were new to their posts.

5. **The people and the famine.**—We have criticized the Government of Bengal for their failure to control the famine. It is the responsibility of the Government to lead the people and take effective steps to prevent avoidable catastrophe. But the public in Bengal, or at least certain sections of it, have

also their share of blame. We have referred to the atmosphere of fear and greed which, in the absence of control, was one of the causes of the rapid rise in the price level. Enormous profits were made out of the calamity, and in the circumstances, profits for some meant death for others. A large part of the community lived in plenty while others starved, and there was much indifference in face of suffering. Corruption was widespread throughout the province and in many classes of society.

It has been for us a sad task to inquire into the course and causes of the Bengal famine. We have been haunted by a deep sense of tragedy. A million and a half of the poor of Bengal fell victim to circumstances for which they themselves were not responsible. Society, together with its organs, failed to protect its weaker members. Indeed there was a moral and social breakdown as well as an administrative breakdown.

PART II

DEATH AND DISEASE IN THE BENGAL FAMINE

CHAPTER I.—MORTALITY

A.—Total mortality.

1. According to figures published by the Bengal Public Health Department, 1,873,749 people died in Bengal in 1943. The average number of deaths reported annually during the previous 5 years, 1938 to 1942, was 1,184,903, so that deaths in 1943 were 688,846 in excess of the quinquennial average. The reported death rates per *mille* in Bengal in the five years preceding the famine ranged from 19·6 to 25·0, with an average of 21·2. In the famine year of 1943 the rate rose to 30·9 per *mille*.

Nearly all the famine mortality occurred in the second half of the year. During the first 6 months mortality was only 1·9 per cent. in excess of the quinquennial average. From July to December 1943, 1,304,323 deaths were recorded as against an average of 626,048 in the previous quinquennium, representing an increase in mortality of 108·3 per cent.

2. Death continued to take its toll in 1944. In the first 6 months of 1944, 981,228 deaths were recorded, an excess of 422,371 over the quinquennial average. The death rate during the year from July 1943 to June 1944 reached 37·6 per *mille*. The complete mortality figures for 1944, which are not available at the time of writing, may show that, as far as excess mortality is concerned, the year 1944 was almost as disastrous as the previous one.

B.—Accuracy of mortality statistics.

3. All public health statistics in India are inaccurate. Mortality figures indicate trends in the death rate but can rarely be accepted as absolute. Even in normal times, deaths are not fully recorded and the number of births registered may be 20 to 25 per cent. below the number of births that have actually occurred.[1] The famine mortality statistics issued by the Bengal Public Health Department, it may be remarked, tell a sufficiently tragic story as they stand. Many people have, however, maintained that they grossly underestimate the actual number of deaths. Thus, witnesses appearing before members of the Commission in Dacca estimated deaths in the district in 1943 as one million, whereas the figure recorded by the Public Health Department was 149,000 (70,000 in excess of the quinquennial average). Professor K. P. Chattopadhyaya, Department of Anthropology, Calcutta University, made an estimate of the total mortality in 1943—3·5 million deaths—which has received wide publicity. This was based on surveys of sample groups in the worst famine areas, in which the mortality rate was 10 per cent, and it was assumed that two-thirds of the population of the province were equally affected by the famine. The method of investigation followed cannot be accepted as statistically sound; to estimate the provincial death rate from a sample of this nature is unjustifiable. When the famine was at its height dead and dying people were all too visible in famine-stricken areas, and it is natural that in such circumstances exaggerated estimates of mortality should have gained credence.

4. While the Commission cannot accept popular views on mortality, it is nevertheless of the opinion that the official figures under-estimate the total

[1]Report of the Public Health Commissioner with the Government of India, 1936.

number of deaths. In rural Bengal, as elsewhere in India, the primary collector of mortality statistics is a village functionary to whom deaths are reported by relations of the deceased in the village. The village *chowkidar* [1] (previous to 1944), reported deaths to the Union Board office, whence by several stages the records ultimately reached the office of the Director of Public Health. The *chowkidar* also reports the cause of deaths. In normal times the system scarcely lends itself to scientific accuracy and in 1942 and 1943 other factors making for errors and omissions were introduced. In certain places the salaries of *chowkidars* were not paid and they deserted their posts to obtain work on military projects and aerodromes. During the famine *chowkidars* were not immune from starvation and disease and some of them died. The replacement of dead and vanished *chowkidars* was no easy matter and several weeks or months might elapse before successors could be found, during which deaths presumably went unrecorded. Further, in the height of the famine thousands of people left their homes and wandered across the countryside in search of food. Many died by the road-side—witness the skulls and bones which were to be seen there in the months following the famine. Deaths occurring in such circumstances would certainly not be recorded in the statistics of the Director of Public Health.

5. There was a remarkable fall in 1943, in the number of deaths recorded in infants under one month. Deaths in this age group numbered 101,406, the quinquennial average being 138,780—a *decrease* of 26·8 per cent. This reduction in neo-natal mortality may be to a considerable extent due to a fall in the number of live births; the recorded birth-rate actually fell from 28·0 (quinquennial average) to 18·8 per *mille*. It seems probable, however, that during the famine a large proportion of deaths of infants under one month was not recorded and that a similar factor operated in the reported fall in the birth-rate. The lower mortality reported in infants under one month—an age group which normally makes a large contribution to total mortality—must be borne in mind in assessing the number of deaths by comparing deaths in 1943 with the quinquennial average.

6. At the end of 1943 a considerable effort was made, by civil and military medical authorities, to improve the registration of deaths. Emergency medical workers were instructed to supervise the recording of deaths by *chowkidars* and to check and accelerate the whole system. The result was an unquestionable improvement in the collection of mortality statistics and the figures for the first half of 1944, can probably be regarded as reasonably accurate. A graph showing recorded mortality, month by month, is given on page 113. It is significant that there was a fall in January 1944, after registration had been improved. No doubt the actual number of deaths fell at this stage owing to the provision of food supplies, but the health situation remained very serious. If the figures recorded in 1943 were a gross under-estimate (*e.g.*, half the actual number of deaths) one would expect that any real fall in the death-rate in January would be offset by the greater accuracy of registration, and that the result would have been a rise in recorded mortality.

7. In spite of the conditions produced by the famine, there was no universal breakdown in 1943 in the system of recording deaths. We made careful inquiries on this point from local officials and other witnesses. After due consideration of the available facts we are of the opinion that the number of deaths in excess of the average in 1943 was of the order of one million—that is, some 40 per cent. in excess of the officially recorded mortality. We have found no valid reason for accepting estimates in excess of this figure. On the other hand, the high excess mortality in 1944 must be added to the toll of

[1] The *chowkidar* or village watchman is a part-time village servant, usually illiterate, and paid about Rs. 6 or Rs. 7 a month.

mortality. On this basis we must conclude that about 1·5 million deaths occurred as a direct result of the famine and the epidemics which followed in its train.

C.—Age and sex mortality

8. Various views were expressed to the Commission as regards the age and sex groups on which mortality fell most heavily. In some areas women and children appeared to be the principal victims, since many of the men had left home to seek employment elsewhere. The destitutes who thronged the relief kitchens in Calcutta and other centres seemed to be for the most part children, women, and old people of both sexes, and mortality among such wandering destitutes was high. On the other hand, opinions were given that in villages from which little or no migration took place, more men died than women. The effect of the famine on the age distribution of the population of Bengal is a question which deserves careful investigation. In view of errors and omissions in the recording of deaths to which previous reference has been made, it is, however, by no means easy to reach satisfactory conclusions. The data available for study include the public health statistics for 1943 and the results of various inquiries on sample groups submitted to the Commission.

9. Male and female deaths reported in 1943 numbered 998,428 and 875,321 respectively, a difference of 123,107 to the disadvantage of males. Actually more male than female deaths are normally reported in Bengal, which is due to the higher proportion of males in the population, and to the excess of male births (108 male to 100 female), which leads to more deaths among infants of the male sex.[1] If, however, the average number of male and female deaths in the previous quinquennium is compared with the figures for 1943, it is found that the increase in male deaths was 62·5 per cent, as compared with 53·2 per cent in the case of female deaths. The preponderance of male deaths is confirmed by a sample survey carried out in various rural areas by Mr. T. C. Das, Lecturer in Social Anthropology, University of Calcutta. Of 4,833 deaths investigated, 56·7 per cent were male and 42·3 per cent female. The same trend is shown in the records of deaths in famine hospitals in various centres.

10. The excess in male deaths was more marked in the adult age groups. Up to 10 years the increase in mortality was almost equal in both sexes. In the age group 10 to 15, the rise in the number of male deaths was somewhat greater than in the case of female deaths, but the difference is not striking. In the groups between 10 and 60, 515,290 deaths in males were recorded as against 439,273 in females, the percentage increases in mortality over the quinquennial average being as follows:—

Age group	*Percentage increase over quinquennial average of deaths in 1943.*	
	Male	*Female*
15-20	98·3	48·8
20-30	82·9	59·1
30-40	98·8	88·9
40-50	103·6	90·9
50-60	93·2	76·3

[1]The Census Report of 1941 gives 32,360,401 males and 29,099,976 females.

11. It must, however, be mentioned that the results of a series of sample inquiries in rural areas, analysed by Professor P. C. Mahalanobis, Statistical Laboratory, Presidency College, Calcutta, are not in agreement with the provincial sex mortality data. The investigation covered 2,622 families (13,652 individuals), inhabiting villages in 7 sub-divisions. In the groups as a whole, the percentage mortality among females in 1943 was higher than the percentage mortality among males. (Infants of both sexes below one year were left out of the calculation). There was, however, considerable irregularity in the proportionate sex mortality in the various sub-divisions, and in some sub-divisions the male mortality, on a percentage basis, exceeded the female. The aggregate figures are influenced by the data from one sub-division in which, for some reason, female deaths greatly exceeded male deaths.

12. As regards mortality by age, the decrease in the reported number of deaths in infants under one month has already been referred to. The number of deaths in infants aged 1 to 12 months increased, but the total deaths under one year declined as a result of the reported fall in neo-natal mortality. A large number of deaths occurred in the age groups 1 to 5 and 5 to 10. The number of deaths in old people over 60 was also high, 247,556 as compared with the quinquennial average of 154,405. The age groups 1 to 10 and 60 and over contributed between them 274,810 of the excess deaths in 1943, but since the mortality in these groups is normally high, their excess mortality was slightly lower than that in the intermediate age groups.

13. Mortality in Calcutta in 1943 shows different trends from those shown by the data for the whole province. The proportionate increase in male and female deaths was reversed, the former being 52·7 per cent in excess of the quinquennial average and the latter, 72·2 per cent. The percentage increase in female deaths exceeded that in male deaths in almost all the age groups. The total number of male deaths reported was greater than that of female deaths, but this is due to the preponderance of males in the industrial population of Calcutta. According to the 1941 census, males in Calcutta outnumbered females by about two to one.

14. The greatest excess mortality in Calcutta was recorded in the age groups 1 to 5, 5 to 10, and over 60, the percentage increase in mortality in these groups being 223·1, 85·1 and 192·6 respectively. The mortality statistics thus confirm the impression that women, children, and old people were in the majority in the famine-stricken population which sought food and relief in the capital. It may be added that the recording of deaths in Calcutta is likely to be more accurate than elsewhere in Bengal, since no dead body can be disposed of by cremation or burial without notifying the municipal health authorities.

15. Finally, attention should be drawn to one factor which may influence the records of age and sex mortality in the districts. Omissions in the registration of deaths may not have been equally distributed in the different age and sex groups. We have referred to unrecorded road-side deaths. It is not unlikely that these included more women and children than men.

16. The above analysis is based largely on the mortality figures of the Public Health Department as they stand. The quotation of recorded mortality figures, including digits down to the tens and hundreds, and the calculation of percentages to one place of decimals, tends to give a false air of accuracy. We must again emphasize that all the figures given are inaccurate and should not be regarded as indicating more than general trends in mortality.

17. We incline to the view that in the province as a whole famine mortality was greater among men than in women. There were, however, undoubtedly places such as Calcutta where the reverse was the case. Assuming the higher male mortality to be a fact, it is by no means easy to suggest reasons for it. Possibly men, with larger food requirements than women, suffered more acutely as food supplies dwindled away to nothing. Men may have attempted, more often than women, to remain at work in spite of increasing starvation, and thus used up their bodily reserves more rapidly. Again, women and children may have sought relief at food kitchens more readily than men. It is known that large numbers of families have been deprived of their bread-winners and large numbers of women have been left widows. Responsibility for the care of the widows and orphans of the famine has been accepted by Government as part of the rehabilitation programme. Our tentative conclusions about sex mortality emphasize the extent of the task involved.

18. A considerable fall in the birth-rate must unquestionably have occurred. This effect of famine is referred to in earlier reports on famine in India. Thus, it was said that in Orissa in 1866 and 1867, the birth-rate was reduced almost to nothing. According to a report on the Madras famine of 1876-7, in 9 famine districts the birth-rate fell from 26 per *mille* in 1876 to 20·3 per *mille* in 1877, and to 13·8 in 1878. The number of births in these two years was calculated as being 200,000 less than in two average years. In certain districts the birth-rate fell to 4 to 5 per *mille*. The reported fall in the birth-rate in Bengal in 1943 from 28·0 (quinquennial average) to 18·8 means a loss of 500,000 to 600,000 births. While the accuracy of this figure may be questioned, there is no reason to doubt that births were greatly decreased in the Bengal famine, as in earlier famines. The decrease will influence the age composition of the population in future years and the curve of population growth. The latter will, of course, also be affected by the total famine mortality, and notably by the mortality among females of all ages up to the end of the child-bearing period.

19. The falling-off in the number of live births during famine is presumably due largely to an increase in the incidence of abortion, miscarriage, and still-birth resulting from malnutrition and disease. It is well known that a woman's capacity to bear living children is impaired by malnutrition, while malaria frequently leads to abortion. The disruption of family life must also be an operative factor, particularly in the later stages of famine.

D.—Course of mortality

20. In May and June, 1943, the death rate began to rise in the districts of Rangpur, Mymensingh, Bakarganj, Chittagong, Noakhali, and Tipperah. The most striking increase was in Chittagong and the neighbouring district of Noakhali, where, after a steep rise in May, the number of deaths was twice the quinquennial average in June, and 3 to 4 times the average in July. It was in fact in these districts that the famine first made itself evident. In July the reported death-rate was above the average in all districts except Hooghly, Jessore, and Malda, but the rise was of a comparatively small order. From August onwards, the number of deaths rose rapidly, reaching its peak in December. The actual numbers recorded monthly are shown below, in comparison with the quinquennial average. It will be noted that the famine mortality curve follows the quinquennial mortality curve, which also attained its highest point in December. This suggests that during the last few months of the year, the presence of famine accentuated the lethal effect of disease present in lesser degree in normal times.

Number of monthly deaths reported in Bengal from July 1943 to June 1944, compared with the average in the previous quinquennium.

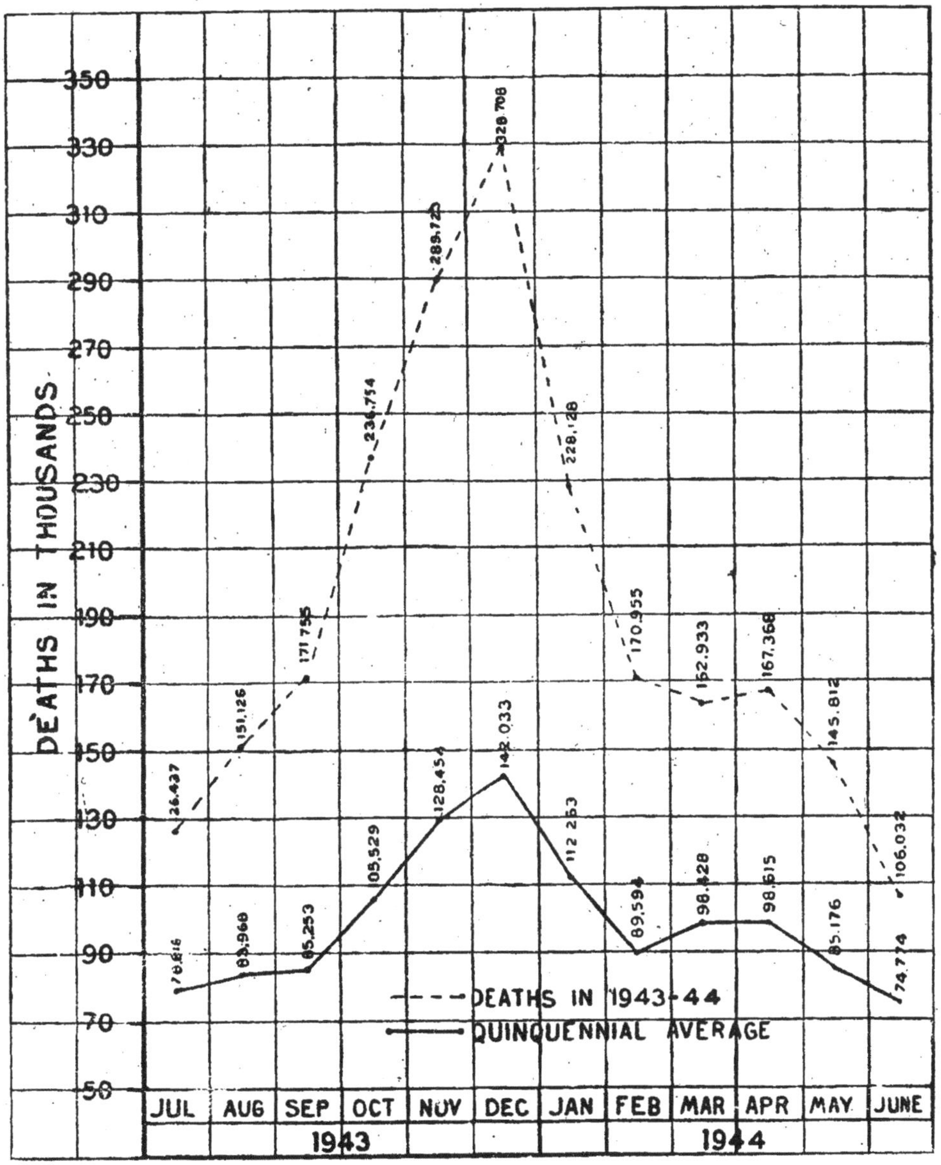

21. The death-rate in Calcutta, unlike that in the province as a whole, reached its peak in October, 1943. The decrease in November and December was no doubt due to the distribution of food, the increase in hospital accommodation, the better care and treatment of patients, and the removal of destitutes to camps outside the city.

22. Study of the mortality recorded in the various districts in Bengal in 1943 and 1944, reveals some important facts. Some districts are normally surplus in rice supplies, others deficit, while a third group is more or less self-supporting. In 1943, the usual order in this respect was disturbed in various ways. Thus, Midnapore is normally a surplus district and was taken as such for purposes of the Bengal Government's Procurement Scheme in 1944. In 1943, however, it was heavily deficit as a result of the cyclone, which produced famine conditions and serious health problems in certain districts before the great famine began. Again, rice supplies in various districts which are normally surplus, notably certain districts in West Bengal, were reduced as a result of the short crop. No satisfactory information about rice supplies in any district, in relation to the needs of the population, is in fact available. It is thus difficult to compare mortality and the degree of scarcity district by district. Comparison is also affected by the migration of famine victims, who in general tended to wander from the worst areas to places where they had at least some hope of obtaining food.

23. In spite of these facts—to which must be added the general inaccuracy of the mortality figures—certain rough conclusions can be drawn. Early in 1943, certain districts were regarded as "buying areas" by the Government of Bengal. These were: Bakarganj, Burdwan, Birbhum, Bogra, Dinajpur, Jalpaiguri, Malda, and Rajshahi. It is impossible to say how far these districts were genuinely surplus; in Burdwan, for example, crops in two sub-divisions had been damaged in 1942 and 1943, by insect pests and flood. But at least scarcity was less acute in them than in certain other parts of the province. Chittagong, Dacca, Faridpur, Tipperah, and Noakhali, normally deficit areas, were unquestionably seriously short of supplies in the famine year. The excess mortality recorded in these districts in 1943 was in general considerably higher than in the buying areas. It ranged from 51·1 per cent in Faridpur to 121·0 per cent in Chittagong, the excess in Tipperah, Dacca, and Noakhali being 118·6, 88·7, and 95·9 per cent respectively. In the districts declared buying areas, excess mortality ranged from 2·8 per cent (Malda) to 60·5 per cent (Birbhum). In none of the others did it exceed 45 per cent. In the remaining districts of Bengal, excess mortality exceeded 50 per cent in Murshidabad (96·5) Howrah (71·5). 24-Parganas (76·1), Midnapore (58·1), Rangpur (55·4), and Nadia (82·4). Of these, Midnapore was in a special position, while Howrah and 24-Parganas, which are near Calcutta, were subject to the drain of the Calcutta demand. 24-Parganas had also suffered to some extent from the cyclone. In certain sub-divisions of Murshidabad, the *aman* crop of 1943-44, was a total failure. In the Nilphamari sub-division of Rangpur, there had been failure of crops for 2 successive years as a result of drought.

24. Thus, in a very broad way, mortality during the first six months of the famine was related to the degree of local scarcity. But in almost all the districts, whatever their position as regards production and supplies of rice, there was some increase in the death-rate. The rise in price was general throughout Bengal and led to starvation even in districts which were not obviously deficient in their total supplies. Further, epidemic diseases were not confined to the areas in which food shortage was most acute.

25. In the first six months of 1944 there was a general rise in the death-rate in the districts which had not suffered severely in 1943, while it continued on a high level in most of the latter. In Birbhum, Dacca, Rangpur, 24 Parganas. Murshidabad, Malda, and Tipperah, excess mortality in the first six

months of 1944 exceeded 90 per cent. Tipperah, Rangpur, Malda, and Dacca being the worst affected. In all the other districts, except Darjeeling which is an isolated hill district dissimilar in nature to the rest of Bengal, it ranged from 26 to 86 per cent. A very appreciable fall in excess mortality occurred in Chittagong (31·3 per cent, as compared with 204·1 in the previous six months), but in Tipperah the death-rate remained extremely high, being 111·3 per cent in excess of the quinquennial average. Of all districts in Bengal, Tipperah suffered most severely during the famine.

The mortality figures show that almost the whole of Bengal, in greater or lesser degree, was affected by the famine and the outbreaks of epidemic disease associated with it. The extent of the area involved made the problem of combating epidemics and providing medical relief an enormous one.

CHAPTER II.—CAUSES OF DISEASE AND MORTALITY

A.—Health previous to the famine

1. In normal times, malaria, cholera, and small-pox are endemic in Bengal and serious epidemics of these diseases are of frequent occurrence. The state of nutrition of a considerable section of the population was poor. The same can of course be said of many other parts of India. The calamity of famine fell on a population with low physical reserves and circumstances were favourable for a flare-up of epidemic disease. The association between health conditions in normal times and the high famine mortality must be underlined.

B.—Lack of food

2. A high proportion of the deaths which took place in the early stages of the famine can best be described as deaths from starvation. It is true that disease of some kind or another was usually present in starving patients, adding to the seriousness of their condition. Very commonly such patients suffered from "famine diarrhoea", often seen as an uncontrollable diarrhoea which led to dehydration, rapid weakening and death. Other kinds of disease were also frequently present in starving destitutes. There was a considerable excess mortality from malaria and cholera as early as July, 1943. The difference between death from simple starvation and death occurring in a starved individual who is suffering from disease is of medical interest, but a negligible difference when the broad facts of famine mortality are under consideration.

3. We can perhaps roughly distinguish between two phases of famine mortality and disease. During the first months of the famine, the emphasis was on starvation, with or without coincident disease, as a cause of death. At a somewhat later stage, epidemic diseases took precedence over starvation. The peak in cholera mortality occurred in October and November 1943, while in the case of malaria December stands out as the worst month. By the end of the year, with the reaping of the *aman* crop, and the provision of food to the famine victims through the medium of relief kitchens, etc., deaths from sheer starvation diminished. When this stage was reached the main medical and public health problem became that of epidemic disease, notably malaria. But even when relief measures had been in operation for some time, and adequate food supplies for the province as a whole were available, the recovery of sections of the population from under-and mal-nutrition was slow, and survivors belonging to the classes affected remained in a poor state of health. Throughout the famine the provision of suitable nourishment to patients in famine hospitals was of primary importance in treatment, although it was in the early stages that the problem of resuscitating cases of starvation by suitable therapeutic measures was most acute.

C.—Disease in Calcutta famine hospitals.

4. Epidemic diseases were prevalent among famine victims in Calcutta as in other parts of Bengal. For example, investigations carried out in Calcutta towards the end of 1943 showed that some 40 per cent of destitute patients harboured malaria parasites. But in general the picture seen in the Calcutta emergency hospitals from August to November 1943 was that of acute starvation and its effects. Many of the patients in the hospitals were picked up on the streets in a state of extreme weakness and collapse, often on the point of death. They were for the most part emaciated to such a degree that the description "living skeletons" was justifiable Weight was often reduced by

as much as one-third of the normal; that of men who normally weighed 120 to 130 lbs. fell to 80 to 90 lbs. When this degree of emaciation is reached as Alexander Porter points out in his book "The Diseases of the Madras Famine of 1877-8", "life is held by a slender thread which the least untoward circumstance is sufficient to snap."

5. Many suffered from mental disorientation, showing a very marked degree of apathy and indifference to their surroundings. When taken to hospital, such patients made little effort to help themselves and received medical attention with an indifference which sometimes amounted to passive obstruction. They did not care how dirty or naked they were. Those with famine diarrhoea would repeatedly soil their beds and pay no attention to the protests of the attendants. In a few cases maniacal symptoms were present. The mental state of many starving destitutes indeed sometimes disconcerted workers in famine hospitals, who were not aware that it was a pathological condition induced by starvation. There was some tendency to regard starvation cases as needlessly dirty and uncooperative and, since they made little effort to help themselves, not worth helping. Actually, the clouding of the mind induced by starvation cleared in a few days, if the patient could be rallied by suitable dietary and medical treatment.

6. The exact causes of so-called "famine diarrhoea" are at present unknown. They may include the following:

(a) Unsuitable food which is not digested and leads to irritation of the intestines. The spectacle of starving destitutes ransacking refuse bins was common in Calcutta during the height of the famine.

(b) Impairment of the digestive functions of the intestines, and actual anatomical changes in the intestinal wall, due to the consumption of a diet grossly inadequate in quantity and defective in quality.

(c) Infection with dysenteric organisms.

A high death rate from "dysentery and diarrhoea" has been reported in earlier famines in India. In the nineteenth century, the term "famine diarrhoea" was often used. If the recorded mortality from dysentery and diarrhoea during the course of earlier famines is studied, it is found that the number of deaths ascribed to this cause rose and fell according to the severity of famine conditions, that is, the degree of starvation. A similar phenomenon is observable in the mortality statistics of Calcutta during the second half of 1943. When the famine was at its worst, famine diarrhoea was perhaps the most formidable problem with which the medical relief agencies had to deal.

7. Many patients showed famine oedema or dropsy, the dropsical swelling often masking the gross underlying emaciation. Dropsy invariably makes its appearance under famine conditions; for example, it was widely prevalent in the under-fed population of Central Europe during and just after the last war. Protein deficiency is usually considered to be the chief cause. In the Bengal famine victims, it was often associated with anaemia. An interesting observation was that malaria not infrequently developed in patients who had rallied after a few days' stay in hospital. The temperature would rise and malaria parasites would be found in the blood. This may be explained in two ways: either the parasite was unable to multiply in a starved body and revived together with its host, or during the phase of starvation, it was present as in the later febrile stage, but, owing to the low state of the patient, produced no febrile reaction.

Anaemia was prevalent in patients in famine hospitals at all stages of the famine. This was no doubt largely due to the combined effects of under-nutrition and malaria.

8. The treatment of cases of acute starvation cannot be considered in detail in this report. A research unit in Calcutta, financed by the Indian Research Fund Association, made a study of this subject and published a brochure entitled "The Treatment and Management of Starving Sick Destitutes", which contains much useful information. The essentials of treatment are the provision of nourishment in suitable form and good nursing. Nutritious food must be administered at first in small quantities and then in gradually increasing amounts as the patient recovers. Good results were obtained in cases of severe inanition by the injection of "protein hydrolysate", an extract of meat containing protein in pre-digested form. Disease present in starving patients must of course be appropriately treated.

9. Many collapsed cases admitted to the Calcutta hospitals died within a few hours. Probably no form of treatment could have saved them. Sometimes very weak patients survived for a few days in hospital and appeared to be rallying when they suddenly died. This phenomenon, which was observed by Alexander Porter in the Madras famine of 1877-8, illustrates his remark that in the circumstances "life is held by a slender thread".

10. Starving destitutes did not show vitamin deficiency diseases, which are usually associated with chronic malnutrition, with the emphasis on qualitative rather than quantitative defects in the diet. The rarity of such diseases throughout the famine was somewhat surprising. In general, the condition of destitutes in Calcutta—and no doubt in other centres—in the early stages of the famine was indicative of acute starvation, into which they had fallen within the space of 2 to 3 months, and not of prolonged under-nutrition. The destitutes who left their homes to seek relief were not simply short of food. They had no food. This is consonant with other facts on record about the onset of the famine.

D.—Disease takes precedence over starvation.

11. From about December onwards, there was a change in the clinical picture seen in famine hospitals. Most of the beds were filled with cases of malaria. The number of cases of famine oedema gradually diminished during the early months of 1944. Cases of acute starvation and extreme emaciation became relatively rare. Patients in general were thin and weak, and obviously required plenty of nourishing food to restore them to health. The majority were anaemic. There was, however, a genuine improvement in the state of nutrition. Cases of dysentery were frequent, but the "famine diarrhoea" which was so serious a problem in the earlier part of the famine, largely disappeared. Scabies a skin disease, became almost universal among destitutes in famine camps and hospitals. In many cases the greater part of the skin surface was involved in the lesions of scabies, complicated by impetigo and localised septic infection. The epidemic of scabies was probably due to various causes. In the first place, conditions of life among destitutes, *e.g.*, lack of clean clothing, lack of opportunity for washing, overcrowding or close contact in famine camps, etc., facilitated the transmission of the infecting agent. It has also been suggested that lack of oil for inunction of the skin was an important factor. Secondly, the unhealthy state of the skin itself, resulting from malnutrition, perhaps reduced its resistance to secondary infection. It is worth adding that healthy famine relief workers sometimes contracted scabies in the course of their work and that in general the disease in destitutes responded to the familiar treatment with sulphur ointment.

12. Another condition which was common in famine hospitals was "tropical ulcer" or "Naga sore", an ulcer of the skin and subcutaneous tissues usually situated in the anterior aspect of the lower part of the leg or the ankle. It usually begins with some slight wound or abrasion which refuses to heal. In

normal times tropical ulcer is common among plantation labourers who are in a poor state of nutrition and anaemic as a result of malaria and hookworm. Presumably malaria and malnutrition were responsible for its prevalence during the Bengal famine.

A good deal of Kala-azar was seen in the famine hospitals and some doctors think that its prevalence increased in 1944. There were a few cases of cancrum oris—a distressing condition in which tissues in the neighbourhood of the mouth putrefy and are destroyed. In the Russian famine of 1920, cancrum oris was widespread, but for some reason it was not common in the Bengal famine.

It was anticipated that with the onset of the cold weather there would be numerous deaths from pneumonia. This, however, did not occur; there was very little pneumonia. Again, eye-disease of various kinds often results from malnutrition and vitamin deficiency, but eye-disease was rare in patients in famine hospitals and out-patient clinics. The relative absence of vitamin deficiency disease has previously been mentioned. This again was contrary to expectation, since a high incidence of such disease had been prophesied as acute starvation gave place to more chronic malnutrition. In fact, the picture of disease in the Bengal famine failed in many respects to conform to the anticipations of doctors and nutrition experts.

E.—Epidemics

(i) Mortality.

13. Severe epidemics of malaria, small-pox and cholera were associated with the famine. The malaria season in Bengal normally extends from July to December. A severe and widespread epidemic, beginning in June, occurred during the latter half of 1943, reaching its peak in December and continuing in 1944. From July to December 1943, 479,039 deaths from malaria were recorded, an excess of 266,208 deaths (125·1 per cent) over the quinquennial average. In the first 6 months of 1944, malaria mortality figures were of the same order; 400,901 deaths were recorded, which was 223,664 deaths (126·1 per cent) above the average. Excess deaths from malaria accounted for 41·5 per cent of excess deaths in 1943 and 53·0 per cent of excess deaths from January to June 1944. In December 1943, the reported deaths from malaria were 202·6 per cent in excess of the quinquennial average.

14. Certain districts suffered more severely than others. The largest number of malaria deaths was recorded in Nadia, Murshidabad, Mymensingh, Faridpur, and Tipperah. As regards percentage increase over the quinquennial average, Howrah, Murshidabad, Dacca and Tipperah head the list. While in general mortality from malaria was exceptionally high in the admittedly deficit districts previously mentioned, the epidemic affected all districts in greater or lesser degree.

We realise that the figures of malaria mortality are likely to be inaccurate, and more inaccurate in 1943 than in 1944. For the certain diagnosis of malaria, which may be confused with other fevers, a blood examination is necessary and the proportion of cases in which this was done was of course infinitesimal. The figures, however, suffice to show that a most formidable epidemic of malaria was associated with the famine, and indicate its general course. Bengal is normally a very malarial province, having in fact the highest incidence of malaria of any province in India except the small province of Coorg. But no epidemic approaching in severity that of 1943-4 has occurred within its recent history.

15. There was no abnormal rise in mortality from cholera in the first half of 1943. The epidemic began in July and reached its peak in October—November. In Bengal, March and April are normally the months of highest prevalence. After November there was a gradual fall in cholera deaths, and by the

end of May 1944 they declined almost to the normal level. The total number of deaths from cholera reported from July 1943 to June 1944 was 218,269, that is, 309·7 per cent in excess of the quinquennial average for 1938-42. The whole of Bengal was involved in the cholera epidemic and there was no close correspondence between cholera mortality and general mortality. The greatest number of cholera deaths was reported in Mymensingh, Dinajpur, Bakarganj, Tipperah, and Noakhali.

16. As compared with malaria and cholera, small-pox was a relatively unimportant cause of mortality in 1943. Reported deaths numbered 22,005, the quinquennial average being 7,991. A severe epidemic, however, began in December 1943 and raged during the first half of 1944, reaching its peak in March and April. From June onwards it declined. During the months January to June 1944 the number of deaths from small-pox was 125,471, that is, 118,841 in excess of the average. Some 28 per cent of the excess mortality during this period is accounted for by deaths from small-pox.

(ii) The relation of famine to the epidemics:

17. A famine-stricken population is a sick population. Famine means not only lack of food in the quantitative sense but also lack of essential food constituents which are needed for bodily health. The functioning of every tissue and organ in the body is impaired by insufficiency of food. Susceptibility to infection may be increased, and resistance to disease when contracted will be reduced. Attacked by the same disease, an ill-nourished and debilitated individual is more likely to succumb than a healthy one. The former's response to treatment is likely to be unsatisfactory, and recovery, if recovery takes place, prolonged. The disorganization of life produced by famine furthers the spread of disease of various kinds, including the major epidemic diseases. We have estimated that there were some 1·5 million deaths in excess of the average in 1943 and the first half of 1944. It is impossible to separate these into groups and to assign a proportion to starvation and under-nutrition, another proportion to epidemic disease, and yet another to non-epidemic disease. The famine and its effects on the life of the people must be held generally responsible for the high excess mortality recorded under all the headings in the mortality tables.

18. The relation between epidemics and famine requires, however, more detailed discussion. The Commission was specifically asked to report on the causes and prevention of epidemics in famine. We must also inquire how far mortality in the Bengal famine could have been reduced by effective public health measures. The problem of famine disease and its prevention was discussed by the Famine Commission of 1901 whose views, given below, are worthy of close attention:

"Before we consider, as required by our instructions, 'in what manner the famine affected the death rate of the various provinces and districts' and enquire into 'the causes of any variation', it is necessary to explain our opinion of the connection with famine of the different diseases which commonly appear in its course, *viz.*, fever, cholera, dysentery and diarrhoea, and small-pox. The last is inconsiderable, and only so far connected with famine as vaccination falls into disuse owing to the engagement of the vaccinating staff on other duties. Dysentery and diarrhoea are peculiarly famine diseases, directly caused by insufficient and unwholesome food or by reduced powers of digestion and assimilation as the result of continued privation. Again, it is practically impossible to prevent the outbreak of cholera when large masses of men are collected together in the hot weather under famine conditions: but efficient organization and careful sanitary arrangements can stay the spread of the epidemic and when these precautions are not taken, a considerable share, at any rate, of the resultant mortality must be deemed to have been preventible. Of fevers it can only be said that they often are in origin climatic, but that their fatality is owing to the reduced power of the people to resist them, largely due to famine."

19. The severe diarrhoea which complicated many cases of starvation is unquestionably a famine disease. Dysenteric organisms were found to be present in some 30 per cent of intestinal fluxes in destitute patients in Calcutta, but it must be remembered that a large percentage of the population is infected with such organisms in normal times. Even in infected cases, the condition of the intestines induced by starvation may have been an important etiological factor. Though its underlying pathology is at present obscure, "famine diarrhoea" may be regarded as a genuine clinical entity, and an important cause of mortality in the Bengal famine. It could have been prevented only by preventing the famine, and its effective treatment, in collapsed and emaciated cases, was extremely difficult.

20. The fatality rate of almost any serious disease is likely to be increased by undernutrition and starvation. We have, however, no satisfactory information about hospital fatality rates in the case of the major epidemic diseases during the famine. Lack of food may also facilitate the transmission of disease by increasing susceptibility to infection. In the case of small-pox, there is no evidence that this factor is operative. The epidemic during the famine can be ascribed to social disorganization which increased opportunities for contagion, and to the unprotected state of the population, that is, the insufficient proportion vaccinated. The small-pox epidemic could have been largely prevented by widespread vaccination in previous years and up to the time when it flared up.

21. As regards cholera, other factors may be involved in epidemics associated with food shortage and famine. In the conditions produced by the famine there was, of course, every opportunity for the pollution of water supplies and the spread of the disease through obvious channels of infection. But, apart from this, two possible causes may be mentioned. In the first place, food shortage and famine make people more careless about what they eat and drink, and opportunities for infection are thereby increased. Secondly, the acid secretion of the stomach tends to be diminished in people who are short of food. It has been suggested that while the healthy stomach with its normal secretions may act as a barrier against the cholera *vibrio*, which enters the body by the mouth, the stomach of an ill-fed individual provides a less effective "acid-barrier". This, however, is speculation and is not based on satisfactory scientific evidence.

We agree with the views of the 1901 Commission that much of the cholera mortality "must be deemed to have been preventible". Apart from the disinfection and purification of water supplies, public health workers have to-day at their disposal another weapon against cholera in the shape of cholera vaccine. A cholera epidemic can be checked, even in a famine-stricken population, by familiar sanitary methods and by the inoculation of vaccine on a wide scale. We shall inquire later whether the anti-cholera measures in the famine were in fact adequate and efficient.

22. The relation between malaria and famine is a more complicated problem. As regards fatality, medical witnesses told us that destitutes attacked by malaria often failed to respond to appropriate treatment and succumbed readily to the disease, while healthy people attacked by malaria in the same area recovered after treatment in the usual way. This would conform to the views of the 1901 Famine Commission and of earlier Famine Commissions on "fevers" and famine. Malaria is the most prevalent and lethal of the "fevers" both in normal and famine times in India. Fulminant epidemics of malaria have often been associated with food scarcity and famine. To give one example, in 1897, an epidemic of fever, occurring in famine districts in the Central Provinces, was the subject of a special inquiry. The theory was advanced that

the fever was of a "specially malignant type" but this was not supported by the majority of observers. "Almost all the medical officers employed agreed in holding that the fever was ordinary malaria fever, which, though it attacked all classes more or less, was specially fatal only in the case of those who had suffered from privation."[1]

Fever epidemics in typical Indian famines due to drought have followed a somewhat different course from malaria in the Bengal famine. They have tended to occur after the famine had been relieved, when the long delayed rains had arrived and the people were returning to their normal village occupations. During the height of a "drought famine", the parching of the land checks mosquito breeding. "The rainfall, which occurs after a few years of drought is often excessive, giving rise to floods, and this in itself usually creates circumstances favourable for the transmission of malaria. There are other epidemiological factors which may play a part in such outbreaks. The years of drought preceding an epidemic may so lower anopheline density and longevity that little or no malaria transmission takes place for several consecutive years. The absence of malaria transmission during such prolonged periods allows the immunity of the population to fall to a low level, especially in the younger children, many of whom may never have been exposed to malarial infection. In malaria epidemics, the mortality among children is often exceptionally severe and forms a high proportion of total mortality. Widespread destruction of cattle may result in the deviation of cattle-feeding anophelines to man"[2].

S. R. Christophers, in his investigations of the epidemiology of malaria in the Punjab, studied the relation between famine and the disease.[3] He noted that, of twelve great epidemics of malaria which devastated the Punjab in the latter half of the nineteenth century, seven followed seasons of famine or acute scarcity. Taking the price of food stuffs as an index of scarcity, he found a high correlation between scarcity and mortality from fever; the epidemics of 1870, 1872, 1878, 1879, 1881, 1887, 1890, 1892, 1900 and 1908 all occurred during periods of high prices. He found, however, an equally high correlation between famine and rainfall and concluded that "even if scarcity is in reality involved in epidemic causation, we should not expect to find it acting in the absence of the necessary factor of rainfall. We must not look for the effect of famine in this respect in the famine districts at the time of the famine, for at this time the essential factor, excess of rainfall, is absent". In the Punjab, years of scarcity or famine were usually followed by excessive rainfall and periods of high prices.

23. These observations do not throw much light on the epidemiology of malaria in the Bengal famine. In Bengal there was no preceding drought followed by heavy rains and indeed in the water-logged delta of Bengal climatic conditions can have little effect on the breeding of mosquitoes. Mosquitoes could thrive when the famine was at its height and the epidemic raged at this period. It is, however, significant that so experienced and distinguished a malariologist as Sir Rickart Christophers should have regarded food scarcity and famine as being possible factors in the genesis of severe malaria epidemics.

As in earlier famines, it has been suggested that the malaria which caused so many deaths in the Bengal famine was of an exceptionally virulent type. A stationary malaria-ridden population acquires some degree of immunity to the local strain or strains of malaria parasite. If a new strain is introduced

---

[1] Report of the Indian Famine Commission, 1898

[2] R. Passmore and T. Sommerville, Journal of the Malaria Institute of India 1940. 3,447.

[3] Proceedings of the Imperial Conference, Simla, 1909.

" Malaria in the Punjab ".—Scientific Memoirs of the Goverment of India. No. 46.

immunity is weakened and the new strain may be highly virulent. In Bengal circumstances were propitious for the dissemination of unfamiliar strains; there was considerable migration of sections of the population in certain areas, and previous to the famine there had been an influx of refugees from Burma, many of whom were malarious and may have been the carriers of exotic strains. It is very difficult, from the evidence available, to reach a satisfactory conclusion on this point. We may, however, suggest that the high mortality rate from malaria can be largely accounted for without pre-supposing any change in the virulence of the infecting organisms. This opinion, tentatively expressed, is similar to that of previous Famine Commissions.

24. Malaria control in Bengal by the prevention of mosquito breeding or the destruction of adult mosquitoes is a formidable problem for which no solution has as yet been found. Anti-malarial measures of this nature were impossible during the famine. The only way of mitigating the epidemic was by supplying anti-malarial drugs in abundance and by treating as many patients as possible. The main responsibility of medical and public health authorities was to provide facilities for treatment. We shall revert to this question later, but it may be said at once that the responsibility was inadequately fulfilled.

25. An attempt has been made in the preceding paragraphs to discuss the relation between famine and epidemic diseases. The subject should not, however, be closed without reference to our present lack of knowledge of all the factors concerned in the rise and fall of epidemics and their interaction. The Croonian Lecture of Professor W. W. C. Topley entitled "The Biology of Epidemics", given before the Royal Society in 1941, brings out the complexity of the problem. It may be difficult to account satisfactorily for the cause and course of epidemics even in a well-fed static human population, even indeed, in a closed colony of experimental animals. To do so in the case of a socially disorganized famine-striken population is an impossible task.

CHAPTER III.—MEDICAL RELIEF AND PUBLIC HEALTH WORK

A.—HOSPITALS AND STAFF.

1. The steps taken by the Government of Bengal, with the assistance of the Government of India and the military medical authorities, to meet the grave medical and public health situation created by the famine will be briefly described. During the earliest months of the famine some use was made of the A.R.P. medical organization, which had at its disposal a certain number of beds in existing hospitals and emergency A.R.P. hospitals. In the middle of August 1943 arrangements were made for doctors to attend to destitutes collapsing in the streets of Calcutta from starvation, and to provide hospital accommodation for them. By the end of September, over 2,000 emergency beds had been opened in Calcutta and its suburbs for the treatment of sick destitutes, and medical staff was recruited for the emergency hospitals and wards. The A.R.P. medical organization in the city was pressed into service. During the same months orders were issued by Government to district authorities sanctioning the opening of emergency hospitals in such places and on such a scale as the emergency demanded. By January 1944 it was reported that some 13,000 beds were available and the number in July 1944 reached 18,250. These were provided largely by the construction of Relief Emergency Hospitals containing 100, 50 and 20 beds according to local necessity. In the early months of 1944 "satellite treatment centres" were opened in association with 1,400 dispensaries, for the treatment of patients in villages remote from dispensaries.

In November 1943 military medical resources were placed at the disposal of Bengal. Military hospitals, 16 in number and situated in various centres throughout the province, provided 2,100 beds and some 50 mobile military medical units were organized. The latter were subsequently replaced by civil units when the military personnel was withdrawn. Mobile units, staffed for the most part by medical students, were also organized by the Bengal Government. In February 1944, the number of such units was about 250, but this was later reduced to 80 owing to the return of the students to colleges.

2. Steps were taken to transfer district and subdivisional hospitals from the control of local authorities to that of the Provincial Government, in order to improve their efficiency. In June 1944, 11 hospitals had been taken over by the Provincial Government, 44 were on the point of being taken over and negotiations for the transfer of the remainder were in progress.

3. The Director General, Indian Medical Service, visited Bengal during the first week of September, 1943, and made arrangements for the distribution of milk through the Indian Red Cross Society; an appeal for funds for this purpose was made in the same week by the Vicerine. At a meeting of the Nutrition Advisory Committee, Indian Research Fund Association, held in Delhi on October 1st and 2nd, 1943, the famine in Bengal was discussed and immediate arrangements made to establish a research unit in Calcutta to study methods of treating cases of starvation and famine disease. Early in October there were consultations in Delhi between the Minister for Public Health and Local Self-Government, Bengal, and the Department of Education, Health and Lands, Government of India, about the health and medical requirements of Bengal, and efforts were made by the latter to obtain doctors and nurses for famine work. The Director-General, I.M.S., newly appointed in October, and the Public Health Commissioner with the Government of India arrived in Bengal in the first week of November 1943 to advise and assist in the organization of medical relief and public health measures. Other visiting experts during 1943

included the Director of Medical Services in the Army, the Director, Malaria Institute of India, and the Director of Nutrition Research.

4. In November 1943 an I.M.S. officer was made available to the Bengal Government for the post of Director of Public Health to replace, in the interests of efficiency, the provincial service officer previously employed. Seven I.M.S. officers were released from military service, and returned to Bengal for duty at various dates during the first half of 1944. They were mostly employed as Civil Surgeons. The military authorities, in November 1943, lent the services of one Assistant Director of Hygiene, 10 Deputy Assistant Directors of Hygiene, and 56 medical officers for employment as health officers in sub-divisions. A senior officer was appointed as Medical Adviser for Famine Relief. The Assistant Director of Hygiene was concerned with general supervision, the Deputy Assistant Directors of Hygiene assumed the duties of Assistant Directors of Public Health in various parts of the province, and the medical officers were employed as health officers in sub-divisions. The duties of the additional health staff included the improvement of village sanitation and disinfection of water supplies, the carrying out of inoculations and vaccinations, the treatment of malaria cases, and the supervision of the work of the subordinate public health staff. They were also instructed to ensure the prompt reporting of vital statistics to the Director of Public Health. Before they proceeded to the districts the officers were given a brief course of instruction at the Health Unit in Singur, an organization attached to the All-India Institute of Hygiene and Publc Health.

At the end of May 1944 it became necessary, owing to military requirements, to withdraw part of this staff, but two Deputy Assistant Directors of Hygiene and 40 military sub-divisional officers were left with the Government of Bengal to give time for arrangements to be made to replace them.

5. There was great difficulty in obtaining enough civilian medical officers of satisfactory calibre to meet the emergency. Other provinces were approached to supply medical officers, but since the medical cadres of all provinces had been depleted by the release of medical officers for service with the army, little help was forthcoming. The Central Provinces provided 2 medical officers, and the Government of Burma lent the services of 27 doctors who were in India awaiting the reconquest of Burma and return to their own duties. The attempts of the Government of Bengal to recruit medical officers within the province were far from successful. It was found that doctors were reluctant to serve in rural areas under the conditions produced by the famine, and moreover the pay offered was not attractive enough. There was a general increase in sickness among well-to-do people who could afford to pay for medical treatment and hence good money to be made in private practice. Up to February 1944 some 160 doctors—a quite insufficient number—were recruited. At the instance of the Government of India rates of pay were increased in March, 1944, and by the end of June 328 doctors had been obtained for famine medical work. This was about half the number which the Government of Bengal estimated to be necessary.

6. There is a great shortage of nurses in India in normal times, the reasons for which need not be discussed here. In the whole country there are only some 7,000 trained nurses, which works out as one nurse for every 56,000 of the population. A large proportion of these are at present serving with the army. During the famine the problem of obtaining additional nurses was insoluble. Neither Provincial Governments nor missionary organizations were able to help. The only way to meet the emergency was to obtain untrained male and female attendants, put them in hospitals and hope that they would learn something about nursing from the instructions of the docters and practical experience. Clearly such attendants cannot be described as nurses in the

usual sense of the term. The medical work of famine hospitals was handicapped throughout by the lack of satisfactory nursing staff.

7. The sweeper is a functionary of vital importance in Indian hospitals, performing the essential tasks delegated to him by the customs of the country. His services were of particular importance in emergency hospitals without sanitary appliances or drainage. Great difficulty was encountered in obtaining sweepers for the famine hospitals. There was a shortage of sweepers in Bengal owing to the demands of the military and the swollen population of Calcutta. Two hundred sweepers were recruited in the United Provinces—a number altogether insufficient to meet requirements. Although their pay was nearly double that of Bengali sweepers, and the difference led to discontent among the latter, some of the U. P. sweepers deserted after brief service. In the early months of the famine, when many patients were suffering from diarrhoea and beds and wards were continually befouled, the shortage of sweepers was almost as great an obstacle to the efficient running of hospitals as the shortage of doctors and nurses. The problem remained unsolved throughout the famine.

B.—Medical Supplies.

8. The lethal epidemic of malaria made quinine preparations and substitutes the most important of all drugs during the emergency. In peace time the normal consumption of quinine in India is about 200,000 lbs. In 1943 some 79,000 lbs. of quinine and 20,000 lbs. of cinchona febrifuge were allotted to Bengal. In 1944, 65,000 lbs. of quinine, 30,000 lbs. of cinchona febrifuge, 500,000 quinine ampoules and 382 million tablets of mepacrine and quinacrine were supplied to the province. The latter are recently introduced synthetic preparations, resembling the German preparation "atebrin". Mepacrine has been widely and successfully used by the army in the Burma campaign. Large amounts of anti-malarial drugs were in fact supplied to Bengal during the famine and the epidemic of malaria which continued throughout 1944, the cost of those distributed free in 1944 being no less than Rs. 21,00,000

9. One million sulphaguanidine tablets were sent from the United Kingdom under arrangements made by the Secretary of State. The main use of sulphaguanidine tablets is in the treatment of bacillary dysentery. The effect of this drug on cholera is at present under investigation.

10. The following supplies of vitamin tablets and preparations were obtained: one million compound vitamin capsules from army stocks; 50,000 vitamin B1 tablets from local stocks; one million vitamin B1 tablets and one million halibut oil capsules by air from the United Kingdom, the despatch being arranged by the Secretary of State: one million halibut liver oil capsules presented by Boots Pure Drug Co.; 700 gallons of shark liver oil from supplies in India. In the second half of 1944 a further supply of 2,900,000 composite vitamin B tablets was expected from England.

11. The civil emergency hospitals, mobile units, etc., had to be supplied with drugs, blankets, sheets, disinfectants and other necessary articles. This was the responsibility of the Government of Bengal. The military units which came into action at the end of 1943 were fully equipped, but equipment for the expansion of certain military hospitals was later provided by the Government of Bengal. Additional drugs were also supplied by the civil authorities to medical units after the initial stage. Food supplies for military hospitals were a civil responsibility.

Existing hospitals in Bengal were in general poorly equipped and there was a deficiency in the province of most medical supplies, so that there was little to build on in the task of creating hospital accommodation. After November 1943 the problem of medical relief was taken up in earnest, and by degrees the supplies required by the hospitals were obtained and distributed—no easy task under war conditions. Needless to say, the standard of equipment of the emergency hospitals was not high, but in general it sufficed for the care and treatment of destitutes. The Government of India made available in November 1943 the services of the officer in charge of the Calcutta Medical Store Depot, his duties being to advise on the procurement of medical supplies, and to assist in their storage and distribution, pending the completion of satisfactory provincial arrangements for these purposes by the Government of Bengal. A Centre Store Depot was opened by the Government of Bengal in May 1944. The military undertook the distribution of medical supplies, and after their withdrawal in April 1944 fresh difficulties were encountered. In May the Government of Bengal reported that medical supplies were adequate but that there was a breakdown in the distribution arrangements in some areas.

C.—Anti-epidemic measures.

12. The number of vaccinations against small-pox and inoculations against cholera carried out monthly from July 1943 to May 1944 is shown below. The figures are those of the Director of Public Health.

1943	Vaccinations	Inoculations
July	114,167	721,615
August	84,167	609,306
September	71,224	568,142
October	72,781	762,019
November	167,160	610,367
December	463,738	610,854
Total for July—December 1943	973,237	3,882,303

1944	Vaccinations	Inoculations
January	1,776,166	945,436
February	3,335,542	1,141,880
March	5,139,101	2,605,882
April	7,303,137	4,339,636
May	5,700,030	2,595,186
Total for January—May 1944	23,253,976	11,628,020

By the end of May, 1944, according to these figures, over a third of the population had been inoculated against small-pox and about one-fifth against cholera. It was one of the duties of military and civil medical officers employed in famine relief to carry out inoculations and vaccinations. After very considerable delay, some 1,000 sanitary assistants were recruited by the Government of Bengal for this purpose. By October 1944 the number of inoculations and vaccinations reported had reached 18 and 32 millions respectively.

13. Bleaching powder is essential in combating epidemics of cholera. It is needed to disinfect clothing, the houses in which cholera occurs, and water supplies. Bleaching powder has been in short supply in India during the war and early in the war was placed under the control of an officer of the Government of India, the Controller of Heavy Chemicals. Supplies required by Provincial Governments, local bodies, etc., could be obtained only by application to this officer. In the emergency in Bengal this proved a cumbrous procedure, and indeed in the early months of the cholera epidemic little attempt was made by the Government or local bodies in Bengal to secure the necessary bleaching

powder. In November, 1943, at the instance of the Public Health Commissioner, the Controller of Heavy Chemicals placed 50 tons at the disposal of the Director of Public Health.

14. The water used for domestic purposes in rural Bengal comes from tube wells, tanks and rivers. Cholera is readily spread by infected tank and river water. Tube wells, when in proper order, provide a safe source of water supply and do not require treatment in a cholera epidemic. Unfortunately a large proportion of the tube wells in Bengal—one estimate given to the Commission was one-third—were out of order. The sinking, maintenance and repair of these wells are the responsibility of the District and Union Boards, the necessary funds being supplied partly from their own resources and partly from Government grants. Owing to the war the price of the materials required for tube wells has risen steeply and local Bodies, with the limited funds at their disposal, were unable to keep the wells in a satisfactory state. It may be added that there is no regular system for the inspection and repair of tube wells, and no capable engineering staff, and the state of the wells under the local bodies may be ascribed as much to indifference and inefficiency as to lack of money.

15. The severe cholera epidemic made the repair of tube wells a matter of urgent public health importance. The deficiency of wells in proper working order naturally increased the use of tank and river water and thus facilitated cholera infection. In November 1943 the Government drew the attention of all District Boards to the vital need of ensuring uncontaminated water supplies and called for information about the numbers of derelict tube wells and the quantities of materials required to put them in order. The practical results of this step were negligible. In January 1944 the Government sanctioned the expenditure of 1,500,000 rupees for the repair and maintenance of tube wells. Owing, however, to difficulties in obtaining materials and transport, and other causes suggested above, work on tube wells did not begin until two months later. By August 1944 some 10,000 tube wells had been repaired in the various ways needed to make them serviceable and a source of safe water supply.

D.—Distribution of Food

16. In famine food is the most important medicine and hence a reference to the provision of food to famine victims will not be out of place in this section of our report. During the second half of 1943, from August and September onwards, a large number of kitchens for the free distribution of cooked food were opened throughout Bengal. The number reached 6,625 in the beginning of November and it was reckoned that during this month about 2·1 million people were being fed daily. According to figures supplied by the Government of Bengal, some 110,000,000 free meals were provided; this includes meals supplied after the Midnapore cyclone in October 1942. Free kitchens were also set up by charitable agencies in both Calcutta and the mofussil, with the emphasis strongly on Calcutta, where distress was most evident to the well-to-do and voluntary relief workers easily obtainable. Nearly half the kitchens in Calcutta were run by charitable organizations.

17. Doles of uncooked food were given on a wide scale in the districts, the number of recipients reaching 257,000 in November 1943. Apart from free doles, foodgrains were sold at cheap rates to the poorest sections of the community. During the period of greatest distress, 1,801 cheap grain shops were selling foodgrains to about 492,000 families, *i.e.*, over two million people. There were also canteens selling cooked food at a cheap rate and it was reckoned that 120,000 people took advantage of them over a long period.

18. The quantities of food supplied as free doles of uncooked grains or in the form of gruel at the kitchens were very meagre. In a circular issued by

the Government of Bengal on August 20th, 1943, the following scale was laid down:—

Gratuitous relief—

(a) *Free gruel at 2 chataks (4 oz.) of foodgrains per head.*

(b) *Uncooked foodgrain doles per head per day.*

(i) 4 *chatacks* (8 *oz.*) *for adults who normally do manual work.*

(ii) 3 *chatacks* (6 *oz.*) *for other adults, and*

(iii) 2 *chatacks* (4 *oz.*) *for minors aged* 2-14.

It was added that "expectant and nursing mothers and if possible growing children should be given 50 per cent. more than the above, preferably as a second meal". In Calcutta foodgrains for gruel kitchens were provided by the Department of Civil Supplies, which put a Relief Control Officer in charge of the kitchens. In a note dated August 28th the Department of Civil Supplies prescribed a rate of 3 *chatacks* (6 oz.) of foodgrains *per capita* daily.

In September, when the supply position had somewhat improved, it was decided to increase the quantities of food given as gruel and doles. A correction slip to the original instructions was issued on September 21st, by which the quantity of grains in the gruel was raised to 6 oz., while the allowances of uncooked grains for classes (i), (ii) and (iii) became 12, 8 and 4 oz. respectively. Government did not receive any reports from District Officers expressing their inability to introduce the new allowances for want of adequate supplies and presumably these were issued without delay throughout the districts.

The gruel supplied in the kitchens usually consisted of a mixture of grains in which millets predominated. In Calcutta equal quantities of rice, *bajra*, *jowar* and *dhal* were included. Some of the charitable organizations supplied more rice in the gruel when they could obtain it. Small quantities of other ingredients such as vegetables, spices and sugar were also usually added to the mixture. The gruel as issued did not at the best supply more than 600—800 calories for adults and about half this number for children. The millets, notably *bajra*, were unfamiliar and unpalatable food and it was widely stated that they were so indigestible that they produced intestinal irritation, diarrhoea and death in numerous destitutes.

19. Towards the end of 1943, the gruel kitchens were gradually closed down and the feeding of destitutes in poor houses, homes, orphanages, etc., assumed importance. The scales of diet varied from district to district. In some places they were reasonably generous; for example, in the Contai sub-division of Midnapore a scale for destitute homes was introduced in December 1943, providing for an adult 16 oz. of cereals and 4 oz. of *dhal*, the whole diet yielding more than 2,000 calories. In April 1944, the question of diet scales was taken up by Government. It was found on investigation that the calorie value of the diet in relief institutions was in general much below requirements and the Public Health Department recommended the following generous scale:—

For Adults

Rice or rice and wheat	16 ounces=1 lb. (wheat not to exceed 8 oz.
Pulses (*Dhal*)	3 ounces.
Non-leafy vegetables (Potato, Turnip, Brinjal, etc.)	6 ounces.
Leafy vegetables (cabbage, *sag*, amaranth, etc.)	2 ounces
Fat and oil	2 ounces.
Salt and condiment	In sufficient quantity.
Fish	2 ounces. (If not possibel every day, at least every other day.)

Children below 12 years should get milk as available according to the following scale in addition to a proportionate amount of an adult's diet :—

For ages 2—5	12 to 16 ounces.
For ages 6—12	16 to 20 ounces.

Pregnant and lactating mothers should get over 12 to 16 ounces milk daily in addition to an adult's diet.

E.—Hospital Feeding

20. It has been remarked that in hospitals the provision of a good diet was a vital part of treatment. The dietary treatment of cases of acute starvation is a difficult problem which was studied by research workers in Calcutta. Recommendations based on these findings were passed on to hospitals throughout the province. It was observed that starved patients not infrequently refused the fluid diet appropriate to their condition and begged for a large meal of rice. When this was refused they sometimes absconded. Alexander Porter reports similar occurrences in the Madras famine of 1877-8.

21. The ordinary hospital diet provided for debilitated patients in famine wards and hospitals was by no means perfect from the standpoint of nutrition, but the condition of patients consuming it usually improved and they put on weight. The standard of diet was not uniform in all hospitals and places. There were difficulties of supply and some doctors in charge of famine hospitals made little effort to overcome those and provide the best diet possible in the circumstances. But on the whole the famine hospital diets were not unsatisfactory.

F.—Milk

22. The distribution of evaporated and dried milk was undertaken by the Indian Red Cross Society. At the beginning of September 1943, the army handed over 200 tons of milk to the Society, and with this supply distribution was begun in Calcutta and the districts. Subsequently, generous consignments were received from abroad, notably from the United States. By September 1944 some 1,850 tons of processed milk had been supplied to Bengal. Distribution was carefully organized and the milk reached those who were most in need. It was given largely to infants, young children up to 10 years and expectant and nursing mothers at gruel kitchens, and in hospitals, destitute homes, famine camps and orphanages.

At the kitchens it proved invaluable for children who were too ill to take the gruel. A rigid rule was made that the milk must be consumed at the kitchen itself, in order to avoid the possibility of its being sold by recipients. Relief workers in general were struck by the improvement in under-nourished destitute children which took place when they were given milk for a few weeks.

23. Transport of milk supplies from Calcutta to the districts presented considerable difficulties in the early months of the famine. These were alleviated when military transport became available for relief work. Hundreds of tons of milk were transported to outlying places with speed and reliability. We record with pleasure that at one point the United States Air Force co-operated by flying some tons of milk to Dacca, in response to an urgent call from the District Magistrate. To facilitate distribution in the districts the Indian Red Cross Society in 1944 appointed 18 paid agents. This arrangement was found to be more satisfactory than entrusting distribution to District Magistrates, overburdened by other work.

24. The quantities of evaporated and dried milk distributed in Bengal monthly from September 1943 to June 1944 were as follows:—

	Calcutta	*Mofussil*	*To the Surgeon-General for hospitals*
	Tons	Tons	Tons
1943—September	15	33	..
October	15	56·75	..
November	15	68	..
December . . .	10	120·5	..
1944—January	10	125·5	50
February	10	122·5	25
March	10	121·5	25
April	11	121·5	17
May	11·5	208	17
June	11·5	157	20

CHAPTER IV.—THE FAILURE TO PREVENT HIGH MORTALITY

1. An objective account has been given of the measures taken to provide medical relief, check epidemics and supply food to the famine-stricken population. They are by no means unimpressive, at least as regards their scale. A very considerable effort was made by the Bengal Government to succour the millions of people affected by famine and disease. But clearly the various measures taken were on the whole unsuccessful, since the excess mortality according to our estimate may have reached 1·5 millions. The causes of the failure must now be critically examined.

A.—Famine and health services in general

2. In the story of the events leading up to the famine it has repeatedly been pointed out that only action, taken before a certain stage in the descent into catastrophe was reached, could have fully retrieved the situation. This is equally true in the health sphere. Once the position as it existed in August and September 1943 had developed, with some millions of people starving, socially disorganized and already a prey to epidemic disease, no health service, however well-staffed and organized, could have prevented heavy mortality.

We must, however, inquire whether, at the various stages of the famine, it would not have been possible to reduce mortality by more effective health measures.

B.—Previous defects in the Public Health Organization

3. If a public health organization is to be capable of meeting emergencies, it must reach a certain degree of efficiency in normal times. In Bengal the public health services were insufficient to meet the normal needs of the population and the level of efficiency was low. The same can of course be said of public health organizations in all parts of India, but that in Bengal was below the standard of certain other provinces. The Department of Public Health and Local Self-Government (Medical) under the charge of a Minister, is responsible for public health. At the centre there is a Director of Public Health, who at the time of the famine was an officer recruited from the Provincial Service. (The post is not a "reserved" I.M.S. post, though it may and has been filled by I.M.S. officers). The provincial health department includes 6 Assistant Directors of Public Health, 2 concerned with school hygiene and malaria research respectively and 4 for superintending public health work in the 4 Divisions.[1] Previous to the famine, three special Assistant Directors had been recruited, two for work in subdivisions of the Midnapore district badly affected by the cyclone, and one for public health work connected with A.R.P. and Civil Defence. In the malaria section there are an engineer, an entomologist and a qualified assistant. Other officers in the provincial health department include the Director of the Public Health Laboratory, the Superintendents respectively of the Bengal Vaccine Laboratory (for cholera vaccine), the Bengal Vaccine Institute (for small-pox vaccine), Maternity and Child Welfare, and Vital Statistics, and an Inspector of Septic Tank Installations. In numbers the provincial health services were at about their usual strength in 1943. A post of assistant malariologist was unfilled and there were two vacancies for epidemiologists.

4. Public health work in the districts is the responsibility of the District Boards. In each district there is a District Health Officer, half of whose salary is paid by Government, but who is actually a servant of the District Board.

[1]The Burdwan Division, the Presidency Division, the Rajshahi Division and the Dacca and Chittagong Division.

Subordinate health workers in the districts are also servants of the local Body. The health organization in rural Bengal in general may be illustrated by describing the organization in a typical district—Dacca. The population of Dacca is some 4·5 millions and its area 2,738 square miles. There is a District Health Officer at district headquarters on a salary grade of Rs. 300—20—500 per month, the present holder of the post having reached his maximum salary in 1932. The district is divided into 32 health circles, the population of which varies from 60,000 to 250,000 and the area from 36 to 174 square miles. In each health circle there are 3 subordinate health workers, *viz.*, a sanitary inspector, a health assistant and a medicine carrier. In addition some 100 vaccinators are appointed temporarily for about 6 months in the year. The pay of the sanitary inspectors is Rs. 50—5—70 per month, with a travelling allowance of Rs. 15, house allowance of Rs. 3, and office allowance of Rs. 3. The health assistants are not on a salary grade, their pay being fixed at Rs. 22 per month with Rs. 5 travelling allowance and Rs. 2 house allowance. The medicine carriers receive Rs. 17 per month, while the vaccinators get from Rs. 12 to Rs. 20 according to their experience, during the period of their employment. This is the normal organization, without reference to additional staff employed during the famine.

5. Clearly one sanitary inspector, even with the help of a health assistant, a medicine carrier and a few temporarily employed vaccinators, cannot deal adequately with the health problems of a population which may exceed 200,000 and inhabit an area of over 150 square miles. Further, touring in rural Bengal is in general slow and not infrequently interrupted during the rains. This makes the work of the local health staff more difficult and also reduces the amount of supervision which can be exercised over their work by the District Health Officer.

6. In addition to inadequate staff, there were other defects in the health organization in Bengal which were repeatedly brought to the attention of the Commission. Steps have since been taken to remedy a few of these, but the use of the past tense in the paragraphs which follow does not imply that much reform has as yet been carried out. Since the district health staff was in the employ of the local Bodies, the Director of Public Health had no disciplinary control over them and no powers of selection or transfer. He could not dismiss or transfer a lazy and inefficient health officer. In the case of an emergency he had no powers to mobilize the limited resources of health personnel in the province. He could indeed give technical advice, but advice might not result in action. When epidemics occur, swift and drastic action is necessary. No general could conduct a campaign without full control of the forces at his disposal.

7. The pay and prospects of District Health Officers were not conducive to efficiency. They usually remained throughout their entire careers in the districts to which they were first appointed, having reached the maximum grade of salary long before retirement. Transfer from one district to another never occurred, so that the refreshment brought about by changes in work and environment was absent. Senior appointments to which District Health Officers could aspire in the provincial health department were few in number. Professional contacts were lacking and the officers fell out of touch with recent developments in the field of public health. The result was that they tended to get into a rut and lose the enthusiasm necessary for successful work in the health sphere.

The pay of subordinate members of the service was insufficient and had not been adjusted in accordance with the rise in the cost of living. Financial allotments for travelling on the part of all the staff were often inadequate. In view of the large areas to be covered, it was particularly important that District Health Officers and their subordinate staff should have adequate facilities for touring. In one district, the Commission was informed that no travelling allowance had been paid for 15 months previous to the famine. The part-time vaccinators were very poorly paid and were forced to do other work in order to live. In the circumstances lack of drive and limited achievement on the part of the rural health services were only to be expected.

8. Another factor of importance was the position of the district health personnel as employees of the local elected bodies. Such bodies are often swayed by party politics and technical officers in their employ tend to get drawn into the political sphere. The Commission learnt of instances in which District Health Officers and the subordinate health staff were employed in activities other than public health, including political activities. The District Health Officer was often at the beck and call of the Chairman of the District Board. It has been claimed that District Boards are likely to understand local needs better than Government experts. This may be true as regards some of the responsibilities of District Boards, but it is not true as regards public health. The general public has not yet become "health conscious". Hence it was difficult or impossible for local elected bodies to understand the modern public health movement and its requirements and obligations.

C.—Vital statistics

9. Reference has already been made to the inaccuracy of vital statistics in Bengal as elsewhere in India. Another point of importance in connection with the famine was the delay in their compilation. Under the system operative in 1943, the village *chowkidar* sent his mortality report to the Union Board office. The President of the Union Board was responsible for collecting the figures from the various villages in the Union and forwarding them to *thana* headquarters, where they were collated by the sanitary inspector and in due course sent to the District Health Officer. In some districts they were sent to Sub-Divisional Officers and not to sanitary inspectors. In 1943 the Director of Public Health had two offices, one in Calcutta at which he himself worked, and another in Rajshahi which housed his statistical staff. Part of the public health staff was removed to Rajshahi from Calcutta in 1942 as an A. R. P. measure. The result was that it took many months for the health expert of the Provincial Government to receive information about the trend of mortality in the districts. The usual period was 3 to 6 months; in the case of certain districts, considerably longer. In November 1943 no figures for total deaths in 5 districts later than December 1942 were available in the office of the Director of Public Health. The latest completed figures for any district were those of April 1943. The reporting of outbreaks of certain epidemic diseases was somewhat more rapid. When the President of the Union Board was informed by the village *chowkidar* of an outbreak of small-pox or cholera, he sent on the information by postcard to the sanitary inspector at *thana* headquarters, who sent it to the District Health Officer, who sent it to the Director of Public Health.

In such circumstances it was impossible for the Director of Public Health to maintain vigilant watch over the health of the population and to give timely warning of deterioration and the need for urgent action. A health department in such a position is seriously handicapped when an emergency arises.

The most serious block in the sluggish channel by which mortality records reached the Director of Public Health was at the Union Board offices. In January 1944 an attempt was made to hasten the flow by removing the obstruction and making sanitary inspectors responsible for collecting figures from *chowkidars*. This produced some acceleration, which was not however uniform throughout the province, since many delays still occurred in certain districts.

D.—Previous Defects in hospital services

10. Curative medicine in Bengal suffered from much the same disabilities as preventive medicine. Nearly all hospitals and dispensaries in the districts

were financed by local bodies; only in Dacca was there a large hospital supported out of provincial revenues. The Surgeon General, an I.M.S. officer, is in general responsible for curative medicine throughout the province. In each district there is a Civil Surgeon, who is a Government officer and appointed by the Government on the advice of the Surgeon-General. Assistant Surgeons in charge of Sub-Divisional hospitals are also on the provincial cadre while sub-assistant surgeons in charge of small hospitals and dispensaries in the rural areas are employed by local bodies. Before the war some of the Civil Surgeons in Bengal were I.M.S. officers, but during the war the large majority of these were withdrawn for military service. Their places were taken by officers in the Bengal Medical Service, usually promoted Assistant Surgeons. A number of Indian Medical Department medical officers had also reverted to military duty, their posts being filled by provincial service officers. The total strength of all grades of the medical services in July 1943 was 425 against a sanctioned strength of 510, a shortage of 85. The number of Bengal Medical Service (Upper) officers was 125 compared with a sanctioned strength of 166, while the corresponding figures for the Bengal Medical Service (Lower) were 255 and 273 respectively. Recruitment to full strength in both grades previous to famine was delayed by a decision to employ only officers above military age, and also, in the case of the senior grade, by questions relating to the communal distribution of posts. In November 1943 the order restricting recruitment to candidates over military age was withdrawn. It may be observed that the Bengal Medical Services generally had not been very seriously depleted, except as regards I. M. S. and I. M. D. officers. Recruitment from the Bengal Medical Services into the army had not been extensive.

11. While the Surgeon-General was nominally in control of Civil Surgeons and Assistant Surgeons, disciplinary action against an inefficient and disobedient officer could be taken only through Government and was a lengthy process. Civil Surgeons in turn had little power of control over the subordinate medical staff in the district, which looked to local bodies for orders and policy. According to the usual procedure, all additional expenditure on the part of the Provincial Government had to be sanctioned by the Finance Department. Delay in administrative procedure which may have been of relatively little significance in normal times proved serious in the famine emergency. The financing of hospitals throughout the districts was the responsibility of local Bodies. The general organization of the medical services and hospitals was in fact such as to render mobilization and development to meet the emergency extremely difficult.

12. In the opening months of the famine Civil Surgeons in general were not aware of, or at least did not report, the development of a critical situation in their districts. Their lack of knowledge of what was happening appears to have been partly due to inability or disinclination to tour their districts. There seems to have been lack of contact and co-ordination between Civil Surgeons and District Magistrates in certain districts with regard to the medical emergency created by the famine. The Surgeon-General stated in evidence that the medical authorities at provincial headquarters did not become aware of the existence of unusual conditions until August 1943, when sick destitutes began to throng the streets of Calcutta.

13. In general the standard of efficiency reached by Civil Surgeons and subordinate medical personnel left much to be desired. Discipline and sense of duty were defective and morale low. This is in comparison, not with an ideal standard, but with standards in certain other provinces in India. Many of the Civil Surgeons had obtained their appointments at a late stage in their careers after years of service in a subordinate position. Hence they were not suited to take vigorous initiative when initiative was required. The hospitals throughout Bengal, with certain exceptions, were poorly equipped and badly run.

Representatives of the District Boards who appeared before the Commission ascribed the inefficiency of the rural public health and medical services to financial stringency. The income of District Boards has not increased *pari passu* with the increasing demand for expenditure on roads, water supply, public health services, hospitals, etc. Their powers of taxation are limited and they depend largely on grants from the provincial revenues. The Provincial Government themselves suffered severely from financial stringency for many years and were not able to provide adequate funds for public health and medical purposes. There can be no doubt that lack of money, both from provincial and local revenues, was a serious obstacle to the development and maintenance of public health services and the provision of well-equipped hospitals, but this does not excuse the state of affairs revealed in 1943 when the health and medical services were called upon to deal with the famine emergency.

E.—The Famine Period

14. In view of the state of medical and public health organizations in Bengal before the famine, it is scarcely surprising that they failed to rise to the occasion. On the health side, no satisfactory attempt was made during the early months to deal with the situation; there was in fact almost a complete breakdown of health services, affecting both the centre and the periphery.

15. **Cholera.**—At this time the need for the inoculation of cholera vaccine on a wide scale was urgent. The Bengal Vaccine Institute normally produces 500,000 doses of cholera vaccine per month, and abundant supplies of cholera vaccine, amounting to 12·5 million doses, were available in India as a whole. In spite of this, adequate quantities of vaccine were not available in the districts throughout the critical months of 1943, and in general cholera preventive work during this period was unsatisfactory. At the end of the year, with the help and stimulus of the military medical organization, the anti-cholera campaign by means of inoculation on a large scale was begun in earnest. It was prosecuted with vigour throughout the first half of 1944, during which period the epidemic was brought under control.

The repair of tube wells, urgently recommended by Government to local Bodies in November 1943, was not begun until many months later when the cholera epidemic had waned. While due weight must be given to the difficulty of obtaining labour and materials, the long delay reflects little credit on the engineering section of the Public Health Department and the local authorities concerned.

16. **Small-pox.**—As regards small-pox, no widespread epidemic, calling for urgent action occurred in 1943. The chief failure was the insufficient number of vaccinations carried out previous to the famine, which meant that the population was inadequately protected against an epidemic of small-pox. Reference must, however, be made to the delay in appointing additional workers for carrying out vaccinations and other public health work. In August, 1943, the Director of Public Health put forward a proposal to Government for the recruitment of 40 doctors and 10 sanitary inspectors for anti-epidemic work. Nothing resulted. In November, plans were formulated for dealing with health problems on a wider scale. It was decided, in view of the difficulty in obtaining qualified doctors and trained sanitary assistants, to engage untrained matriculates and give them a brief course of training. After some unnecessary delay due to an attempt to adhere to the communal ratio in selection, these were recruited and trained and by January 1944, 736 were at work in the districts.

17. During 1944 the vaccination of the population was pushed forward with great energy. One witness remarked to the Commission that the achievement represented by the vaccination figures could scarcely be equalled in any country in the world, even in Russia. It must, however, be noted that the

small-pox epidemic was not brought under control until June 1944. This may be accounted for in various ways. Most important is the low percentage of the population vaccinated when the epidemic began. Mention must, however, be made of the possibility that some of the lymph used had lost its potency. Until the beginning of the epidemic most of the lymph used was prepared in Bengal; later lymph was obtained from all over India to supplement local supplies. Lymph has a short active life. Again, the technique of vaccination may have been to some extent faulty; the unqualified workers recruited by Government received only a brief training. Another obvious possibility is that the workers engaged in vaccination did not in fact carry out all the vaccinations entered in their returns. Care was, however, taken by military and other medical authorities to check the accuracy of their records and little or no evidence of wilfull exaggeration was detected. It must of course be borne in mind that there was no segregation of small-pox cases and abundant opportunities existed for contagion in the prevailing social circumstances.

The vaccination campaign was unquestionably a most praiseworthy effort on the part of the military and civil public health organization. There was at first considerable resistance on the part of the public to vaccination and inoculation. One military officer engaged in the task was assaulted. Sometimes men would allow themselves to be inoculated or vaccinated, but would object to their womenfolk receiving the same treatment. Much tact and ingenuity were applied to bring home the necessity for protection against disease before its appearance. Public meetings were held in *thanas* and conferences with local influential officials arranged. Vaccinations and inoculations were often given at centres for more popular relief measures, *e.g.*, the distribution of food or clothing. Roads leading to markets were picketed and wayfarers induced to accept preventive treatment. By degrees prejudice was dispelled and people learnt to submit willingly to the procedure.

18. The military sub-divisional health officers played an important part in this as in other forms of health work. They superintended the work of the subordinate health staff and stimulated the latter to unwonted activity. They occupied, in fact, a pivotal position in the emergency health organization. We shall refer later to the permanent need for sub-divisional health officers as part of the health services of the province.

19. **Quinine.**—The distribution of anti-malarial drugs was thoroughly unsatisfactory. Previous to the Japanese war supplies of quinine needed by hospitals and dispensaries were purchased from Government by the local bodies concerned, and quinine for private patients was obtained through ordinary commercial channels. The conquest of Java cut off the main source of world supplies of quinine. Accordingly it became necessary to ration quinine in the various provinces and regulate its distribution. In Bengal, the Director of Public Health was responsible for the distribution of quinine to the districts, while District Magistrates were in charge of distribution within the district.

In 1943, reasonably good supplies were available with the Government of Bengal, but a large proportion of these failed to reach the districts. The officer who was Director of Public Health up to November 1943 stated in evidence before the Commission that demands for extra quinine were not received from the District Magistrates, and accordingly additional supplies were not sent. Within the districts quinine was not satisfactorily distributed and was found to be in short supply as the malaria epidemic rose to its peak in the later months of the year. One difficulty with regard to quinine distribution was its very high price in the black market, which reached Rs. 300 per pound. Not only famine victims but also well-to-do people were suffering from malaria; the latter were prepared to pay substantially for treatment. When quinine was sent to the districts it had to proceed under an armed guard, and when it reached district headquarters was placed under lock and key in the local gaol. A District Magistrate in need of quinine had to arrange for the armed guard to proceed to Calcutta. A more convenient arrangement would have been for an armed guard to set out from Calcutta with stocks for several districts and visit them in turn. Naturally these precautions to secure the inviolability of consignments of quinine, no doubt necessary, did not oil the wheels of distribution. The situation was reached at which there was a large and urgent demand for quinine, stocks were available in Calcutta and the districts and patients with malaria were dying for want of quinine. It was reckoned that in November 1943 there were about 43,000 lbs. of quinine available in Bengal undistributed.

20. Later the distribution of anti-malarial drugs was improved. Civil Surgeons were made responsible for distribution in districts in place of District Magistrates. Ultimately anti-malarial drugs became available for malaria patients in hospitals and dispensaries throughout the province. But even as late as the second half of 1944, in spite of numerous efforts, the general distribution of quinine was far from satisfactory. Quinine remained a substance of high financial value and the temptation to those who handled it to make sales on the black market remained. The Director of Public Health stated publicly in December 1943 that "a vast quantity of quinine issued by the Government had gone into the black market." He added that there was a bigger margin of profit on the sale of quinine than on the sale of mepacrine and that unscrupulous dealers were carrying on propaganda against the new synthetic drugs so that the public might keep on demanding quinine.

21. **The creation of hospital services.**—Reference has already been made to the sum total of achievement in this important branch of famine relief. A large number of emergency hospitals were constructed and staffed, in spite of many and serious difficulties. Previous to the famine, hospitals were not popular in rural Bengal. People were reluctant to enter them as in-patients, which is scarcely surprising in view of the low standard of nursing: In many hospitals there were no night nurses or attendants and a patient might die at night without attention. It is greatly to the credit of those responsible for the creation of the famine hospitals that the latter become popular, largely because they provided better medical care and nursing than had previously been available in local hospitals.

22. Certain criticisms of the emergency hospital organization must, however, be made. During the early stages of the famine, when things were at their worst, progress was slow. Conditions in certain famine hospitals at this time, notably the Behala hospital in Calcutta, were indescribably bad. Destitutes picked up in the streets were usually taken to the Behala hospital in the first instance. Visitors were horrified by the state of the wards and patients, the ubiquitous filth, and the lack of adequate care and treatment, in spite of their appreciation of the efforts of the nursing superintendent who was striving, against formidable odds, to alleviate these conditions. In the districts little was done during the early months. On September 20th, 1943, the Government issued general instructions to District Magistrates and Civil Surgeons, giving them full authority to build additional hospitals, to open up new wards in existing hospitals, and recruit the necessary additional staff. The districts were in fact given *carte blanche* to spend what was needed for emergency medical relief. The results were meagre. The hospital situation in the districts in the early stages of the famine is illustrated by the following extract from a report presented to the Commission:—

"Hospital accommodation was entirely inadequate to start with, both in town and country. Moreover, it was only in some of the larger towns that any proper hospitals existed. The condition of patients was usually appalling, a large proportion suffering from acute emaciation, with 'famine' diarrhoea. It was exceedingly difficult to improvise additional hospital accommodation, or to secure medical and nursing staff. Sanitary conditions in nearly all temporary indoor institutions were very bad to start with, owing to the insanitary habits of the inmates, lack of sweepers and inefficient supervision and management."

23. In November after the visit of the Viceroy and the arrival of the military there was a change in atmosphere. Medical officers of the Government of India and Bengal and military medical officers, working in collaboration, took the health situation in hand and drift was replaced by drive. Careful plans were drawn up for the construction, equipment and staffing of wards and hospitals and these were circulated to the districts. Under strong pressure the district authorities began to move. In a number of districts—Dacca and Faridpur are examples—progress in hospital construction was rapid and by January, 1944, the necessary hospital accommodation was available. In some, however, several months elapsed before effective action was taken. Such delays were due to various causes, including difficulties of supply and defects in the administrative machinery, and insufficient initiative on the part of the District Magistrates and Civil Surgeons concerned. There was also some lack of knowledge of the requirements of different districts. When plans were made certain districts were singled out as being most severely affected by the famine and their need for famine hospitals received special attention. As we have seen, a high excess mortality occurred in practically all districts during the first half of 1944, so that there was an urgent demand for medical relief almost everywhere in the province.

24. The obstacles encountered in getting the famine hospitals constructed and in working order are vividly described in the reports of touring medical officers presented to the Commission. In one place there would be difficulty in finding contractors and materials for building, in another lack of necessary drugs and equipment, in another shortage of satisfactory staff. Problems of transport and distribution were by no means entirely solved with the coming of the military. Many Civil Surgeons were unable or unwilling to exercise adequate supervision over the work of hospitals in their districts by frequent tours of inspection. The old sub-divisional hospitals, pressed into the service of famine relief, were found to be in many respects unsatisfactory. The opening of "satellite treatment centres" in association with dispensaries was on the whole an unsuccessful venture. The dispensary doctors, who had in-patients to look after in small emergency hospitals erected in the neighbourhood of dispensaries, did not give adequate attention to the "satellite centres".

25. The doctors recruited for famine work were in general of poor calibre. Their training had given them little knowledge and experience of hospital organization and little sense of duty and discipline. The young Indian army officers employed in medical relief were far more conscientious and efficient and did excellent work under difficult conditions. The poor standard of the civilian doctors must be ascribed largely to defects in their medical education. The army doctors had a very similar educational background, but after graduating had learnt orderly habits, discipline and teamwork as part of their military training. The difference between army and civilian doctors, which struck many observers during the famine, is hopeful in connection with the future development of medical services in India, since it shows that the standard of the medical profession could be decisively raised in a very short period by changes in medical education.

26. Up to November 1944, 25,551 and 203,702 patients were admitted to famine hospitals and wards in Calcutta and the districts respectively. For the mofussil hospitals these figures are from December 1943, but in the case of the Calcutta hospitals some admissions previous to that date are included. The number of deaths was 8,912 in Calcutta and 22,992 in the districts, 34·8 and 11·3 per cent. respectively of total admissions. These are very high hospital mortality rates and reflect the serious condition of the patients who received medical care. They also reflect the inadequacy of treatment in many hospitals.

The higher death rate in the Calcutta hospitals can be explained in various ways: in general the condition of destitutes who reached Calcutta from the districts during the famine was bad, and many were picked up in the streets in a moribund state and taken to hospital to die; in Calcutta most of the destitutes who were seriously ill reached hospital, while in the mofussil a larger proportion of such destitutes probably died without receiving hospital attention; the most acute phases of the medical emergency in Calcutta were during the months August to November, 1943, before the effort to put medical relief on a satisfactory basis was fully initiated.

27. **Provincialization of District Health Services.**—The famine emergency revealed the serious defects of the public health organisation in the districts. In certain other provinces, notably Madras, an improvement in the efficiency of health services has been produced by placing District Health Officers on a provincial cadre under the control of the Director of Public Health. The provincialization of district health services in Bengal was strongly urged by the Public Health Commissioner with the Government of India in November 1943, and at this stage the Government of Bengal was on the brink of action in the matter. The District Boards learnt, however, of the proposal to deprive them of the control of their health officers, and on December 21st a deputation of chairmen of District Boards met the Hon'ble Minister for Public Health and Local Self Government and protested against the impending move. The reasons for the proposal, the gravity of the public health situation, the necessity for vigorous and immediate action, were explained to the delegates who, however, argued strongly in support of the *status quo*. The Government acceded to their wishes, but obtained an assurance of complete co-operation with the Director of Public Health and a promise that the rates of pay for health personnel laid down by Government would be restored and enforced throughout the districts. An opportunity was thus given to the District Boards to prove their mettle under the old system. The Government asked the Director of Public Health to watch the situation and report any failure to fulfil the assurances given. Subsequent reports of the Director of Public Health showed that the state of district health organizations remained unsatisfactory in many respects.

In May 1944 the Government of India issued a Public Health (Emergency Provisions) Ordinance which gave power to take over the administration of health services. No action has, however, been taken with regard to the district health organization. The Commission has recommended that District Health Officers in Bengal should be enlisted in a provincial cadre, public health in Bengal being reorganized along the lines laid down in the Madras Public Health Act, 1939.

F.—Health services in Bengal and other Provinces.

28. A critical account has been given of the defects of the medical and public health services in Bengal and of their general failure to cope with the situation created by the famine. We do not wish to imply that such defects are peculiar to Bengal or that medical and health services in all other provinces, faced with similar emergency, would necessarily have acquitted themselves better. In certain provinces, medical and health services are organised on a more efficient basis than the Bengal services; in others they are not. All may deem themselves fortunate in having escaped the severe test to which those of Bengal were put.

G.—Destitute Kitchens.

29. The methods of feeding followed in the free kitchens have been severely criticised. There is no doubt that the quantity of food provided was below normal requirements—it was in fact a starvation ration. Apart from quantity, the food was unsatisfactory in nutritive quality, *e.g.*, in its content of protein

and vitamins. It was widely stated that the unfamiliar millets usually included in the gruel caused many deaths. In the districts recipients had often to walk 2-3 miles to obtain their 800 calories or less. The management of kitchens was not always what it should have been; abuse and corruption were far from infrequent.

On the other hand, the supply position during August to November 1943 made it difficult to provide a more satisfactory ration. There can be little doubt that the free kitchens run by Government and relief agencies, in spite of their shortcomings, did in fact save a large number of lives. Organized on a wide scale, they at least provided some food to many thousands of starving people. Many of the destitutes who made use of them could not, at least at the time when they first received relief in the form of food, have tolerated large meals. It is probable that most of the deaths ascribed to the inclusion of *bajra* and other millets in the gruel occurred in destitutes who were very weak and ill when they came to the kitchens. In the circumstances the swallowing of badly cooked gruel containing unfamiliar millets might produce intestinal irritation and precipitate famine diarrhoea and death. There is no evidence that this happened in any considerable number of starving destitutes. Those in a less desperate condition are unlikely to have suffered serious ill effects by consuming grains which are the staple food of many millions of healthy people in India. In other parts of India, healthy rice-eaters have been able to take millets without untoward results, beyond some intestinal discomfort during the first days or weeks of the change. In general reports of the ill effects produced by the gruel supplied by the kitchens seem to have been greatly exaggerated.

H.—Recovery and the future.

30. If an individual who has suffered from famine is freed from disease and given the right sort of food, physical recovery is usually rapid and complete. The rapidity with which starved children returned to normal when they were properly cared for and given good food often astonished relief workers. The restorative effect of milk was particularly striking. A child admitted into a home in a diseased and emaciated state could be transformed in a few months into a healthy and happy child, without any permanent physical scars.

While under such conditions individuals could quickly recover from the effects of starvation, it must be emphasized that in general the famine may produce serious after-effects in the sphere of public health. There was still much malnutrition among sections of the population in 1944. An impetus may have been given to various diseases previously present in Bengal. For some years tuberculosis has been on the increase and the famine has probably hastened its spread; while we could obtain no evidence on this point, the deduction seems justified from what is known of the epidemiology of tuberculosis. Kala-azar may also have become more prevalent. Again, the famine provided malaria parasites with remarkable opportunities for extending their range and the malaria problem is likely to be most formidable during the coming years.

31. In the circumstances considerable effort is needed, first to restore health to the low pre-famine level, and next to bring about general improvement. Health conditions in Bengal are likely to remain abnormal until the end of 1945 or for a longer period and the need for the additional organizations created for famine work has not disappeared. Further it is essential, in the interest of future development, that what has been gained should not be lost. We have referred to the inadequacy of the medical and health services in normal times No doubt there may be certain hospitals opened during the famine which are now no longer needed in the places in which they are located, and some of the additional health workers employed on special tasks in various famine areas may now appear to be superfluous. But Bengal as a whole needs more hospitals and health workers and every effort should be made to turn over the temporary

famine and medical relief organization to the permanent service of the province. For example, 40 military officers were still employed at the end of 1944 as sub-divisional health officers pending their replacement by suitable civilian officers. The military personnel cannot be indefinitely retained and it is important that these posts should not fall vacant. The sub-divisional health officers proved of the greatest value during the famine. It may be added that there are 84 sub-divisions in Bengal and a health officer in each sub-division is a reasonable objective.

It is not the responsibility of the Commission to define long-term health policies in Bengal. We have recommended that District Health Officers should come into a provincial cadre because this seems an immediate necessity. The reorganization of health and medical services in India is being considered by the Health Survey and Development Committee, and the report of that Committee will be available to guide the Government of Bengal in the future development of curative and preventive medicine.

I.—General Appreciation

32. The Bengal famine resulted in high mortality the basic cause of which was lack of food. The lethal epidemics of malaria, small-pox and cholera were associated in various ways with the famine and its disruptive influences on social life. The health situation which arose in 1943, was beyond the control of any health and medical service. The health and medical services in Bengal were, however, unfitted to meet the emergency because of defects in organization and inadequacy and inefficiency of staff, and some of the mortality which occurred could have been prevented by more vigorous and timely measures. During the famine period up to November 1943, there was almost a complete breakdown in the health services. In November the atmosphere of defeatism was partially dispelled and much effective work was subsequently done in the medical and public health spheres. Even at this later period, however, there were many unnecessary delays and failures. The story is, in fact, throughout one of belated efforts to bring the situation under control. This is said with full understanding of the numerous and formidable difficulties and full appreciation of all that was eventually done to overcome them.

CHAPTER V.—HEALTH IN OTHER PARTS OF INDIA.

1. The disastrous effect on the population of Bengal of lack of food has been described in detail. We shall now briefly inquire into the health position in the rest of India during the same period. During 1942-4 the food situation in various parts of the country gave rise to anxiety. Local shortages of various kinds of food occurred, and districts, in Bombay and Madras suffered from drought and came under the operation of the Famine Code. In general appropriate steps were taken by the governments concerned to prevent hunger and catastrophe was avoided. It is, however, important to ascertain whether the food situation in India outside Bengal has had any obvious effect on public health.

A. Birth rate.

2. The recorded birth-rate in British India remained steady at about 34 per *mille* from 1920 to 1940. In 1941 it fell to 32·1 and in 1942 to 29·4. In 1943 there was a remarkable fall to 25·6, a decline being recorded in all provinces. Of the major provinces, the largest recorded falls occurred in the following:

Province	Birth-rate 1938-42	Birth-rate 1943	Difference per cent
Bihar	28·6	18·2	– 10·4
Bengal	28·0	18·8	– 9·2
Bombay	37·2	29·7	– 7·5
Punjab	40·3	33·0	– 7·3
Assam	26·5	19·6	– 6·9
United Provinces	31·5	24·9	– 6·6

Relatively insignificant falls were recorded in the Central Provinces, Madras, Orissa and Sind.

Since population pressure has been held responsible for all the woes of India, a fall in the birth-rate must be regarded as an occurrence of great importance. With a population of 400 millions, a birth-rate of 34 per *mille* would add 13,600,000 babies to the population every year, while a rate of 26 per *mille* would add only 11,400,000 babies. The difference is 2,200,000, which is a very substantial difference. To the question whether the fall is a real one or a product of statistical omissions and fallacies we can only reply once more that vital statistics in India, whatever their inaccuracy, do indicate trends in the vital indices. Sources of error remain relatively constant from year to year. It can legitimately be concluded that a real fall has occurred, but its cause can be only a matter for speculation. In Bengal the fall in 1943 can be largely accounted for by the famine, but that occurring in other provinces is less easily explained. One of the major factors, in certain provinces at least, must be recruitment to the army and the transfer of male workers from rural to industrial areas usually without their families. If this is the main cause, it shows how strong the impact of the war has been on social life in India. There is little reason to suppose that, outside Bengal, shortage of food has been an important factor in the reduction of birth-rate. Thus, a striking fall occurred in the Punjab, which certainly has not suffered from food shortage—which has, in fact been more abundantly supplied with food than ever before. In the Punjab there has been heavy recruitment of young men for the army. In Bihar, where considerable industrial development has taken place, the recorded fall was greatest. In general no relationship can be elicited between the degree of fall in the various provinces and the prevailing food situation during 1942 and 1943.

B. Death rate.

3. The death rate returned for India in 1942 was 21·2 per *mille*, the lowest on record. Since the decade 1911-20, in which the recorded death-rate was about 34 per *mille*, there has been a fairly steady decline, with annual fluctuations. In 1943, there was a rise to 23·4, an increase, of 1·1 per *mille* over the 1938-42 average. This is largely accounted for by famine deaths in Bengal, but significant increases were reported in Orissa and Madras as follows:—

	Death-rate 1938-42	*Death-rate* 1943
Orissa	26·8	30·9
Madras	22·5	25·5

4. The Punjab showed a rise from 24·6 to 25·4, the main cause of which was a serious epidemic of malaria. In all other provinces there was a decline in 1943. A fall in the birth-rate must in ordinary circumstances lead to a fall in the death rate, since infant deaths make a heavy contribution to total mortality. Thus a rise in the death-rate in the age groups above infancy might be masked by a reduction in the number of infant deaths. Leaving aside, however, possibilities of this nature, it is clear that in the greater part of India in 1943 no gross deterioration in health conditions, reflecting itself in rise in the death rate, took place. The famine in Bijapur in Bombay was successfully handled and there was no abnormal mortality.

5. The province of Orissa demands more detailed consideration. Orissa is a surplus province as regards rice but purchases of rice by agents and merchants from Bengal during the free trade period pushed the price almost up to the Bengal level, so that in parts of Orissa, as in Bengal, the poor could not buy enough food. The total recorded number of deaths in Orissa in 1943 was 233,584, an increase of 17·9 per cent over the quinquennial average of 198,150. In the district of Balasore, bordering on Bengal, the increase in mortality was 40·7 per cent. In this district 1,105 deaths from starvation were recorded, but many of the victims were destitutes from Bengal. The rise in the death-rate in the province as a whole was due largely to epidemics of cholera and malaria, but there was also an increase in the number of deaths reported under the head "dysentery and diarrhoea". During the months August to December, 11,194 deaths were recorded as against a quinquennial average of 7,563. The Director of Public Health, Orissa, in giving evidence before the Commission, expressed the opinion that the increased mortality in Orissa in 1943 was due to food shortage, migration within the province, and the influx of destitutes from Bengal. Some of the latter died in Orissa and moreover they carried with them epidemic diseases which spread among the Oriyas. An increase in vitamin deficiency diseases was observed in 1943. The Director of Public Health also laid stress on the poor quality of the diet consumed by the bulk of the population in Orissa, even when rice is available in sufficient quantities. There is a serious shortage of milk, fish, pulses, and vegetables, and in normal times standards of nutrition are low.

6. Much of the excess mortality in Madras in 1943 can be ascribed to the severe cholera epidemic. The relation between cholera and food shortage has been discussed in a previous section. The Director of Public Health, Madras, informed the Commission that the cholera epidemic in 1943 spread from district to district in the usual manner of such epidemics. The very severe outbreak in Malabar waned in August 1943, without any improvement in the food situation. He felt that the appearance and spread of the disease could be explained on epidemiological grounds without particular reference to food scarcity. The famine in the Ceded Districts, which affected a large population, was kept under control by the operation of the Famine Code and was not accompanied by exceptional mortality. The economic condition of the people in this part of Madras is low even in the years intervening between recurrent famines, and in famine years the reduction in malaria incidence due to drought may offset other inimical health conditions. Study of mortality rates in the deficit district of Malabar, where rice supplies are short and the population has been strictly rationed at a low level of intake, shows that mortality was well above the average during the first 6 months of 1944 and that the increase was most marked in the age groups 5 to 10 and 10 to 15. The Commission is not in a position to make a detailed investigation of vital statistics in Madras with reference to the possible effect of the food situation on mortality. That task is the responsibilty of the Provincial Health Department. The effect of the food situation on health in Madras (as elsewhere in India) requires most careful watching, but at least it can be said that Madras has passed through the crisis of 1942-4 without catastrophic results in the health sphere.

7. No satisfactory mortality statistics for Cochin and Travancore are available for study. Evidence was presented to the Commission in Travancore of a fall in the weight of infants at birth and a fall in the weight of elementary school children, records of earlier years being used as the basis of comparison. It seems probable that under-nutrition and malnutrition are responsible for the change observed. Here again it is essential that the health authorities should keep a vigilant watch on health conditions and report any evidence of deterioration.

8. In Bihar there were no abnormal health conditions in 1943 and the death rate was below the quinquennial average. In 1944 severe epidemics of malaria and small-pox broke out in North Bihar and the serious public health situation in this area was ascribed to malnutrition by certain newspapers and political leaders. The Commission had no opportunity of visiting Bihar to study the position. No evidence has however been put before it in support of the view that the outbreak of epidemic disease was associated with food shortage and malnutrition.

9. While there is no statistical evidence that food shortage had led to a serious increase in mortality outside Bengal and Orissa, it must be emphasized that the study of mortality rates is a crude method of investigating the effect of the food situation on health. The possibility that the health of certain groups in the population has been adversely affected cannot be dismissed. During recent years some sections have consumed more food than before the war. The high price of grain has enabled villagers to pay their dues by selling a smaller proportion of their produce than formerly and thus retain more for their own use. Large groups of workers in industry are being paid high wages which allow them to increase their intake of food. In some industrial areas cereal supplies for workers are heavily subsidized, while in others very substantial dearness allowances, which more than cover the increase in the price of grain, are being paid. On the other hand there are groups whose wages have not risen proportionately to the rise in the cost of living, *e.g.*, lower middle class people in clerical and other occupations, and their health may have

suffered through restriction in diet. In a broad survey of health conditions, deterioration in one group may be masked by improvement in another.

10. Special reference must be made to the high cost and scarcity of protective foods such as milk, fish and vegetables. The intake of such foods on the part of the poorer classes in general is low in normal times. Among certain groups it has been further reduced by high prices. Lower middle class families cannot afford to buy protective foods even in the limited quantities to which they were accustomed before the war. This is bound, in the long run, to lower standards of health and careful investigation would probably reveal that some deterioration has already taken place. It is of the utmost importance that the food problem of India should not be regarded solely as a problem of providing enough cereals and distributing them equitably so that everybody gets enough to eat. The objective must be the provision of a well balanced diet containing protective foods in adequate amounts.

11. **Recommendations.**—The Commission recommends that District Health Officers should be brought into a provincial cadre under the control of the Director of Public Health, for reasons which have been made clear in the preceding chapters. With regard to the status and duties of health officers, we are of the opinion that legislation along the lines of the Madras Public Health Act, 1939, is desirable. We do not feel it incumbent on us to make specific recommendations about the reorganization of health and medical services in general, which includes such questions as the status of subordinate health personnel in the districts. The nature of the health and medical organization required to meet the needs of Bengal is a problem for detailed consideration by experts. We have referred to the Health Survey and Development Committee which is concerned with the health problems of India and will deal with provincial requirements and organization in respect of medical and health services. We have no doubt that the Government of Bengal will give their full attention to the recommendations of this Committee.

12. We commend the steps which are being taken to provincialize hospitals at district and sub-divisional headquarters. The state of local hospitals revealed by the famine indicates the need for this measure.

13. Our terms of reference include "the provision of emergent medical relief and the emergent arrangements for the control of epidemics in those areas and in those aspects in which the present system may be found to be faulty". These questions have been dealt with in the chapters on "Death and Disease". We have shown that satisfactory "emergent medical relief" depends on the existence of a satisfactory organization in normal times. This applies, not only to Bengal, but to the whole of India. Apart from any possible danger of a recurrence of famine, the need for the improvement and development of health and medical services in Bengal is indeed obvious.

14. In conclusion we may add that, whatever future advances are planned, the need for the existing emergency medical and health organization will persist until the end of 1945, and possibly for a considerably longer period. We may further point out, that not only should there be no premature retrenchment, but that full use should be made of developments during the famine as a foundation for further progress.

PART III

FOOD ADMINISTRATION & REHABILITATION IN BENGAL

CHAPTER I.—THE SYSTEM OF SUPPLY AND DISTRIBUTION

A.—Supplies and Prices after the Famine.

1. The famine of 1943, ended with the harvesting of the *aman* crop in December of that year. This crop was probably the largest in the history of Bengal. The following table shows the acreage and yield of the *aman* crop reaped in December 1943, as compared with that of the preceding two years according to estimates made by the Government of Bengal:

The Aman Crop

Year	Acreage (in million acres)	Yield (in million tons)
1941	16·91	7·40
1942	16·21	5·02
1943	18·18	8·53

According to these figures the *aman* crop acreage increased by 1·27 million acres in 1943, as compared with 1941. The figures are, however, not comparable because the method of estimating the acreage was changed in 1943. As we have explained the normal acreage assumed for statistical purposes in the past does not agree with the acreage as recorded in the settlement records and in consequence there has been a systematic under-estimation of the acreage of the *aman* crop.[1] We have been told that in preparing the estimate for the *aman* crop reaped at the end of 1943, an attempt was made to correct the acreage figures with reference to the figures given in the settlement records. The revised acreage is, however, still below the settlement figure of 19·22 million acres and hence we think that probably it is even now an under-estimate. We understand that with a view to obtaining accurate agricultural statistics the Government of Bengal have recently sanctioned two schemes: one, a plot to plot enumeration of all crops and the other a random sample survey of the jute, *aman*, and the *aus* crops. It is proposed to continue both surveys for a period of three years and then to decide on future policy. The cost is heavy, being Rs. 43 lakhs in the first year and Rs. 31 lakhs in each of the two succeeding years. We trust that as a result of this large expenditure accurate figures of acreage will be obtained.

2. As we have said, the *aman* crop reaped in December 1943, was an excellent one. During 1944 the supply position was satisfactory and the Government of Bengal were able to accumulate, by the end of the year, a reserve stock of over 600,000 tons of rice and paddy in terms of rice. It is unlikely that the whole of the surplus passed into the hands of the Government and if that be so, the carry-over at the beginning of 1945 was in all probability equal to several weeks' supply. The *aman* crop reaped in December 1944, was not as good as the bumper crop of the previous year and according to the estimates prepared by the Government of Bengal, the yield of the former is less by 1·44 million tons than that of the latter. It is probable, however, that this reduction will be offset by the increase in the carry-over at the beginning of 1945, as compared with that at the beginning of 1944.

[1] Para 9 of Appendix II.

3. The bumper *aman* crop was the principal factor in the restoration of confidence and the fall in prices during 1944. There were also other factors. The Government of India undertook the responsibility of providing Bengal with a supply of rice sufficient for the needs of Greater Calcutta during 1944. This was obtained from other parts of India under the Basic Plan. This arrangement was made in order to help in the restoration of normal conditions by taking the Calcutta demand completely off the Bengal market. In 1943 the Calcutta demand had been the largest single disturbing factor in that market. Rationing was introduced into Greater Calcutta in 1944. Employers whose employees number a thousand or more, were prohibited from purchasing rice and paddy for supply to their employees except through Government. Rice mills were brought under control and prohibited from selling rice except to the procurement organization of the Government, or under permit, to a limited number of approved wholesale dealers. All employers of labour supplying foodgrains to their employees were prohibited from having in their possession, except under permit, more than two months' requirements of rice and paddy. Consumer stocks were limited by an order forbidding any person, other than a producer or a trader licensed under the Foodgrains Control Order, holding more than 20 maunds of rice and paddy without a permit. Exports from surplus districts were prohibited. A procurement organization was established for making purchases on behalf of Government in order to meet the requirements of the deficit areas, for making supplies to employers of labour who were prohibited from making private purchases, and to build up a provincial reserve. Finally, the organization for the general enforcement of food controls was developed during the year.

4. The system of price control by the fixation of maximum prices, introduced in August 1943, continued during 1944. These prices were successfully lowered at relatively short intervals. Two sets of statutory maxima are now in force in different areas of the province. They are as shown below:

Price per maund.

	Rice.	Paddy.
	Rs. a. p. Rs. a. p.	Rs. a. p. Rs. a. p.
Wholesale traders .	13 8 0 and 14 12 0	7 8 0 and 8 4 0
Agriculturists . .	12 12 0 and 14 0 0	7 4 0 and 8 0 0

On the reaping of the *aman* crop market prices fell sharply from the abnormal levels of 1943. Thereafter they remained fairly steady until about August 1944, when there was a further fall. At the end of the year they were approximately at the same level as at the end of 1942.

B.—Conditions in the Immediate Future

5. Conditions in Bengal during 1944 were specially favourable in two respects. One was the bumper *aman* crop reaped in December 1943, and the other was the special arrangements made by the Government of India for supplying the needs (rice) of Greater Calcutta from other parts of India. It is necessary to realize the exceptional character of these two factors and to be sure that food administration in Bengal is so organized, that it will function effectively under less favourable conditions. It is true that there is a tendency for the rice acreage to increase—this may be maintained in view of the prevailing prices —but it is unlikely that the yield per acre of the *aman* crop during the next few years will be as high as it was in December 1943. Again, lean years consequent on poor *aman* crops appear to occur regularly in Bengal. The sequence in the past has been 1928, 1936, 1941 and 1943. It cannot be said when the next lean year will occur. We may hope that it will be long in coming, but it would be imprudent to assume that such an event will not happen before

imports of rice from abroad once again become available on the same scale as before the war.

6. The supplying of rice for Calcutta from other parts of India in 1944 was recognized at the time to be a special arrangement. It has since been decided that this arrangement will not continue in 1945, and allocations under the Basic Plan will be made to Bengal in the same manner as to other provinces and states, that is, with reference to their actual need for imports. This does not, of course, mean that Calcutta will not receive supplies from other parts of India. As regards wheat the necessary allotments will be made. In respect of rice the needs of Bengal will be reviewed at appropriate intervals by the Government of India, in consultation with the Government of Bengal, and allocations, if necessary, made from the stocks available to the Government of India under the Basic Plan. In making these allocations due regard will be paid to any special circumstances arising in Bengal from its proximity to the war zone, as well as to the special needs of other parts of India. It is, however, clearly necessary that Bengal should make the fullest use of its own resources. During 1944 much was done towards the improvement of food administration in Bengal. Rationing of Calcutta was a major advance. The results of procurement have been satisfactory and Government have been able to build up a large reserve of rice and paddy. But there is still room for improvement in the organization which has been developed for procurement specifically and for the enforcement of controls generally, before it can be regarded as adequate to meet more difficult conditions than those prevailing during 1944. We shall now consider the improvements required.

C.—Urban Rationing

7. Apart from Greater Calcutta which includes the cities of Calcutta, Howrah, and 30 other municipal towns, with a total population of about 4 millions, the only towns in which a true system of rationing has been introduced are Chittagong and Kurseong. In a considerable number of other towns "partial rationing" schemes are in force. These, however, are not true rationing schemes for, every person, in addition to the ration he draws from Government supplies, is free to obtain further foodgrains from the ordinary retail shops. There is also no restriction on private trade in rationed foodgrains. What these schemes seek to assure is a minimum ration, generally of 2 seers per adult person per week, and even that is not guaranteed, for it is liable to be reduced if Government stocks are inadequate.

8. We attach great importance to the rationing of the urban population and Bengal, in this matter, has lagged considerably behind many provinces. We note that even Dacca, a town with a population of over 200,000, has not been rationed. We recommend that the Provincial Government should undertake as rapidly as possible the rationing of every truly urban centre. Many of the small municipal towns in Bengal are in reality only overgrown villages and include within their boundaries a considerable amount of agricultural land. We do not suggest that these small towns which are, strictly speaking, not urban areas, should be rationed. It would not be worth while. What we propose is that the rationing of towns with a population of about 25,000 or more should be carried out as quickly as possible and that, thereafter, in the light of the experience gained, a decision should be taken whether towns with a smaller population should also be rationed.

D.—Enforcement

9. **The Foodgrains Control Order.**—We regard this Order as a most important weapon in the armoury of food administration in Bengal, for it is the only means by which the stocks in the hands of traders can be watched and controlled. It has, however, not been administered efficiently in Bengal. We consider that

immediate steps should be taken to enforce the provisions of the Order strictly. This will entail drastic action, for the registers are at present encumbered by the names of thousands of persons who are not traders by profession. Originally, licences were not granted to new entrants in the trade, or to those who had been in business for less than three years, unless the District Magistrate was satisfied that a public purpose would be served by granting the licence. In May 1943 when free trade was introduced into the Eastern Region, these restrictions were removed and orders were issued that the licensing authority "should issue licences freely to new entrants to business and to those who have been in the trade, irrespective of the period during which they have been in business, provided the applicants are able to satisfy the licensing authority that they have made arrangements for carrying on business, and possess storage accommodation, and have an office where accounts will be kept and business transacted". We understand that this step was taken because of the great need for obtaining the maximum amount of supplies from outside the province. The result was the issue of thousands of new licences. In one district which a Member of the Commission visited, out of 3,500 licensees over 2,000 had not submitted any return for many months. In these conditions efficient administration is impossible. We consider it very important that drastic steps should be taken without delay to restore order out of this chaos.

10. **Embargoes.**—The enforcement of embargoes round surplus districts prohibiting the export of rice and paddy, except under permit, presents special difficulty in many parts of Bengal because of the large number of rivers and *khals*. Control of transport by rail and river steamer is a simple matter and that of movement by road does not present great difficulty. But the control of country boat traffic, when that traffic, as in Bengal, travels by innumerable rivers and *khals*, throws a heavy burden on the administration. There is little doubt that cordons round many of the surplus districts are not effective because the country boat traffic is not properly controlled. And yet procurement will suffer unless these cordons are enforced strictly. A large staff is essential but an increase in staff will not of itself solve the problem. The staff, particularly the supervisory staff, must also be provided with adequate transport, that is, with launches, if success is to be achieved in controlling country boat traffic. In the riverine districts of Bengal, launches are just as essential for the efficiency of administration as are motor cars in areas where communication is by road. We realise the difficulty of obtaining launches for the civil administration under conditions imposed by the war, but we trust that it will be possible for arrangements to be made by which a reasonably adequate number of launches are made available to the Government of Bengal. It should then be possible for the Provincial Government to enforce these cordons effectively.

E.—Requisitioning

11. We attach great importance to requisitioning. We consider it essential that Government should be prepared to undertake requisitioning as and when necessary, whether from traders or from producers, if the flow of supplies is not maintained by voluntary sales. If it were practicable to adopt in Bengal monopoly procurement schemes on the lines of those in force in Bombay and Madras, requisitioning as a separate measure would be unnecessary. The compulsory sale of the levy quota in Bombay and the assessed surplus in Madras is a form of requisitioning. It is the impracticability of adopting such schemes which makes requisitioning in Bengal a matter of such importance.

12. One point should be made clear at this stage. When we speak of requisitioning from the producer we are not thinking of requisitioning from the cultivator who has a small surplus over and above his own needs. That we regard as not only impracticable but also dangerous. The compulsory purchase of the surplus of such a producer is only possible where means exist for making a reasonably correct estimate of the crop he has reaped and of the needs of

himself and his family. In Bengal the agency for making such an assessment does not exist. What we contemplate, therefore, is not the requisitioning of the surplus of the small, but of the large cultivator. In practice, requisitioning will be limited to holdings with an acreage above a prescribed minimum.

13. If requisitioning is to be successful it must be prepared for in advance. This is particularly necessary in Bengal where, owing to the absence of village records and a village revenue establishment, particulars are not readily available as regards large cultivators. We understand that the District Enforcement Staff has been directed to collect information, but, so far as we could learn, little progress has been made. It is important that plans for requisitioning should be kept in readiness. What is required is a list of large cultivators so that, should requisitioning become necessary, information will be ready at hand as regards potential "hoarders". It will be impossible to prepare these lists in secret and we think it would be a mistake to attempt to maintain secrecy. If Government are prepared to undertake requisitioning it is desirable that the public should not be kept in ignorance of Government's policy and should realise why requisitioning may be necessary. Like every other activity of food administration it is essential that the policy of requisitioning should have the support of public opinion. Only then can it be successful. The hoarder must not be in a position to rely upon public sympathy. Public opinion must make him realize that hoarding grain is anti-social. Indeed, the more village opinion condemns the holding up of stocks the less need there will be for requisitioning. We attach, therefore, importance to propaganda directed to explaining Government's policy in regard to requisitioning.

14. Although occasions may occur in which requisitioning on a wide scale may be necessary and indeed imperative, we trust that these will be rare of absent. We regard general requisitioning as an extreme measure that should be resorted to only in a grave emergency such as that arising from an exceptionally poor crop. On the other hand, we regard individual requisitioning as part of the normal procedure of procurement, that is to say, as a measure which should be taken whenever, in an area, the flow of grain to the markets is slowing down owing to large cultivators holding back their stocks. This policy has been adopted with success in other provinces, for instance in the Central Provinces and Madras. In the main rice producing areas of Madras, as in Bengal, procurement normally depends upon voluntary sales by the cultivators. Usually, no difficulty is experienced during the months immediately following the harvest. Later in the year, however, the flow of grain slows down and at such times the Grain Purchase Officers have been authorized to resort to requisitioning. We understand that requisitioning, or even the threat of requisitioning, of the surplus stocks of a relatively small number of individuals usually has the desired effect. The practice is that the cultivator whose grain is requisitioned is given the option to enter into a voluntary contract for the sale of his surplus within a reasonable time after the service of the requisitioning notice. This procedure has worked satisfactorily and, in the large majority of cases, the cultivator sells his grain voluntarily and compulsory acquisition proves unnecessary.

15. We understand that the Bengal Government are considering a proposal that the large cultivator should be brought within the scope of the Foodgrains Control Order. We support that proposal. Although we have recommended that lists of large cultivators should be prepared, we recognize that their preparation, in the absence of village records showing the areas held by individual cultivators, will not be such a simple operation as would at first sight appear. Extensive and intensive inquiries will be necessary and if the lists are to be accurate the work of the staff engaged on the inquiries will require close supervision. Finally, even when the lists have been prepared it will be necessary, prior to the issue of requisition notices, to decide which cultivators have hoarded

their stocks. This will necessitate further inquiries. There is an administrative advantage, therefore, in a procedure which places upon the large cultivator the duty of submitting returns. It is also possible that an obligation to submit returns may of itself discourage him from holding back his surplus grain. He will realize, provided there is an adequate inspection staff, that he is under continual observation. Again we understand that the large cultivator is sometimes also a trader and that, by reason of being a producer, he evades the provisions of the Foodgrains Control Order. We recognize, of course, that the number of cultivators who are required to submit returns should not be unwieldy. It has been suggested that the numbers would not be too large if a limit of 25 acres was adopted, that is to say, if those who cultivate 25 acres or more of land were brought under the scope of the Order.

16. Requisitioning of stocks may be necessary not only in the case of the large cultivator; action may also have to be taken against the trader. But such action will not be possible, except in a haphazard manner, unless up-to-date records of stocks are maintained. This can only be ensured by the efficient administration of the Foodgrains Control Order to which we have already referred.

F.—Rice Mills

17. Rice mills constitute a most important part of the procurement machine, for they form "bottle necks" through which paddy, except in so far as it is hand-pounded, passes in order to emerge as rice. Their efficient use in procurement schemes therefore is of the greatest importance. In Madras, Bombay, and the Central Provinces rice mills are under official control. We were not able to visit the rice-producing areas in Bombay and the Central Provinces, but from what we heard from official as well as non-official witnesses, we are satisfied that the system of official supervision has been a success in those provinces and that the co-operation of the rice millers has been obtained. In Madras we were able to visit two of the important rice purchasing centres, Bezwada and Tanjore, and had the opportunity of acquainting ourselves with the working of the system in that province. There too official control has operated with ease and success. The main rice surplus areas of Madras are in the north and south deltas and comprise seven districts which are well supplied with rice mills. Practically all the purchases by the official purchasing agents, Grain Purchase Officers, are made from the mills in these districts. The Grain Purchase Officers, who are selected Deputy Collectors belonging to the Provincial Service, are five in number and each is in charge of a separate area. During the period December 1942 to October 1943, the purchases made by these officers amounted to 721,000 tons, and during the ten months from November 1943 to August 1944, to 700,000 tons. The staff employed is not large and consists of 5 grain Purchase Officers, 5 Grain Movement Officers, 29 *Tahsildars* and Deputy *Tahsildars*, 66 Food Inspectors, Marketing Assistants, Grain Purchase Supervisors, etc., and 166 Clerks.

The cost to Government is very low. At the Bezwada centre the cost (excluding pensions) is about 3 pies per maund of rice purchased, while that at Tanjore is only about 1 pie per maund. Again, milling charges are not high, being about 11 annas a maund, including profit, in the southern delta, and about one anna less in the northern delta. The mills are closely supervised by the Grain Purchase Officers' staff throughout all the milling processes in order to ensure that quality is maintained and the under-milling order complied with. We visited several of the mills and found rice, both in store and in the course of production, to be of good quality. We understand, however, that at an earlier stage the quality of rice obtained from the mills and distributed by the Grain Purchase Organization, left much to be desired.

18. An important feature of the scheme is the manner in which storage difficulties have been avoided. Monthly quotas are allotted to deficit districts.

certain Indian States, the Defence Services, and the Railways, and are distributed among the Grain Purchase Officers. Each of these officers, therefore, knows the monthly demands which he has to meet and regulates his purchases from the mills accordingly. Deficit districts are supplied by merchants selected by District Officers and these merchants are also allotted monthly quotas. The merchants apply to the Grain Purchase Officer and deposit the cost of the rice in advance. The Grain Purchase Officer arranges with a mill for the delivery of the consignment at the despatching point where it is inspected by the merchant. The miller is paid after the merchant has accepted the consignment. The same procedure is followed as regards purchases for the Indian States, the Railways, and the Defence Services. The Grain Purchase Officer accepts no responsibility for transport but he keeps the railway authorities informed of probable despatches and assists the exporting merchants as far as possible. The system has worked successfully. Storage accommodation, beyond that provided by the mills, has not been found necessary and the demands for transport have been spread out uniformly throughout the year.

19. In Bengal, rice mills are under the control and supervision of the Chief Agents and it is they who are responsible for the inspection of the milling processes, for taking delivery of the rice and for making payments. The Bengal Rice Millers' Association gave evidence before us and it is clear from what they told us that the rice millers are suffering under a sense of grievance. They said quite frankly that they object to being placed under the control of other members of the trade, that is the Chief Agents. They urged that if the rice milling industry must be controlled by the State, control should be exercised directly through Government officials and not through private firms. They regarded this as a matter of principle and maintained that the present system was bound to lead to friction and misunderstanding. It is essential that the full co-operation of the Bengal rice millers should be obtained and, after our visits to other provinces, we have no hesitation in recommending that Bengal should, as regards the control and supervision of rice mills, fall into line with other provinces. We realize that the Bengal Government fear that Government officers will not be able to deal with the rice miller as efficiently as the Chief Agents have done. but if Government officers in other provinces are able to accomplish this task with success we see no reason why Government officers in Bengal should not be able to protect Government interests and at the same time deal fairly with the mills. The rice millers made no complaint against the Chief Agents individually It is of course possible, indeed probable, that their views are influenced by circumstances in which, rightly or wrongly, they feel that they have not had a fair deal at the hands of the Chief Agents. We realise that personal differences between the millers and the Chief Agents may have strengthened the former's view in favour of direct relations with the Government instead of through the Chief Agents. But, quite apart from the possibility of individual cases of friction and misunderstanding, we take the view that the proper course is for the mills in Bengal to be brought directly under official control. As we have said, we see no reason, in the light of experience in other provinces, why officials in Bengal should not be able to exercise efficient supervision and control over rice mills.

20. In relation to the size of the crop, the number of rice mills in Bengal is small as compared with that in Bombay, Madras, the Central Provinces, Sind, and the Punjab. Further, in Bengal the mills are unevenly distributed. The surplus rice districts in West Bengal are well provided with mills and a large number are concentrated in and around Greater Calcutta. On the other hand, the majority of the surplus districts in East and North Bengal are badly provided with mills. For instance, Khulna has only nine very small mills, and Jalpaiguri only seven, of which only one has a capacity of over 500 maunds a day. Bakarganj, another heavy surplus district in East Bengal, has 64 mills but only

12 have a capacity of over 200 maunds a day. We understand that the Bengal Government are considering a proposal for the better distribution of rice mills either by the transfer of existing mills or by the erection of new ones. We agree that a better distribution of mills would be advantageous from the point of view of procurement. There is one point, however, to which special attention should be drawn. Hand-pounding of rice is a village industry of considerable importance in the rural economy of the province. Roughly one half of the market supply is dehusked by manual labour in the villages. We attach importance to the maintenance and extension of village industries. Hand-pounding of rice is a small industry specially suited to rural conditions in Bengal; it provides employment for a large number of landless persons and serves as a subsidiary means of livelihood for the smaller cultivator. We accordingly recommend that in any plan for increasing the total output of milled rice as opposed to one for redistributing existing mills, the existence of this important village industry should not be overlooked.

G.—Monopoly Procurement

21. Schemes under which the producer is required by law to sell the whole or a part of his surplus grain to Government are in operation in several of the provinces and states in India. An officer of the Food Department of the Government of India, who recently made a tour of the provinces and states in which "monopoly" schemes are in operation, has made the following observations in his report:—

"It is interesting and important to observe that in those areas which have gone forward towards a Government monopoly, there is not one single instance where any doubt is felt that the basic principle is right. In no case is there any thought of withdrawing even to a minor degree. On the contrary, the tendency is quite the reverse and in virtually every case the determined policy is to go forward to make the monopoly more complete."

We visited several provinces and states in which "monopoly" schemes are in force and our inquiries point to the same conclusion. Where such schemes exist they appear to be working on the whole satisfactorily, though no doubt they will be further improved as experience is gained. The advantage of "monopoly" procurement is that it enables the authorities to ensure a more equitable distribution of the available food resources. We shall now describe the schemes in operation in the Madras and Bombay Presidencies and then decide, in the light of conditions in Bengal, whether they are suitable for introduction into that province.

22. **Bombay.—The failure of the voluntary system.**—Up to the spring of 1944 procurement operations in the Bombay Presidency depended upon voluntary sales by the producer. During 1943 District Officers made purchases locally. Purchases were, however, not on an extensive scale and in the autumn of that year the Provincial Government came to the conclusion that if black markets were to be eliminated and the food resources of the Presidency equitably distributed it was essential that a more extensive scheme of procurement should be adopted. They, therefore, announced their intention to purchase 10 per cent of the millet production and 25 per cent of the rice production. The scheme was of a "voluntary" character and cultivators were under no obligation to sell any portion of their produce to Government. The scheme was only partly successful and the quantity procured fell short of the target figure. This was attributed to lack of co-operation on the part of the big landlord and the large cultivator. The failure of this scheme led the Bombay Government to adopt in the spring of 1944 a scheme of monopoly of purchase and distribution

23. **The Bombay Monopoly Scheme.**—The main elements of this scheme are—

(a) a compulsory and graded levy from the cultivator of a portion of his surplus grain; the levy quota must be sold to Government;

(b) a Government monopoly of purchase of whatever the cultivator sells over and above the levy quota;

(c) strict control over movements; and

(d) a Government monopoly of distribution in all rural and urban areas.

In 1944 the scheme was introduced into three districts. In spite of certain difficulties experienced in its actual working, it was considered to have worked successfully and it has been decided to extend the scheme, subject to certain modifications in the method of calculating the levy, to all areas in the province where rice is not the predominant crop.

No private trade in a monopoly foodgrain is allowed except that the producer is permitted to sell, within the village, retail quantities for the *bona fide* consumption of the buyer and his family. All movement beyond the village boundary is prohibited except under permit. Government is entirely responsible for distribution and both rural and urban areas are rationed. In the rural areas family ration cards are issued to those who have no stocks and those whose stocks are inadequate to last them till the next crop is reaped. Rations are drawn from controlled shops, and in the rural areas these shops are so situated that no villager has to go more than 5 miles for his supplies.

The District Officer, with the assistance of the revenue staff—this has been strengthened considerably—is in charge of the procurement and distribution operations. In most districts purchases are effected by Government officers directly from the producer. In some districts, however, co-operative societies are entrusted with the task of making purchases and in others, traders are employed as purchasing agents on a commission basis.

Under the system of land revenue administration in Bombay, complete and up-to-date records are maintained by the village accountant for each village and it is primarily on the basis of these records that the levy is calculated. The prices paid by Government for the grain purchased from the cultivator are fixed and remain in force for the whole crop year.

24. **Madras.**—The District of Malabar is a heavily deficit area in regard to rice, the staple foodgrain. Formerly it drew a large proportion of its supplies from Burma. The Madras Government have not been able to supply rice to the full extent of the needs of the district and in order to ensure a satisfactory distribution of the total supplies available from internal and external sources, a scheme of monopoly of purchase and distribution was introduced in the district in October 1944. The main features of this scheme are two. First, the cultivator is required to sell the whole of his assessed surplus, not only a proportion of it, as in Bombay, to Government at the notified price, and secondly, the entire population of the district is rationed.

No private trade whatsoever in monopoly foodgrains is permitted and all movement beyond the village boundary is prohibited. In view of the shortage of supplies, the ration has been limited to 12 ounces of foodgrains per adult per day instead of the normal figure of 1 lb per adult per day. This standard of 12 ounces has also been adopted for the purpose of determining the quantity which the producer is allowed to retain for his own consumption.[1] As in Bombay the District Officer is in charge of procurement and distribution. Purchases are, however, not made by Government officers but by local traders acting as government agents. The distribution of foodgrains to the licensed retailers

[1] It is understood that this amount has recently been increased.

is also made by approved local traders. The assessment of the surplus with each producer is made by the village accountant under the supervision and direction of the district revenue staff. The prices paid to the cultivator for his surplus produce are fixed by Government.

25. For the successful working of a monopoly scheme on the lines of those in force in Bombay and Madras, it is imperative that Government should possess an agency which can (a) prepare a reasonable and accurate assessment of the crop reaped by each cultivator; (b) can purchase and collect the quota due from each cultivator or in the alternative, supervise and, if necessary enforce the sale of that quota to approved purchasing agents; and (c) can undertake the distribution of supplies to the whole population other than those who grow sufficient grain for their own needs. In Bombay and Madras (and in other parts of India where similar monopoly schemes are in operation), the foundation for this agency exists in the form of a highly developed revenue administration. As we have explained in Chapter II, this administration consists of, first a revenue staff in each village or group of villages charged with the maintenance of village records, and secondly, a staff of revenue officers whose duty it is to assist, supervise, and control the village staff. There is no such staff in Bengal, nor can it be brought into being within a reasonable time. Its recruitment and training would certainly be a matter of years, and we are of the opinion that any attempt to improvise such a staff within a short time would result in failure. It is not only a question of appointing and training thousands of officers. The subordinate revenue staff in the provinces of Bombay and Madras has been in existence for many years and possesses great influence and authority among the villagers. But that influence and authority cannot be acquired in a day. And finally there is the question of cost. The charge would be a very heavy one. We see no prospect, therefore, of the successful introduction into Bengal of monopoly schemes of purchase on the lines of those in operation in the provinces of Bombay and Madras.

26. In Orissa, and the Central Provinces and Berar, schemes are in operation which, while they do not require the producer to sell the whole or part of his surplus grain to Government, create in favour of Government a limited monopoly of purchase over the marketable surplus, that is, over that part of the crop which the producer brings for sale to the market. Under these schemes, as in Bengal, sales by the producer are voluntary. Where they differ from the Bengal system is that Government acquire not only a monopoly of purchase of all the rice produced by the rice mills but also a limited monopoly over that part of the marketable surplus which does not pass through the mills. We shall now describe these schemes and then consider whether they are suitable for introduction in Bengal.

27. **Orissa.**—The scheme which has been in operation in Orissa since the harvesting of the rice crop in 1943, aims at directing the flow of all rice and paddy sold in wholesale quantities into the hands of Government. It has three essential features. First, the prices of rice and paddy which the producers are entitled to demand and receive, have been fixed for the whole of the crop year. Secondly, purchase or sale by any person, whether a cultivator or not, of any quantity of rice or paddy exceeding 10 maunds in any one transaction has been prohibited unless it be by or to a Government agent.[1] Thirdly, no person holding a licence under the Foodgrains Control Order is entitled to hold a stock of more than 100 maunds of rice and paddy at any one time unless he is an agent or a sub-agent of the Government.[1] The object of the exemption of the purchase and sale of quantities up to 10 maunds in a single transaction is to enable purchases and sales to continue unhampered at the small village markets and elsewhere as an essential part of the system of distribution in the

[1] **It is understood that these limits have since been reduced.**

province. Purchases are made by agents selected from the trade. Each agent makes purchases in a definite area and in order to bring the purchasing agency within easy reach of the cultivator, the agents have been encouraged to appoint sub-agents. The agent is responsible not only for the purchase of foodgrains but also for custody, packing, and safe storage. Purchases are, as far as possible, spread over 8 months of the crop year. The District Officer is in charge of all the operations. We understand that this scheme has been on the whole successful and that the target figure, which includes a provincial reserve, has been achieved.

28. **The Central Provinces.**—In the rice producing areas paddy is brought to the mills and rice to the markets by the small trader and to some extent by the primary producer. Paddy is either sold outright to the miller or, after being milled on a commission basis, is sold in the market. In other areas where mills are few in number, hand-pounded rice is also sold in the market. Under normal conditions, rice in the markets is bought partly by local retail dealers but chiefly by the larger dealers either for export to the consuming areas, or resale to other dealers for export. The millers are frequently wholesale traders and exporters, but in certain areas they sell their rice in the main markets. Normally therefore it is either at the mills or at the market that rice passes into the hands of the large wholesale dealer and it is at this point that the Government monopoly of purchase normally comes into operation. The actual sanction by which this monopoly is effected is by an order under clause 4 of the Central Provinces and Berar Foodgrains (Control of Distribution) Order prohibiting any person from selling rice at places specified in the Order except to Government or their agents. The monopoly extends only to rice and not to paddy.

When the scheme was first introduced, it was found that, on the issue of an order giving Government the monopoly of purchase at an established market, sellers, in order to avoid selling to Government at the controlled price, transferred their operations to places outside the declared markets. To prevent this evasion these places were treated as market equivalents and an order passed prohibiting sales at these places otherwise than to Government. The number of such places declared as market equivalents depends upon local circumstances. If rice is not flowing freely into the markets (or the market equivalents), requisitioning of paddy from the cultivator is resorted to without hesitation. Purchase prices are fixed on the basis of delivery at railhead, and for purchases in the interior prices are reduced by the differential necessary to bring the grain to railhead. Variations are also made to allow for differences in quality. A large number of agents drawn from the trade (including the millers) are employed in making purchases. Agreements are entered into with the agents by which they bind themselves to act as Government agents only and not to trade independently. The functions of the agents are to pay for the rice, take delivery of it on behalf of Government, bag it, weigh it, mark the bags, and transport it to Government warehouses. The agents work under the close supervision of Government officers. A Food Inspector is always present at the time a purchase is made either in the market or at the mill and if there is a difference of opinion between the seller and the Food Inspector as regards the quality of the rice, the matter is referred to the local Food Officer whose decision is final. The scheme has worked successfully in the surplus rice districts of the Chhattisgarh Division.

29. An essential feature of the schemes in force in the Central Provinces and Orissa is that Government purchases are made at fixed prices. We do not, however, regard this as a serious objection to the introduction of similar schemes in Bengal. Reductions in the ceiling prices at relatively short intervals were necessary during 1944 in view of the abnormal prices prevailing at the end of

1943. Prices have now (the beginning of 1945) reached a more reasonable level and it seems to us that the time has come when it is not only possible but also desirable for Bengal to adopt a more stable price policy. Other provinces have followed a policy of maintaining a uniform price level for as long a period as possible. In Orissa prices have been fixed for both rice and paddy for the whole of the crop year and in Madras, the Central Provinces, and Bombay, prices have been maintained at a steady level over a long period. It is clearly desirable that the cultivator should be assured that Government have no intention of forcing prices down to an unduly low level. Further, it is essential that the acreage under rice should increase rather than decrease, and this can only be ensured if the cultivator is assured of a reasonable price for his grain. It is also to the advantage of the rice miller to know that prices will remain steady. Apprehensions that prices may fall must inevitably restrict his purchases of paddy and, in consequence, his outturn of rice. Again, a stable price will make Government relations with the miller easier. We accordingly recommend that the prices at which purchases on Government account will be made, should be fixed for as long a period as possible. We would prefer that this period should correspond to the crop year but, if that is not possible, we suggest that it should be for at least six months. We also consider that the prices should not be kept secret. It is desirable that the cultivator, the trader, and the miller should know the prices fixed by Government for their purchases.

30. We now return to consider whether the schemes in operation in the Central Provinces and Orissa are suitable for introduction in Bengal. In the Central Provinces monopoly purchase by Government extends to rice and not to paddy. It will not be possible to maintain this distinction in Bengal, except perhaps in a few districts which are well supplied with rice mills, because the procurement organization purchases large quantities of paddy. No difficulty, however, should be experienced in extending the monopoly to paddy. But it is doubtful whether the system in force in the Central Provinces is suitable for adoption in all districts in Bengal. We have in mind the districts in which communication is mainly by water. In these areas, rice and paddy are largely bought and sold by merchants who move about in boats. To a large extent the boat is the market, and much of the grain is not brought to an established market as in the Central Provinces. In these conditions, it would be difficult to prevent evasion of orders prohibiting the sale of rice and paddy at markets or market "equivalents", to persons other than Government agents. The only way to prevent widespread evasion would be by full monopoly. This we consider impracticable. Bengal has not the administrative machinery for full monopoly procurement, nor do we regard the establishment of such an organization a practical proposition. Full monopoly purchase also implies full responsibility for distribution. And here again, we do not consider this practicable. Subject, however, to the reservation as regards districts in which communication is mainly by water, we are of opinion that the system of monopoly procurement in force in the Central Provinces may prove suitable for adoption in Bengal. As regards the scheme in operation in Orissa, we do not anticipate that any insuperable difficulty will be experienced in introducing a similar scheme in Bengal.

31. We are of opinion that Bengal should advance towards the monopoly ideal. We therefore recommend that the schemes in force in Orissa and in the Central Provinces should be studied with a view to the introduction of a system of monopoly purchase as an experimental measure in a selected district or districts in Bengal.

H.—The Procurement Machinery

32. The procurement organization which was set up at the end of 1943 and was in operation during 1944 consists of

(i) a Purchasing Board, and

(ii) four sole purchasing agents, called the Chief Agents.

The Purchasing Board, the functions of which are of a purely advisory character, consists of the Commissioner of Food and Civil Supplies, who acts as its Chairman, one representative of the Railways, two representatives of the Chambers of Commerce, and the four Chief Agents. Its duty is to advise Government on questions of policy such as the price at which purchases should be made, the quantities to be purchased from time to time, and the areas in which purchases should be accelerated or retarded. Four firms of standing have been appointed as purchasing agents, and districts, in which they conduct their buying operations, have been allotted to each of them. Their purchases are made at prices fixed by Government, on the advice of the Purchasing Board and the methods of buying are through rice mills, through sub-agents appointed from among the local rice and paddy dealers, and directly through local dealers, co-operative societies and cultivators. This system was in operation throughout 1944.

33. It will be recalled that a substantially similar procurement organization was set up on two occasions during 1943 and the agency employed for making purchases under the "denial" scheme was of the same type. We have explained in an earlier chapter our view that this type of organization is not suitable for procurement in conditions of shortage.[1] In saying this we are not criticizing the manner in which any of the chief agents performed his functions during 1944. As we have said, procurement in that year was successful—more successful than was expected during the early part of the year. Government were able to purchase over one million tons of rice and paddy, and at the end of the year had built up a reserve of over 600,000 tons. The success of the year's operations reflect the success with which the Chief Agents carried out their tasks. The point we are considering is the suitability of this type of purchasing organisation in more difficult conditions when measures of coercion may be necessary in order to maintain the flow of grain. At first it might appear that a commercial firm with experience in the buying and selling of foodgrains would be a more suitable agency than a purchasing organization manned by officials. This, however, has not been the experience of the large majority of the provinces. Madras, Bombay, Orissa, Bihar, United Provinces, the Central Provinces, and the Punjab, have all preferred an official agency and, as we have pointed out, even more significant is the fact that when a change has been made, it has been the substitution of an official for a trade agency. The result of this experience, combined with the failure of the "private" agency in Bengal in the difficult times of 1943, offer lessons which, in our opinion, should not be disregarded, and are conclusive.

34. We would briefly summarize the reasons for our preference in favour of an official purchasing agency in the following terms:—

(i) The system of agents selected from the trade raises a problem of selection. It gives rise to jealousy and friction which often lead to difficulties for the agent actually chosen. Such jealousy and friction hinder co-operation between the Government and the trade, which is so important for the success of control measures. The views expressed by the Bengal Rice Millers' Association, to which reference has already been made, are relevant as illustrating this point.

(ii) It is important that the procurement agency should have the full support and co-operation not only of the local traders and the rice millers but also of public opinion generally. This is particularly necessary when the flow of grain into the market shows signs of slowing down and pressure has to be brought to bear on the producers and local traders to part with their grain. The public does not readily believe that private firms are imbued with a spirit of public service and the more difficult procurement conditions become, the more ready

[1] Part I, Chapter X, paragraphs 29 to 32.

the public is to assume that their object is gain at the public expense. It is just at the stage when coercion is necessary that lack of confidence in the private agency may gather momentum and prove very embarrassing.

(iii) There is a fundamental difference between normal trading and the procurement of supplies on behalf of the Government. The latter in the last resort must depend on coercion, in the form of requisitioning. Requisitioning involves the use of legal powers which must be entrusted to responsible state officials and not to private individuals. It can be undertaken more effectively, and with less risk of misunderstanding as to its necessity in the public interest, by officers who are part of the official purchasing agency than by officers who are normally outside the procurement organization and are occasionally called in to support the operation of that organization.

(iv) The continuity of an official agency is assured though individual officers may change. A system of agents chosen from the trade, on the other hand, involves danger of lack of continuity. For, should a Chief Agent retire for any reason the benefit of his experience and organization in the areas allotted to him is lost and procurement may suffer while a new organization is establishing itself and acquiring familiarity with the work involved.

(v) It has been found necessary to buttress the present procurement organization in Bengal by a Government establishment, parallel with that of the Chief Agents, for the purpose of supervising and assisting them. Originally, provision was made for a staff of 7 Regional Deputy Directors, one Additional Deputy Director, 37 Assistant Directors and Officers of equal standing, and 450 Inspectors. The duties of this very considerable staff were defined generally as being "to supervise procurement operations as well as distribution under the scheme", and specific reference was made to the inspection of the stocks purchased, requisitioning of godowns and stocks, and the control of rice mills. We understand that recommendations have recently been made to the Government for the enlargement of this staff. There is in addition a considerable establishment entrusted with the responsibility for the storage and movement of supplies. Given the position that official establishments on this scale are necessary, we feel they would be more adequately, as well as more effectively, employed if they are also entrusted with the duty of making purchases from rice mills and local traders.

35. For these reasons, we recommend that an official procurement agency be established in place of the Chief Agents. We fully recognize the fact that careful preparations will have to be made before the change we recommend can be carried out. The transition will not be effected in a day; the pace of the change-over must necessarily be a matter for practical administration in Bengal. We desire to add that there should be no undue delay in taking the necessary measures; and having regard to the considerations which we have set out in Section F, the procurement of rice from rice mills should be entrusted to an official agency as an initial step in this process of transition.

I.—Organization in the Districts

36. During 1944, the staff employed in the districts in the administration of food and civil supplies and connected matters was considerably strengthened. In every district there is an Assistant Director, and under him, a number of Licensing and Returns Officers, and Inspectors. During our inquiries we gained the impression that there was some uncertainty as to the authority responsible for controlling this staff. According to the orders issued by the Government of Bengal early in 1944, this staff was placed under the Regional Deputy (or Additional Deputy) Director of Civil Supplies, an officer whose jurisdiction extends over a group of districts and who is directly responsible to the Civil Supplies Department of the Provincial Government. It was also at the same time pro-

vided that the district staff was to be "subject to the supervision of the District Magistrate". This arrangement reflected the uncertainty prevailing at the time about the respective functions to be undertaken by the District Magistrate and the Deputy Director of Civil Supplies. It was expected that the uncertainty would be removed in course of time, as a result of mutual settlement between these officers with reference to local conditions; and that some definition of functions would emerge as a result of the practical working of the *aman* procurement scheme. This expectation, however, was not realised, and during 1944, officers, generally speaking, were not clear about their functions and powers. We consider it desirable that the responsibility for procurement, distribution, and enforcement of controls should be clearly defined.

37. We think there can be no doubt that the District Magistrate, except for certain clearly specified purposes, should be the authority responsible to the Government for food administration in his district, and that the staff employed for this purpose should be controlled by an officer or officers subordinate and responsible to him. We understand that the Provincial Government have recently decided that the District Magistrate, assisted by a staff over which he will have complete control, shall be solely responsible for all matters concerning the distribution, storage, and movement of supplies within the district from the point or points at which they are made available for use within it. The uncertainty as regards the authority responsible for distribution within a district has therefore been removed and we need say nothing further on this point. We consider however, that the District Magistrate should also be responsible for the enforcement of controls within his district, and we recommend that this principle should be observed. We agree that in those districts where a staff is specially employed for the purpose of making purchases on behalf of Government, or controlling and supervising such purchases, the District Magistrate and his staff should have no responsibility in the matter of procurement and operations connected therewith. We suggest, however, that in districts classed as deficit districts, the District Magistrate should be authorised to undertake procurement, should this prove necessary, in local surplus areas in order to provide supplies for other parts of the district.

38. There has also grown up recently a large staff which, while it performs a number of functions relating to the Jute Regulation, the Rural Reconstruction, and the Agricultural Development Departments, is also employed in connection with the distribution of controlled commodities. We understand that this consists of 10 Assistant Development Commissioners, 30 District Development Officers, 82 Chief Inspectors and Inspectors in Charge, 154 Range Inspectors, 1,000 Assistant Inspectors, 1,000 *Amins*, 6,000 Development Assistants, and 12,000 part-time Local Crop Recorders. A considerable proportion of this staff belongs to the Jute Regulation Department, and the remainder represents the staff sanctioned in 1943 and 1944 for the "Grow More Food" campaign and the collection, by a plot to plot enumeration, of agricultural statistics. The "jute" staff was utilized during 1943 in connection with the food drive and subsequently in relief measures. About the end of 1943, Government decided to introduce a scheme for the equitable distribution of controlled commodities, *e.g.*, kerosene, salt, sugar, and in a very limited field, foodgrains, throughout the province. Again, in 1944 Government formulated a scheme for the "modified rationing" of foodgrains in the smaller towns and rural areas. This scheme has so far only been brought into force in certain rural areas in the Chittagong District. But, if we understand the position correctly, the intention is to introduce it as a relief measure should it become necessary to undertake the distribution of foodgrains at subsidized rates in other parts of the province. This scheme also contemplates the utilization of local food committees, the work of which will be supervised by the Jute Regulation Staff. It is possible that the functions we have referred to are such that they can be combined with advant-

age in one organization but we consider it a defect that the staff should be, as at present, organized independently of the District Magistrate in a separate hierarchy directly subordinate to the officer who holds the posts of Chief Controller of Jute Regulation, Director of Rural Reconstruction, and Special Officer, Rural Rationing. We have drawn attention more than once in our report to the weakness in the district administration in Bengal arising out of the absence of revenue and village establishments similar to those in the *ryotwari* provinces. Apart from the *Amins* and the part-time Local Crop Recorders, we assume that a considerable proportion of the establishment to which we have referred, will be retained permanently. It seems to us, therefore, that the existence of this staff affords an opportunity for organizing a subordinate administrative establishment under the control of the Circle Officers, which will be of great value in enabling the District and Sub-divisional Officers to maintain closer contact with the villages. We understand that the whole question of the organization of administration in Bengal is at present under review, and we recommend that the suggestion we have set out above be borne in mind in any scheme of reorganization.

J.—Other matters.

39. **Co-operative Societies.**—Although an attempt was made in 1944 to utilize co-operative societies as agents for the purchase of grain from producers, little success was achieved. On the one hand, the co-operative societies attribute this lack of success to the "unsympathetic attitude" of the employees of the Chief Agents with whom they had to deal, whereas, on the other hand, we understand that the Chief Agents complain that the societies refused to sell paddy and rice at the prices at which they (the Chief Agents) were authorized to buy. We cannot say what truth there is in these allegations and counter-allegations, but we think it unfortunate that the co-operative societies should have this sense of grievance. We consider that not only in Bengal but throughout India, endeavour should be made to develop co-operative societies as part of the procurement organization because they are perhaps the most effective way of obtaining the support of the cultivator in procurement operations. At the same time, however, we recognize that the rate of progress cannot be spectacular. Indeed, there is a real danger in attempting too rapid an advance and the history of the co-operative movement, certainly in Bengal, affords a clear warning of that danger. An official agency is now operating in the Bakarganj district and what we suggest is that a scheme should be worked out for the utilization of the marketing and agricultural credit societies in that district as part of the procurement machine. We feel convinced that the wise course is to concentrate on a particular area and to postpone, except in regard to the few large and well established marketing societies in other areas, any attempt to introduce on a wider scale procurement through co-operative societies until further experience has been gained.

40. **Corruption.**—Many persons who gave evidence before us spoke with great concern of the extent to which corruption prevails in connection with food administration (and other matters) in Bengal. Food administration, particularly in conditions created by war, unfortunately offers special opportunities for dishonesty and the atmosphere in Bengal has been charged, for some considerable time, with rumours of widespread corruption among both officials and non-officials. We have little doubt that the conditions prevailing in Bengal in 1943, encouraged the growth of peculation and dishonesty and it is possible that this explains why the evil seems to be more serious in that province than in other parts of India. The disease demands drastic treatment. A cure will only be effected by vigorous action in three directions. First, rigorous disciplinary action against officials of whatever standing guilty of corruption, secondly, strict enforcement of controls and the punishment of those who break the law, and

thirdly, the mobilization of public opinion against every form of corruption. The eradication of the evil is necessary for the full recovery of Bengal and for her future progress.

41. **Public Co-operation.**—In paragraph 25 of Chapter X in Part I, we have drawn attention to the existence in other provinces of *ad hoc* advisory bodies which have been of assistance to the Provincial Governments in reaching satisfactory decisions on matters of food administration and in obtaining support of public opinion in executing them. We have also referred to the fact that a proposal to set up such a body in Bengal was considered and that Government and the Opposition could not agree on its functions. In spite of the difficulties experienced in the past, we recommend that a Provincial Advisory Council should be established and that it should be composed of officials and non-officials, the latter representative of producers, traders, and consumers. We also recommend that District Advisory Committees should be established for the assistance of local food administrations in those districts in which such a body does not at present exist. In particular, we consider that it would be an advantage if a separate advisory body were to be established for Greater Calcutta. We are clear that the functions of these bodies should be of a purely consultative and advisory nature; they should not possess any executive power. The responsibility of Government for the maintenance of the supply and distribution of food is to-day no less important than that for the maintenance of law and order. Government must, therefore, accept full responsibility for all measures taken in regard to the food of the people and cannot share that responsibility with food councils and committees. We have recommended the formation of these bodies not with the object of absolving Government and their officers of responsibility for securing and distributing food supplies, but because we consider that they will enable public opinion to play a more effective and helpful part in shaping food policy, in devising measures and reviewing their execution, and also in assisting to remove questions affecting the food of the people from the sphere of party politics.

42. **Summary.**—Our main recommendations arising out of this chapter are:—

(1) The rationing of towns with a population of about 25,000 or more should be carried out as quickly as possible, and in the light of the experience gained, rationing of smaller towns considered.

(2) (a) Immediate steps should be taken to review licences issued since May 1943 under the Foodgrains Control Order, and to remove from the register of licensees persons who are not traders by profession.

(b) Cultivators holding land exceeding a prescribed acreage limit should be brought within the scope of the Foodgrains Control Order. A limit of 25 acres is suggested as suitable.

(3) Embargoes round the surplus districts should be effectively enforced: an adequate number of launches should be made available for the purpose.

(4) Requisitioning should be undertaken, as and when necessary, from traders and large producers, if the flow of supplies is not maintained by voluntary sales. Public opinion should be enlisted in support of requisitioning by suitable propaganda directed to explaining the policy of Government.

(5) An official procurement agency should be established in place of the present system of procurement through Chief Agents chosen from the trade. The pace of the change-over must necessarily be a matter for practical administration in Bengal. It is desirable, however, that there should be no undue delay in taking the necessary measures. The procurement of rice from rice mills should be entrusted to an official agency as an initial step.

(6) The systems of monopoly procurement in force in Orissa and the Central Provinces should be studied with a view to the introduction of a system of monopoly purchase, as an experimental measure, in a selected district or districts in Bengal.

(7) (a) The respective functions of District Magistrates and Deputy Directors of Civil Supplies in regard to the procurement and distribution of supplies and the enforcement of controls should be clearly defined.

(b) The District Magistrate should be responsible for all matters concerning the distribution, storage and movement of supplies and the enforcement of controls in the district.

(c) In those districts where a staff is specially employed for making purchases on behalf of Government or for controlling and supervising such purchases the District Magistrate and his staff should have no responsibility in regard to procurement and operations connected therewith. In other districts, the District Magistrate should be authorized to undertake procurement, should this prove necessary, in local surplus areas in order to provide supplies for other parts of the district.

(8) The existence of a large staff under the Jute Regulation, Rural Reconstruction, and Agricultural Departments affords an opportunity for organizing a subordinate administrative establishment which will be of value in enabling District and Sub-divisional Officers to maintain closer contact with the villages The possibility of such a reorganization should be considered.

(9) It is no longer necessary to reduce prices at relatively short intervals. A more stable price policy is recommended.

(10) Co-operative societies should be developed as part of the procurement machine. It is recommended that a beginning should be made in the utilization of the marketing and agricultural credit societies in the Bakarganj district as part of the procurement machinery.

(11) Vigorous action against corruption is called for in three directions. Fist, disciplinary action against officials of whatever standing guilty of corruption, secondly, strict enforcement of controls and the punishment of those who break the law, and thirdly, mobilization of public opinion against every form of corruption.

(12) (a) A Provincial Food Advisory Council, composed of officials and non-officials, should be established. Producers, traders, and consumers should be adequately represented on this council.

(b) A separate advisory body for Greater Calcutta should be established as also District Advisory Committees in those districts where they do not at present exist.

CHAPTER II.—REHABILITATION

1. **Short and long term schemes.**—In previous chapters we have described the effect of the famine in Bengal and the relief measures taken during the emergency period. The first necessary steps were to provide food, to get the wanderers back to their homes, and to bring the health situation under control. By the beginning of 1944, adquate supplies of food were available, the majority of wandering destitutes had returned to their villages, and throughout the year the health situation slowly improved, until at its close the death rate was not far above the usual unsatisfactory level. But more is needed to repair the damage inflicted by the famine.

We do not propose to deal here with long term schemes for improving the economic condition of the population. These concern the whole of India and will be considered in a later report. In order to remove any threat of future famine, far-reaching developments in irrigation, animal husbandry, and industry are required. But such developments will take time. Meanwhile there is an immediate problem of rehabilitation in Bengal. We obtained abundant evidence, both during our tours in rural Bengal and in the examination of witnesses, of the need for effective measures to hasten the economic recovery of the classes affected by the famine. Such measures should conform with, and ultimately merge into, broader schemes of reconstruction and development.

2. **Restoration of lands.**—Late in 1943 the Bengal Alienation of Agricultural Land (Temporary Provisions) Ordinance was promulgated[1] to enable petty cultivators who sold their land during the famine to get it back. According to the Ordinance, any small-holder who during 1943 transferred agricultural land by sale "for any consideration the amount and value of which does not exceed Rs. 250", can apply to the District Officer for restoration. He must satisfy the latter that "he could not have maintained himself or his family except by making such alienation of such land", and the transferee has the right of being heard. The small holder who regains his land must repay the sum he received from the sale in 10 annual instalments. If the small-holder so desires he may, however, instead of applying for a restoration order, apply for the conversion of the sale into a complete usufructuary mortgage for a period of 10 years. The Ordinance ceased to operate on March 11, 1944, under the provisions of the Government of India Act, 1935, regarding such Ordinances. A Bill was thereupon introduced in the Legislature and passed by the Council; it could not, however, be passed by the Assembly owing to the prorogation of the latter. On September 7, 1944, Government issued a fresh Ordinance embodying the provisions of the Bill. Over 7,000 cases were filed under the original Ordinance. Out of these only a small proportion were disposed of during the period of the first Ordinance and in September 1944 the number of pending cases was 6,498. The disposal of these, and of further cases which may be filed, will place a heavy burden on District Officers and their staff. Considerable importance must be attached to the settlement of cases with the greatest possible speed.

Restoration of land is a very necessary part of rehabilitation. No information is, however, available as to the number of dispossessed small holders who would be entitled to take advantage of the Ordinance. Probably only a small fraction have already applied, or will apply, for restoration. Many of those who sold their land will find it difficult to raise the money necessary to pay the annual instalments, and thus regain immediate possession. If they prefer to apply for the usufructuary mortgage, they will regain their land in 10 years, unless they can pay off the mortgage debt earlier, but meanwhile will have to find other means of earning a living.

3. **Expenditure on rehabilitation.**—Rehabilitation schemes involving the expenditure of Rs. 4 crores have been formulated by the Government of Bengal. The schemes include the establishment and maintenance of workhouses, homes and orphanages for destitutes, free grants for house building, the rehabilitation of artisans, and various irrigation projects. The Revenue Department is in charge of the work of rehabilitation.

4. **Workhouses and destitute homes.**—It is proposed to centralize relief institutions, at present scattered, into 60 institutions consisting of a workhouse, a destitute home, and homes for orphans, deserted children and young women with and without children. Workhouses are planned as centres for encouraging cottage industries. They will provide work for (a) inmates of destitute homes if any, attached to the workhouse, (b) such residents of neighbouring areas as wish to come and work for a living and (c) for local people who may take materials from the workhouses, produce goods in their homes, and return the latter to the workhouse against suitable payment. The kinds of work to be carried out include paddy-husking; cane-work and bamboo work; mat-making; spinning; weaving; net-making; rope-making; toy-making; paper-making; and nail-making. Other suitable handicrafts may be suggested by the Director of Industries.

The care of widows is one of the major problems of rehabilitation, and presumably the majority of adults who will be housed in, or otherwise assisted by, relief institutions will belong to this class.

5. **Orphans.**—The number of orphans requiring care dose not apper to be very accurately known. Preliminary estimates made by District Officers gave a total of over 30,000, but later this figure was reduced to 10,000. The Government of Bengal have accepted the responsibility of looking after all famine orphans, the Education Department being entrusted with their care. Voluntary bodies will also assist. Any private organization which undertakes the charge of orphans must, however, submit proposals to the Director of Education for approval and guarantee to feed the children on an approved type of diet and to educate them in accordance with principles laid down by the Director. It is proposed that the orphans should receive elementary education with particular emphasis on hand work, and that at a later stage they should be given a training in some craft which will provide a means of livelihood and render them independent of state aid.

In August 1944, 11 Government orphanages, with accommodation for about 1,700 children, had been constructed and occupied, or were nearing completion. The bulk of the orphans were still housed in workhouses, temporary orphanages etc., scattered all over the province, their care being the responsibility of District Officers. Some orphanages were also being run by voluntary organisations.

6. **House building.**—Expenditure of Rs. 10 lakhs has been sanctioned for this purpose. Free grants will be given to homeless destitutes to enable them to re-build their huts. There has been particular need for this in the cyclone-damaged areas, but elsewhere also huts need repairing. In the chapter on relief we have told how famine victims sold doors, windows, roofs, etc., in the early stages of the famine.

7. **The rehabilitation of artisans.**—This is a task of great importance. It is proposed to assist workers such as fishermen, weavers, potters, carpenters, etc., by subsidies and loans, and by the supply of raw materials and trade implements at cost price. Fishermen suffered severely during the famine and their rapid rehabilitation is particularly necessary in order to increase supplies of a valuable protective food. Boats, nets and other fishing tackle must be

supplied to set fishermen who lost their belongings at work again. One difficulty which was mentioned to the Commission is the shortage of water-proofing material to prevent the deterioration of nets.

8. **Irrigation.**—Irrigation Schemes, at a cost of Rs. 100,00,000, are projected as follows:—

(a) Rs. 10,00,000 for expenditure on the re-excavation of derelict irrigation tanks, mostly in western Bengal.

(b) Rs. 26,00,000 for the execution of small irrigation projects which do not require much expert supervision by engineers. This will be spent by District Officers.

(c) Rs. 64,00,000 for expenditure on the more important irrigation schemes which are ready for execution, under the supervision of the Irrigation Department.

9. **Comment on rehabilitation.**—Plans have thus been laid for the care and rehabilitation of those who suffered during the famine and considerable sums of money have been allotted for the purpose. It is, however, one thing to draw up schemes and provide money, and another to produce satisfactory practical results. We are by no means satisfied with the progress hitherto made towards rehabilitation and wish to stress the need for more energetic and co-ordinated action.

There seems to be some lack of knowledge about the nature and extent of the problem to be tackled. Thus, it is known that the famine has had important effects on village life and economy, but no clear picture of the changes it has produced is available. Many small-holders sold their land, and many artisans their trade implements and have not the means to resume their normal means of livelihood. The numbers involved are, however, unknown. There has been loss of life which must considerably affect the availability of labour and opportunities for employment. Will the village labourer, on account of the shortage of labour, be better off than before the famine? On a number of such questions there is at present no accurate information, and the Commission heard many conflicting opinions. Clearly it is essential to make a careful study of the whole position, in order to guide rehabilitation policy. Unless this can be done expenditure on rehabilitation, however, generous, may be misdirected and the results obtained disappointing.

A strong staff is needed for rehabilitation, both at the centre and the periphery. We shall refer shortly to the question of central direction. With regard to the actual task of rehabilitation in the rural areas, we fear that the ordinary district staff, overburdened as it is with other work, will not be able to give sufficient time and attention to this important matter. We accordingly are of opinion that special officers, trained in rehabilitation work, should be appointed.

While some good orphanages already exist, the present position with regard to the care of a large proportion of orphans is by no means satisfactory. Plans for their accommodation in Government institutions seem slow in maturing and meanwhile the conditions in which many are living leave much to be desired. We would, therefore, emphasize the need for establishing suitable homes for all destitute orphans without unnecessary delay. We are by no means satisfied that this task is being prosecuted with sufficient energy.

It is essential that when private organizations are entrusted with the care of orphans, Government should have powers of supervision and inspection to ensure that the necessary standards are reached and maintained. Provided such powers are conscientiously exercised, there is every advantage in making use of the services of suitable voluntary bodies, supported by subventions from Government. Children in a well-run voluntary institution would probably receive more sympathetic attention than in a Government institution. On the other hand, voluntary bodies may undertake the care of orphans during the wave of enthusiasm for relief work engendered by the famine, and lose interest in their charges as the years pass. This possibility should be borne in mind in enlisting the help of such bodies.

While the Revenue Department is responsible for the organization of rehabilitation and the allotment of funds, rehabilitation is also the concern of other Departments, *e.g.*, Commerce and Industry, Development, Health, Agriculture, Fisheries, etc. These departments must, therefore, be closely associated with rehabilitation work and the necessary co-ordination between them and the Revenue Department, which is directly responsible for rehabilitation, must be assured. Secretariat delays, *e.g.*, delays in obtaining sanction for expenditure on suitable schemes, should be avoided. For the rehabilitation of the affected classes, instruments and materials (*e.g.*, seed, fishing boats, yarn, etc.), have to be provided immediately, and this demands joint action on the part of the various departments concerned.

Recommendation.—We are of the opinion that a Rehabilitation Commissioner, generally responsible for rehabilitation work in all its aspects, should be appointed without delay, with whatever additional staff is necessary both at the centre and in the districts. Such an officer would be in a position to initiate a survey of the existing situation, with the object of obtaining a clear idea of the economic and social effects of the famine, and of the measures necessary to repair the damage. His main task would, however, be to provide the drive necessary to overcome obstacles and difficulties, and to ensure that the work of rehabilitation was not hindered by lack of contact and co-ordination between the various Departments. Drive and co-ordination are needed to speed up rehabilitation.

CHAPTER III.—PROTECTIVE AND SUPPLEMENTARY FOODS

A. The Present Position

1. **General.**—The famine of 1943, was a famine in rice. Typical Bengali diets are composed largely of rice which may provide 80 to 90 per cent. of total calories. While, in the feeding of Bengal, adequate supplies of rice (and of wheat, to fulfil the Calcutta demand) are the primary necessity, the importance of other foods must not be overlooked. In the first place, such foods supply additional calories and hence a reduction or increase in the quantities available influences requirements of cereals. Secondly, the nutritive value of a diet based largely on rice is unsatisfactory. To be adequate for health, such a diet must be supplemented by other foods which help to make good the deficiencies of rice in respect of protein, vitamins and mineral salts. Such foods are often called "protective" foods, and include milk and milk products, meat, fish, eggs, pulses, vegetables and fruit. Vegetable oil (usually mustard oil in Bengal) and sweet potatoes are not usually placed in the protective group, but they have certain useful properties. Sweet potatoes provide calories and some varieties are rich in pro-vitamin A. Vegetable oil, while it contains no vitamins, is a source of fat and the fat content of Indian diets is in general undesirably low. Further, one part of vegetable oil is equivalent, in calorie value, to about 2½ parts of cereal so that an assured supply of vegetable oil, sufficient to provide one ounce *per capita* daily, would have an appreciable effect on rice requirements.

2. In nearly all parts of India there is, in normal times, a scarcity of protective foods. The poorer classes live on an ill-balanced diet composed almost exclusively of cereals. Intake of protective foods rises with increasing income, but even middle class families may consume too little of them. In Bengal, at the present time, the scarcity and high price of protective foods have led to a general reduction in their intake, never sufficient from the standpoint of nutrition. This has affected mainly the middle classes, accustomed to some variety in diet. The Commission heard many complaints about the difficulties encountered by middle class families in obtaining milk, fish, vegetables, etc. The scarcity is felt less by the poor, who were used to go without such foods, or to consume them only in very small quantities. The fact, however, that their intake of protective foods may not have been greatly influenced by the scarcity does not indicate that their need for them is less than that of the middle classes. More protective foods are required, not only for those who can afford to purchase them in reasonable quantities in normal times, but for the whole population of Bengal.

In the case of rice and wheat fairly adequate data about supplies and distribution are available. The position with regard to various non-cereal foods is more obscure. We propose to discuss the situation in the light of whatever information we have been able to obtain.

3. **Pulses.**—Pulses are a valuable supplement to cereal diets since they supply protein and various vitamins. Bengal is normally deficit in pulses. The Government of Bengal were not able to provide the Commission with any figures relating to the normal production and import of gram (*Cicer arietinum*). Under the Revised Basic Plan nearly 62,000 tons were received in Bengal and the quantity allotted for the period May 1944 to April 1945 is 38,000 tons. It appears, however, that gram is not a popular pulse in Bengal, and a considerable proportion of the 62,000 tons remains unconsumed. A small part of the consignment of 38,000 tons was accepted, but the balance was cancelled at the request of the Government of Bengal since large stocks were already available in the province.

4. Imports of pulses other than gram during the years 1937-40 averaged 120,690 tons. Under the Revised Basic Plan, Bengal was allotted, in April 1944, a quota of 70,050 tons of pulses other than gram for the period November 1943 to April 1945. Previous to April 1944, 11,450 tons were obtained by special arrangement from various provinces and states, which were not debited to the quota of 70,050 tons. Roughly speaking, a quantity equal to about half the usual import is due to Bengal during the present financial year under the Basic Plan.

The quota as originally formulated included the following:

	Tons
Dhal arhar (Cajanus indicas)	20,300
Mung dhal (Green gram, Phaseolus radiatus)	16,200
Masur dhal (Lentil, Lens esculenta)	12,350
Khesari dhal (Lathyrus sativus)	20,000
Urd (Black gram, Phaseolus mungo)	1,200

5. The most popular pulses in Bengal are *masur dhal* and *mung dhal*. Of the pulses included in the allotment, *khesari* and *urd* are in no demand, and the Government of Bengal surrendered the quotas of these pulses. They asked the Government of India to reduce the quota of *dhal arhar* by half and raise those of *masur dhal* and *mung dhal* to 40,000 and 20,000 tons respectively. While these negotiations were proceeding the actual import of pulses into Bengal was small. Up to November 1944, nothing was received except some quantities of *masur dhal* from Bihar.

6. The pulse position in Bengal cannot, therefore, to put it mildly, be regarded as satisfactory. The Commission, during its tours in various parts of India, observed lack of direction and co-ordination with regard to the supply of pulses. In some provinces there was a glut and in others a shortage, and demand and supply appeared to be uncorrelated. Existing difficulties seem to be partly due to lack of knowledge of local preferences for different kinds of pulses. These are important, since local methods of cooking are often based on the use of certain familiar pulses and people may be as reluctant to change their favourite pulse as their staple cereal. There is also some lack of knowledge about the supply and distribution of pulses in normal times.

It is the task of the Government of Bengal to encourage production within the province of the various pulses which the population requires. The despatch of pulses to Bengal under the Basic Plan is, however, the responsibility of the Government of India and the provinces concerned. The whole position needs to be clarified and the existing chaos reduced to order.

7. **Fish.**—More fish is consumed in Bengal than in most other provinces in India. The many rivers, large and small, which flow through the province abound in fish and the mouths of the great estuaries are exceptionally rich fishing grounds. There are also numerous tanks which are a good source of fresh-water fish. Both fresh-water and salt-water fish are important; about 40 per cent of the fish reaching the Calcutta market in 1941 was sea fish and the remainder fresh-water fish.

During 1943 and 1944 there has been a serious scarcity of fish and prices have been high. In April 1944 the price of common varieties sold in the Calcutta market was 2 to 3 times in excess of the pre-war level. The present position is due to a variety of causes. First, the removal of boats under the Denial Policy, and the restriction on the movements of boats, affected the fishing industry in the greater part of the estuarine area. Secondly, fishermen were among the classes seriously affected by the famine. Considerable mortality occurred amongst them and many, reduced to destitution, have not yet been able to resume their trade. A good many have found other employment. Thirdly, there are difficulties in obtaining motor boats, and petrol and kerosene for the few motor boats that are available. Ordinary boats are also in short supply. Fourthly, there is a shortage of yarn and water-proofing material for nets. Fifthly, transport of fish from the fishing grounds is affected by the prevailing conditions on the railways, the lack of motor boats and shortage of ice. Lastly, there is a considerable military demand for fish and ice which reacts on the civil markets.

8. **The Denial Policy.**—An account has already been given of the removal of boats under the Denial Policy. Both large and small boats are used for fishing in the estuarine area. In 1942 most of the larger fishing boats were taken away and the movement of all boats was restricted. In normal times fishing boats may go 10 or 15 miles out to sea. By degrees the restrictions have been relaxed. Except in certain localities, boats are now allowed to go up to 8 miles from the shore and a number of fishing boats requisitioned under the Denial Policy are now in use again. These are being supplied to fishermen either free or on a hire-purchase system. The provision of loans and subsidies to fishermen to enable them to buy boats and fishing apparatus is an important item in the rehabilitation programme. No information is available to the Commission about the construction of new fishing boats.

9. **Motor boats.**—Motor boats are not used to any extent in actual fishing operations in Bengal, which remain primitive and undeveloped. The chief function of motor boats is the transport of fish and ice to and from centres at which fish is collected. While the number of motor boats employed in this way was not large, those engaged in the trade played a useful part in supplying the Calcutta market. During 1942 motor boats and launches were requisitioned for military purposes and have not been returned. Attempts are being made to secure their return and to put a few boats, which are lying idle, into commission. For running motor boats petrol and kerosene are necessary, and this, it appears, involves further difficulties under present conditions.

It is the Calcutta market which is mainly affected by the lack of motor boats. For the provision of fish in villages and towns remote from the main fishing centres and markets, the rehabilitation of fishermen operating in small craft is the chief necessity.

10. **Nets.**—The yarn needed for the manufacture of nets is in short supply and what is available is so expensive as to be beyond the means of the average fisherman. Many nets previously in use have perished during the last two years. Water-proofing is necessary to preserve nets and for this purpose coal-tar is the most satisfactory material. In normal times it was transported from Calcutta to the important fishing centres, but now it is unobtainable. Various local tanning materials, such as gab fruit and saran bark, are used for water-proofing; these are reasonably effective if not as good as coal-tar. The Controller of Supplies, Government of India, was approached in June 1944, for supplies of coal-tar for the Bengal fisheries. He replied that coal tar was unprocurable and suggested the use of a preparation of bark called "cutch". Supplies of the latter were available in Bareilly in the United Provinces. Cutch cannot be used for nets once water-proofed with coal-tar, but appears to be reasonably satisfactory for application to new nets. After some delay two wagon-loads of cutch were obtained from Bareilly in October, 1944.

11. **Ice.**—Ice is essential for the transport of fish to the Calcutta market. Nearly all the ice factories are in Calcutta. Previous to the war, ice factories were established at various fish-collecting centres, but most of those within easy reach of Calcutta had to close down owing to underselling on the part of the Calcutta factories. The present position is that there is little production of ice outside Calcutta, while the factories in the Capital cannot meet the military and civil demand. The Government of Bengal have allotted a quota of 120 tons daily for military use, a quantity which is actually considerably below estimated requirements. The demand for ice in military hospitals in the hot climate

of Bengal is heavy. The Director of Fisheries, Bengal, stated in evidence that within 40 miles of Calcutta fish was being thrown away for lack of ice. Salt for fish preservation is also in short supply. Late in 1944 an Ice Control Board was set up, with the functions of controlling the production and distribution of ice and of allocating available supplies, and an Ice Controller was appointed.

12. Railway transport of fish, which is affected by the shortage of ice, is by no means satisfactory. Insulated wagons are not available. A number of trains carrying fish have been cancelled without alternative arrangements being made for its transport. Trains often run late, to the detriment of so perishable an article of food as fish. Arrangements for loading and unloading fish at railway sidings are defective. Railways in Bengal are at present under heavy strain owing to the additional demands imposed by the war. We would, however, ask the Railway Board to do whatever is possible to improve and accelerate the transport of fish.

13. **Military demand.**—The amount of fish purchased by the Army in Calcutta is only a small fraction of the total quantity estimated to reach the Calcutta market in normal times. It is probable, however, that military demand has been a serious drain on supplies reduced by the conditions in the fishing industry which we have described. In 1944 there was some controversy. into which we need not enter, between military and civil authorities about army purchases of fish. Steps are now being taken by the military to develop their own sources of supply and thereby relieve the Calcutta market.

14. **Tank fisheries.**—A considerable development of tank fisheries is contemplated by the Government of Bengal. Such fisheries in general, supply local demand, so that problems of storage and distribution do not arise. The project involves the cleaning of tanks, their stocking with fish fry, and periodic draining to ensure aeration of the floor of the tank to prevent the formation of poisonous gases. As a preliminary experiment, fry is being distributed free in certain areas in the Sunderbans to villagers who have cleaned their tanks and embanked their paddy fields to make them suitable for fish culture. It is hoped that the encouragement of tank fisheries will considerably increase the fish supplies of the province.

15. **More fish.**—The potential supply of fish in Bengal is enormous. While an increase in the production of milk and meat presents great difficulties, fish is there waiting, so to speak, to be caught and eaten. Meanwhile, for reasons which we have briefly outlined, fish is scarce and dear. Of all measures designed to improve nutrition in Bengal the resolution of the present difficulties in the fish trade, and the development of fisheries generally, are perhaps the most promising. The Commission is glad to note that the Government of Bengal have taken the preliminary step of strengthening the Fisheries Department. In 1942 the Department consisted of a Director of Fisheries and two District Fishery Officers. It is now proposed to employ, in addition to the Director, 4 Deputy Directors, 8 Superintendents, 32 District Fishery Officers and 90 Fishery Demonstrators.

The immediate difficulties regarding nets, motor boats, ice and transport do not appear to be beyond solution. The case for the supply of the necessary materials from within India or abroad is a strong one. We feel that immediate steps should be taken by the Government of Bengal and the Government of India to obtain motor boats, the necessary machinery and materials for the construction of additional ice factories, water-proofing material for nets, and whatever else is needed for the reorganization of the fishing industry in Bengal. Military and civilian demand could be more amicably adjusted and plans laid to turn channels of supply developed by the Military to civilian use when the war is over. Closer co-ordination between military and civil authorities with regard to fish supplies is obviously desirable.

16. **Milk.**—In the "Report on the Marketing of Milk in India", published in 1940 by the Central Agricultural Marketing Department, the daily *per capita* consumption of milk and milk products in Bengal is estimated as 2·8 oz. This is a low figure, which may be compared with 15·2 oz. in the Punjab, 40·3 oz. in Denmark, and 55·6 oz. in New Zealand. The same report gives the daily *per capita* milk consumption in Calcutta as 3·8 oz. In normal times the milk supply of Bengal was in fact grossly inadequate, and a large proportion of the urban and rural populations consumed no milk at all.

During the last two years supplies of milk and milk products have been reduced for various reasons and prices have risen. In the famine year there was high mortality among cattle owing to disease and inadequate feeding and care. Bengal normally imports cattle from neighbouring provinces, but exports are now prohibited by these provinces. Bihar has recently agreed to the export of a very small number. The slaughter of cattle for meat may also have reduced milk supplies to some extent. Bengal's consumption of butter and ghee was normally in excess of production, the balance (some 638 and 12,858 tons in the case of butter and ghee respectively) being obtained from provinces which now restrict their exports. In 1944 the Governments of the United Provinces, Bihar and Madras were asked to allot export quotas from these provinces to Bengal. As a result 440 tons of butter were obtained from Bihar and 1,837 tons of ghee from the United Provinces.

The Government of Bengal have themselves prohibited the export of milk and milk products from the province except under permit. To conserve the cattle population a Meat Control Order enjoining two meatless days per week throughout the province has been issued.

17. The increase in the population of Calcutta has accentuated the demand on the city's limited milk supply. Military purchases of milk are of importance in Calcutta, and in other places in Bengal. The Army consumes large quantities of tinned milk, imported from abroad, but fresh milk is also consumed, particularly in hospitals; actually some 50 per cent of the total military consumption of milk is in the form of fresh milk. In one important town the military offtake of fresh milk amounted in 1944 to 102 tons monthly, which must represent a considerable proportion of the total milk supplies available. Some 75 per cent of the total military requirement was, however, being provided in the form of tinned milk.

18. The total production of milk in Bengal can be substantially increased only by far-reaching developments in agriculture and animal husbandry. Improvement in milk marketing is also essential to the growth of the dairy industry. Meanwhile the existing problem of scarcity and high price has to be faced. Among the immediate measures which would help to relieve the situation are the following: An increase in the import of milch cattle and dairy products; prohibition of the use of milk for non-essential purposes; a rationing system whereby infants, young children, and expectant and nursing mothers are given prior claims on available supplies; a reduction in military demand.

19. With regard to imports, we may urge that other provinces should consider sympathetically the requirements of Bengal, where the need for nourishing food is particularly pressing, in respect of cattle and milk products. We understand that the Government of Bengal contemplate prohibiting the manufacture of luxury articles, such as ice-cream, for which milk is required. This has already been done in Bombay. Such a measure would not, of course, increase total supplies, but it would presumably have some effect towards making more fluid milk available and reducing its price.

20. The Commission was very favourably impressed by the Bombay Municipal Corporation's scheme for the distribution of milk to infants, initiated in 1944. Under this scheme, which is financed by the Government of Bombay, 8 oz. of milk daily can be bought at half price by those entitled to benefit.

The actual cost of this quantity is 1½ annas. Milk-cards are issued at Rationing Offices in the different wards and the milk is issued to card-holders in the early morning at numerous distributing centres, in return for cash payment. The supplies for the various centres, bought from contractors, are inspected by the Health Department of the Municipality to ensure their freedom from adulteration. At the beginning of January 1945 the scheme was extended to include children up to 6 years of age and expectant and nursing mothers. At that time 36,705 milk cards were registered under the scheme and about 18,500 lbs. of milk were being distributed daily at 192 centres.

21. We hope that other municipalities in India will follow the lead of Bombay. The first step would be to discover whether sufficient quantities of milk are obtainable and, if they are not, to reorganize the milk supplies of the municipality concerned in order to provide them. There is nothing to prevent card-holders re-selling the milk at market prices, but it is assumed in Bombay that family affection will ensure that the milk reaches the child for whom it is intended in the great majority of cases, and little evidence of abuse has been obtained. We realize that conditions in Calcutta and Bombay are not the same. Milk supplies in Calcutta are probably smaller, in relation to the size of the population, than in Bombay, and for various other reasons the organization of a scheme of this nature might tax the resources of the Calcutta Corporation. Nevertheless we feel that the authorities in Bengal should give the matter their earnest attention.

22. Military demand can be reduced by the greater use of tinned milk and the development of military dairy farms. Nutritionally speaking, imported tinned milk is generally superior to local fresh milk and there is no objection to its use in military hospitals. Soldiers, however, get tired of tinned milk and relish fresh milk for a change. The quantity of processed milk which can be made available for military use in Bengal depends on the supplies of the United Nations, the distribution of which is a matter of high policy with which we have no concern. We can, however, suggest that there is a strong case for relieving local markets in Bengal as far as possible of military demands for milk.

23. **Meat.**—As compared with fish, meat is not an important food in normal times in Bengal. Its present dearness and scarcity seriously affect only the small section of the population accustomed to consume it regularly. The reasons for its scarcity are very similar to those which have led to a shortage of milk. Though the bulk of army consumption of meat has been in the form of tinned meat and meat imported from other provinces, the military demand on local supplies has been very considerable. It is now, however, being reduced. Schemes for breeding pigs and poultry for army purposes have been developed and it is anticipated that by the middle of 1945 frozen meat will be available in substantial quantities.

We are informed that Regional Control Boards consisting of civil and military representatives have been, or will be, set up in each division to control available supplies of fresh meat. The Bengal Government have urged the military authorities to reduce Army consumption of local meat to the greatest extent possible.

24. **Eggs.**—Eggs, always an expensive article of diet, were in 1944 almost beyond the means of all but the wealthy. The estimated annual production in Bengal in 1938 was some 500 million eggs, which works out at less than one egg per month per head of population. Military demand, including the large American demand, amounts to a considerable fraction of total production, though the Army cannot obtain all the eggs it requires. Steps are being taken by the military to increase supplies of eggs by the creation of duck farms. It has been found that ducks are less liable to disease in Bengal than poultry, and easier to handle generally. We commend to the Government of Bengal the

idea of encouraging duck-rearing in the province, on the basis of the experience gained in the military venture.

The export of poultry and eggs from Bengal is now controlled, no one being allowed to take more than one bird and 6 eggs out of the province, except under permit. We understand that the Government of Bengal are now taking some steps to develop poultry farms and encourage the rearing of poultry in villages.

25. **Vegetables.**—Both Indian vegetables and vegetables of the European type are produced and consumed in Bengal. The latter grow well anywhere in the province during the cold weather and can be grown in the hills throughout the year. In 1944 there was a shortage of all kinds of vegetables for the civilian market, and prices in Calcutta were 2 to 3 times in excess of the pre-war level. A large farm for the production of vegetables for the Army has been created in Darjeeling, a small proportion of its produce being available for the civilian market. The Bengal Government have also developed vegetable farms in Darjeeling and a scheme has been sanctioned for the creation of farms in other centres. It is proposed to put 5,000 acres near Calcutta, and 1,000 acres somewhere in East Bengal, probably near Dacca, under cold weather vegetables. No serious attempt has been made by Government to control the price of vegetables.

26. The supply of home-grown potatoes in Bengal is normally insufficient for the needs of the province. The average annual imports from 1937 to 1942, which included imports from Burma, were about 62,000 tons. Since 1942 the import from Burma, which amounted to 40 per cent of the total imports, has ceased, and provinces which previously supplied potatoes to Bengal have restricted or prohibited exports. A small export to Bengal was allowed in 1944 by the Government of Madras, and in September 1944, the Government of Bihar temporarily removed the ban on exports. The shortage of seed potatoes is an obstacle to an immediate increase in the production of potatoes within the province. Sweet potatoes are widely grown in Bengal, but no data about the quantities produced are available. Their price in the Calcutta market in 1944 was one to three annas per pound. Ordinary potatoes were selling at about 8 times this price.

27. The present scarcity of vegetables of all kinds obviously calls for a vigorous "grow more vegetables" campaign. We feel that this is an important matter which should receive the special attention of Government. As regards control of price, we would draw attention to the fact that in England the price of vegetables has been fixed by the Government, although the Government does not itself purchase vegetables for distribution, and that prices have been successfully kept in check. Vegetables are rapidly perishable. If reasonable prices are fixed and made known to the public, and the public learns to insist on paying no more than the fixed rate, opportunities for refusing sale and subsequent disposal in the black market are limited. In Bombay vegetables are sold at fixed rates in ration shops. The sale of even a limited quantity of vegetables at controlled prices would help to keep the general price level down. We have little information about the fruit position; but it appears that fruits, like vegetables, are scarce and dear. The quantities reaching the Calcutta market are considerably less than before the war. The scarcity is no doubt due to approximately similar causes to those which have reduced supplies of other supplementary foods.

28. **Mustard oil.**—About half of Bengal's supply of mustard seeds for the manufacture of oil formerly came from other provinces. Here again, imports have almost entirely ceased owing to embargoes on export imposed by other provinces. The actual quantity imported annually from 1937 to 1942 averaged

about 170,000 tons. This would yield some 60,000 tons of oil, equivalent in calorie value to perhaps 140,000 tons of rice.

B.—Comment on protective and supplementary foods.

29. We have emphasized the value of non-cereal foods from the nutritional standpoint. Another point to which attention must be drawn is that the aggregate contribution made by such foods to the quantitative food needs of the province is by no means negligible. Pulses, fish, potatoes and vegetable oil are the most important in this respect. We have dealt with the matter in some detail because we feel that it must be given a prominent position in the programme of reconstruction in Bengal. Clearly, there is not one single problem, but many both large and small which require solution. Few of these appear, however, to be insoluble. We would lay immediate stress on the need for the following: an improvement in distribution of pulses on an all-India basis, with particular reference to the requirements of Bengal; more motor boats for Bengal and more ice and its better distribution; more potatoes for seed and consumption; an energetic effort to grow more vegetables; closer collaboration with the military about the question of military purchases. With regard to the last, the establishment of Regional Control Boards, including military and civil representatives, to co-ordinate military purchases of various foods, is strongly to be recommended. We hope that the efforts of the army to develop its own sources of supply will be intensified and that when the war is over arrangements will be made to utilize and develop certain of these sources to meet civilian needs. It may be added that many of the problems considered in this Chapter concern not only the Bengal Government, but also Governments of provinces which normally fulfilled Bengal's demands for non-cereal foods, and the Government of India. We are aware that shortage and dearness of supplementary foods are not peculiar to Bengal at the present time. A similar situation exists in many other parts of the country. It is, however, particularly urgent and serious in Bengal.

C. The Substitution of rice by wheat.

30. In view of the present all-India shortage of rice, the use of wheat and other cereals in place of rice is a question of importance. During the famine large supplies of wheat and millets were sent to Bengal and helped to relieve food shortage. They were supplied to rice eaters through the free kitchens but efforts to persuade people to eat them in their homes in place of rice met with little success. Reference has already been made to the unpopularity of *bajra* and other millets. Wheat is somewhat more acceptable, but in general is consumed with reluctance by habitual rice-eaters. When in Bengal, we were informed of the difficulties of increasing the offtake of wheat and we visited numerous grain stores in which quantities of wheat, mainly in the form of *atta*, were deteriorating for lack of demand. In Travancore we found a similar situation. It may be added that from the standpoint of nutrition, the partial substitution of rice by wheat is a good thing, since wheat is richer in protein and certain vitamins than rice.

31. The reasons why little progress has been made in increasing the consumption of wheat by rice-eaters may be briefly analysed. Wheat as a staple food is eaten in two principal forms: as bread, or as unleavened cakes, known as *chappaties*. In this country bread is eaten only by well-to-do people and bakeries are confined to towns and cities. The domestic baking of bread is unknown, except possibly in limited areas in the North-West. To make *chappaties* an iron grid is needed, and it takes skill and experience to produce a light and palatable *chappati*. The poor rice-eater does not possess the necessary iron utensil and if he did would not know how to use it. Further, *chappaties* as a food differ in bulk and consistency from a bowl of rice. The rice-eater is accustomed to bulky meals of soft consistency which give him a

feeling of repletion, and does not relish more concentrated food which needs chewing.

32. In certain parts of the country wheat is eaten in small amounts by rice-eaters in the form of special preparations made from *atta* or semolina. Generally speaking, this habit is confined to the middle classes. Such preparations add variety to a diet largely composed of rice, but are not taken as a staple article of diet to replace rice. In the same way, people in Europe or America may take some rice in the form of curries or puddings, while the bulk of their diet is made up of other foods.

33. In wheat-eating areas whole wheat is stored as such and ground into *atta* in mills or stone *chakkies* before being made into *chappaties*. It is not stored in the form of *atta*. In Bengal there are few wheat mills outside Calcutta and the people do not possess stone *chakkies*. Hence wheat sent to Bengal has to be ground before distribution, mainly in Calcutta, and the resulting ground flour or *atta* readily goes bad on storage. There would be no point in distributing unground whole wheat, since it is difficult to use wheat in this form, and as has been said the people have no facilities for grinding it. In Bombay, on the other hand, *chakkies* are generally available and wheat can be distributed unground

34. We noted that in Travancore tapioca is preferred to wheat as an alternative to rice largely because people are used to it and it can be cooked in the same way as rice. Tapioca is an inferior starchy food, containing less than one per cent. of protein as compared with 11 to 12 per cent in wheat. We may also refer to the experience of Ceylon which, before the outbreak of the war with Japan, imported over two-thirds of her rice supplies and has since been forced to consume Australian wheat as an alternative. The following is an extract from a recent report on the food situation in Ceylon:

"The change-over of the diet of the people from rice to substitutes was not done in one stroke nor without disappointments and tears. At first, whole wheat was issued and used by the population in the same way as rice. Government too put out propaganda, during the early days of the change-over, trying to teach people how wheat could be boiled like rice after being broken up or roasting, or how local preparations could be made from ground wheat exactly in the same manner as with rice flour. Failure of this plan to produce in wheat an exact substitute for rice was soon discovered and, under stress of necessity, the preparation and serving of wheat flour in the form of bread (baked in European style) was popularised, in addition to the use of flour (maida) for whatever local forms of preparations for which it was suitable. Vigorous propaganda was carried out through schools, local Government Bodies and health officers, in all the languages of the country by lectures, demonstrations and posters, explaining the value of bread and the methods of preparation of the more successful varieties of dishes according to styles with which the people were familiar. It was pointed out that while there was bread available to eat there was no necessity to starve; and bread was available outside the ration. Government vigorously encouraged the establishment of bakeries throughout the country, including the rural areas and estates. Large numbers of bakeries have in fact been so established and the consumption of bread (as baked in European style) has increased considerably. Bread is eaten with curry or chutney".

35. The problem of increasing the consumption of wheat and other cereals by rice eaters is obviously a most difficult one and we do not find it easy to make constructive suggestions. As long as rice is available, rice eaters in general will consume it in preference to other grains and in such circumstances "eat more wheat" campaigns are not likely to be very effective. Propaganda based on nutritional arguments might, however, carry some weight with certain sections of the public. Even when shortage of rice makes the consumption of alternative foods necessary, mere visual and verbal propaganda by itself cannot

achieve much in changing the habits and preferences of the mass of the population. Such propaganda must be reinforced by practical demonstration. Suitable recipes must be devised and popularized by sale in canteens, government restaurants, etc. Before undertaking an educational campaign, it is essential to be fully informed about the cooking habits and tastes of the people and their facilities for adopting unfamiliar methods of cooking (utensils, etc.). More use could be made of women for studying domestic food questions, and the improvement of methods of preparing and cooking food, and also for teaching the public about desirable changes in diet—for work, in fact, on what has been called the "Kitchen Front" in England. Domestic science institutions have played a useful part on the "Kitchen Front" in England and other countries and we feel that they could also do so in India.

36. If school-feeding schemes are developed, alternative cereals could be used for school meals, as in Cochin, and their offtake thereby increased. Further, if children learn to take such foods, they may carry the preference into later life. Children are more flexible in their dietary habits than adults.

37. Whatever methods are adopted in the attempt to encourage the use of wheat in place of rice, progress is likely to be slow. We feel, however, that in view of the position of Bengal as regards rice supplies, steady and persistent efforts should be made in that province to increase the consumption of wheat, particularly in urban areas. It is obviously easier to influence people in cities and towns than the rural population. A greater offtake of wheat under existing rationing schemes is most desirable in connection with Bengal and all-India food policy. The problem of how to wean rice-eaters from their determined preference for a food in short supply and reluctance to turn to alternative grains is, as we have already pointed out, not peculiar to Bengal, but is of all-India importance.

J. A. WOODHEAD, *Chairman*
S. V. RAMAMURTY
MANILAL B. NANAVATI
M. AFZAL HUSAIN*
W. R. AYKROYD

R. A. GOPALASWAMI, *Secretary*
New Delhi, the 10th April 1945

---

* Signed subject to separate minute.

MINUTE BY MR. M. AFZAL HUSAIN

The following minute sets out briefly the conclusions, which I have reached in respect of the questions of the existence of a carry-over, and the effects on the economy of Bengal of the inter-provincial trade barriers. It has been shown, in Section A of part I of the minute, that during recent years, and particularly in the beginning of 1943, there was no carry-over. In Section B the course of events leading to the famine of 1943 has been traced from 1941, and it has been shown that the shortage (considered in Section C) was really large and could not be made up without imports from other provinces. Section D shows that the shortage was aggravated by Calcutta remaining on the Bengal market. It has been shown (Section E) that imports became impossible, because of the barriers which were set up in the way of inter-provincial trade. Thus Bengal had to face a very serious problem during the war and the Government had a very difficult task (Sections F and G).

In Part II of the minute a brief account has been given of the general unpreparedness of India to meet a food emergency.

I. THE CAUSES OF THE BENGAL FAMINE

A—The fallacy of carry-over

In Chapter X of the Report, under Section B, the causes of the Bengal Famine have been discussed, and one of the causes mentioned is:-

> "a shortage in the stock of old rice carried forward from 1942 to 1943" (p. 77).

In Appendix II, the problem of the, "production and consumption of rice in Bengal", has been dealt with very fully, and is summarised in Chapter III, C. It is stated that "the carry-over at the beginning of 1943 was probably sufficient for about 6 weeks' requirements" (p. 15). In other words it was 11·5 per cent of the annual requirement.

The idea that there has been, even during recent years, a substantial 'carry-over' of rice in Bengal, has been responsible for the miscalculations that led to the Bengal disaster, and, on 'looking back', this impression still causes a great deal of confusion. This conception of "huge stocks somewhere" may prove dangerous in the future as well, as it is likely to give a sense of false security. It is necessary, therefore, that the true nature and significance of 'carry-over' should be fully understood. The theory of 'carry-over' is a survival from the era of plenty when Bengal produced far in excess of the requirements of its population and exported rice. The unconsumed stocks constituted the 'carry-over'. Those days are long past. Absolutely no data are available regarding the stock position of rice (or any other foodgrain) from month to month, or year to year, in Bengal, or any other part of India. Such data, in fact, are not available for any rice eating country of Asia, with the single exception of Japan. According to Wickizer and Bennett, "Japan is about the only Oriental country which has followed a regular practice of storing considerable quantities of rice". And even in Japan "normally the carry-over at the close of a season is equivalent to one month's or six weeks' consumption, but at the end of the bumper crop year 1933-4 it was approximately twice as great".[1]

---

[1] The Rice Economy of Monsoon Asia, 1941.

Wickizer and Bennett sum up the position thus: "Rice stocks are commonly held in many hands: by growers for the need of the family, and by numerous intermediaries and distributors scattered throughout the market. Such holdings are necessarily small, and are intended generally to meet requirements only until the next harvest. Except where governments have intervened in order to influence a rice price situation, rice stocks do not ordinarily become concentrated, nor are they carried over for more than one season. Hence annual production of rice tends to correspond closely with annual utilization". The last sentence of this quotation is significant. In arid zones, where rainfall is scarce and uncertain, where a good crop is obtained once in five years or so, and where fluctuations in production are wide, climatic conditions, types of food-grains—jowar and millets—psychology of the people, all tend to bring about the storage of an occasional surplus crop. These factors do not operate in a region of abundant rainfall; at least, not to any appreciable extent.

2. There are other causes also of the illusion about the existence of a carry-over. Some 'high class' varieties of rice improve in storage and are kept for more than a season. The rich few who have more than they need may store rice. Traders have a small stock left at the end of the year. There may be isolated pockets of carry-over in some heavily surplus districts. Such stocks, however, are too insignificant to alter the general food supply situation of a province of over 60 million people, with an overall deficit production.

3. The real cause of the misunderstanding, however, is that "most rices are not really suitable for consumption until at least two or possibly three months have elapsed from the date of harvesting......". The new rice has "an insipid watery taste", cooks into "a meshy glutinous consistency", a "pasty mass" which "cannot be digested as satisfactorily as grains which retain their individuality". Therefore, "wherever it is possible to exercise preference, no consumer will eat rice which has only just been harvested".[1] Thus the year of production and that of consumption normally do not coincide. The point may be elucidated by a statement of what actually happens. The *aman* crop is harvested from November to December, and may be said to be assembled by the beginning of January; the *boro* crop is harvested by March-April, and the *aus* crop in August-September. The year of production may be regarded as from January to December. Ordinarily the year of consumption will be, approximately, let us say, from March-April to March-April next year.

Jan/Feb/Mar/Apr/May/Jun/Jul/Aug/Sep/Oct/Nov/Dec/Jan/Feb/Mar

(...... Production Year ....)

(........... Consumption Year ....)

Only that quantity which is left over as *surplus* after full twelve months' consumption is strictly speaking a 'carry-over'. But the quantity in stock during January to March-April is not 'carry-over'; it represents the actual requirement for the last two or three months of the year of consumption. The year of consumption is not rigidly fixed. It slides over the year of production backwards and forwards according to the quantity of stocks available for consumption. When the quantity during the previous year is short of full requirements, the consumption of the new *aman* starts earlier, and when the quantity is in excess of requirements it starts later. This overlapping acts as a 'shock absorber', and is of great importance. The crop assembled in January is certainly available for early consumption, but if consumed prematurely will leave a deficit at the end of the year of consumption, unless the crop produced is more than the requirement of 12 months and will, therefore, meet the additional requirements up to the end of the normal year of consumption.

[1]Report on the Marketing of rice in India and Burma, 1941.

4. Ever since the annual production, or supply, has begun to be only equal to, or less than the actual requirements, the deficiencies due to very short crops have been met, not to an appreciable degree from the accumulated reserves of previous years, but mainly by an earlier consumption of the *aman* harvest. It was Bengal's good fortune that years of serious crop shortages have been well spaced and have invariably been followed by years of very heavy crops. For instance:

1 { 1928 with 7·1 million ton short-crop, was followed by
1929 with 9·2 million ton crop; and eight years later,

2 { 1936 with 7·8 million ton short-crop, was followed by
1937 with 10·7 million ton crop; and again,

3 { 1941 with 7·4 million ton short-crop, was followed by
1942 with 10·3 million ton crop.

Therefore, during recent years, it is not so much on his accumulated reserves, carried forward from year to year, that the subsistence farmer of Bengal has existed, but on the 'advances' that he has been able to draw. The deficit of a poor crop he made up by starting consumption of the next crop before its normal period of 'maturity'. He lived by borrowing and this applied to money and food equally. When his 'debts' increased beyond a certain limit he collapsed. It may be stated that the triennium 1941-3 was the first in the recent history of Bengal when a bumper crop year (1942) was preceded and succeeded by years of very poor crops (1941, 1943).

5. In Appendix II, a study is made of the actual conditions in Bengal relating to the yearly requirements of rice. The correctness of the statistics of acreage, yield, consumption, and even population has been rightly questioned. It has been recognised that the acreage estimate is too low and so is that of the yield, and an increase of 20 per cent over the Director of Agriculture's estimate has been made (Statement III). With statistics so hopelessly defective, either no attempt at all should be made to evaluate the position, or the conclusions drawn from the estimates available should be subjected to various tests and their reliability determined. In what follows, the second alternative has been employed in determining whether a 'carry-over', *i.e.*, a surplus really existed in Bengal.

6. "India, without Burma, is not self-sufficient in the production of food-grains. Before the war a comparatively small and diminishing exportable surplus of wheat was offset by a large and increasing import of rice". In pre-war years India's dependence upon rice imports was progressively increasing.[1]

	1937-8	1938-9	1939-40	1940-1
Net Imports of Rice and Paddy (in tons).	+1,165,072	+1,253,098	+2,138,600	+1,097,198

In view of these large and increasing imports, any substantial 'carry-over' of rice could not be a reality in India.

Similarly, since 1934 Bengal has been, except for a single year (1937), an importing province, in other words not completely self-sufficient in respect of the production of rice. It was, therefore, not producing more than it actually needed. This must be admitted. It is true that the volume of net imports did not correspond with the variations in production, but the significant fact is that year after year imports were made and their quantity showed a tendency towards increase. In such circumstances any appreciable accumulated carry-over was not likely to emerge, for imports would not be made if the demand

[1] Report of the Foodgrains Policy Committee. 1944.

could be satisfied from the carry-over. According to the estimates made this carry over, from 1932 to 1940, varied between 13 and 33 per cent. of the total crop harvested (Statement I, Appendix II). (*See* paragraph 12 *infra*).

7. From 1934 to 1941 there was no increase in rice production in Bengal (Appendix II, Statements I and III). Yield per acre had shown a downward tendency [Appendix II, paragraph 9 (ii)]. The population, on the other hand, had increased from 53 million in 1934 to 60·3 million by 1941. Therefore, during this period the food position was steadily deteriorating. From being an exporter, Bengal had become an importer. From solvency in regard to food it had reached the stage of insolvency. If there ever was a 'carry-over' in the sense of surplus over consumption, it must have vanished years ago.

8. Another test of whether supplies were adequate would be an assessment on the basis of actual food and seed requirements and production. On the basis of *per capita* consumption, as worked out by Prof. Mahalanobis, there has been since 1936 (except for the year 1937) a definite shortage in the quantity of rice available. It is difficult to reconcile this unquestionable shortage with any surplus or 'carry-over'. A more detailed study of figures will be fruitful. Reference may be made to the statement below, which is based on the data of supplies as given in statement III of Appendix II. It should be made clear that any notion of the quantity consumed being absolutely inelastic is inadmissible. In fact during years of plenty a person eats a little more, and during years of scarcity he eats less; and the margin is fairly wide, and may range from a mere subsistence ration to the full satisfaction of hunger. Further, during scarcity there is increased use of other available food such as tubers. Ignoring these considerations, and even admitting, merely for the sake of argument, a progressive accumulation of surpluses—which is very unlikely—there was a deficit in 1941 of 1·55 million tons. The previous 'carry-over', if any, must have disappeared by the end of 1941, a year of poor crop. The adjusted supply figures (involving a 20 per cent increase over the estimates of the Director of Agriculture Bengal) and the data of actual consumption requirements obtained by Prof. Mahalanobis, fit in admirably with the supply and consumption position in Bengal during the last 15 years and give a picture very close to the reality. These data also fit in with the change-over of the province from the position of a net exporter to that of a net importer. These figures, therefore, provide a very good test of the food resources of the province in respect of rice.

Year	Population (Million)	Adjusted supply ('000 tons) including net imports or exports	Net imports (+) or exports (—) ('000 tons)	Seed ('000 tons)	Net available supply ('000 tons)	Requirement at 3·58 seers per week (tons)	(—) Deficit (+) Surplus (Million tons)	Progressive total of Col. VIII or Carry over (Million tons)
	II	III	IV	V	VI	VII	VIII	IX
1928	49·0	7,563	+161	422	7,141	8,377,873	—1,237*	..
1929	49·44	9,662	—250	411	9,251	8,436,005	+815	—422
1930	49·68	9,009	—311	437	8,572	8,504,137	+68	—354
1931	50·1	9,940	..	441	9,499	8,565,947	+933	+579
1932	51·1	9,945	—239	440	9,505	8,736,924	+768	+1,347
1933	52·1	10,771	—31	438	10,333	8,907,901	+1,425	+2,772
1934	53·1	9,927	+414	425	9,502	9,078,878	+423	+3,195
1935	54·1	9,840	+150	424	9,416	9,249,855	+166	+3,361
1936	55·1	8,251	+155	448	7,803	9,420,832	—1,618	+1,743
1937	56·1	11,218	—185	446	10,772	9,591,809	—1,180	+2,923
1938	57·1	9,981	+133	446	9,535	9,762,786	—228	+2,965
1939	58·1	9,596	+482	445	9,151	9,933,763	—783	+1,912
1940	59·1	9,882	+358	440	9,442	10,104,740	—663	+1,249
1941	60·3	7,954	+323	482	7,472	10,275,717	—2,804	—1,555
1942	..	10,774	—2	467	10,307	10,446,694	—140	—1,695

Consumption per million per annum—170,977 tons.

* It may appear that a 'negative' carry-over has no meaning. Reference is invited to paragraphs 3 and 4 of this minute, as stated deficiencies are made up by early consumption of the crop of the succeeding year.

A comparison of columns VI and VII shows that since 1936 net available supplies have been considerably short of the minimum requirements, as calculated on the Mahalanobis formula, every year with the exception of 1937. Before 1936 supplies were in excess of requirements; Bengal then was an exporting province. Surpluses and deficits are shown in column VIII. Further, when supplies were adequate the people were able to eat more, and perhaps lay by some stocks. Since 1936-7, the people have been on short rations.

The figures in column IX, provide a test for the accuracy of the assumption of a carry-over. If there was an accumulated surplus, it had disappeared by 1941, and 1943 opened with nothing more than the *aman* crop of 1942, assembled by January, 1943.

9. The test supplied by the economic condition of the people leads one to the same conclusions. The distribution of holdings given on p. 6 of the Report is as follows:—

More than 5 acres . . .	2	million families
Between 2-5 acres . . .	2	„ „
Less than 2 acres . . .	3·5	„ „

It is stated that 5 acres will be the minimum area required to keep the average family in reasonable comfort, but the size of holding will have to be 7 acres if the land is capable of growing nothing but *aman* paddy. If the number of holdings above 5 acres capable of growing *aman* paddy only is taken to be 0·5 million, the number of families which live below the level of 'reasonable' comfort will be 6 millions. What happens to these 6 million holders when the crop is very short? Such families could just balance income and outgo in a normal year. They cannot have any carry-over of either money or grain. In many cases a substantial portion of the crop goes to the money-lender. The only possibility is that during years of short-crops consumption of rice must be reduced in order to meet the constant factor of the standing charges. Alternative foods such as sweet potatoes are grown and consumed and make up for the deficit. During normal years the consumption increases, and carry-over is possible only when the production is much above the requirements. Such occasions have become rare since population increase has outstripped food supply.

10. The nutritional standard of the people of Bengal supports the above contentions. Since the days (1933) when Sir John Megaw (p. 7, para. 9) conducted his inquiry, there has been a marked deterioration in the food position. There has been no increase in production and a steep rise in population. The Foodgrains Policy Committee arrived at the following conclusion "........ though it is true that taking India as a whole ...... and taking an average of years, she may broadly be described as only slightly less than self-sufficient in foodgrains as a whole, nevertheless the self-sufficiency implied by this statement at the very best is self-sufficiency at a very low level of *per capita* consumption. There is very little room, taking the country as a whole, for the process of tightening the belt. We have it on the authority of the highest nutritional expert in this country, Dr. Aykroyd, that there is at all times serious under-nourishment of some third of the population".[1] With a considerable proportion of the population living at a level of under-nourishment, if not starvation, it is difficult to accept the hypothesis of large surpluses or stocks remaining unconsumed year after year, and getting accumulated, even to the extent of

[1] Report of the Foodgrains Policy Committee, 1943, p. 33.

33 per cent. of the annual production (paragraph 8 above and statement). Under-nourishment of a large section of the population and huge accumulations of stocks cannot go together.

11. The results of the "anti-hoarding" campaign or the "food drive" which was undertaken in Bengal in June 1943 (excluding Calcutta, Howrah and a few other areas) supports this conclusion. From the data available the following conclusions may be drawn.

1. Population of the area of this drive	55·748	million	
2. Total requirement of this population from 16th June to 31st December in terms of rice at 3 seers *per capita* per week[1]	4·4	„	tons
3. Actually consumed by this population from 1st January to 15th June, at the same rate	3·8	„	„
4. Stocks on 16th June, 1943 (at 25 per cent excess of those actually discovered)	1·17	„	„
5. Total consumed and in stock *i.e.* 3 *plus* 4	4·97	„	„
6. Total consumed by the remaining population (6·5 million) up to 15th June 1943, at the above rate. . . .	0·44	„	„
Total consumed and in stock on 16th June 1943	5·4	„	„
Estimated *aman* crop assembled in January 1943	6·0	„	„
Balance unaccounted for	0·6	„	„

Even allowing for undiscovered stocks if there had been a large carry-over, much bigger stocks would have been found. (There had been import of rice and other grains as well during this period). Similarly the Calcutta Food census in July 1943 discovered stocks of the order of 31,000 tons, which is just one month's rice consumption of that city. Had there been a substantial 'carry-over', the stocks would have been larger.

12. In Appendix II, Section B, the relation of supply of rice to requirements for the ten years 1928 to 1937 has been examined, and the conclusion arrived at is stated thus:

"...*prima facie*, it would appear that stocks carried over from year to year must have been accumulating in the province during the period" (page 209, paragraph 13).

Similarly in Section C, the supply position in relation to requirements for the years 1938 to 1942 has been examined, and the following conclusion is arrived at:

"The state of current supply during 1941 supports the conclusion reached in paragraph 14 above, namely, that the stocks carried over from year to year must have been considerable." (page 210, paragraph 16). Again, in Section D, the supply position in relation to requirements for the year 1943 has been discussed and it is stated:

"The carry-over at the beginning of the year was sufficient for the requirements of about 6 weeks" [page 212, paragraph 23(ii)(b)].

[1] This figure is lower than Prof. Mahalanobis' estimate of actual consumption.

It is to be determined if these conclusions are correct. The table below has been compiled from the lata of surpluses and deficits as given in **Appendix II**, Statement IV.

I Year	II +Surplus —Deficit (Million tons)	III Progressive total of Col. II (Million tons)	IV Net—Export (—) Imports (+) ('000 tons)
1928	—1·20	..	..
1929	+0·79	—0·41	..
1930	+0·01	—0·42	..
1931	+0·80	+0·38	..
1932	+0·69	+1·07	..
1933	+1·39	+2·46	..
1934	+0·44	+2·9	+414
1935	+0·24	+3·14	+150
1936	—1·50	+1·64	+155
1937	+1·35	+2·99	—185
1938	..	+2·99	+133
1939	—0·51	+2·48	+482
1940	—0·34	+2·14	+358
1941	—2·43	—0·29	+323
1942	+0·29	..	—2

Column III of this table shows the stocks of rice in the province at the end of each year, on the assumption that accumulation of surpluses was taking place; while Column IV shows the net imports or exports of the province. If, as the Report has concluded, accumulated stocks were available in the province in each of the years 1931 to 1940, and during certain years those stocks were very large, it becomes impossible to explain the net imports in these years for the following reasons. The population of Bengal may be divided into the four classes:—

(a) those who grow their own food but whose production is just equal to or less than their requirements;

(b) those who buy their requirements;

(c) traders;

(d) big land-holders who have surplus over their requirements.

Of these it is only classes (c) and (d) who would hold surplus stocks of rice. The big landlords would accumulate unnecessarily large stocks only if they were unable to find a market for them. Therefore, stocks would come to be concentrated in the hands of traders. And it is this class which imports rice. If the traders had been accumulating stocks, would they still import and thus add to their unsold stocks? No wise trader would hold stocks much in excess of his annual turnover. The existence of net imports is thus incompatible with the accumulation of large stocks.

13. In 1942, according to Statement IV, of Appendix II (p. 216), the current supply, seed deducted, was 10·31 million tons and consumption 10·02 million tons, leaving a surplus of 0·29 million tons, equal to 1·5 weeks' supply. Is it too much to say that this so-called 'surplus' was completely wiped out by the cyclone of October 1942 in the districts of Midnapore and the 24-Parganas, and by the export of 185,000 tons which was allowed to take place during 1942? There was definite shortage during November-December, as is evident from

the prevailing distress, and this supports the conclusion that the supplies had been exhausted.

Conclusion

One is, therefore, forced to the conclusion that in Bengal, and in fact in the rest of India as well, there are no surplus stocks of such magnitude as to serve as "huge" reserves. What we find is a hand to mouth existence, at a very low level of consumption. Events of the last two years have proved this conclusively. In spite of the 'Grow More Food' campaign, the food situation still causes anxiety. At any rate, this much is certain that Bengal had no carry-over of rice worth considering in the beginning of 1943.

B—The Course of Events Leading to the Famine

14. The cycle of events which terminated in the famine of 1943 may now be described. One need not labour the point that every event has a history and its true cause cannot be determined by a study merely of factors involved at the moment of its occurrence, but must be traced to its past. To borrow a phrase from biology, every event has a phylogeny. Therefore, the immediate causes of the famine of 1943 have to be traced from 1941. These events may be traced year by year.

1941.—(Appendix II, Statement III). The *aman* crop which was assembled in January 1941 was 5·178 million tons (adjusted figures by addition of 20 per cent to the Director of Agriculture's figure)—the shortest crop for fifteen years and with *boro* and *aus*, supplemented by 323,000 tons imports, and after deduction of seed requirements, gave 7,472,000 tons of rice, for the consumption of 60·3 million people, which was the population of Bengal at that time. According to the estimate of 3·58 seers *per capita* per week (the estimate of Prof. Mahalanobis) the total quantity required for 12 months was over 10·25 million tons. Thus there was a shortage of 2·8 million tons, *i.e.*, 14 weeks supply. Normally the *aman* crop would come into consumption, let us say, from March-April 1941. The total crop being short, it was barely enough for nine months, and was, therefore, consumed by about the end of the year 1941. Nothing was available for the last two or three months of the consumption year 1941-42 (January-February-March 1942).

1942.—The *aman* crop assembled by January 1942 was 8·876 million tons—the highest since 1937. The *boro* crop of 1942 gave 206,000 tons and the *aus* 1·694 million tons. There were no imports. The total quantity available for consumption (*minus* seed requirements) was 10·3 million tons. This crop would normally have come into use from March-April, but as the previous crop was very short and had been consumed by the end of the year 1941, the new crop was drawn upon most probably from about the beginning of January 1942. It would have sufficed for twelve months, *i.e.*, till the end of December 1942, and possibly even beyond that period with some effort, but during this year various unforeseen factors adversely affected the position:—

(i) A quantity of rice was exported (187,500 tons in the year, of which 184,618 tons were exported between January and July 1942). [Report p. 28].

(ii) There was short supply of wheat during later part of 1942:—57,377 tons [Chapter V—para. 23].

(iii) The disastrous cyclone of October 1942 destroyed large stocks of rice in important surplus districts in Bengal, *viz.*, Midnapore and the 24-Parganas. The quantity destroyed has not been determined but is described as very large.

(iv) There was an influx of refugees, estimated at several lakhs.

(v) There was a very large increase in the strength of the Defence Forces in Bengal, and also rapid increase in the industrial population, labour for military works etc., etc., which directly or indirectly depleted the foodgrain resources of the province.

In view of these considerations (a) of heavier demands and (b) of serious loss, it would not be incorrect to hold that by the end of the year 1942 the year's production had been completely consumed.

This view is supported by the fact that reports of distress were made early in December (Appendix VI), and by the end of the month hunger-marches had started. The price of rice had risen enormously, and there was shortage in some places even in the villages. This was at the time when the *aman* crop was being harvested. The situation at that time has been described in the Report (Chapter V, paragraph 29):—

"The evidence presented by these contemporary documents leaves no room for doubt that the upheaval in the Bengal markets towards the end of 1942, was due to the fact that in November and December of that year, that is, before the bulk of the *aman* crop had been reaped, unusual purchases were being made by persons who were convinced, quite correctly, that the yield of the *aman* crop would be so short and stocks in hand so low, that a crisis in supply was inevitable and was fast approaching".

In face of these observations any material 'carry-over' at the end of 1942 was a mere myth.

1943.—Therefore, it may be assumed, with considerable justification, that 6·024 million tons *aman* crop, assembled by January 1943, came into consumption almost immediately, if not even earlier during the harvest, *i.e.*, November-December 1942.

According to the Rice Marketing Report, on the average of the years 1934-35 to 1936-37, out of the total production of 8·4 million tons, 3·9 millions were kept for domestic consumption and 376,000 tons for seed. The marketable surplus was 3·87 million tons. It is generally the *aman* crop which comes into the market, and when it is taken into consideration, that—

(i) this crop was very short (1·5 million tons short of the previous fifteen years average),

(ii) there was a general feeling of insecurity, on account of the military situation,

(iii) prices were rising rapidly,

(iv) there was no carry-over, not even for the usual period of 'maturing' of the harvested crop, and

(v) all these facts were being widely advertised, the conclusion is irresistible that the cultivator retained a larger quantity than the normal for his own use, and the marketable surplus was reduced, perhaps to 2 million tons, in a market which used to get double that quantity during times of peace and stability. Consumers began to secure supplies in excess of immediate requirements, priority concerns to lay by stocks to ensure supplies for their labour, traders to make money, all joined the mêlée. The sources of supply having dried up, panic set in. This was a critical stage. Effective action was not taken, stocks had been captured, and those left without food had to pay prices which many could not afford. Famine had really begun from the commencement of the year 1943 although its results became manifest some months later, and its effects even continued in the heavy death-rate during the first half of 1944.

C—The real extent of the shortage

15. The conclusions arrived at in the Report regarding supplies are given in paragraph 15 (iii), p. 15 and in paragraph 23 of Appendix II, of the Report (p. 212), and these may be summarised thus:—

(1) The current supply during 1943, was sufficient for the requirements of about 43 weeks (8·36 million tons).

(2) The carry-over at the beginning of the year 1943, was sufficient for the requirements of about 6 weeks (1·16 million tons).

(3) Therefore, the absolute deficiency of supplies was of the order of the requirement for 3 weeks, *i.e.*, 0·58 million tons.[1]

With these conclusions it is difficult to agree. From what has been said above (p. 15), it is evident that there was no carry-over of any significance at the end of 1942. The *aman* rice crop available for consumption from January to September 1943 (when the *aus* crop becomes available), was approximately 5·5 million tons (adjusted figures with 20 per cent increase over Director of Agriculture's estimates). If all grain available had been procured and distributed equitably, it would have provided 2·44 seers *per capita* per week for a population of 63 million for 9 months. At a rate of 3 seers *per capita* per week, with a perfect system of control and distribution, 6·7 million tons would have been the required quantity, and, at 3·2 seers *per capita* per week 7·2 million tons. It is evident, therefore, that the absolute shortage, at a very conservative calculation, could not have been less than 1·5 million tons. The Government of Bengal had placed their demands for all foodgrains at 1·36 million tons, of which rice was 0·9 million tons. These were indeed very modest estimates. The Director of Agriculture informed the Commission that an enormous area had been put under sweet potatoes during 1943. This must have helped to mitigate the effect of the shortage. Taking everything into consideration one is forced to the conclusion that the shortage was large and far more than 0·58 million tons. It was certainly of a magnitude, that by mere manipulation of supplies actually available in the province, it could not have been wiped out. This was not realised early enough. The 'carry-over' mentality had bred complacency. To avert disaster, a timely supply in regular and substantial instalments of foodgrains to the extent of *at least* a million tons was absolutely necessary. The quantity of foodgrains which actually arrived in Bengal was of the order of 0·65 million tons, but it came sometimes in driblets, sometimes in torrents, and most of it came too late, towards the end of the year.[2]

All the rice that came into Bengal was within the country and if the large quantities which came after May had come earlier deaths might have been avoided. Regular arrivals would have produced confidence and kept the prices down.

D—CALCUTTA ON THE BENGAL MARKET

16. The shortage considered in the last section was aggravated by the fact that, throughout the famine of 1943, Calcutta, was on the Bengal market.

---

[1] If the actual shortage was of the magnitude of 0·5 million tons, *i.e.*, a little in excess of the net Burma imports, then would not free trade have supplied this deficiency from the o-called 'stocks' all over the country ? Had not the rest of India accumulated the same arry-overs which, it is suggested, Bengal possessed ? The theory of carry-over thus stands xploded.

[2] The arrivals of rice and wheat into Bengal during 1943 were :—

	Rice.	Wheat.
January, February, March	17,452, tons.	26,000 tons.
April	15,827 „	38,000 „
May, June, July	100,324 „	99,000 „
August, September	30,689 „	
October, November, December	99,334 „	176,000 „

On 'looking back' the feeling grows strong that the most obvious and correct step, which was taken in 1944, should have been taken in 1943. With the first signs of distress, Calcutta should have been immediately *taken off* the Bengal market. This was obvious. For wheat Calcutta had been off the Bengal market always. The average imports of Burma rice were roughly equal to the rice requirements of Calcutta. Therefore, for many years Calcutta had been virtually off the Bengal market both for rice and wheat. During the year of a short crop, after cyclone and flood, with the enemy knocking at the gates. the population increasing through an influx of refugees, increased concentration of war industries, and a huge army depleting the market of milk. fish, egg, poultry, vegetables, and fruit, Calcutta was *on* the Bengal market, armed with a huge purchasing power. The inevitable result was famine in Bengal. This should have been easily foreseen. This is a lesson for the future.

E—THE STORY OF THE BARRIERS

17. From what has been said above it is evident that there was no carry-over in the beginning of 1943, the previous year's crops had been consumed by the end of 1942, the *aman* crop available was very short, imports from Burma were not possible, the external and internal situation was disquieting, panic had set in, prices were soaring. The only thing which could stem the tide was an assured supply of foodgrains. There were obstacles. To appreciate the difficulties of Bengal a review of the conditions leading to these obstacles is necessary.

18. In Chapter IV, paragraphs 1 and 2, are described changes in the economic and administrative organisation of the country as a result of the control of trade by Governments. In this change, which has been rightly described as 'tremendous', the period when 'barriers' were springing up to prevent the movement of grain from one district to another and from one province to another has been very correctly described as "a critical and potentially most dangerous stage". The erection of barriers may be regarded as a necessary step in the assumption by Government of control over trade (para. 4), but was the step taken at the right time and in the right direction? And, these are the two essential attributes of a wise step. Government control over trade was admittedly a most urgent wartime necessity, but stopping the flow of trade, without creating adequate channels for the flow of food supply, is like putting a dam across a river first and planning to dig irrigation channels afterwards. The consequences of such a mistake are evident. It may be argued that in the absence of a well-planned scheme of food control and distribution, on an all-India basis, barriers set up by Provinces and States independently, without co-ordination or even mutual consultation, essentially to protect their own interests, had become *inevitable*. Nevertheless, it cannot be denied that, as anticipated, these barriers led to the conditions which, were responsible, in no small measure, for the scarcity and famine that visited Bengal —the province which had the singular misfortune of being in the war zone, and falling a victim to floods, a devastating cyclone, a short crop, political unrest and enemy action, and with 'denial' and defence measures leading to dislocation of internal economy. I, therefore, agree with the following view: "If there was a single root cause . . . . for the initial dislocation of the whole 'food economy' and 'food morale' of this densely populated area . . . it was the incautious use of newly created provincial barriers."

In paragraph 32, p. 24, the possibility of such a danger is recognised. It is stated that if the machinery of control could not be completed speedily "any serious and sudden deterioration in internal supply arising out of natural causes, was liable to lead to disaster," and this is exactly what happened in Bengal.

19. The dangers inherent in those barriers, or measures restricting trade, did not come as a surprise. They were evident and had been fully anticipated. Categorical statements prophesying disaster as the consequence of such measures had been repeatedly made. The Bihar Central Advisory Committee on Price Control meeting on 18th December 1939, emphasised "the need of some form of inter-provincial control"[1] and this opinion was communicated to the Government of India as early as the 8th January 1940.

20. In the Third Price Control Conference of the official representatives of the Centre, Provinces and States, held at Delhi in October 1941, the President (Sir Ramaswami Mudaliar) stated "the Government of India wished to keep inter-provincial trade as free as possible, but if the control was applicable within a particular area he saw no objection to it". The views expressed were: It was "feared that restriction of inter-provincial or inter-State movement of supplies would lead to difficulties" (Bihar). It "was clear that the Central Government's intervention was necessary in respect of inter-provincial trading for provincial boundaries were not economic boundaries" (Madras). It was suggested that the "control should extend from the producing stage right down to the final stage" "imports should be flattened", and "the possibility of not merely controlling prices but also regulating the movement of rice to the competing consuming provinces" should be considered (Assam). The scramble for rice supplies in the Central Provinces, was leaving a deficit in the province's own requirements.

A foretaste of such unco-ordinated control had already been experienced when, on account of scarcity in Arakan, the Burma Government had prohibited export of rice, just as some Provincial Government had prohibited export of rice from their own areas to adjacent areas. The Government of Burma had finally lifted the embargo, but by that time the favourable season for shipping rice had practically ended.

The President emphasised: "We do not contemplate at all the possibility of provincial barriers for export of this product (rice) or any product for the matter of that", and he added: "If any Government finds itself in such an unfavourable position as a result of the activities of its surrounding provinces or States, it can come to the Government of India who will use their good influence to get over the difficulty".

It is clear from the above that by October 1941, difficulties had arisen, and barriers were considered dangerous, and need for a central controlling agency, was evident.

21. The Fourth Price Control Conference met on 6th/7th February 1942. (A day previously the Rice Conference had met at the instance of the Bihar Government. At this Conference Bihar and Assam had expressed the opinion that provincial control of exports would lead to chaos.) By then the problems had "become more complicated, their solutions were more urgent and the administrative difficulties greater than they had ever been." Bans "had been put by certain Administrations, both Provincial and State, on the movements of commodities", the President (Sir Ramaswami Mudaliar) remarked "At first flush it looks as if such a ban was eminently justified and that the Provincial or State authority concerned had a duty towards the population in its charge to see that the movement of goods, when scarcity conditions were about to prevail, was checked so far as its area was concerned, that is to say, that foodstuffs available within the area are not transported beyond its border. One or two Provincial Governments have done it; and some States have done it; and I must also admit with thankfulness that some Provincial Administrations have stoutly resisted the temptation to put such a ban . . . .

1 Perhaps this referred to Price Control only.

The free movement of commodities up to the last stage is the most vital factor that will check the growing rise of prices and will also try to preserve for the consumer adequate supplies in every area . . . . India may be geographically called a 'continent'; it is after all one country and under one Administration; and consequently the Central Government is concerned with the safety and the conditions of living of all the people within this geographical area, India." He continued: "The Central Government cannot, therefore, view with equanimity any attempt at tying up stocks of a particular commodity, within a specified area, and leaving other areas to look after themselves . . . . If this movement is widespread then it will create the most chaotic conditions, nay, absolutely famine conditions in several parts of the country . . . . . The theory of self-sufficiency has led to ruin so far as Sovereign States are concerned; and if that theory of self-sufficiency were to be incorporated in provincial and State units in this great Federation, not only ruin but something worse will be our lot. We have agreed, not with enthusiasm, to such bans as a very temporary measure in certain areas. But the decisive view of the Government of India is that such bans on export do much more harm than good, and to the utmost possible extent should be avoided." He also referred to the anxiety of certain governments to build up stocks.

While on the one hand certain provinces considered that their first care was the supply of food to those who lived within their jurisdictions, and help to other provinces could not be given to the extent of facing a shortage themselves (Punjab, Madras), on the other hand a higher degree of control over transport and supplies was demanded (Bombay), to the extent of an all-India control of stocks (C. P.). It was stressed that the unit was not the province or the district, but the whole of India, and a shortage of any particular commodity had to be shared equally (N. W. F. P.), by means of control at the Centre (Bihar) and that bans on exports should not be placed (Bihar), as restrictions on inter-provincial trade would be suicidal (Mysore). It was claimed that in certain emergent circumstances, such as the danger of a famine, stoppage of exports from a particular area would be justifiable. The President, summing up the discussion stated "that the process of tightening up the belt must be a universal process and not a process which must apply only to those unfortunate provinces which were in short supply with reference to any particular commodity". He drew the conclusion "that broadly speaking there should be no attempt on the part either of the Provinces or States to put a ban on the export of commodities but that when a proper transport authority which would co-ordinate the interests of various Provinces and States began to function at the Centre, it could be left to that authority so to adjust the transport that there was no draining of all resources of one province to its own disadvantage and to the advantage of accumulating stocks in the neighbouring province or State. He, however, agreed that if there were a famine condition in a local area, something must be done on the spot, and he did not "object to a particular kind of emergency power being used by district officer or local officer".

22. Barriers continued to be put up. In March 1942, the Central Provinces, after a scramble for rice, had stopped export of foodgrains to places outside the province. The Government of India had in some cases issued directions against such steps. When the Food Production Conference met in April 1942 the question of barriers came up for a good deal of discussion. The President (Mr. N. R. Sarker) stated in his opening remarks: "...... that in case intensive and planned efforts (to Grow More Food) failed to make good the shortage of a commodity, then substitution of this commodity by some other surplus foodstuff shall have to be considered. And, even if this remedy failed to fill up the gap, then it would be for the various governments to consider how

far an all-round cutting in the consumption of the commodity must be voluntarily accepted by all the Provinces and the States."

Sir Ramaswami Mudaliar said: "The Central Government has been up against this problem of every province, of every State, of every area thinking in terms of its own population, and not willing to recognise the needs of the population elsewhere in India.......... That is a most dangerous doctrine to be preached.......It would bring about such confusion in trade, commerce and transport that it would harm the interests of the whole country......When we have gone to the extent of including a country like Ceylon into (our) economic orbit in respect of food production and food supply, it seems to me the most unnatural thing to suggest that each province or State will look after itself and only when there is a surplus and to the extent that (province or) State judges there can be a surplus, having provided for all the contingencies which might arise in the future and having provided for all that is necessary for the province (or State), would it allow export from its territory......That sort of attitude, ... would completely break up the economic structure of the country......We have been resisting this idea that each area should look after itself first, leaving others alone.........I do venture to suggest that we cannot take the view that each province or State must first look after itself and then to other provinces or States." He further emphasised his point of view by taking a specific example. "Taking wheat consumption as 10 million tons, and supposing there is only 9 million tons in the country, we know how it is distributed to various provinces from the surplus; would it be an impossibility to say that Punjab will have nine-tenths and all the other importing provinces will have nine-tenths of their normal imports?" In the same meeting Sir Pheroze Kharegat explained this point of view further. He stated that if in spite of the best efforts of the surplus and deficit areas, there was a shortage of a particular commodity in the country, for instance rice, then "*the whole lot of rice available in the country should be treated as one and it should be distributed equitably between all the Provinces and States throughout the country, so that all may suffer equally and benefit equally* ...... Where there is a deficit in a particular commodity in the country as a whole, it should be distributed as equitably as possible humanly, and as equitably as transport facilities may allow" The underlying idea was equality of sacrifice of all consumers. As a logical corollary to this proposition representatives of many Provinces and States stressed the need for a *Central authority with executive power.* No steps were taken to set up such an authority.

The Food Department which was established in December 1942 set out on the task of disentangling the food tangles.

The Second All-India Food Conference was held on the 24th-26th February, 1943. The Secretary of the Food Department once again preached the gospel of 'equality of sacrifice'. He stated "Although ...... shortage of production was ...... in the neighbourhood of 4 or 5 per cent, the main difficulty was to distribute the deficiency over the whole body of consumers. If equitably distributed no one would feel the deficiency but if the whole weight was to fall on certain unfortunate localities then the shortage in these areas would be severe. Every area therefore must be prepared to take its share of the shortage." It was emphasized that "the only solution to the difficulty must be for all areas in surplus to surrender slightly more than their actual surplus". It was necessary that the stocks collected, whether for the use of the province where these were collected or for another Province or State, should become the property of the Central Government. The gravity of the position in Cochin and Travancore was emphasized, and it was stated that it could only be "alleviated" in a satisfactory manner if the Central Government were to exercise a considerable measure of centralised control". Mr. Pinnell (Bengal) held that, "there was one rice crop in the North East India, that was the concern of every province. There was need for co-ordination of purchase and that co-ordination could only be exercised by the Central Government. There must be one authority if an effective control over prices and supplies was to be secured and he expressed that very early arrangements for such purpose should be made." It was emphasized that the artificial boundaries between the Punjab and Delhi ought to be removed. The control measures introduced by Provinces and States which placed an embargo on exports were reacting harshly on small territories (Coorg). Mr. Maqbool Mahmud (the Chamber of Princes) considered a co-ordinated scheme on an all-India basis as essential. The representatives of the Government of India held that "if control was to be effective, it must be a strong control", and dwelt on the absolute necessity that provision be made for the last word and decision in any matter resting with the Central Government. It was felt that certain provinces were not prepared to give up anything beyond the food balance left there after providing for their own normal consumption, however, serious the position, and it was therefore, 'urged that the Government of India should control surpluses on the lines of equality of sacrifice' (Sind). Centralised control, and even a high degree of centralised control, was considered to be the only way in which the problem of the country could be solved (Bombay, Madras, Bihar). Such control did not materialise.

23. This is the story of the barriers. The food position continued to deteriorate. Isolated actions had been taken, natural flow of food supplies had been stopped, no controlled channels on an all-India basis had been created, the country had drifted into independent food-kingdoms. Price control without control of supplies, disappearance from the market of commodities thus controlled, black market, de-control, ineffective requisitioning, wranglings over the quotas of the 'Basic plans', failure to obtain supplies for the 'rescue plans' of Bengal, present a sorry spectacle. Frustration is writ large on the history of this period. As clearly foreseen and predicted, disaster and famine were the result. The weakest organ was attacked and succumbed to the disease. Bengal, the province which had suffered from a series of calamities, was the victim, and sank deeper and deeper into famine conditions.

F—The Problem for Bengal

24. The facts which emerge from a study of the position as it developed in Bengal during the later part of 1942 and the early months of 1943, justify the following conclusions.

There was a serious shortage of foodgrains, far more serious than Bengal had faced previously for at least twenty years. The shortage was such that it could not be met by husbanding Bengal's own resources, without large-scale supplies from outside the province. The position was aggravated by acute psychological factors which were the results of the war, and of the military situation at the time. Burma had fallen, refugees were pouring in, retreating troops were coming into Bengal, the danger of invasion was imminent, Calcutta had been bombed, there was danger of further air raids, serious doubts existed as to the capacity of British troops to stem the Japanese 'Blitzkrieg', the 'denial' policy had been put into action, political unrest of serious magnitude had manifested itself within the province and in the neighbouring areas, the 'quit India' demand had been made, political dissensions in Bengal were serious, cyclone and floods had destroyed human life, cattle, and crops and stores of foodgrains, and there was an atmosphere of tension. No one knew what was coming. Everyone played for safety; food, the most urgent requirement of man, was to be conserved. The producer wished to lay by stocks for his own consumption; consumers were anxious to secure supplies. Employers of big industries wished to make adequate provision to feed their employees. Essential services had to be maintained. Traders knew that money could be made. The marketable quantity had diminished. The combination of these formidable factors created unprecedented conditions. A series of calamities, each one of unprecedented magnitude, followed in such quick succession that the administration was overwhelmed. It was a '*Dunkirk*' on the food front in Bengal. It was in these circumstances that the Government of Bengal had to discharge its tremendous responsibilities.

A full and complete control over supplies and distribution of all available foodgrains might have saved Bengal—excellent in theory but not so in practice under the then existing conditions. Statutory price control had been tried and it had failed. Procurement operations in December and January had not been successful. Another attempt was made on the 9th of January but abandoned on the 17th of February. This obtained 2,200 tons. The Foodgrains Purchasing Officer did not purchase more than 3,000 tons. By the beginning of March stocks were down to such a low level in Calcutta that it looked as if the city must starve within a fortnight unless large supplies arrived quickly. Price control was abrogated on the 11th of March and then the Food Purchase Officer was able to obtain 17,000 tons from 12th to 31st March. Early in March the Government of India started their 'rescue plan' which was to obtain 60,000 tons within three weeks to a month, but succeeded in obtaining only half the required quantity. The Basic Plan had not started functioning as, by March 1943 when the need of Bengal became acute, the Government of India's arrangements for supply of foodgrain were not complete. The preliminary figures of the first Basic Plan were issued on the 13th April 1943. By the end of April the stocks of rice in Calcutta were again running low and reports of distress in the districts clearly indicated famine. By April it was clear to everybody, including the Government of India, that the Basic Plan would not function.

G—Into the Breach

25. About the end of March 1943 the Ministry went out of office. For a month the Governor of Bengal was in charge of the administration. It was at this time that the Muslim League party was invited to accept responsibility, and a Coalition Ministry was sworn in on the 23rd of April. This was the most critical period in the recent history of Bengal and the new Ministry had to face the unprecedented problem of impending famine, during a world war, with imminent threats of invasion. There cannot be two opinions that in this crucial period an All-Parties Ministry was obviously the only right thing. Various attempts were made to secure such a combination, but they proved abortive. Congress was in any case out of it, having refused to "co-operate". The European Group had adopted the policy of not sharing responsibility in the cabinet. The Hindu Mahasabha was prepared to join, but on the condition that the Muslims outside the Muslim League had a share. This the Muslim League was not prepared to accept. The blame must be shared equally by all the parties for this *impasse*.

On 'looking back' one cannot help feeling that the Muslim League party took a great risk in accepting office, so as to continue a parliamentary form of government, at a time when it was evident that a terrible famine was approaching and formidable difficulties lay ahead. The difficulties were such as demanded for their solution undivided attention, vigorous action, full support and complete co-operation from everyone in Bengal and outside. They knew they could not obtain such full co-operation. On the other hand, when called upon to shoulder a grave responsibility, at the most difficult period in the history of the province and country, a refusal would have meant abdication of all constitutional rights. It would have meant a desire to *rule* during peace and prosperity and to seek safety during trials and tribulations. It would have meant political *hara kiri.* They decided to fill the breach. Criticism of the Ministry in the Legislatures and in the Press was bitter and unrelenting. There was no respite. Such was the atmosphere in which the Ministry had to function.

As stated (report page 84, para. 24) a non-political organization in charge of food would have been the second best alternative to an all-parties government. The Government have been accused of not grasping the hand of co-operation offered to deal with the food problem. In an atmosphere charged with suspicion, bred of intensive propaganda, it is a pity that mutual understanding was not achieved.

26. The situation had become grave and menacing by the end of April. The short supplies had been eaten into for four months, further reducing the available quantity and more particularly the quantity in the market. The Basic Plan of the Government of India had not functioned even by this time. The country had become divided into numerous independent food monarchies, all thinking of their own limited interests. The new Ministry tried to grapple with the deteriorating situation which it had inherited. It groped, fumbled, sometimes blundered, sometimes floundered. But it continued its efforts. The magnitude of the problem had not been appreciated. Even the diagnosis of the disease had been wrong. At one time there was doubt regarding the shortage of grain supply in Bengal. The "carry-over" spectacles had coloured the vision. There were no data to go by. In the circumstances the "propaganda of plenty" was prescribed. The remedy, if successful, would have been trumpeted as a wonderful achievement. However, the treatment proved wrong. It failed, it engendered mistrust. The need was food, and not propaganda; propaganda alone could not appease hunger. Valuable time was lost. Another prescription was indicated. The traditions in which generations in India had been brought up was:

"If half a loaf a man of God eats, the other half he gives to those in need" (Saadi).

Instead, the more materialistic doctrine of self-preservation dominated. The geographical, economic and racial unity of India had receded into the background.

27. The condition caused grave anxiety. Food had to be obtained at any cost, anyhow. Persuasion and entreaties had failed. The evident solution was to pay the price and save life. *Basic Plan, Modified Free Trade and Free Trade* presented the possible alternatives, and a graded series to choose from. Absolute shortage of supplies was the real cause of the disease; high prices, like high temperature, were merely the symptom. Hence, the demand of the Bengal Ministry, in the beginning of May 1943, was for a guarantee from the Central Government that the quota of foodgrains according to the Basic Plan would be made available within a *few months*. May had arrived. August-September would bring in the *aus* crop. Three to four months of grave shortage lay ahead. Was the demand for the *approved quota, within a few months*, unreasonable or excessive? The Government of India presumably were not prepared to give the guarantee demanded. The Basic Plan had not started functioning. Was the middle course of Modified Free Trade rapid enough to resolve an acute emergency which had arisen? Modified Free Trade was a younger sister of the Basic Plan. It might have matured slowly and borne fruit. The urgency of the situation, however, called for quick action. It is not possible to determine the ethical value of a measure by detaching it from its context. It may be urged by some that free trade in war-time was wrong in principle. In the peculiar circumstances, however, which obtained in India in 1943, when some parts of the country were unwilling to share in the 'equality of sacrifice', free trade was the only course which had at least some chance of averting the impending disaster. But those

who had accepted the expediency of free trade had not taken into account the power of obstruction of the local administrations. Free trade, hemmed in by transport priorities and other difficulties, was strangled by strong local measures. The provinces requisitioned and froze stocks, put traders behind the bars. Buying was like trying to get stuff from behind doors bolted and locked and well guarded. Free trade was not allowed to function and it is not possible to determine what results would have been achieved if it had been allowed to function, even for a short while. During the operation of free trade the economic unity of India was on trial. Free trade engendered much bitterness and much mud-slinging. It was withdrawn. The Government of India stood vanquished for the time, and the Government of Bengal shared their defeat. At least one thing happened, namely, as is evident from later events, the shock of Free trade resuscitated the Basic Plan. In this role free trade was a significant factor in resolving difficulties which months' discussions had failed to resolve. It must also be remembered that if rice and wheat had come into Bengal during May-July 1943 in the same trickle at which they were coming from January to April 1943, the distress would have been acuter. Free trade produced over 90,000 tons of rice and saved Bengal for a while—at least for a while.

28. It was in these circumstances that the Third All-India Food Conference was called in July 1943. In this conference the Government of India lost the 'Free Trade', but regained the 'Basic Plan'. What was considered impossible became possible. Foodgrain was procured and moved into Bengal. Unfortunately it was too late. Had the quantity which reached Bengal during the third and fourth quarters of 1943 been sent during the first and second quarters, the whole story would have been different.

29. All along the Government of Bengal failed to appreciate the enormity of the problem facing them. This applied also to the handling of foodgrains in quantities amounting to hundreds of thousands of tons.

An experienced witness deposed that the quantities of foodgrain moved after May 1943 was greatly in excess of those moved in peace-time in two ways, "......... first, in peace-time civil supplies moved in an even flow according to requirements. In this case next to nothing had moved for months, and the supplies were 'bunched' as we call it in technical transportation parlance; secondly: Bengal is a war area and army stores were moving in considerable quantities ...." In reply to an enquiry as to the time necessary to build up an adequate organisation in an emergency the witness stated, "......... it is a colossal business .... Government has not got the staff and when they have recruited men have to be trained." Asked whether it was possible to have foreseen that the movements of the grain coming in would be so tremendous, the witness replied: "I think it would have been very difficult indeed to have foreseen it because it was an entirely new situation in India .... and it must have been extremely difficult for the Provincial Government to realise beforehand that difficulties would arise in transportation in areas not far from the front-line .... I do not think that with peace-time resources they would have been able to deal adequately with such emergencies in war-time ....".

It should have occurred to those in authority, that only an army, with trained staff, tried organisation, well equipped with transport, could cope with such a big job. A soldier grasped the problem and solved it.

30. *Inefficiency and corruption.*—These running sores of society, are serious obstacles to stability and progress, economic and social, and during an emergency lead to complete breakdown. They can neither be created nor destroyed in a day. The conditions of distress in a social organisation which lacked vigour led to defeatism, fatalism and inefficiency. Profiteering, a war-time disease, in face

of a serious shortage of food supplies, led to increased corruption. If India hopes to march on the path of progress, she must get rid of inefficiency and corruption, and every possible means should be adopted for the eradication of these evils as early as possible.

II. UNPREPAREDNESS OF INDIA TO MEET FOOD EMERGENCY

31. On 'looking back' one is astonished at the unpreparedness of India to meet the food situation during an emergency. In England a complete food scheme had been worked out before the war started. It has not been possible to ascertain whether His Majesty's Government had, at any stage, suggested a similar study of the food problem of India in case of war. It may be said that India had passed through the last Great War without any food difficulty, and, therefore, the position did not demand attention. On the contrary, for years, numerous investigators and writers on economic, agricultural, medical and nutritional problems had been pointing to the seriousness of the food situation in India. Stationary, if not declining, food production, rapidly increasing population, under-fed millions, disease and high mortality had been the topics of serious thought and discussion. Was the Government ignorant of the normal food situation in the country? Did not dwindling exports and increasing imports for a pre-eminently agricultural country indicate danger?

Even after war had been declared, the food question received little attention. Even after Japan entered the war, food was still considered a problem of secondary importance. The Bihar Government's warning of 1940 was not heeded. A series of Price Control Conferences and Food Conferences had urged a better and co-ordinated control of food. They caused not a stir, till the situation was out of hand.

32. The Allies were carrying on a world war on several fronts, with unity of objective, and unity of action. The Russians were sacrificing men in millions. The Americans and the British were fighting in the deserts of Africa thousands of miles from their homes. All resources of men and material had been pooled. American factories were working for England and Russia, and British factories manufactured equipment for all the Allies. Russia had to be provided with munition and supplies. She could be supplied through Iraq and Iran with greater facility. A passage had to be obtained and a passage was obtained. Again, to carry on the war effectively the independent countries of the Middle East were organised for food supply. Unity of effort was achieved.

In contrast, what happened in India? India was fighting starvation and famine. The Government of India used persuasion, made demands for foodgrains in the name of the unity of India, and equality of sacrifice. These failed. The last effort was free trade. The power of money, to get out grain which had not been produced, was employed. But free trade was resisted and it failed. Unity of effort was not achieved. Till July nothing effective was done. Free trade failed, but led to the working of the Basic Plan. Grain was produced from *within* the country. It was too late to save thousands who had marched too far on the path of starvation. Deaths continued during 1943 and during a part of 1944.

33. October 1943, in the fifth year of the war, witnessed a sudden change in the attitude of the Government of India. At the Fourth Food Conference held in October 1943 the President (Sir J. P. Srivastava) said "...... we must think of each other and not of ourselves ...... In the mobilisation of India's resources the Government of India will have to take and implement, decisions which may at times conflict with what appear to be local or sectional interests. Whenever possible, and to the greatest extent possible, the Government of India

will proceed after consultation with you and with your consent, but if circumstances should compel us to proceed otherwise, I look to you to accept and implement those decisions which we, and we alone can take on behalf of all ...... We can no longer afford either failure or prospect of failure and I, in the discharge of the duty which is mine, shall not hesitate to exercise whatever degree of superintendence and control at every stage may be necessary, or to invoke the use of whatever powers are essential to ensure success". This is what had been urged from the beginning of 1940. An early decision on these lines would have saved Bengal. This decision, one is constrained to say, was arrived at when the famine had almost spent itself.

M. AFZAL HUSAIN.

APPENDIX 1

Agricultural families and their holdings

1. The results of investigation into the means of livelihood of the population of Bengal ave been tabulated at pages 121 to 125 of Volume IV of the Census of India, 1941. The form of the Tables differs from that of the Imperial Tables of 1931 by reason of the more detailed classification of dependants. As a measure of economy extraction did not proceed beyond the category of the class.

2. All occupations providing means of livelihood have been divided into four classes, namely, (A) production of raw materials, (B) preparation and supply of material substances, (C) public administration and liberal arts, and (D) miscellaneous. The cultivation of land naturally falls under (A). As indicated already, there are no separate figures for occupations falling under this class other than the cultivation of land. It is seen, however, from page 69 of the Statistical Abstract for British India, published in 1942, that " extraction of minerals " accounts for only 0·3 per cent and " fishing and hunting " for 1·4 per cent of the total; we may, therefore, roughly assume 2 per cent to be the allowance to be made under this class for occupations other than the cultivation of land.

3. It is seen from page 123 of the Census Tables, Volume IV, that the number of persons for whom particulars have been furnished, was 1,193,754 in the province of Bengal. It is presumed that this was a representative sample. The summary at page 122 shows that the numbers enumerated under the heads P, PS, and TD together add up exactly to this total. The figures thus added are shown below :—

Class and type of occupation	Number of persons	Percentage to total
A—Production of raw materials	883,584	74·0
B—Preparation and supply of material substances	161,141	13·5
C—Public administration and liberal arts	38,253	3·2
D—Miscellaneous	110,776	9·3
Total	1,193,754	100·0

The following explanations have been furnished for the terms P, PS, and TD :—

P : Principal means of livelihood without subsidiary means of livelihood ;
PS : Principal means of livelihood with subsidiary means of livelihood ;
TD : Total dependants on this means of livelihood.

From this (and with reference to what has been said at paragraph 2 above) it may be concluded that all persons deriving the whole or a major part of their income from the cultivation of land, whether as owners of land, cultivating tenants or labourers working on the land, together with the members of their families dependent on them, amount to 72 per cent of the total population (60·31 millions) of Bengal, that is, 43·4 millions.

4. The subsidiary table at page 4 of the Census of India Tables, Volume IV, shows that in 1941, the number of persons per thousand houses in Bengal was 5,412. Assuming on the average that the size of a family is equal to the average number of inhabitants per house, the number of families in a population of 43·4 millions comes to 8 millions.

5. At the instance of the Land Revenue Commission, Bengal, certain special enquiries were made in 1939. The results have been tabulated as Appendix IX at pages 88-123 of Volume II of the Report of that Commission. Table VIII(*b*) (pages 114-115) shows that the 19,599 families enquired into held 85,470 acres and that the average holding of these families was 4·36 acres. Table No. VI(*a*) (pages 107-108) shows that the total area of all land held in *khas* by ***raiyati*** and ***under-raiyati*** holders in Bengal is 31·06 million acres. If the average holding of the sample which was investigated was roughly the same as the average of the province as a whole, the total number of families dependent on the cultivation of land should be 7·1 million.

6. The question arises whether the estimate of 8 million families arrived at on the basis of 1941 census figures is too high or whether the above estimate is too low. The figure of 8 millions is probably too high because it includes persons who are merely rent receivers. It also appears not unlikely that the estimate of 7·1 millions is too low, particularly if the families enquired into were not sufficiently representative of the poorest classes of cultivating families. There is some reason to think that this may have been the case, as will now be explained.

7. It is seen from Table No. VIII(*d*) (page 117) that 22·5 per cent of the families enquired into were " living mainly or entirely on agricultural wages ". As a footnote to the Table points out, the corresponding figure according to the census of 1931 was 29·2 per cent. This

is one indication that the sample was inadequately representative of the class of cultivating families for the province as a whole. This is also corroborated by information furnished at page 121 of the Census of India 1941, Bengal Tables (Volume IV). This shows that out of a total of 453,689 persons who were wholly or principally dependent on the cultivation of land, 121,804 persons were agricultural labourers and their dependants. In other words, the percentage according to the 1941 census was 26·8. Similarly, Table No. VIII(*d*) (page 117) referred to above shows the percentage of families living mainly or entirely as *bargadars* (*i.e.*, crop-sharing tenants) was 12·2 per cent. The corresponding percentage obtained from information given at page 121 of the Census of India 1941, Bengal Tables is 15·3 per cent.

8. It is, however, not surprising that estimates based on different methods of sampling vary, more especially since the census figures of dependants are not based on the treatment of the family as an ascertained unit. The census figures themselves have varied from one decennium to another. The inference which, we think, can safely be drawn is that the number of families in Bengal who depend mainly or entirely on the cultivation of land is approximately 7·5 millions.

9. Table No. VIII(*b*) (pages 114-115) shows that the proportion of families with less than 2 acres is 46·0 per cent of families with between 2 and 5 acres is 28·6 per cent of families with between 5 and 10 acres is 17·0 per cent; and of families with above 10 acres is 8·4 per cent. We accept these results, subject to the uncertainty indicated already and make the following deductions :

(*i*) Less than 2 million families hold more than 5 acres each and about one-third of this number hold more than 10 acres each.

(*ii*) About 2 million families hold between 2 and 5 acres each.

(*iii*) All others, who constitute about one half of all the families who depend wholly or mainly on the cultivation of land, are either landless or hold less than 2 acres each.

10. Table No. VIII(*d*) (page 117) shows that the proportion of families living mainly or entirely as *bargadars* is 12·2 per cent and the proportion of families living mainly or entirely on agricultural wages is 22·5 per cent. Reference has already been made at paragraph 7 above to the reasons for believing that the actual percentage for Bengal as a whole was probably rather higher. The available figures permit the following inferences to be drawn :

(*i*) The cultivating families of Bengal include roughly about one million families who live mainly or entirely as *bargadars, i.e.,* crop-sharing tenants.

(*ii*) The number of families who live mainly or entirely on agricultural wages is about 2 millions.

APPENDIX II

Production and consumption of Rice in Bengal

1. Preliminary.—It is necessary to make an estimate of the supply of rice available in Bengal during 1943, and to determine how this supply compared with—

(*a*) the supply available in previous years, and

(*b*) the requirements of the province duri 1943.

No conclusions can be formed on these matters exerpt by a survey of all available statistical information relating to a series of years ; and, as there are defects and gaps in the information available, any conclusions finally reached must necessarily be tentative. The object of this note is to assess the effect of errors and omissions in available statistics and formulate the conclusions which appear to be the most probable.

2. Definitions.—Some of the terms used in this note are defined below.

(*i*) *Year.*—Except where otherwise stated, this means the calendar year.

(*ii*) *Rice.*—Means de-husked paddy and includes paddy in terms of rice. It also includes rice-products.

(*iii*) *Old rice.*—Of the rice available in the province during any year, the rice grown or imported during previous years is called " old rice ", but it does not include the yield of the *aman* crop harvested at the end of the immediately preceding year.

(*iv*) *Carry-over.*—The ' carry-over ' of any year means the stock of " old rice " physically nexistence in Bengal on the first day of the year.

[*Note.*—This definition is sufficiently accurate for practical purposes. A stricter definition would be that the " carry-over " of any year means the stock of all rice physically in existence in Bengal on the first day of the year, *minus* the yield of the *aman* crop harvested in the immediately preceding year. A difference exists between the two definitions, only in so far as any portion of the *aman* rice harvested in the closing months of a year may be consumed in that year. This happens only in very lean years, and the quantities thus consumed are small in proportion to the *aman* supply as a whole.]

(*v*) *Aman supply.*—In relation to any year, the ' *aman* supply ' means the entire yield of the *aman* crop grown in the immediately preceding year.

(*vi*) *Boro supply* and *aus supply.*—In relation to any year, these terms mean the yield of the *boro* and *aus* crops grown and harvested during the year.

(*vii*) *External supply.*—By this is meant the excess of imports over exports. When exorts exceed imports, " external supply " is negative.

(*viii*) *Current supply*.—In relation to a year, this means the sum of *aman*, *boro*, *aus*' and external supplies (that is to say, production *plus* imports *minus* exports).

(*ix*) *Total supply* means the sum of the carry-over and the current supply (that is to say, the carry-over *plus* the *aman*, *boro* and *aus* supplies, *plus* imports, *minus* exports).

(*x*) *Requirements* means the quantities estimated as required for seed and for consumption. The estimates are made on the basis of prevailing average rates—variations due to abnormal conditions being disregarded.

(*xi*) *Consumption*.—This is primarily meant to signify human consumption.

[*Note*.—Wastage and the use of rice for purposes other than seed and human consumption are not separately allowed for, nor is allowance made for consumption of cereals other than rice. The two factors are deemed to offset one another in the province as a whole.]

(*xii*) *Surplus* or *Deficit*.—The difference between *aman*, *boro* and *aus*, and external supplies on the one hand, and requirements on the other, is a 'surplus' when the supply exceeds requirements, and a 'deficit' when the supply falls short of requirements.

(*xiii*) *Supply in terms of weekly requirements*.—This means the number of weeks during which any given supply (whether carry-over, *aman*, *boro*, *aus*, external, current, or total) may be expected to be consumed, at the prevailing rate of consumption and after deducting seed requirements.

(*xiv*) *Shortage of supply* and *absolute deficiency*.—A distinction is drawn in this note between "shortage of supply" and "absolute deficiency". The latter exists when total supply falls short of the requirements of the year and is an advanced stage of 'shortage'. Supply is taken to be short when it is so relatively to the average supply of a period assumed to be the standard for purposes of comparison. In this note, the supply during 1943 is compared with the average of the immediately preceding 5 years as the standard ; and the latter, in its turn, is compared with the average of 10 years preceding 1938.

SECTION A—REVIEW OF INFORMATION AVAILABLE

3. Population.—According to the census, the population of Bengal was 60·31 millions in 1941. The rate of increase at ten-yearly intervals had been 2·8% from 1911 to 1921, 7·3% from 1921 to 1931, and 20·3% from 1931 to 1941. It has been suggested that these figures do not reflect the real rate of increase, but an over-statement of actual numbers in the 1941 census or an understatement in the 1931 census or both. This may be true, but there are no reliable data to indicate the degree of error, if any, involved. There is, therefore, an element of uncertainty about the actual population in any particular year which must necessarily affect all estimates of the aggregate consumption of rice in the province as a whole.

4. Rates of consumption of cereals—(*i*) *Standards* (per adult and *per capita*).—The standard advised by the Government of India for purposes of rationing, and generally followed throughout India, is one pound a day per adult. The standard adopted in the rationing of Calcutta is 4 seers per week per adult, equivalent to 19 ounces per day. These standards are not based on ascertained actual consumption. It is generally assumed that the consumption of 100 persons of all ages is equivalent to that of 80 adults. On this basis, the standard rates of *per capita* consumption are 80% of those of adult consumption.

(*ii*) *Actual off-take of Greater Calcutta under Rationing*.—The average weekly off-take, on the basis of 22 weeks' actuals, was 5,529 tons of rice and 3,562 tons of wheat and wheat-products, or 9,091 tons in all. The number of registered ration card holders in Greater Calcutta was 4·10 millions. Of these 3·36 millions are adults, 0·68 million are children entitled to a half ration, and the rest are infants not entitled to any cereal ration ; in other words, the total in terms of adults is 3·70 millions. If these figures represent the actual population, then the actual average off-take would be as follows :—

Average off-take	*In seers per week*	*In ounces per day*
Per adult	2·68	13
Per capita	2·41	11

But the number of registered ration cards cannot safely be assumed to be equivalent to the number of the total population, for the former include "dead cards" which, though registered are not used. The proportion of "dead cards" among those registered with Government stores is 16 per cent and it is believed that the proportion is smaller among cards registered elsewhere. Hence the actual average off-take is somewhere between the figures given above and those given below which are obtained by multiplying the figures by 100/84.

Average off-take	*In seers per week*	*In ounces per day*
Per adult	3·20	15
Per capita	2·87	14

(*iii*) *Estimates furnished by Professor Mahalanobis, Honorary Secretary, Indian Statistical Institute, Calcutta.*—Professor Mahalanobis has analysed the results of five different surveys conducted at different times between 1936 and 1942. Some of these were made at the instance of the Bengal Government and others were undertaken by the Indian Statistical Institute or the Viswabharati Institute of Rural Reconstruction. The following estimates, relating to the consumption of cereals, are based on his report :—

Per capita *consumption of all cereals*	*In seers per week*	*In ounces per day*
General average rate for Bengal	3·58	17
Sectional average rates—		
(*a*) Rural population	3·65	17
(*b*) Calcutta middle classes	2·79	13
(*c*) Mofussil Urban middle classes . .	2·75	13
(*d*) Industrial working classes	3·47	16
(*e*) Families whose monthly expenditure is Rs. 10 or less	2·95	14

[*Note.*—The number of families whose monthly expenditure was Rs. 10 or less, was 3,212 as against a total of 15,409 families in the sample ; and the number of persons included in such families was 11,788, as against a total of 81,554 in the sample.]

(*iv*) *Other estimates.*—Many other estimates have been made in the past which need not be referred to here. These were reviewed by the Foodgrains Procurement Committee, appointed by the Bengal Government during 1944. This Committee drew attention to the wide divergence between the estimates, and concluded that the general average rate of consumption in the province as a whole was probably higher than 4 seers per week per adult. If this view is accepted, the *per capita* rate is not less than 3·20 seers per week or 15 ounces per day.

(*v*) *Conclusions.*—(*a*) *General average.*—The available data do not permit of conclusions being drawn with certainty. It is probable that the true average rate is somewhere between the following limits :—

Per capita *consumption*	*In seers per week*	*In ounces per day*
Lower limit	3·2	15
Upper limit	3·6	17

(*b*) *Sectional averages.*—The rate of consumption of cereals is higher in the villages than in the towns and cities and higher for the working classes than the middle classes.

(*vi*) *Under-nourishment.*—A low rate of cereal consumption does not necessarily mean under nourishment. The figures supplied by Professor Mahalanobis show that the relatively lower rates of cereal consumption of the urban middle classes are associated with relatively higher rates of consumption of protective and supplementary foods. But the figures for "families whose monthly expenditure is Rs. 10 or less" indicate a cereal consumption rate of 14 ounces per day with a very low rate of consumption of other foods. This class, which accounts for one-seventh of the total number, is probably under-nourished even in normal times. It is probable that the actual proportion of the population which is under-nourished in normal times is larger than one-seventh, but precise information on this point is not available.

5. Direct estimates of annual consumption.—If, as mentioned already, the probable rate of consumption per head per week is anything between 3·2 seers and 3·6 seers, the probable annual consumption of a population of *one million* during *one year* might be anything between 153,000 tons and 172,000 tons. As the population of Bengal during 1941 was (according to the census) 60·3 millions, the probable annual consumption of the province may have been anything between 9·2 million tons and 10·4 million tons during 1941. The elements of uncertainty inherent in any estimate of total consumption of the province during any particular year include the following :—

(*a*) There is a range of error of over one million tons, arising out of the uncertainty about the average rate of consumption.

(*b*) The population of Bengal during 1941 may have been less than the census figure of 60·3 millions. If the true figure was smaller by as much as, say, 3 millions, the figure of consumption would have to be reduced by nearly half a million tons.

(*c*) An estimate of consumption for any earlier or later year depends on an allowance being made for the increase of population. This might, in view of the doubts mentioned already, be anything between 0·7 per cent per annum and 2 per cent per annum.

(*d*) For the following reasons it cannot be assumed that an average rate of consumption per head remains constant over a series of years:

(*i*) The proportion of the population which is under-nourished in normal times may be increasing. There is, however, no means of determining the effect of such a change on tota consumption.

(*ii*) The poorer classes in rural areas, whose standard of consumption is normally low probably reduce their consumption in lean years and increase it in years of good harvest Likewise the urban poor increase their consumption in periods when the prevailing level of wages and employment rises more rapidly than the price of cereals, and decrease it when the opposite occurs. It is, however, not possible to make any satisfactory allowance for such variations, because neither the numbers of the classes whose consumption may vary for these reasons, nor the range of the variation, is known.

It may thus be concluded that the information available is such that any estimate of the annual consumption of the province based on population statistics and an assumed average rate of individual consumption is likely to err by as much as 2 million tons—or about 25 per cent of the estimate. So wide a margin of error blocks this method of approach.

6. Basis of indirect estimates of consumption.—The annual consumption of the province may be estimated indirectly, without making any assumptions about the rates of individual consumption. Thus, if information is available as regards (*i*) the stock in hand in Bengal at the beginning of the year (*ii*) the stock added to it in the course of the year as a result of production and the balance of imports and exports, and finally, (*iii*) the stock carried forward at the end of the year, then (*i*)+(*ii*)—(*iii*) represents consumption and seed. Estimates of consumption have been made on this basis. Attention must, however, be drawn to the following difficulties:—.

(*i*) Information is available about production, imports, exports and seed requirements. These are, however, subject to errors which in Bengal and other permanently settled areas are of considerable magnitude.

(*ii*) There is no information available about stocks carried over from year to year. An attempt may be made to overcome this difficulty taking a long period of years and assuming that the difference between the stocks at the beginning and end of the period is negligible in comparison with the consumption during the period as a whole. This is a reasonable method of procedure, but can give only the average annual consumption over the whole period and not the consumption of any particular year. In order to deduce the latter, some assumption has to be made as to the rate at which consumption varied from year to year during the period, and this is subject to uncertainties referred to in item (*d*) of paragraph 5 above.

7. Statement I explained.—(*i*) *Production.*—Information furnished by the Government of Bengal about the estimated acreage and yield of crops during 1943, and during the 15 preceding years, is given in tabular form in Statement I. The figures are based on crop forecasts prepared over a series of years by the Director of Agriculture, Bengal. The three rice crops (*aman*, *boro* and *aus*) are shown separately. The *aman* crop in any particular year is the crop which came into supply during that year, having been harvested towards the end of the preceding year. The *boro* and *aus* crops are those which are harvested during the year against which they are shown.

(*ii*) *Imports* and *Exports.*—Particulars of imports and exports, as furnished by the Bengal Government, are included in the statement. These are based on statistics compiled by the Department of Commercial Intelligence and Statistics. They relate to the financial year, except for 1943 for which figures for the calendar year are furnished (figures for earlier years have not been separately worked out in terms of the calendar year, since the difference involved is unlikely to be material for purposes of this analysis).

(*iii*) *Current supply.*—Current supply during each year is production *plus* imports *minus* exports. This has been determined for each year and shown in the statement.

(*iv*) *Seed requirements.*—In the Report on the Marketing of Rice in India and Burma, it has been estimated that the seed requirements of 21·27 million acres in Bengal are 376,000 tons, *i.e.*, an average of 1·77 tons per hundred acres. On this basis, the seed requirements of the sown area of each year have been worked out and shown in the Statement.

8. Statement II explained.—(*i*) *Consumption* (*Average over 15 years*).—Figures of current supply (less seed), as determined from Statement I, are set out in column 2 of Statement II against the years noted in column 1. The average of the figures of current supply during 15 years (1928-1942) is taken, for the reasons explained in paragraph 6, to be the average annual consumption in this period as a whole. This amounts to 8·14 million tons.

(*ii*) *Consumption* (*year to year*).—To deduce from this figure an annual estimate of consumption some assumptions must be made about the variation in consumption from year to year.

It is assumed that consumption increased at the rate of 0·10 million tons each year during the period.[1] The results are set out in column 3 of Statement II.

(*iii*) *Surpluses* and *Deficits*.—If we compare current supply (less seed) with consumption, the difference is either the surplus or the deficit according as supply exceeds or falls short of the requirements.[2] These figures have been determined and set out in Statement II.

(*iv*) *Current supply, surpluses,* and *deficits, in terms of weekly requirements*.—(*i*) 'Weekly requirements' may be estimated by dividing the estimates of annual consumption by 52. The number of weeks during which current supply may be expected to be consumed is obtained first by deducting seed requirements from current supply and then dividing by the figure representing 'weekly requirements'. This has been worked out and shown in Statement II. Similarly, surpluses and deficits are also expressed in terms of weekly requirements.[3]

9. STATEMENTS III AND IV EXPLAINED.—Statements I and II have been compiled on the basis of statistics of production, imports and exports, as available; and without alteration. But it is known that they are subject to certain errors and omissions. It is now necessary to consider the latter and make reasonable allowances for them.

Statements III and IV are the result of a revision of Statements I and II in the light of the following considerations:—

(*i*) *Estimates of acreage*.—The figures of acreage under the *aman*, *boro* and *aus* crops of different years as set out in Statement No. I are those given by the Director of Agriculture, Bengal. There is an important difference between the manner in which these figures are arrived at in Bengal (and certain other permanently settled areas) on the one hand, and the *ryotwari* areas of India, on the other. In the latter, the figures are arrived at by an enumeration of survey fields under crop, and the ascertainment of areas from land registers and village records.

In Bengal, the figures are arrived at by estimating the area in a particular year as a proportion of an assumed *norm*. It has been ascertained in evidence, that these *norms* were assumed in the past without any reference to areas under crop as recorded in settlement reports of different districts in different years. A comparison of the total of areas thus recorded in settlement reports with the acreages furnished in crop forecasts indicates that there has been a systematic under-estimation of acreages over a long period of years. This is also the opinion of an experienced administrative officer of Bengal, as well as of Professor Mahalanobis who has studied the

---

[1]This implies an increase of consumption at the rate of 1·34 per cent per annum in 1928, diminishing slowly to 1·13 per cent per annum in 1942. Whether the allowance is reasonable or not depends primarily on what the rate of increase of population has been. Here it has been assumed that the rate of increase is not as small as 0·73 per cent per annum (as a comparison of the census figures of 1921 and 1931 suggests) nor as high as 2·03 per cent per annum (as a comparison of the census figures of 1931 and 1941 suggests). It is probable that the actual rate of increase of population has been more steady, approximately equivalent to the mean of these two figures, *i.e.*, 1·38 per cent per annum. If this is accepted, and given the proportion of the poorest classes to the total population, an increase in the assumption made in Statement II about the variation from year to year is not unreasonable.

It should be immediately added that the derived figures are intended to be estimates of quantities required for consumption. It is possible that the actual consumption during any particular year may be a little below or a little above requirements—this depending on conditions of season and prices. In years of very poor (or very good) harvests, it is not merely possible but probable, that actual consumption may be significantly in defect (or in excess as the case may be of estimated consumption. These facts must be borne in mind, in drawing conclusions from the estimates of consumption, which are estimates of the quantities likely to be consumed by the population as a whole, at the average rate of consumption of the different classes of the population, in the immediately preceding years.

[2]It is probable that surpluses, worked out in this manner, may in years of very good harvests be larger than the actual surpluses—to the extent to which the poorer classes consume more than normally. It is probable also that deficits, estimated in the same way may, in years of very poor harvests, be larger than the actual deficits—to the extent to which the poorer classes consume less than normally.

[3]There is an advantage in expressing supply figures in terms of weekly requirements which may be explained as follows:—

The object of this note is to draw, from statistical data which may be subject to large errors conclusions which are as little as possible vitiated by such error. It is a well known rule of statistical analysis that the error in a ratio between two terms is very nearly the difference between the errors in the two terms. If the errors in the terms are in the same direction, they tend to neutralize one another; and, if they are also nearly equal, the error in the ratio is very small. As estimates of weekly requirements are deduced from figures of current supply, the error in the a tter is likely to be reflected by an error of the same order in the former. The errors thus tend otlneutralize one another.

subject. It may, therefore, be regarded as well established that there is an under-estimation. The correction to be made can be deduced from the following figures :—

	Area sown (in million acres)	
	Aman	*Boro and aus*
Standard (1938-1942)	15·99	6·40
Total of Settlement Reports	19·22	6·32

These figures justify the assumption that the estimated acreages of *aman* crop are likely to be closer to the true figures, if they are increasd by one-fifth. Figures, revised on this basis, are set out in Statement III annexed to this note.

(*ii*) *Estimates of yield.*—After the acreage is estimated, the yield is estimated by a process involving two factors, *viz.* (*a*) the assumption of a 'normal' rate of yield per acre, and (*b*) the estimation of the actual rate of yield of the year as a proportion of the 'normal'.

Errors incidental to the latter are unavoidable, but will probably not affect the comparability of estimates made in different years. As regards 'normal yield rate', this is settled at quinquennial intervals by means of crop-cutting experiments. The assumed rates are shown below :—

Period	*Assumed 'normal' rate of yield in maunds per acre*		
	Aman	*Boro*	*Aus*
1928-32	13·5	15·0	12·4
1933-37	12·5	14·5	11·1
1938-42	12·4	13··6	10·9

The 'normal yield' is the absolute value attached to a 12 anna crop, and has been defined as the yield which "in the existing circumstances might be expected to be attained in the year if rainfall and season were of a character ordinary for the tract under consideration, that is neither very favourable nor the reverse". If (as is implicit in this definition) the effect of the season is regarded as constant, the only factors which influence the yield rate per acre are the extension of cultivation to marginal lands, alteration in the fertility of the soil or changes in methods of cultivation. These are factors the effect of which is perceptible only over a long period. In reply to an enquiry on this point, the Director of Agriculture as well as the Department of Civil Supplies, Bengal, have agreed that the assumed rates of 1928-1932 were overpitched. It seems therefore, reasonable to assume that the *aman* yield figures of 1928-1942 should be reduced by 1/15th, and the *aus* yield figures should be reduced by 1/12th, in order to make them comparable with the corresponding figures of succeeding years.[1] As regards the *boro* rates, the differences between successive years are unduly wide, though nearly equal; but, in view of the very small proportion which this crop bears to the total, it is not worth while disturbing the *boro* figures. Figures of yield, revised in this manner, are exhibited in Statement III.

(*iii*) *Imports* and *Exports.*—The figures of imports and exports set out in Statement II are not estimates. They are based on the actual registration of receipts and despatches made by Port and Railway authorities and the statistics, compiled by the Department of Commercial Intelligence and Statistics, are far more accurate than estimates of yield of crops. The figures, however, do not include movements across the provincial frontiers by road or by country-boat. Such movements take place in both directions and, except for the trade with Assam and Arakan, probably balance one another. On the balance of recorded movements, the position during each of the three quinquennial periods was as shown below :—

Period	Net Imports (+) Net Exports (—) (*in thousands of tons*)
Average (1928-32).	—128
Average (1933-37).	+51
Average (1938-42).	+159

[1] On this basis the rates of normal yield of the *aman* and *aus* crops are as follows :—

	(*In maunds per acre*)	
	aman	*aus*
1928-32	12·6	11·4
1932-37.	12·5	11·1
1938-42	12·4	10·9

It has been suggested that the effects of the economic depression on agricultural economy generally may be a possible cause of diminution of the rates of normal yield.

The quantities are relatively small. The unrecorded movements are probably smaller It is proposed to assume that unrecorded movements are equivalent to net imports of roughly 50,000 tons per annum in the second quinquennium and 100,000 tons in the third quinquennium This would probably suffice to remove the possibility of the true extent of the dependence of Bengal on external supply being under-estimated. Figures of external supply, revised on this basis, are exhibited in Statement III.

10. COMMENTS ON ORIGINAL AND REVISED FIGURES.—(*i*) The most important difference between Statements I and II based on original figures, and Statements III and IV based on revised figures, is the increase in the supply figures which results from increasing the *aman* acreage by one-fifth. There is evidence suggesting that the revised figures are nearer the truth. In paragraph 5 above, it has been pointed out that the probable limits of consumption during 1941 were 9·2 and 10·4 million tons. This result was deduced from direct estimates of consumption, without reference to supply statistics. According to Statement II, the consumption requirements are estimated for this year as 8·74 million tons; while, according to Statement IV, the estimate is 9·90 million tons. These estimates were arrived at without any reference to estimates of actual consumption, but indirectly from supply statistics. The fact that the estimate arrived at in Statement IV lies between the probable limit, while the estimate arrrived at in Statement II is smaller than the lower limit by nearly half a million tons, suggests that the revised figures are likely to be more accurate.

(*ii*) Other changes, *viz.*, reduction of yield rates in the quinquennium 1928-32 and increase of net imports in the subsequent decade, are quantitatively of smaller importance.

(*iii*) In the course of further discussion in this note the figures contained in Statements III and IV will be referred to, as they are regarded as likely to be nearer the truth than the corresponding figures of Statements I and II. Both sets of figures are, however, available for comparison, when necessary.

SECTION B—SUPPLY IN RELATION TO REQUIREMENTS FROM 1928 TO 1937

11. In this section it is proposed to examine the relation of supply to requirements during the ten years 1928 to 1937. The points to be considered are—

(*i*) the relative importance of the different elements in current supply during the period as a whole, *viz.*, the yields of different crops and external supply;

(*ii*) the variations of supply, and surpluses and deficits in different years;

(*iii*) the carry-over and total supply in years of serious shortage of current supply.

In the next section, these points will be examined in relation to the period 1938 to 1942. Later figures of 1943 will be compared with those of the two previous periods.

12. The following table shows average current supply, in the ten years 1928 to 1937 :—

	Supply in terms of weekly requirements[1]
(*i*) *Aman* supply	42
(*ii*) *Boro* and *aus* supply	12
(*iii*) External supply	..
Current supply	54

The yield of the *aman* crop, the most important source of supply, provided on the average the food required by the province for 42 weeks. The *boro* and *aus* crops provided 12 weeks' food. (Of these two crops, the *aus* is much more important. The *boro* accounts for a little more than one week's food). Taking the period as a whole, the external supply was quantitatively negligible. During the first half of the decade, the province was a net exporter of less than one week's supply per annum; and, towards the end, it was a net importer of less than one week's supply per annum. Thus current supply, on the whole, exceeded requirements by a margin equivalent to nearly two weeks.

13. The variations of current supply from year to year, during this ten-year period, are shown below :—

Year	Current supply in terms of weekly requirements	Year	Current supply in terms of weekly requirements
1928	45	1933	60
1929	57	1934	55
1930	52	1935	53
1931	57	1936	44
1932	56	1937	59

[1]Rounded to the nearest week.

Two years stand out from this table, *viz.*, 1928 and 1936, as years of serious shortage in current supply. During the remaining 8 years there was no shortage of current supply, and in a number of years it was substantially in excess. Surpluses exceeded deficits by a considerable margin ; and, *prima facie*, it would appear that stocks carried over from year to year must have been accumulating in the province during the period. Are these inferences consistent with experience ?

14. There is no doubt that there was a serious shortage of current supply during 1928 and 1936. It is known that the yield of the *aman* crop harvested in the years immediately preceding 1928 and 1936 was unusually low, and there was serious distress among the poorer classes in parts of the province. Relief measures were undertaken on a considerable scale during those years. So far, the figures are confirmed by known facts. But the question arises, in respect of 1936, why, if stocks had been accumulating as the figures suggest, considerable distress should have occurred during that year ? Two answers are possible : One is that the surpluses of previous years were not, in fact, substantially carried over, but were eaten up because, when crops are good and prices low, actual consumption by the poorer classes is in excess of the " requirements " indicated by the figures. The other possibility is that the surpluses indicated by the figures were substantially carried over ; that the province as a whole did possess during 1936 a carry-over which, together with current supply, was more than sufficient for requirements ; that distress nevertheless, occurred because large numbers among the poorer classes whose income was diminished by the failure of the crop, were too poor to buy the supplies which were physically available. The latter is probably the correct view. It is true that the consumption of the poorer classes is variable. Large numbers who live on the margin of subsistence consume more when they can and less when they must. But the range of this variation should not be over-estimated. The following considerations suggest that increase of consumption could not have wiped out the whole, or even a large part, of the surpluses of the years preceding 1936 :—

(*i*) The cultivators and non-cultivating landholders who have a surplus in excess of their normal annual requirements are likely to consume an adequate ration even in normal times and unlikely to increase their consumption in years of good supply or low prices. Though this class may not be larger in numbers than those who produce less than their annual requirements, it is likely to be in physical possession of a large proportion of the total surplus produce. This is likely to have been carried over in full,—as stocks in the hands either of producers or traders.

(*ii*) From 1930 onwards for a number of years, the price of rice was abnormally low. This meant that the poorer cultivators,—who could have increased their consumption—were obliged to sell a larger quantity of produce than normally, in order to secure the same amount of cash for paying rent, debts, and other pressing cash obligations.

(*iii*) The period of abnormally low prices also coincided with a fall in the level of employment. Therefore, labourers who could have increased their consumption in prevailing conditions were probably handicapped to some extent by diminution of their earnings.

It may, therefore, be concluded that during 1936 there was a carry-over which largely exceeded the deficit in current supply during the year ; and that distress prevailed, not because the supplies required for the adequate nourishment of the poorer classes were unavailable, but because these classes could not afford to buy them. This is an important conclusion, in connection with the supply position in 1943.

SECTION C—SUPPLY IN RELATION TO REQUIREMENTS FROM 1938 TO 1942.

14. The following table shows the average current supply in the 5 years 1938 to 1942 :—

	Current supply in terms of weekly requirements[1]
(*i*) *Aman* supply	38
(*ii*) *Boro* and *aus* supply	10
(*iii*) External supply	1
Current supply	49

If we compare these figures with those in paragraph 12, it appears that, on the whole, current supply was in deficit during this period. The *aman* crop provided on the average a supply which was 4 weeks shorter than in the previous decade. The *boro* and *aus* crops provided a supply which was 2 weeks less. On the other hand, the province had become a net importer during the period, and external supply accounted for rather more than one week's supply. The difference between the two periods can be explained as follows :—First, the rate of increase of cultivation of rice was falling behind the rate of increase of population, and there was thus a long-term tendency towards decreasing surpluses and increasing deficits. Secondly, this tendency was

[1]Rounded to the nearest week.

to some extent offset by a preponderance of good seasons in the previous period, and emphasized in this period by a preponderance of unfavourable seasons. This is illustrated by the figures in the following table :—

	Total area sown (In millions of acres)	Average rate of yield per acre (In tons)
Average (1928-1932) . . .	23·71	0·39
Average (1933-1937) . . .	24·53	0·40
Average (1938-1942) . . .	25·53	0·37

15. The variations of current supply from year to year during this five-year period are shown below :

Year	Current supply in terms of weekly requirements
1938 . . .	52
1939 . . .	49
1940 . . .	50
1941 . . .	39
1942 . . .	54

On comparing these figures with those furnished in paragraph 13 above, 1941 stands out as a lean year even more clearly than 1928 and 1936 in the ten-year period previously considered. There was only one year (1942) when there was a surplus and the surplus was relatively small. Thus it appears that stocks must have been drawn upon during this period, and particularly heavily during 1941. Distress occurred in rural areas during this year, and relief measures were undertaken on a considerable scale.

16. The state of current supply during 1941 supports the conclusion reached in paragraph 14 above, namely, that the stocks carried over from year to year must have been considerable. The deficit in the current supply was as much as 13 weeks. It is difficult to believe that the whole, or even a large part, of this deficit could have been met by restriction of consumption. Undoubtedly, the actual consumption of large classes of the poor must have been reduced to a significant extent. Let us suppose that onehalf of the population restricted their consumption in varying degrees, so that one-sixth reduced its in-take of rice by half for 6 months, one-sixth for 4 months, and the remainder for 2 months and that all this was *in addition* subject to such under-nourishment as exists in normal years. The reduction of consumption thereby effected would amount to only 4 weeks' supply.

17. It is arguable that there must have been a large consumption of the new *aman* crop reaped at the end of 1941 and this helped to make the deficit good. This is, no doubt, true. There is evidence that in 1941 there was noticeable increase of such consumption. Here again we may ask how much could this have amounted to ? The interval between the reaping of the *aman* crop and the end of the year is small, and those sections of the poorer classes who have to get their supply from the markets, and not directly from the fields, would still consume only earlier grown or imported rice. Making allowance for all these factors, it still remains probable that in 1941, as in 1936, there was not an absolute deficiency of supply. The total supply, consisting of the carry-over and current supply, must have been smaller than in 1936, but not necessarily short of the requirements of the province as a whole. The distress prevailing in the year 1941 was, as in 1936, primarily due to the lack of purchasing power in the hands of the poorer classes who were affected by the crop failure.

18. An attempt can be made to discover whether there was any stock left at the end of 1941, as the carry-over[1] at the beginning of 1942, in the following manner. The carry-over at the beginning of 1928 is unknown. Supposing it was entirely wiped out by the deficit of that year, we may consider only the surpluses and deficits of succeeding years as set out below :—

Year	Surplus (Million tons)	Year	Deficit (Million tons)
1929 . . .	0·79	1936 .	1·50
1931 . . .	0·80	1939 . . .	0·51
1932 . . .	0·68	1940 . . .	0·34
1933 . . .	1·40	1941 . . .	2·43
1934 . . .	0·44		
1935 . . .	0·24		
1937 . . .	1·35		
	5·70		4·78

These figures indicate the existence of nearly one million tons, as the carry-over at the beginning of 1942—that is, about 5 weeks' supply for that year. (This might have been rather more, if the

[1] The stock of all rice at the beginning of 1942 *minus* the yield of the *aman* crop harvested in 1941, see paragraph 2 (iv) above.

carry-over at the beginning of 1928 had been larger than the deficit during that year). There is of course little direct evidence in support of this conclusion. All that can be said is that it is a reasonable inference drawn from the analysis made in this note. It is not rendered improbable merely because actual consumption is variable and not identical with the assumed figures of ' requirements '. If consumption increased in good years and decreased in bad years, the surpluses would no doubt be smaller, but the deficits would also be smaller.

SECTION D—SUPPLY IN RELATION TO REQUIREMENTS IN 1943.

19. The following table shows the particulars of current supply during 1943 :—

	Supply in terms of weekly requirements[1]
(*i*) *Aman* supply	29
(*ii*) *Boro* and *aus* supply	13
(*iii*) External supply	1
Current supply	43

If we compare the figures with those of the *average* of the preceding 5 years (as set out in paragraph 14 above), current supply was short by about 6 weeks. This was mainly due to the low yield of the *aman* crop reaped at the end of the previous year which provided food sufficient for only 29 weeks, as compared with the average, *viz.* 38 weeks. There was a shortage in the *aman* supply to the extent of about 9 weeks. The *boro* and *aus* crops yielded more, thus reducing the shortage of current supply. External supply was about the same during 1943 as compared with the average.

20. Thus, 1943 was a lean year, comparable with the three years 1941, 1936 and 1928 already considered. Current supply in these years is compared below :—

Year	Current supply in terms of weekly requirements
1943	43
1941	39
1936	44
1928	45

The shortage of current supply was a little more serious during 1943 than in 1936 and 1928, but less serious than in 1941. This table brings out the need of forming some idea of the carry-over. If consumption is so variable that it can adjust itself to large variations in current supply and variability of consumption is of much greater importance than the carry-over, it is difficult to understand why an unprecedented tragedy befell Bengal during 1943, when current supply was larger than in 1941 by nearly 4 weeks' supply. It is clear, however, from the examination of the supply position in past years—

(*i*) that the total supply consisting of the carry-over, as well as current supply, has generally exceeded annual requirements by a considerable margin in past years ;

(*ii*) that distress occurs even when such a margin is adequate, primarily because the poorer classes in rural areas affected by crop failure, lack the purchasing power necessary for buying supplies even though they are physically available in the province ; and that this was so both during 1941 and 1936[2].

21. If the conclusion stated in paragraph 18 is accepted some estimate of the carry-over during 1943 may be reached. The carry-over at the beginning of 1942 was about 5 weeks requirements. During 1942, current supply exceeded annual requirements, and there was a small surplus of between one and two weeks' requirements. This suggests that the carry-over at the beginning of 1943 was about 6 weeks' requirements. If this is correct, the total supply during 1943 was probably as follows :—

	Supply in terms of weekly requirements
(*i*) Carry-over	6
(*ii*) Current supply	43
Total supply	49

Thus, it is probable that total supply during 1943 was not adequate for the requirements of the year. In other words, there was an absolute deficiency, the probable magnitude of which was equivalent to about 3 weeks' requirements.

[1] Rounded to the nearest week.

[2] It is not possible to say anything about 1928, as the supply position prior to that year has not been examined.

22. It must, however, be emphasized that there is no direct information available about the carry-over of any year, and that the basis for assessment of surpluses and deficits involves many assumptions, none of which is conclusively provable. It can, therefore, be argued that the carry-over at the beginning of 1943 was smaller or larger than has been estimated in the previous paragraph. Some of the points in favour of either view are referred to below :—

(*i*) The conclusion that the carry-over at the beginning of 1942 was about 5 weeks' supply was based on the assumption that the carry-over at the beginning of 1928 was so small that it was wiped out by the deficit in that year. It may have been larger. This is possible, but there is some reason to believe that it may not have been very large. The *aman* crop of 1926 which came into supply during 1927, was also a poor one ; and this makes it likely that the carry-over was not large at the beginning of 1928.

(*ii*) It may be urged that there was never any large carry-over during these years, and that whatever existed was completely exhausted at the end of 1941 ; and that since the current supply in 1942 was only a little more than sufficient for annual requirements, there could have been practically no carry-over at the beginning of 1943. The reasons for believing that there had been a substantial increase in stocks during the years of depression and a few years thereafter have already been explained.

(*iii*) Lastly, mention should be made of the results of the 'food drive' conducted in June 1943 by the Bengal Government. In its course a census of stocks was taken and the requirements for the remainder of the year, as well as the anticipated yield of the *aus* crop, were ascertained. The conclusion reached by the Bengal Government was that there was an absolute deficiency of 1·06 million tons—roughly equal to 5 weeks' requirements on the basis of the present analysis. The results are, however, not conclusive because it was known at the time that stocks were under-estimated, on account of under-statement by the owners as well as concealment. The Bengal Government assumed that the under-estimation was equivalent to one-fourth of the ascertained stocks. There is no way of determining whether this allowance was adequate. If it was not, the deficiency would have been less. The statistical results of the food drive are indeed of value in that they suggest that there was an absolute deficiency. The total of ascertained stocks at the time of the drive was 0·94 million tons. Unless, therefore, the stocks which were under-stated or concealed largely exceeded the ascertained stocks, it is evident there must have been some deficiency. On the whole, therefore, the results of the 'food drive' are consistent with the conclusions about the supply position reached in the preceding paragraphs.

23. To sum up, the supply position in 1943 may be described as follows :—

(*i*) *Comparison with previous years.*—(*a*) There were three years, within a period of 15 preceding years, when the shortage in current supply was comparable with that in 1943.

These were 1941, 1936 and 1928. In these years, the shortage was due to the failure of the *aman* crop, there was distress among the poorer classes in rural areas affected by the crop failure, and relief measures were undertaken on a considerable scale. The current supply during 1943 was smaller, in relation to requirements, than in any previous year except 1941.

(*b*) The carry-over was smaller in 1943 than in 1941 and much smaller than in 1936.

(*c*) The total supply, including the carry-over, was probably smaller in 1943 than in any of the preceding 15 years.

(*ii*) *Estimated supply in relation to requirements of the year.*—(*a*) The current supply during 1943 was sufficient for the requirements of about 43 weeks.

(*b*) The carry-over at the beginning of the year was sufficient for the requirements of about 6 weeks.

(*c*) The total supply during the year was sufficient for only about 49 weeks. It is, therefore, probable that there was an absolute deficiency of supply, of the order of 3 weeks' requirements.

STATEMENT I.—UNADJUSTED CURRENT SUPPLY AND SEED REQUIREMENTS IN BENGAL. (Figures in '000)

Year	*Aman* crop		*Boro* crop		*Aus* crop		External supply			Current supply	Seed requirements
	Acreage	Yield	Acreage	Yield	Acreage	Yield	Imports	Exports	Net imports (+) or exports (—)		
1	2	3	4	5	6	7	8	9	10	11	12
		Tons		Tons		Tons	Tons	Tons	Tons	Tons	Tons
1928	13,210	4,731	400	160	5,649	2,119	668	507	+161	7,171	368
1929	15,357	7,405	398	162	5,031	1,589	270	520	—250	8,906	359
1930	14,794	6,453	400	160	5,082	2,107	208	519	—311	8,409	384
1931	15,120	6,943	380	156	6,163	2,190	571	571	..	9,289	386
1932	15,571	7,150	394	152	5,795	2,209	360	599	—239	9,272	385
1933	15,590	6,958	394	198	5,775	2,254	549	630	—81	9,329	380
1934	15,499	6,226	399	200	5,571	1,842	978	614	+364	8,632	372
1935	14,760	6,222	408	209	5,851	2,015	433	333	+100	8,546	372
1936	14,837	5,003	404	189	5,757	1,903	570	465	+105	7,200	392
1937	15,804	7,692	432	209	5,865	1,963	244	479	—235	9,629	390
1938	15,923	6,873	414	198	5,727	1,403	710	677	+33	8,507	390
1939	15,836	5,963	425	201	5,742	1,758	1,156	774	+382	8,304	388
1940	16,096	6,504	418	194	5,416	1,525	752	494	+258	8,481	387
1941	14,917	4,315	437	203	6,485	2,250	759	536	+223	6,991	422
1942	16,914	7,396	444	206	6,507	1,694	274	376	—102	9,194	410
1943	16,207	5,020	480	218	6,500	2,390	275	11	+264 (*a*)	7,892	472

(*a*) Calendar year figure as per " Trade " Statistics.

STATEMENT II.—CONSUMPTION, SURPLUSES AND DEFICITS IN BENGAL.
(In millions of tons)

Year	Current supply less seed	Consumption	Surplus (+) or Deficit (—)	In terms of weekly requirements: Current supply	In terms of weekly requirements: Surplus (+) or Deficit (—)
1	2	3	4	5	6
1928	6·80	7·44	—0·64	47·5	—4·5
1929	8·55	7·54	+1·01	59·0	+7·0
1930	8·03	7·64	+0·39	54·6	+2·6
1931	8·90	7·74	+1·16	59·8	+7·8
1932	8·89	7·84	+1·05	59·0	+7·0
1933	8·95	7·94	+1·01	58·6	+6·6
1934	8·26	8·04	+0·22	53·4	+1·4
1935	8·17	8·14	+0·03	52·2	+0·2
1936	6·81	8·24	—1·43	43·0	—9·0
1937	9·24	8·34	+0·90	57·6	+5·6
1938	8·12	8·44	—0·32	50·0	—2·0
1939	7·92	8·54	—0·62	48·2	—3·8
1940	8·09	8·64	—0·55	48·7	—3·3
1941	6·57	8·74	—2·17	39·0	—13·0
1942	8·78	8·84	—0·06	51·6	—0·4
Total 1928-42 .	122·08				
Average 1928-42 .	8·14				
1943	7·42	8·94	—1·52	43·2	—8·8

STATEMENT III.—ADJUSTED CURRENT SUPPLY AND SEED REQUIREMENTS IN BENGAL.

(Figures in '000)

Year	*Aman* crop		*Boro* crop		*Aus* crop		External supply	Current supply	Seed requirements
	Acreage	Yield	Acreage	Yield	Acreage	Yield	Net imports (+) or exports (—)		
1	2	3	4	5	6	7	8	9	10
		Tons		Tons		Tons	Tons	Tons	Tons
1928	15,852	5,299	400	160	5,649	1,943	+161	7,563	422
1929	18,429	8,293	398	162	5,031	1,457	—250	9,662	411
1930	17,752	7,228	400	160	5,082	1,932	—311	9,009	437
1931	18,144	7,776	380	156	6,163	2,008	..	9,940	440
1932	18,686	8,008	394	152	5,795	2,024	—239	9,945	440
1933	18,708	8,350	394	198	5,775	2,254	—31	10,771	435
1934	18,598	7,471	399	200	5,571	1,842	+414	9,927	425
1935	17,712	7,466	408	209	5,851	2,015	+150	9,840	424
1936	17,804	6,004	404	189	5,757	1,903	+155	8,251	448
1937	18,964	9,231	432	209	5,865	1,963	—185	11,218	446
1938	19,107	8,247	414	198	5,727	1,403	+133	9,981	446
1939	19,003	7,155	425	201	5,742	1,758	+482	9,596	445
1940	19,315	7,805	418	194	5,416	1,525	+358	9,882	440
1941	17,900	5,178	437	203	6,485	2,250	+323	7,954	482
1942	20,297	8,876	444	206	6,507	1,694	—2	10,774	467
Total 1928-42 . .	276,271	112,387	6,147	2,797	86,416	27,971	+1,158	144,313	6,608
Average 1928-42 . . .	18,418	7,492	410	186	5,761	1,865	+77	9,620	441
1943	19,449	6,024	480	218	6,500	2,390	+264 (a)	8,896	537

(a) Calendar year figure as per " Trade " Statistics.

STATEMENT IV.—CONSUMPTION, SURPLUSES AND DEFICITS IN BENGAL.

(In millions of tons)

Year	Current supply less seed	Consumption	Surplus (+) or Deficit (—)	In terms of weekly requirements: Current supply	In terms of weekly requirements: Surplus (+) or Deficit (—)
1	2	3	4	5	6
1928	7·14	8·34	—1·20	44·5	—7·5
1929	9·25	8·46	+0·79	56·8	+4·8
1930	8·57	8·58	—0·01	51·9	—0·1
1931	9·50	8·70	+0·80	56·8	+4·8
1932	9·50	8·82	+0·68	56·0	+4·0
1933	10·34	8·94	+1·40	60·1	+8·1
1934	9·50	9·06	+0·44	54·5	+2·5
1935	9·42	9·18	+0·24	53·4	+1·4
1936	7·80	9·30	—1·50	43·6	—8·4
1937	10·77	9·42	+1·35	59·4	+7·4
1938	9·54	9·54	..	52·0	..
1939	9·15	9·66	—0·51	49·2	—2·8
1940	9·44	9·78	—0·34	50·1	—1·9
1941	7·47	9·90	—2·43	39·3	—12·7
1942	10·31	10·02	+0·29	53·5	+1·5
Total 1928-42 .	137·70				
Average 1928-42 . .	9·18				
1943 . . .	8·36	10·14	—1·78	42·8	—9·2

APPENDIX III

TABLE I.—RICE SUPPLY (INDIA) DURING 10 YEARS

(In millions of tons)

Period	Production	Imports (*a*)	Exports (*a*)	Net imports (+) or exports (–)	Production *minus* exports net *plus* imports
1	2	3	4	5	6
5 years ending 1937-38 (Average) . .	25·84(*c*)	1·96(*b*)	0·24(*b*)	+1·72	27·56
1938-39 . . .	23·96(*c*)	1·56	0·31	+1·25	25·21
1939-40 . . .	25·73(*c*)	2·43	0·29	+2·14	27·87
1940-41 . . .	22·19(*d*)	1·37	0·28	+1·09	23·28
1941-42 . . .	25·35(*d*)	1·07	0·36	+0·71	26·06
1942-43 . . .	24·90(*d*)	0·02	0·28	—0·26	24·64
5 years ending 1942-43 (Average) . .	24·42	1·29	0·30	+0·99	25·41
10 years ending 1942-43 (Average) . .	25·13	1·62	0·27	+1·35	26·48

NOTE.—Paddy in the case of trade figures has not been converted into Rice, the proportion being very small.

(*a*) Trade figures taken from the Memorandum of the Food Department, Government of India.

(*b*) Calculated on the basis of figures taken from the Report on the Marketing of Rice in India and Burma (1941).

(*c*) Taken from "Estimates of Area and Yield".

(*d*) "Crop Forecast" published by the Department of Commercial Intelligence and Statistics.

TABLE II.—WHEAT SUPPLY (INDIA) DURING 10 YEARS

(In millions of tons)

Period	Production	Imports	Exports	Net imports (+) or exports (—)	Production *minus* exports net *plus* imports
1	2	3	4	5	6
5 years ending 1937-38 (Average)	9·81(*a*)	0·02(*c*)	0·22(*c*)	—0·20	9·61
1938-39	9·96(*a*)	0·17(*d*)	0·36(*d*)	—0·19	9·77
1939-40	10·77(*a*)	0·10(*d*)	0·08(*d*)	+0·02	10·79
1940-41	10·03(*b*)	0·02(*d*)	0·14(*d*)	—0·12	9·91
1941-42	10·04(*b*)	0·02(*d*)	0·28(*d*)	—0·26	9·78
1942-43	11·03(*b*)	(Negligible) (*d*)	0·03(*d*)	—0·03	11·00
5 years ending 1942-43 (Average)	10·37	0·06	0·18	—0·12	10·25
10 years ending 1942-43 (Average)	10·09	0·04	0·20	—0·16	9·93

(*a*) "Estimates of Area and Yield of Principal Crops in India."
(*b*) "Crop Forecasts and Publications issued by the Department of Commercial Intelligence and Statistics."
(*c*) "Report on the Marketing of Wheat in India (1937)."
"Accounts relating to Sea-borne Trade and Navigation of British India."
"Trade at Stations adjacent to Land Frontier Routes."
"Annual statement of the Sea-borne Trade and Navigation of Burma."
(*d*) "Memorandum of the Food Department, Government of India."

APPENDIX III

TABLE III.—INDEX NUMBERS OF AVERAGE MONTHLY WHOLESALE PRICES[1]

	Primary Commodities			Manufactured Articles	
	General	Rice (Calcutta)	Wheat (Lyallpur & Karachi)	General	Cotton manufactures
Week ending 19th August 1939	100	100	100	100	100
1939—					
September	107·6	111	117	110·4	105
December	135·9	114	156	144·5	126
1940—					
March	128·0	114	140	133·9	123
June	112·4	121	117	120·0	118
September	110·3	133	133	111·6	110
December	114·0	140	160	119·7	117
1941—					
March	111·8	139	146	127·2	127
June	122·3	163	148	142·9	143
September	138·3	169	193	166·3	190
December	139·5	172	212	157·8	198
1942—					
March	139·4	159	202	162·5	193
June	152·3	207	214	166·5	212
September	160·4	218	223	179·1	282
December	175·6	218	232	221·5	414

[1] Issued by the office of the Economic Adviser, Government of India. The base period is the week ending 19th August 1939.

APPENDIX V

Distribution of Supplies in Bengal (1943).

1. There is no accurate information about the quantities of rice and paddy stocks held in Calcutta at the beginning of 1943. The Foodgrains Control Order came into force on the 15th December 1942. For various reasons, it was not satisfactorily enforced. According to the returns received, total stocks in Calcutta at the end of January 1943 were 3·84 lakh maunds of rice and 0·80 lakh maunds of paddy, or roughly 16,000 tons of rice and paddy in terms of rice, a quantity which would cover the requirements of Calcutta for about three weeks. The stocks held by dealers must clearly have been in excess of this. An officer of the Civil Supplies Department, Bengal, pointed out that many dealers had not taken out licences by this time, not all licensed dealers submitted returns, and there were glaring discrepancies between the stocks reported under the Foodgrains Control Order and the returns secured under a separate Order under the Defence of India Rules at the same time.

2. The following figures, based on Trade Statistics compiled by the Department of Commercial Intelligence and Statistics, throw some light on the position.

	Rice and paddy (in terms of rice) (In Tons)	
	1941	1942
Imports into Calcutta	583,930	271,475
Exports out of Calcutta	280,343	156,950
Net retention in Calcutta	303,587	114,525

The normal annual rice consumption of the area served by the supplies received into the Calcutta trade block cannot be stated precisely, and the quantities arriving by country boat which should also be taken into account, are unknown. The area is somewhat smaller than the area of Greater Calcutta at present under rationing, but it can be safely assumed that the normal annual consumption would be somewhere between 200,000 and 250,000 tons. It is, therefore, likely that the net retention in Calcutta during 1942 was short of annual requirements by several months, and that while stocks in Calcutta at the end of 1941 were above the normal level, they were severely depleted by the end of 1942. Stocks held on the first day of 1943 were probably much smaller than those held on the corresponding day of previous years, though it is impossible to say how many weeks' stocks were actually carried in the aggregate by consumers, mills, and traders.

3. Imports into Calcutta, of rice and paddy (in terms of rice), during the first quarter of 1943 were as follows :—

	(In Tons)			
	January	February	March	Total
(i) From within Bengal by rail and river steamer [1]	6,253	4,521	13,383	24,157
(ii) From outside Bengal by rail and river steamer [1]	1,077	3,607	5,639	10,323
(iii) By sea and coast [1]	259		212	471
(iv) By country boat [2]	3,219	1,674	2,960	7,853
Total	10,808	9,802	22,194	42,804

Exports out of Calcutta during the first quarter of 1943 were as follows :—

	(In Tons)			
	January	February	March	Total
(i) To Bengal districts by rail and river steamer [1]	1,040	2,334	3,154	6,528
(ii) To outside Bengal by rail and river steamer [1]	243	170	1,210	1,623
(iii) By sea and coast [1]	2,087	81	69	2,237
(iv) By country boat [2]	438	66	..	504
Total	3,808	2,651	4,433	10,892

[1] Trade Statistics compiled by the Department of Commercial Intelligence and Statistics.

[2] Based on figures furnished by Civil Supplies Department of the Government of Bengal.

4. On this basis, the net retention in Calcutta during the first three months of 1943 was as follows :—

Month	Rice and paddy (in terms of rice) (In Tons)
January	7,000
February	7,151
March	17,761
Total	31,912

These figures indicate the seriousness of the position in Calcutta during these months.

5. The Bengal Government have furnished the Commission with figures showing arrivals on Government account into Calcutta, month by month, despatches to deficit districts, the deliveries made to employers' organizations and essential services, and to the general public in Calcutta through "Controlled Shops" and "Approved Markets". The relevant figures for the first three months of 1943 are shown below :—

	Rice and paddy (in terms of rice) (In Tons)		
	January	February	March
(i) Arrivals in Calcutta	1,200	6,361	15,727
(ii) Despatches out of Calcutta to the districts	..	392	2,074
(iii) Deliveries to Employers' Organizations and Essential Services	..	4,445	12,487
(iv) Deliveries to Controlled Shops and Approved Markets		6,988	

6. Imports into Calcutta during the second quarter of 1943 were as given below :—

	Rice and paddy (in terms of rice) (In Tons)			
	April	May	June	Total
(i) From within Bengal by rail and river steamer [1]	13,824	14,267	13,483	41,574
(ii) From outside Bengal by rail and river steamer [1]	11,746	11,675	27,796	51,217
(iii) By sea and coast [1]	..	..	..	..
(iv) By country boat [2]	2,010	2,125	1,014	5,149
Total	27,580	28,067	42,293	97,940

Exports out of Calcutta during the same period were as given below :—

	Rice and paddy (in terms of rice) (In Tons)			
	April	May	June	Total
(i) To Bengal districts by rail and steamer [1]	2,042	1,415	5,343	8,800
(ii) To outside Bengal by rail and steamer [1]	79	69	128	276
(iii) By sea and coast [1]	13	4	30	47
(iv) By country boat [2]	..	249	..	249
Total	2,134	1,737	5,501	9,372

7. The quantities of stocks which were retained in Calcutta according to the foregoing figures were as follows :—

Month	Rice and paddy (in terms of rice) (In Tons)
April	25,446
May	26,330
June	36,792
Total	88,568

The figures reflect the improvement in supply produced by a number of measures namely, the Rescue Plan, De-control in Bengal, and the introduction of Free Trade in the Eastern Region.

[1]Trade statistics compiled by the Department of Commercial Intelligence and Statistics.
[2]Based on figures furnished by Civil Supplies Department of the Government of Bengal.

8. The distribution of supplies passing through the hands of the Bengal Government during the second quarter is shown below :—

Rice and paddy (in terms of rice)
(In Tons)

	April	May	June	Total
(i) Arrivals in Calcutta . . .	17,550	13,186	18,870	49,606
(ii) Despatches out of Calcutta to the districts	5,405	7,006	3,126	15,537
(iii) Deliveries to Employers' Organizations and Essential Services in Calcutta	16,361	12,399	7,303	36,063
(iv) Deliveries to Controlled Shops and Approved Markets in Calcutta .	7,578	6,516	4,188	18,282

9. Imports into Calcutta during the third quarter of 1943 are given below[1] :

Rice and paddy (in terms of rice)
(In Tons)

	July	August	September	Total
(i) From within Bengal by rail and river steamer . .	7,914	8,081	6,141	22,136
(ii) From outside Bengal by rail and river steamer	28,933	11,906	9,998	50,837
(iii) By sea and coast	..	1	3,460	3,461
Total .	36,847	19,988	19,599	76,434

Exports out of Calcutta during the same period are given below :—

Rice and paddy (in terms of rice)
(In Tons)

	July	August	September	Total
(i) To Bengal districts by rail and river steamer	6,353	2,390	4,059	12,802
(ii) To outside Bengal by rail and river steamer	945	1,413	57	2,415
(iii) By sea and coast	75	101	3	179
Total .	7,373	3,904	4,119	15,396

10. The distribution of supplies passing through the hands of the Bengal Government during the 3rd quarter of 1943 is shown below :

Rice and paddy (in terms of rice)
(In Tons)

	July	August	September	Total
(i) Arrivals in Calcutta . . .	16,776	8,789	10,742	36,307
(ii) Despatches to the districts from Calcutta	9,690	3,713	5,753	19,156
(iii) Deliveries to Employers' Organizations and Essential Services in Calcutta	7,315	4,344	6,243	17,902
(iv) Deliveries to Controlled Shops and Approved Markets in Calcutta .	5,301	4,396	4,647	14,344

11. During the last quarter of 1943, imports into Calcutta were as below :—

Rice and paddy (in terms of rice)
(In Tons)

	October	November	December	Total
(i) From within Bengal by rail and river steamer	3,997	5,921	10,760	20,678
(ii) From outside Bengal by rail and river steamer	19,854	23,955	25,169	68,978
(iii) By sea and coast	7,760	2,653	7,394	17,807
Total .	31,611	32,529	43,323	107,463

[1] The figures for the 3rd and 4th quarters do not include the arrivals by country boat as no records were maintained for two months and the amounts were small for the other months.

Exports out of Calcutta during the same period were as below :—

	Rice and paddy (in terms of rice) (In Tons)			
	October	November	December	Total
(i) To Bengal districts by rail and river steamer	2,470	7,820	4,468	14,758
(ii) To outside Bengal by rail and river steamer	14	751	96	861
(iii) By sea and coast	14	1	5	20
Total .	2,498	8,572	4,569	15,639

12. The distribution of supplies passing through the hands of the Bengal Government during this quarter is shown below :—

	Rice and paddy (in terms of rice) (In Tons)			
	October	November	December	Total
(i) Arrivals in Calcutta	23,662	31,016	32,639	87,317
(ii) Despatches to the districts from Calcutta	7,484	11,108	9,201	27,793
(iii) Deliveries to Employers' Organizations and Essential Services in Calcutta	7,421	9,639	3,104	20,164
(iv) Deliveries to Controlled Shops and Approved Markets in Calcutta .	5,922	2,462	2,484	10,868

13. There is a difference between the figures furnished by Bengal Government for despatches to the districts from Calcutta and the trade statistics of exports from Calcutta to Bengal districts by rail and river steamer. The figures are as follows :—

	Rice and paddy (in terms of rice) (In Tons)	
	(Despatches Government figures)	Exports (Trade Statistics)
1st quarter	2,466	6,528
2nd quarter	15,537	8,800
3rd quarter	19,156	12,802
4th quarter	27,793	14,758
Total	64,952	42,888

The two sets of figures are not strictly comparable chiefly because the " Despatches " include movements by road and country boat while the "Trade Statistics " do not.

14. The total quantity of wheat despatched to Bengal from other provinces and from abroad during 1943 amounted to 373,000 tons and the total arrivals were 339,000 tons. The total amount received on Government account was 322,000 tons out of which 120,000 tons were despatched to the districts. The arrivals quarter by quarter were :—

	(In Tons)
1st quarter	26,000
2nd quarter	38,000
3rd quarter	99,000
4th quarter	176,000
Total . .	339,000

The arrivals during the 1st quarter were less than half the normal off-take. Those during the second quarter were better but they were still much below requirements.

15. The production and consumption of millets in Bengal are normally negligible. In view of the general shortage of rice and of the urgent need of Bengal for supplies, the Central Government arranged, under the Basic Plan, for the importation of millets into Bengal. Over 65,000 tons of millets were despatched during the year, out of which about 55,000 tons arrived. The arrivals were heavy in September and October. The United Provinces despatched 43,000 tons, and the Punjab 13,000 tons ; and the remainder was despatched by a number of States. Out of the arrivals, 46,000 tons were sent to the districts.

16. The following table shows the figures of despatches to the districts of Bengal as furnished by the Government of Bengal :—

(In Tons)

District	Rice and paddy in terms of rice	Wheat and wheat-products	Millets	Total
24-Parganas	8,157	5,114	6,524	19,795
Nadia	1,367	2,080	165	3,612
Murshidabad	679	3,348	552	4,579
Jessore	184	898	56	1,138
Khulna	2,266	7,543	3,469	13,278
Burdwan	3,200	10,755	1,023	14,978
Birbhum	..	1,729	..	1,729
Bankura	..	4,710	..	4,710
Midnapore	4,963	11,607	3,928	20,498
Hooghly	2,461	6,004	1,287	9,752
Howrah	11,049	4,997	1,128	17,174
Rajshahi	..	654	..	654
Dinajpur	..	631	..	631
Jalpaiguri	540	2,175	232	2,947
Darjeeling	323	5,154	325	5,802
Rangpur	105	3,069	745	3,919
Bogra	..	313	112	425
Pabna	1,301	2,690	2,773	6,764
Malda	..	202	..	202
Dacca	6,727	15,019	4,831	26,577
Mymensingh	956	4,693	3,259	8,908
Faridpur	4,709	5,597	6,187	16,493
Bakarganj	1,485	2,671	1,092	5,248
Chittagong	9,814	9,469	4,083	23,366
Tippera	2,922	5,092	2,918	10,932
Noakhali	1,744	3,809	1,201	6,754
Total	64,952	120,023	45,890	230,865

ANNEXURE I TO APPENDIX V

EXTRACT FROM A NOTE ON "ARRANGEMENTS FOR RECEPTION AND DESPATCHES IN CALCUTTA PRIOR TO THE FORMATION OF THE DIRECTORATE OF MOVEMENTS IN NOVEMBER 1943" SUPPLIED BY THE CIVIL SUPPLIES DEPARTMENT, BENGAL.

The following problems confronted the Department :—

(*i*) Creation of a widespread organization covering all the points of arrivals and despatches and rapid transmission of information to the headquarters;

(*ii*) Creation of a superior staff at the headquarters to control these arrangements and undertake frequent inspection of the work of the subordinates;

(*iii*) A careful watch over the accommodation in godowns and adoption of prompt steps in advance to meet any difficulty that may arise in this respect, and

(*iv*) To assist the Clearing Agents in their difficulties about transport, etc., which became apparent very soon.

Staff.—The Department began to look for staff at a time when other competitors, (*e.g.*, the Army, the Supply Department of the Government of India, etc.), had already been in the field and taken over practically all suitable personnel available for recruitment. The Department was in dire need of staff not only for its own storage and movement organization but also for the Calcutta Rationing Scheme. All attempts to secure suitable men from the business houses proved abortive. At the beginning of September there were only one Transportation Officer and 4 Inspectors and the first essential was to obtain a sufficient number of inspectors and sub-inspectors for being placed at the different receiving points as well as for supervising despatches at several other points. It requires time to train men for such work but the Department had no time to wait. Inspectors and sub-inspectors were withdrawn from other branches and even from Calcutta Rationing and posted to the terminals and the docks. In this way, the staff was increased to 21 inspectors and 23 sub-inspectors by the end of October. In the meantime recruitment was proceeding under the Controller of Rationing both for his office and for the Directorate. It was soon found that the existing Transportation Officer was hardly able to handle problems and officers superior to inspectors were necessary both for supervising the work of inspectors and for taking charge of the more important reception centres, *e.g.*, Howrah, Kantapukur and the docks. Mr .... and a Sub-Deputy Collector from the Department were deputed to take charge of Kantapukur and Howrah respectively and with great difficulty one Chief Inspector (an *ex*-Transportation Inspector of the East Indian Railway) was obtained for Howrah in the end of September another for other sidings in October and a third in the beginning of November for the docks. The Department was still in search of a suitable Transportation Officer, when Mr.............. was offered by the Regional Commissioner and was appointed as Controller of Transport at the end of September ....But it became apparent soon that besides planning programmes for movements, both *ex*-Calcutta and from outside to the province, he had no time to supervise the despatches with the result that wagons were sometimes not utilised by the Agents. Another officer was therefore appointed on the 8th October to supervise storage and despatches......From the very beginning his entire attention was absorbed at the docks as shipment of foreign foodgrains began to be rushed and considerable despatches had to be made to Chittagong at very short notice. On the 18th October, Mr ....who had experience of transport in the trade was recruited as Storage and Movement Officer but at the very outset he had to be placed under the Controller of Rationing for Calcutta Rationing.

While the organization was thus being improved, it was oon found that the existing clearing agents were not in a position to cope with the work which they were required to do. They were incapable of working under such stress and it was apparent that considerable supervision and training were necessary before they could work at high speed. Moreover, the difficulty of securing adequate road transport from the military sidings to their godowns was one of the principal causes of their inefficiency. This difficulty was due to diversion of lorries and bullock-carts to work under military contractors and also due to the difficulty of securing adequate petrol supplies. Arrangements were made to supply petrol to the agents according to their requirements by the Department and this enabled them to secure more lorries. But this was only a partial solution of the difficulty. The most important clearing and haulage firms were requested to take up this work but they expressed their inability to undertake any liability of this kind under the difficult conditions prevailing in Calcutta. A number of new clearing agents were however, appointed on their producing evidence that they had some transport and possessed adequate godown accommodation. The problem of coping with the daily arrivals still remained. This problem was made more difficult by the fact that the rate of arrivals was irregular and very large quantities were unloaded at very short notice at one or the other of the railway terminals. A further complication was caused by the arrival of a number of ships carrying foodgrains from Australia and Karachi. About 13,000 tons of foodgrains arrived at the port in September and 30,000 tons in October respectively. The conditions of work in the docks were far more difficult due to the following reasons :—

1. Sufficient labour was not available for loading the agents' vehicles ;
2. Railway wagons which were formerly available for removing consignment from the dock sheds to the various points in the city were available only in small numbers ;
3. Due to heavy arrivals of war and other materials and requirements of gate passes facilities for working lorries had been greatly reduced....

In view of the difficult transport situation, it was decided at the end of September to acquire a fleet of 50 lorries to supplement the agents' transport, whenever necessary. Although order had been placed at the beginning of October for 50 lease-lend vehicles with specially fitted bodies only 3 vehicles were delivered on the 22nd October and 22 on the 23rd and the balance on the 18th November. About this time, Army transport was made available and when the Department vehicles were put into commission, transport difficulties were overcome and work went on smoothly.

A further point should be stressed in this connection. Both at Howrah and at Kantapukur a large number of consignments were being received on account of private merchants who were unable to make prompt clearance. Requests were received both from the E. I. R. and the Port Commissioners to remove the congestion caused by private merchants as otherwise the siding would get choked and further booking of supplies would be stopped. In spite of its own troubles the Department had to undertake this work from time to time. These consignments, unless they were removed within a week, were requisitioned and acquired by Government and removed to their own godowns. Some idea of the magnitude of this work may be obtained from the fact that during a period of about 30 days in October-November, the congestion at Kantapukur was reduced from 133,112 bags to 16,677 bags....

In conclusion it may be stated that though the Department had to work under conditions of exceptional difficulty it managed to keep the Railway terminals open and never had occasion to slacken the rate of despatches to districts *ex*-Calcutta.

ANNEXURE II TO APPENDIX V

Storage in the Royal Botanical Gardens

Storage in Calcutta continued to be a serious problem even after the arrival of the Army had expedited distribution to the districts. On the 1st November, the stock in hand was 50,000 tons and the approximate covered storage available in Calcutta was only 40,000 tons. At this stage a considerable amount had to be left in transit sheds at the docks. By the beginning of December stocks had increased to 82,000 tons and covered storage by requisitioning had increased to 80,000 tons. By the end of the month, stocks stood at 159,000 tons and covered storage had risen to

130,000 tons. Imports were still pouring in and could not be delayed. Stoppage of imports could not be contemplated as this would have resulted in a serious shortage when Calcutta was about to be rationed. It was also impossible to delay unloading the ships as the port had to be kept clear. In these circumstances, a depot was started in the open as a temporary measure in the Royal Botanical Gardens. Arrivals in Calcutta continued to exceed the increase in storage accommodation till February. At the beginning of February, the stocks stored in the open rose to 87,000 tons and then gradually diminished to 59,000 tons on 1st March 1944, to 28,000 tons on 1st April, to 26,000 tons on 1st May, to 18,000 tons on 1st June, to 14,000 tons on 1st July and to 4,000 tons on 1st August. In all about 120,000 tons passed through the depot. Of this total quantity 101,500 tons were distributed to the districts and to Calcutta through the rationing organization and 15,000 tons of undamaged stocks were sold to the trade. Of the balance of 3,000 tons, 2,200 tons were sold irrespective of condition and the remainder (the actual figure is 600 tons) became complete loss. On the 1st September 1944 the amount, 3,194 tons, which remained at the Royal Botanical Gardens, was removed for destruction by dumping as totally unfit for issue. This figure of 3,194 tons includes the 600 tons which had become a total loss and about 2,600 tons which had been sold to the trade but had deteriorated badly and had not been removed by the purchasers.

ANNEXURE III TO APPENDIX V

Stocks of Aus Paddy at Jessore

A number of witnesses have referred to the stocks of *aus* paddy at Jessore and especially to those stacked in the station. It has been said that although there was local need for rice these stocks were not released for distribution. It has also been urged that these stocks should have been sent to relieve the distress in other areas and finally it has been alleged that a large part of these stocks were damaged. The Bengal Government have furnished a report on this matter. The salient facts according to that report are as follows: Under the *aus* purchasing scheme of 1943, 3·70 lakh maunds of paddy were purchased of which about 78,000 maunds were purchased by the District Magistrate and the remainder by the Purchasing Agent of the Bengal Government. Over two-thirds of the total amount purchased was procured in November. The District Magistrate who had authority to release stocks for local consumption did not find it necessary to do so except for small quantities in October and November, 2,400 maunds in December 1943 and about 12,000 maunds in January and February 1944. An endeavour was made early in December to release appreciable quantities of paddy through the trade in the Jessore district. But though the price was reduced from Rs. 7-12-0 a maund to Rs. 6-4-0 a maund towards the end of December the off-take was poor, the reason being that the *aman* crop had been reaped. By the end of the year 2 lakh maunds had been despatched; part was sent to deficit districts, a small quantity to the District Magistrate, 24-Parganas, and the balance to Calcutta. In March 1944 the stocks which still remained (1·50 lakh maunds) were sold to the Calcutta rice mills at an average price of Rs. 7-7-0 a maund, 1·06 lakh maunds were moved between the 21st March and 27th May 0·29 lakh maunds were despatched early in July and at the time the report was made the balance was being moved gradually as the stocks were brought to rail-head. Except 75,000 maunds which were kept in the station yard, partly in the open, the entire stocks were stored in warehouses. Even the grain kept in the station yard has not shown any signs of deterioration. Reliance has been placed upon the sale of the *aus* paddy at Rs. 7-7-0 a maund in March 1944, when the market price for *aman* paddy was Rs. 9 a maund, as indicating that the stocks were not seriously damaged.

APPENDIX VI

Extracts from Reports from Commissioners and District Officers

I.—Presidency Division

28th December 1942.—Hunger marches organized by communists.

26th February 1943.—Agricultural labourers in difficulty as agricultural wages have not risen proportionately with the rise in the price of foodstuffs.

26th March 1943.—Acute distress prevails in certain areas of Kandi sub-division of Murshidabad district and number of labourers is gradually increasing at test works. It is necessary to continue test works for a long time.

22nd April 1943.—Cultivating classes in general are in acute distress in Nadia district due to abnormal rise in prices of foodstuffs. Paddy seed has been consumed by cultivators. They require loans immediately for purchase of seed.

5th May 1943.—Widespread distress in Khushtia sub-division of Nadia district due to rise in prices, warranting sanction of immediate gratuitous relief.

10th July 1943.—In 24-Parganas conditions are appalling owing to rice and paddy having been drained away for Calcutta market. Food kitchens being opened in Murshidabad.

10th August 1943.—Nadia district passing through the most acute stage of distress.

11th September 1943.—Food kitchens extending rapidly everywhere. Cases of emaciation numerous.

9th October 1943.—Rice has disappeared, following the previous drop in the controlled price. Village responsibility for running soup kitchens will be enforced.

II.—Burdwan Division

12th December 1942.—Outturn of *aman* in Birbhum and Bankura districts 6 annas ; in other districts also outturn is poor. Sudden and abnormal increase in price of rice.

12th January 1943.—All District Magistrates have given up attempts to control prices of rice and paddy. Shortage of rice in villages in Howrah district.

26th February 1943.—Rice position in Howrah grave. Midnapore apprehends acute shortage in May. Relief operations will be necessary in parts of Bankura, Hooghly and Birbhum.

28th March 1943.—Owing to de-control of prices of paddy and rice, situation getting worse in Burdwan. Economic condition grave. Crime against property increasing, and paddy looting cases have become frequent. Hunger marches going on in some places.

27th April 1943.—Major economic catastrophe apprehended after three or four weeks unless prices came down and sufficient supplies were ensured. Rice not available to feed test work labourers in Katwa and Ulubaria sub-divisions. Increase in crime.

13th May 1943.—Economic conditions approaching a crisis. Rice out of reach of the poor. Rice should be imported if the people are not to starve.

12th June 1943.—Economic position most serious. Bands of people moving about in search of rice. Labourers at test works demanding payment in rice, which is not possible in all cases.

22nd July 1943.—An area of 200 square miles comprising 14 unions in Sadar, 15 in Katwa, and 10 in Kalna, affected by floods. Boats required for relief work. Agricultural loans required immediately in flood-affected areas, where *aman* seedlings have been destroyed. Similar reports from Midnapore.

17th August 1943.—Severe famine conditions likely to prevail after transplantation of *aman*. Many deaths due to malnutrition. Destitutes from villages flocking to towns.

27th September 1943.—Situation in Contai and Tamluk terrible. Disposal of dead bodies in Contai, a problem.

28th October 1943.—Rice scarce in Burdwan. Position in Hooghly and Howrah bad. So also in Contai and Tamluk sub-divisions. Kitchens closed occasionally in Midnapore for want of supplies.

III.—Rajshahi Division

11th December 1942.—Increase in price of rice due to speculative buying by traders.

12th January 1943.—Prices remain high. Outturn of *aman* poor in Rajshahi and bad in Pabna and Malda.

25th February 1943.—Prices of rice going up. Unauthorised exports from the division taking place.

26th March 1943.—Difficult to obtain *aus* seeds with the lifting of control of price of rice. Cases of paddy looting reported from Dinajpur and Rangpur.

2nd April 1943.—Widespread distress in many areas of Bogra due to shortage of foodsupply and high prices.

6th May 1943.—Beggars and landless people are in acute distress and threatened with starvation in Pabna district. Gratuitous relief necessary in Sadar and Serajganj.

26th July 1943.—In spite of good *aus* crop the price of rice is still high.

26th September 1943.—Serious distress in Nilphamari. Deaths from starvation reported from all districts except Malda. Many deaths due to taking food indiscreetly after long period of abstinence.

15th October 1943.—Free kitchens opened in Pabna, Rajshahi, Dinajpur, Jalpaiguri and Bogra.

IV.—Dacca Division

28th December 1942.—Price of rice has risen alarmingly. Profiteering in every article on the increase. Black markets prevail.

12th January 1943.—Economic condition in Sadar and Goalundo sub-divisions of Faridpur daily becoming worse due to failure of paddy crop and high prices of all commodities. Opening of test works on an extensive scale essential and six more officers needed. Distribution of gratuitous relief should also be continued up to July 1943.

10th February 1943.—Price of rice increasing. Difficulty experienced owing to fall of export from surplus districts. People having to go without food in Bhola and Barisal towns of Bakarganj district.

24th March 1943.—Rice position very serious. Situation in Goalundo and parts of Sadar of Faridpur district now much worse than was expected.

25th April 1943.—Food position serious. Huge exports from Bakarganj. Poorer classes will starve.

22nd May 1943.—Great distress in Bhola sub-division of Bakarganj district among landless labourers who can find no employment. Situation aggravated by the fact that a large number of fishermen lost their boats as a result of "denial". Opening of test relief immediately necessary.

23rd June 1943.—Situation in Faridpur has deteriorated still further. Relief operations were for long confined to Sadar and Goalundo but the resources of most of the people in other areas have also been exhausted and urgent steps should be taken to alleviate their distress.

17th July 1943.—Situation in Bhola sub-division is alarming. Town filled with thousand of beggars who are starving. There is not enough rice available.

18th August 1943.—Opening of gruel kitchens necessary in Tangail and Kishoreganj.

16th September 1943.—Food situation in all sub-divisions of Faridpur has further deteriorated. Supply of rice and paddy has become alarmingly insufficient. Free kitchens have been opened in large numbers to save people from starvation. Homes for destitutes and camp hospitals have also been opened.

25th October 1943.—Supplies arriving but no hope of saving those who are starving.

V.—Chittagong Division

11th December 1942.—Sudden rise in price of rice to almost double the previous price.

10th January 1943.—Food problem very serious. Attempt to get emergency supply through Director of Civil Supplies failed. Position in Chittagong town extremely bad as price of rice has been kept below the prevailing price in mofussil.

27th February 1943.—Indications of distress among local people in Chittagong district, particularly of the fishermen class. It is immediately necessary to start test works. Gratuitous relief will also be necessary.

8th March 1943.—Situation serious in Chittagong. Rice position has not improved in Noakhali. Position equally bad in Tippera.

11th April 1943.—There are signs of rice crisis easing in Noakhali. Rice is being distributed by District Magistrate in famine areas of Begamganj and Senbagh at controlled rate. In Chittagong district no famine area. Distress among fishermen prevailing in certain areas. Supplies have started to arrive.

29th May 1943.—Many people starving in Chittagong district owing to high prices. First gruel kitchen started in Chittagong.

28th June 1943.—Number of destitutes in town increased. Eleven deaths in streets.

11th July 1943.—Test and gratuitous relief necessary in Chandpur sub-division of Tippera district, as well as Brahamanbaria and Sadar sub-divisions. Food census has disclosed immediate scarcity in Sadar and prospective scarcity in Brahamanbaria. Chandpur has also suffered from "Denial" policy.

10th August 1943.—Owing to distress in rural areas of Chittagong district, a large number of beggars wandered into the town. With the opening of relief kitchens in villages, they were repatriated. But there is still a number who are sick and disabled. A poor house, an orphanage and a hospital have been opened for them.

9th September 1943.—Deaths still occurring in Chittagong town.

9th October 1943.—Control prices not working except where prices have naturally fallen. The middle class are in trouble.

APPENDIX VII

LIST OF PERSONS INTERVIEWED BY THE COMMISSION

NEW DELHI

		Date
1. The Hon'ble Somerset Butler.	Special Officer, Department of Food, Government of India.	27-7-1944
2. Mr. R. H. Hutchings, C.M.G., C.I.E., I.C.S.	Secretary, Department of Food, Government of India.	27-7-1944 and on 5-12-1944
3. Mr. W. H. J. Christie, O.B.E., I.C.S.	Deputy Secretary, Department of Food, Government of India.	28-7-1944
4. Mr. W. H. Kirby . . .	Rationing Adviser, Department of Food, Government of India.	28-7-1944
5. Lt. Gen. J. B. Hance, C.I.E., O.B.E., K.H.S., I.M.S.	Director General, Indian Medical Service .	29-7-1944
6. Lt. Col. E. Cotter, C.I.E., I.M.S.	Public Health Commissioner with the Government of India.	29-7-1944
7. Mr. D. R. Sethi, C.I.E., I.A.S.	Agricultural Production (and Marketing) Adviser to the Government of India, E. H. & L. Department.	31-7-1944
8. The Hon'ble Sir Md. Azizul Haque, C.I.E., D.Litt.	Member, Executive Council of the Governor General (Commerce, Industries and Civil Supplies).	2-8-1944
9. Mr. D. L. Mazumdar, I.C.S. .	Deputy Secretary, Department of Labour, Government of India.	4-8-1944
10. The Hon'ble Mr. B. R. Sen, C.I.E., I.C.S.	Director General of Food, Department of Food, Government of India.	4-8-1944

11. Mr. N. M. Buch, O.B.E., I.C.S.	Director of Civil Supplies, Punjab . .	5-8-1944
12. The Hon'ble Sir J. P. Srivastava, K.B.E.	Member, Executive Council of the Governor General (Food).	5-8-1944 and on 15-2-1945
13. Mr. J. D. Tyson, C.B.E., I.C.S.	Secretary, E. H. & L. Department, Government of India.	7-8-1944
14. Sir P. M. Kharegat, C.I.E., I.C.S.	Additional Secretary, E. H. & L. Department, Government of India.	7-8-1944
15. Brig. Mac. D. Fraser, I.M.S. .	Inspector of Medical Services, General Headquarters.	8-8-1944
16. Mr. I. E. Jones, I.C.S. . .	Director of Food Purchase, Punjab . .	8-8-1944
17. The Hon'ble Sir S. N. Roy, C.S.I., C.I.E., I.C.S.	Secretary, War Transport Department, Government of India.	8-8-1944
18. Sir Hugh Raper . . .	Member, Railway Board	8-8-1944
19. The Hon'ble Dewan Bahadur Sir A. Ramaswami Mudaliar, K.C.S.I.	Member, Executive Council of the Governor General (Supply).	17-11-1944

CALCUTTA

20. Major General E. Wood, C.I.E., C.B., M.C.	Formerly Secretary to the Government of India, Department of Food.	12-8-1944
21. Mr. O. M. Martin, C.I.E., I.C.S.	Commissioner, Post War Reconstruction, Government of Bengal.	12-8-1944
22. The Hon'ble Mr. Justice H. B. L. Braund, Bar.-at-Law.	Formerly Regional Food Commissioner, Eastern Region.	14-8-1944
23. Mr. L. G. Pinnell, C.I.E., I.C.S.	Formerly Officer on Special Duty, Department of Civil Supplies, Bengal.	15-8-1944 and on 4-9-1944
24. Mr. N. M. Ayyar, C.I.E., I.C.S.	Secretary, Department of Civil Supplies, Bengal.	16-8-1944
25. Mr. H. S. E. Stevens, C.S.I., C.I.E., M.C., J.P., I.C.S.	Food and Civil Supplies Commissioner, Bengal.	16-8-1944 and on 17-9-1944
26. Mr. A. A. McInnes . .	Formerly Foodgrains Purchasing Officer, Bengal.	17-8-1944
27. Mr. M. A. Ispahani . .	Partner, Messrs. M. M. Ispahani, Limited, Chief Agents for Procurement, Government of Bengal.	17-8-1944 and in New Delhi on 1-12-1944
28. Major General W. C. Paton, M.C., M.A., Ch.B. (Edin.), F.R.C.S. (Edin.), K.H.P., I.M.S.	Surgeon-General, Bengal (Offg. Director General, Indian Medical Service).	18-8-1944
29. Lt. Col. K. S. Fitch, M.R.C.S., F.R.C.S. (Edin.), I.M.S.	Deputy Surgeon-General, Famine Relief, Bengal.	18-8-1944
30. Dr. B. Mukerjee, M.B., D.P.H.	Deputy Director of Public Health, Bengal .	18-8-1944
31. Major C. K. Lakshmanan, I.M.S.	Director of Public Health, Bengal . .	18-8-1944
32. Mr. E. W. Holland, C.I.E., I.C.S.	Secretary, Public Health and Local Self-Government Department, Bengal.	19-8-1944
33. Mr. K. C. Basak, I.C.S. . .	Secretary, Department of Education, Co-operative Credit and Rural Indebtedness, Bengal.	19-8-1944
34. Mr. A. C. Hartley, O.B.E., I.C.S.	Controller of Rationing, Calcutta . .	19-8-1944
35. Dr. J. B. Grant . . .	Director, All India Institute of Hygiene and Public Health, Calcutta.	19-8-1944
36. Major General A. V. T. Wakely, C.B., D.S.O., M.C.	Director of Movements, Bengal . .	21-8-1944
37. Nawab Habibullah Bahadur of Dacca.	Formerly Minister, Bengal (Food) . .	21-8-1944
38. Mr. M. Carbery, C.I.E., D.S.O., M.G., M.A., B.Sc., I.A.S.	Director of Agriculture, Bengal. . .	21-8-1944
39. Mr. P. N. Banerjee, M.A., B.L., P.R.S., Bar.-at-Law.	Formerly Minister, Bengal (Revenue) .	22-8-1944
40. Mr. A. K. Fazlul Huq, M.A., B.L.	Formerly Chief Minister, Bengal . .	23-8-1944
41. The Hon'ble Mr. H. S. Suhrawardy.	Minister, Bengal (Civil Supplies) . .	23-8-1944 and on 17-9-1944

42. Mr. L. Aldridge	Formerly Procurement Officer, Middle East.	31-8-1944
43. Mr. K. W. P. Marar, O.B.E., I.C.S.	Secretary, Supply Department, Assam .	1-9-1944
44. Dr. N. Sanyal, M.A., Ph.D. (Lond.), M.L.A.	Chief Whip of the Congress Parliamentary Party, Bengal.	1-9-1944
45. Mr. A. C. Ukil	Nutrition Expert, Congress Parliamentary Party, Bengal.	
46. Mr. Shamsuddin Ahmed .	Representatives of the Nikhil Banga Krishak Proja Party.	1-9-1944
47. Mr. Syed Jalaluddin Hashemi		
48. Mr. Humayun Kabir . .		
49. Mr. Rajani Mukherjee . .	Representatives of the Indian Federation of Labour, Radical Democratic Party.	2-9-1944
50. Prof. Binoyendra Nath Banerjee.		
51. Miss Sobha Mazumdar . .		
52. Mr. Bhowani Sen . .	Representatives of the Bengal Committee of the Communist Party of India.	2-9-1944
53. Mr. Somnath Lahiri . .		
54. Mr. Bhupesh Gupta . .		
55. Mr. Bankim Mukherjee .	Representatives of the Bengal Provincial Kisan Sabha.	2-9-1944
56. Mr. Krishna Binode Roy .		
57. Mr. B. Guha . . .		
58. Mr. Promode Sen . . .	Representative of the Bolshevik Party of India.	2-9-1944
59. Mr. K. N. Gutgutia . .	Representatives of the Marwari Chamber of Commerce.	4-9-1944
60. Mr. C. M. Saraff . . .		
61. Mr. M. L. Khemka . .		
62. Mr. B. D. Tharad . .		
63. Mr. J. K. Mitter . . .	Representatives of the Bengal National Chamber of Commerce.	4-9-1944
64. Mr. B. C. Ghosh . . .		
65. Mr. S. R. Biswas . . .		
66. Mr. D. P. Khaitan . .	Representatives of the Indian Chamber of Commerce.	4-9-1944
67. Mr. G. L. Mehta . . .		
68. Mr. R. L. Nopany . .		
69. Mr. Abdur Rahman Siddiqi, M.L.A.	Representative of the Muslim Chamber of Commerce.	4-9-1944
70. Mr. Manoranjan Chaudhuri	Representatives of the Bengal Provincial Hindu Mahasabha.	5-9-1944
71. Prof. Haricharan Ghosh .		
72. Rai Bahadur C. L. Roy .	Representatives of the Indian Association .	5-9-1944
73. Rai Bahadur B. B. Mukherjee		
74. M . J. M. Datta . . .		
75. Mr. K. C. Neogy . . .		
76. Mr. P. N. Singh Roy . .	Representative of the British Indian Association.	5-9-1944
77. Dr. Sachin Sen, Ph. D. . .		
78. Kumar B. C. Sinha . .		
79. Kumar J. C. Sinha . .		
80. Khan Bahadur Jasimuddin, M.L.A.	Representatives of the Bengal District Boards Association.	6-9-1944
81. Khan Bahadur Nurul Amin .		
82. Rai Bahadur Debendra Mohan Bhattacharya.		
83. Mr. R. E. Russell, C.S.I., C.I.E , I.C.S.	Adviser to H. E. the Governor of Bihar .	7-9-1944
84. Mr. R. A. E. Williams, I.C.S. .	Formerly Secretary to the Government of Bihar, Revenue and Commerce Department.	7-9-1944
85 Mr. J. S. Wilcock, O.B.E., . I.C.S.	Secretary, Supply and Price Control Department, Bihar.	
86. Mr. A. P. Cliff, I.A.S. . .	Director of Agriculture, Bihar.	
87. Mr. C. S. Jha, I.C.S. . .	Secretary, Department of Supply and Transport, Provincial Controller of Supply and Transport and Director of Food Supplies, Orissa.	8-9-1944
88. Mr. H. Lal, I.C.S. . . .	Director, Development, Orissa.	
89. Lt. Col. A. N. Chopra, M.B. B.S., D.T.M. (Liv.), D.P.H. (Eng.), I.M.S.	Director of Public Health and Inspector General of Prisons, Orissa.	
90. Rai Sahib Nihar Chandra Chakravarty.	Additional Assistant Secretary, Department of Agriculture, Bengal.	8-9-1944
91. Mr. B. K. Guha, I.C.S. . .	Additional District and Sessions Judge, 24-Parganas (Formerly Relief Co-ordination Officer, Calcutta).	8-9-1944

No.	Name	Designation	Date
92.	The Hon'ble Mr. T. N. Mukherjee.	Minister, Bengal (Revenue)	9-9-1944
93.	Mr. S. Banerjee, I.C.S.	Secretary, Revenue Department, Bengal	9-9-1944
94.	Rai N. C. Sen Bahadur, O.B.E.	Additional Controller of Rationing, Calcutta.	9-9-1944
95.	Rai U. N. Ghosh Bahadur	Special Officer, Finance Department, Bengal.	
96.	Mr. D. C. Dutt	Special Officer, Rent Drive, Board of Revenue.	
97.	Mr. K. D. Jalan	Representatives of the Marwari Relief Society, Bengal.	11-9-1944
98.	Mr. R. N. Bhojanagarwala		
99.	Prof. K. P. Chattopadhyaya	Representatives of the People's Relief Committee.	11-9-1944
100.	Mr. Panchu Gopal Bhadury		
101.	Mr. K. C. Roy Chowdhury	Representatives of the Bosepukur Relief Committee.	11-9-1944
102.	Babu Natabar Pal		
103.	Mr. S. M. Osman	Representatives of the Muslim Relief Committee.	11-9-1944
104.	Mr. M. S. Vawda		
105.	Mr. T. G. Davies	Representative of the Friends' Ambulance Unit.	11-9-1944
106.	Dr. K. P. Mukherjee	Representatives of the Bengal Public Health Association.	11-9-1944
107.	Mr. P. C. Bhattacharyya		
108.	Mr. K. Chawdhury		
109.	Dr. Shyamaprasad Mookerjee	Formerly Minister, Bengal (Finance)	12-9-1944
110.	Mr. S. C. Sawoo	Representatives of the Bengal Rice Mills Association.	12-9-1944
111.	Mr. C. K. Ghose		
112.	Mr. L. N. Hazra		
113.	Mr. M. K. Kirpalani, I.C.S.	Secretary, Department of Commerce, Labour & Industries, Bengal.	12-9-1944
114.	Major General D. Stuart, C.I.E., O.B.E.	Headquarters, 303 L of C Area	13-9-1944
115.	Prof. P. C. Mahalanobis B.Sc. (Cal.) M.A. (Cantab.) F.S.S. F.N.I., O.B.E., I.E.S.	Hony. Secretary, Indian Statistical Institute, Statistical Laboratory, Calcutta.	13-9-1944
116.	Mr. M. Barman	Representatives of the Calcutta Corporation	13-9-1944
117.	Dr. M. U. Ahmad		
118.	Mr. S. Lahiri		
119.	Mr. K. C. Ghosh		
120.	Mrs. Renu Chakravarty	Representatives of the All Bengal Mahila Atma Raksha Samity.	14-9-1944
121.	Mrs. Ela Reid		
122.	Mrs. Saudamini Mehta	Representatives of the All India Women's Conference (Relief Committee).	14-9-1944
123.	Dr. (Mrs.) Maitreyee Bose		
124.	Mrs. S. C. Roy		
125.	Mrs. Ayesha Ahmad		
126.	Mr. J. K. Biswas, M.A., J.P.	Representative of the Rotary Club	14-9-1944
127.	Mr. V. N. Rajan, I.C.S.	Deputy Controller of Distribution, Department of Civil Supplies, Bengal.	15-9 1944
128.	Mr. W. A. S. Lewis, O.B.E., I.C.S.	Controller of Procurement (Formerly Dy. Director, Department of Civil Supplies, Bengal).	15-9-1944
129.	Mr. Hanumanbux Biswanath	Shellac and Produce Merchant, Calcutta	15-9-1944
130.	Mr. S. K. Chatterjee, M.B.E., I.C.S.	Dy. Director of Civil Supplies, Region VI Dacca.	15-9-1944
131.	Khan Bahadur Maulvi Chowdhury Afsar Ali.	Registrar of Co-operative Societies, Bengal	15-9-1944
132.	Mr. Ashutosh Bhattacharyya	Rice Merchant and Agent to the Government of Bengal.	16-9-1944
133.	Mr. Hamidul Haq Chowdhury	Representative of the Bengal Provincial Muslim League.	16-9-1944
134.	Mr. N. R. Sarker	Formerly Member, Executive Council of the Governor General.	16-9-1944
135.	The Hon'ble Khwaja Sir Nazimuddin, K.C.I.E.	Chief Minister, Bengal.	16-9-1944
136.	Sir John Burder	Representatives of the Bengal Chamber of Commerce.	18-9-1944
137.	Mr. F. C. Guthrie		
138.	Mr. R. H. D. Campbell		
139.	Mr. D. C. Fairbairn		
140.	Mr. P. C. Chowdhury	Representatives of Messrs. Shaw Wallace & Co., Agents for the Bengal Chamber's Foodstuffs' Scheme.	18-9-1944
	Mr. R. H. D. Campbell		
141.	Mr. C. S. Rangaswami	Representatives of the Calcutta Relief Committee.	19-9-1944
142.	Mr. Jnananjan Niyogi		

No.	Name	Designation	Date
143.	Rai Dr. S. L. Hora Bahadur D.Sc., F.R.S.E., F.R.A.S.B., F.Z.S., F.L.S., F.N.I.	Director of Fisheries, Bengal	19-9-1944
144.	Mr. M. A. H. Ispahani	Representatives of the Muslim Chamber of Commerce & Relief Committee.	19-9-1944
145.	Khan Bahadur G. A. Dossani		
146.	Mr. C. J. Minister	D. I. G., C. I. D., Bengal	20-9-1944
147.	Mr. M. M. Stuart, O.B.E., I.C.S.	Collector of Chittagong	20-9-1944
148.	Major General F. H. Skinner, O.B.E.	Headquarters E. C. No. 12, A. B. P. O.	22-9-1944
149.	Mr. F. A. Karim, I.C.S.	District Magistrate, Faridpur	22-9-1944
		BOMBAY.	
150.	Mr. A. D. Gorwalla, C.I.E., I.C.S., J. P.	Supply Commissioner, Government of Bombay.	28-9-1944
151.	Mr. D. S. Bakhle, O.B.E., I.C.S., J. P.	Director of Civil Supplies, Bombay	
152.	Mr. J. Booth, I.C.S.	Director of Civil Supplies, Districts	
153.	Mr. R. N. Samarth, M.B.E.	Controller of Rationing, Bombay	
154.	Mr. G. L. Sheth, I.C.S.	Grains Purchasing Officer, Thana & Colaba and B.S.D. and Deputy Controller of Rationing (in addition).	
155.	Mr. Sankpal	Statistician	
156.	Mr. M. J. Desai, I.C.S., J. P.	Secretary, Revenue Department, Bombay	29-9-1944
157.	Mr. W. J. Jenkins, C.I.E., I.A.S.	Director of Agriculture, Bombay	
158.	Mr. A. V. Thakkar, (Vice-President.)	Representatives of the Servants of India Society.	29-9-1944
159.	Mr. Dinkar D. Desai		
160.	Sir Henry Knight, K.C.S.I., C.S.I., C.I.E., I.C.S., J. P.	Adviser to His Excellency the Governor of Bombay.	30-9-1944
161.	Mr. C. N. Vakil	Representatives of the School of Economics & Sociology, University of Bombay, Bombay.	30-9-1944
162.	Mr. J. J. Anjaria		
163.	Mr. N. N. Wadia	Members of the Standing Committee of Food Advisory Council, Bombay.	2-10-1944
164.	Mr. S. C. Joshi, M.A., LL.B., M.Litt.		
165.	Mr. M. V. Rajab		
166.	Rao Bahadur J. N. Mankar	Secretary, Bombay Humanianiat League	2-10-1944
167.	Prof. D. R. Gadgil, M.A., M.Litt.	Director, Gokhale Institute of Politics & Economics, Servants of India Society Home, Poona.	2-10-1944
168.	Dr. K. A. Gandhi, M.B. B.S., D.P.H., D.T.M. & H., J.P.	Director of Public Health, Bombay	3-10-1944 (Dr. T. B. Patel again at Bijapur on 5-10-1944
169.	Dr. T. B. Patel, M.B., B.S., D.P.H.	District Health Officer, Bijapur	
170.	Sir William Stampe, C.I.E.	Irrigation Adviser to the Government of India, E., H. & L. Department.	3-10-1944
171.	Mr. G. F. S. Collins, C.S.I., C.I.E., O.B.E., I.C.S., J. P.	Adviser (Revenue) to His Excellency the Governor of Bombay.	3-10-1944
172.	Mr. Aziz Ghafoor Kazi, M.L.A., J.P.	Representatives of the Provincial Muslim League, Bombay.	3-10-1944
173.	Mr. I. I. Chundrigar (President)		
174.	Mr. A. K. Sheikh		
175.	Mr. Habib Ibrahim Rahimtoola, (President).	Representatives of the Bombay Muslim Chamber of Commerce.	3-10-1944
176.	Mr. Ghulamhussain Sonawala (Vice-President).		
177.	Mr. M. M. Killedar (Vice-President).		
178.	Mr. Sikander Khan Dehlavi (Secretary).		
		BIJAPUR	
179.	Mr. V. N. Sausman	Land Development Officer, Bijapur	5-10-1944
180.	Mr. S. B. Desai, M.L.A.	Bijapur	5-10-1944
181.	Diwan Bahadur Sardar Deshmukh.	President, District Local Board, Bijapur	5-10-1944

182.	Mr. S. T. Patil	....	5-10-1944
183.	Mr. I. T. Almaula, B.A., LL.B.	Collector of Bijapur	5-10-1944
184.	Mr. H. S. Kaujalgi, B.A., LL.B.	Joint Secretary, Famine Relief Committee, Bombay.	6-10-1944

MADRAS

185.	Mr. A. F. W. Dixon, C.I.E., I.C.S.	Acting Commissioner of Civil Supplies, Madras.	9-10-1944 and 10-10-1944
186.	Rao Sahib M. A. Kuttalalingam Pillai.	Deputy Commissioner of Civil Supplies	9-10-1944 (Madras) 24-10-1944 (Tanjore) & 26-10-1944 (Bezwada)
187.	Rao Bahadur P. V. Subba Rao	Deputy Commissioner of Civil Supplies	9-10-1944 and 10-10-1944
188.	Mr. W. Scott Brown, C.S.I., C.I.E., I.C.S.	Commissioner of Civil Supplies (on leave)	9-10-1944
189.	Sir Purushotamdas Thakurdas, C.I.E., M.B.E.	....	9-10-1944
190.	Mr. C. E. Wood, C.I.E., I.C.S.	Members of the Board of Revenue, Government of Madras.	10-10-1944
191.	Mr. A. R. C. Westlake, C.I.E., I.C.S.		
192.	Dr. R. M. Mathew, M.B.B.S., D.P.H., D.T.M. & H., M.R.C.P.	Director of Public Health, Madras	10-10-1944
193.	Rao Bahadur Dr. B. Viswanath, C.I.E., D.Sc., F.I.C.	Director of Agriculture, Madras	10-10-1944
194.	Janab Abdul Hamid Khan	Members of the Provincial Food Council, Madras.	11-10-1944
195.	Sir P. T. Rajan		
196.	Mr. R. Suryanarayana Rao	Honorary Secretary, People's Food Committee, Madras.	11-10-1944
197.	Sir Hugh Hood, K.C.I.E., C.S.I., I.C.S.	First Adviser to His Excellency the Governor of Madras.	11-10-1944
198.	Mr. H. S. Town	Representative of the Madras Electric Supply Corporation Ltd., Madras Tramway (1904) Ltd., M/s. Binny & Co., The Buckingham Carnatic Co., Ltd., and the Bangalore Woollen Cotton & Silk Mills Ltd.	12-10-1944
199.	Mr. C. Nageswara Row	Joint Secretary of the Rayalaseema Famine Relief Fund, Bombay.	12-10-1944
200.	Mr. A. Khaleeli, I.C.S.	Director of Industries and Commerce, Madras.	12-10-1944
201.	Mr. K. Govindan	Representatives of the South Indian Chamber of Commerce.	12-10-1944
202.	Khan Bahadur Adam Hajee Mohamed Sait.		
203.	Mr. Yusuff Sait		
204.	Mr. C. M. Kothari (President)		
205.	Mr. P. Raghava Nair		
206.	Mr. G. Bapiraju Chaudhury		
207.	Sri Rao Bahadur Thyagaraja Mudaliar, M.A.	Land Lord, Tanjore	13-10-1944
208.	Mr. L. N. Sahu	Joint Secretary, Orissa Relief Committee	13-10-1944
209.	Sri B. Ramachandra Reddi, C.B.E.	Land Lord, Nellore	14-10-1944
210.	Rao Bahadur Govindaraja Ayyangar.	Chief Engineer (Irrigation), Madras	14-10-1944

CALICUT

211.	Mr. E. Kannan, M.L.A. (Madras).	Representative of the Scheduled Castes	16-10-1944
212.	Mr. Sankaran Nambiar	District Agricultural Officer, Calicut	16-10-1944
213.	Dr. K. Viswanath, L.M.S., D.T.M.	District Health Officer, Calicut	16-10-1944
214.	Rao Bahadur K. V. Suryanarayana Aiyer.	Public Prosecutor and Advocate, Member, Provincial Food Council, Madras.	16-10-1944

215. Mr. P. P. Hassan Koya	Advocate, Calicut	16-10-1944
216. Rao Sahib Dr. K. V. Nanukutty Nair, M.R.C.S. (Eng.), L.R.C.P. (Lond.).	Civil Surgeon and District Medical Officer, Calicut.	16-10-1944
217. Mr. V. R. Nayanar	Representative of the Servants of India Society, Calicut Branch.	16-10-1944

COCHIN

218. Sir George T. Boag, C.S.I., C.I.E., I.C.S.	Diwan of Cochin	
219. Sri Rama Varma Thampuran	Secretary to the Government of Cochin	18-10-1944
220. Rao Sahib M. M. Paul	Director of Food Supplies, Cochin	
221. Mr. V. K. R. Menon	Deputy Director of Food Supplies, Cochin	
222. Mr. T. K. Nair	Minister for Development, Cochin State	18-10-1944

TRAVANCORE

223. Sir C. P. Ramaswami Aiyar, K.C.S.I., K.C.I.E., LL.D.	Dewan of Travancore	20-10-1944
224. Mr. G. Parameswaran Pillai	Chief Secretary to the Government of Travancore.	20-10-1944 and 21-10-1944
225. Mr. K. R. Narayana Aiyar	Director of Food Supplies and Additional Secretary to the Government of Travancore.	20-10-1944 and 21-10-1944
226. Dr. C. O. Karunakaran	Superintendent, Public Health Laboratory, Travancore.	20-10-1944
227. Mr. L. Sankaranarayana Pillai	State Food Purchasing Officer	21-10-1944
228. Mr. Chattanda Karayalar 229. Mr. K. P. Amirthanatha Iyer 230. Mr. Sivathanu Pillai 231. Mr. T. Kumara Pillai 232. Mr. P. S. Muhamad 233. Mr. G. Narayana Iyer 234. Mr. D. Krishampotti 235. Mr. V. S. Krishna Pillai 236. Srimathi T. Narayani Ammal	Members of the Sri Mulam Assembly, Travancore.	21-10-1944

TANJORE

237. Mr. T. K. Sankaravadivelu Pillai.	Grain Purchase Officer, Tanjore	24-10-1944
238. Rao Sahib K. P. Krishnan Nair.	Collector, Ramnad District	
239. Diwan Bahadur V. N. Viswanatha Rao.	Collector, Tinnevelly District	
240. Khan Bahadur Md. Ismail	Collector, Tanjore District	24-10-1944
241. Mr. V. K. Krishnaswami Aiyar 242. Mr. Rajaratnam	Revenue Divisional Officers-in-charge of Development.	
243. Mr. Venkatachari	District Agricultural Officer, Tanjore	
244. Chief Rationing Officer, Tanjore.	....	

BEZWADA

245. Rao Sahib Charles John	Grain Purchase Officer, Bezwada	
246. Rao Sahib M. R. Bangara	Collector, Masulipatam	
247. Mr. A. G. Barson, I.C.S.	Sub Collector	
248. Mr. K. S. Patnaik	District Rationing Officer	
249. Rao Sahib V. Hanumanta Rao Nayudu.	Deputy Controller of Food Rationing	26-10-1944
250. Mr. Narasimhachari	District Agricultural Officer	
251. Mr. V. Sadasiva Rao	Rationing Officer for Bezwada Municipality	
252. Food Inspector	....	

NAGPUR

253. Sir Geoffrey Burton, K.C.I.E., I.C.S.	Adviser to His Excellency the Governor of the Central Provinces & Berar (Food and Finance).	27-10-1944 28-10-1944 30-10-1944 and 31-10-1944

No.	Name	Designation	Date
254.	Mr. P. G. Braye, C.I.E., I.C.S.	Commissioner, Berar Division	27-10-1944
255.	Maharaj Nagendra Singh, I.C.S.	Deputy Commissioner, Hoshangabad	28-10-1944
256.	Mr. S. H. Batliwala	Representatives of the Central Provinces Food Advisory Board.	28-10-1944
257.	Dewan Bahadur Sitacharan Dube.		
258.	Khan Bahadur M. E. R. Malak.		
259.	Rao Bahadur Dadu Dwarakanath Singh Seoni.		
260.	Mr. G. A. Gavai		
261.	Mr. V. D. Brahma		
262.	Khan Sahib Haji Ibrahimbhai		
263.	Rao Sahib Suganchan Rathi		
264.	Mr. S. G. Dandige		
265.	Mr. Ramjiwan Chowdhury	....	28-10-1944 and on 31-10-1944
266.	Mr. S. K. Wankhede	Representatives of the Central Provinces Malguzars Association.	28-10-1944
267.	Mr. Y. S. Athalye, B.A., LL.B. (Hony Secretary)		
268.	Mr. R. V. Kalikar		
269.	Mr. D. V. Deshmukh		
270.	Mr. G. R. Joshi		
271.	Rao Bahadur Moharikar	....	28-10-1944
272.	Khan Sahib Kerawala	Officers of the Government of C. P. & Berar	28-10-1944
273.	Mr. R. C. V. P. Neronha	Deputy Director of Food Supplies, Nagpur	28-10-1944
274.	Mr. R. H. Hill, I.A.S.	Director of Agriculture, C. P. & Berar	30-10-1944
275.	Dr. R. J. Kalamkar, Ph.D.	Officer on Special Duty, Department of Agriculture, C. P. & Berar.	30-10-1944
276.	Dr. R. L. Tuli, M.B.B.S., D.P.H., D.T.M., L.M.	Director of Public Health, C. P. & Berar	30-10-1944
277.	Mr. N. S. Krishnan	Representatives of the Controlled Shop Keepers' Association, Nagpur.	31-10-1944
278.	Mr. C. K. E. Naidu		
279.	Mr. Jiwaji Modgare		
280.	Mr. J. R. Dani		
281.	Seth Lalji Ghila Bhai	Raipur	31-10-1944
282.	Rao Bahadur Uttamrao Patil	Representative of the Rice Mills Association	31-10-1944
		....	31-10-1944
283.	Mr. H. S. Kamath, I.C.S.	Secretary, Government of C. P. & Berar (Food)	31-10-1944
284.	Mr. R. K. Patil	Representatives of Shetkari Sangh	31-10-1944
285.	Mr. Kolhe		

APPENDIX VIII

Extracts from papers relating to certain financial aspects of relief.

I

EXTRACT OF PARAGRAPH 29 OF MEMORANDUM FURNISHED TO THE COMMISSION BY THE REVENUE DEPARTMENT, BENGAL GOVERNMENT.

The Revenue Department, who were spending large amounts of money on relief, soon came to realise that relief during this year would be too costly for the Provincial Revenues to bear. They drew up a memorandum in consultation with the Civil Supplies and Finance Departments which was submitted to the Government of India towards the end of May. As the prospects of getting supplies were still fair and it was supposed that with a good *aus* harvest, it might be possible to meet the situation with an expenditure of the order of Rs. 7 crores of which Government of India were requested to bear a substantial share. The response received was however indefinite and not too reassuring. The department, therefore, went on sanctioning funds asked for by the Collectors for carrying on the relief on a large scale but in the normal manner provided by the Famine Manual. During the months of April, May and June the following funds were sanctioned for various kinds of relief to the different districts :—

(*a*) Agricultural loans—about Rs. 106 lakhs.

(*b*) Gratuitous relief—about Rs. 60 lakhs.

(*c*) Test relief—about Rs. 87 lakhs.

In the month of July agricultural operations were reported to be going on in all parts of the province on a large scale. The demand for labour had increased and this to some extent provided a precarious living for a large section of the people who had already been in distress. During this month therefore Government had to spend only about Rs. 26 lakhs for various kinds of relief.

II

Letter dated the 3rd January 1945, from Secretary to the Government of Bengal, Revenue Department, to Chairman, Famine Inquiry Commission.

Will you kindly refer to your Demi-official No. FC (N)/31-3 of the 24th December 1944 regarding paragraph 29 of this department's memorandum on the famine of 1943 and the measures taken in relation thereto ?

Relief work was neither held up nor slowed down at any time because of the lack of funds. As I explained personally before the Commission our real difficulty was in respect of supplies of foodstuff and not of money. At the same time I must admit that the absence of any assurance of substantial financial assistance from the Centre did make us more cautious in our planning of measures of relief than would have been the case if such an assurance had been forthcoming. The effect was wholly psychological. It did prevent us from launching upon more ambitious schemes of relief than those provided in the Famine Manual, for instance giving timely assistance to people in distress so that they might not have had to sell their lands, houses and other assets and also the provision of shelter and clothing on a much larger scale for those in need of them. The actual relief given was almost wholly in the form of test works, doles in cash or kind and loans under the Agriculturist's Loans Act as provided in the Famine Manual, which was not adequate for a widespread famine of extraordinary severity as that of 1943. All that we could do was to spend money on the kinds of relief mentioned above but on a very extensive scale.

We meant by the statement referred to in your letter that for want of any assurance of assistance from the Government of India we could not embark upon any abnormal measures of relief or set up a proper organisation for relief on a very large scale as required by the really abnormal situation in the country during that year, but no brake was actually put on at any time on account of inadequacy of funds. On the contrary you will find from paragraph 30 of our memorandum that there were even cases where some Collectors could not fully utilise the funds sanctioned for relief because of the absence of sufficient supplies.

III

Extract from Relief Commissioner's Note on Relief Operations in Bengal from 27th September 1943 to 29th February 1944.

"...complained to me that relief was curtailed in his area at the most critical stage of the operations, by order of Revenue Department....

IV

Letter No. 794-Misc., dated the 10th July 1943, from Additional Assistant Secretary, Government of Bengal, Revenue Department, to Collector of Midnapore.

Will you please refer to your Memo. No. 2712-R., dated the 8th July 1943 and the last portion of your Memo. No. 2674-R., dated the 5th July 1943 regarding the distribution of gratuitous relief and maintenance loans.

You ask for an additional allotment of Rs. 12,80,000 for distribution as gratuitous relief including Rs. 10 lakhs required for meeting the present demand of the Sub-Divisional Officer, Contai. It appears from your Memo. No. 2424 (3)-R., dated the 16th June 1943 that a sum of Rs. 10 lakhs was drawn under T. R. 27 only on 16th June 1943 for meeting the requirements of the Sub-Divisional Officer, Contai. It is not quite clear why the Sub-Divisional Officer came up with a proposal for a further allotment of Rs. 10 lakhs in the latter part of June as it is most unlikely that the amount of Rs. 10 lakhs drawn on 16th June 1943 could have been spent on gratuitous relief in cash within a short period of a week or so specially in view of the fact that a very large number of people were being engaged in test relief work throughout the month of June. The position may kindly be clarified.

2. It may be observed in this connection that due to various causes distress prevails in almost all the districts of the province and the problem of relieving the same has assumed such proportions that it is beyond the capacity of this Government to cope with the situation without the assistance from the Government of India. We, have, therefore, approached the Government of India for substantial assistance in money and foodgrains for this purpose and pending the decision of that Government it will not be possible to carry on relief measures in the cyclone affected areas of your district on the scale which was contemplated a few months ago. I am therefore to request you to see that relief is restricted to the essential minimum until the above matter is settled.

3. As regards your proposal regarding the distribution of maintenance loans to families who have between 1½ and 5 *bighas* of land. Could you kindly furnish Government with an approximate estimate of the number of families which will fall in this class so that it may be examined what is to be the likely outlay.

V

Copy of letter No. 480-F. R., dated the 21st March 1945, from Officiating Secretary to the Government of Bengal, Revenue Department, to Secretary, Famine Inquiry Commission.

Please refer to your Demi-official letter dated the 24th February,1945 addressed to..... The Government of Bengal generally agree with the views expressed in....'s Demi-official No. 7-F. R., dated the 3rd January 1945. They would, however, like to make the following further observations on the points which have been raised, as it appears that some misunderstanding exists with regard to the statement made in paragraph 29 of this Department's Memorandum submitted to the Commission.

While the Government of Bengal felt very uneasy at the heavy expenditure on relief measures and would have welcomed timely assurance of assistance from the Centre they tried their best not to slow down relief operations for lack of funds. Throughout the province gratuitous relief in the form of free food was given on a scale far in excess of that contemplated in the Famine Manual, owing to the futility of issuing money when food was scarce and not arriving from outside sources, and also owing to the impossibility of conducting large scale test relief works in the rains. Moreover fresh ground was broken by establishing free kitchens, food canteens and cheap grain shops, and distributing clothing. Mr........... 's Demi-official letter No. 94-Misc., dated the 10th July 1943, to the Collector of Midnapore was admittedly somewhat unhappily worded, but it should be interpreted in its historical background. After the devastating cyclone of 1942, affecting large areas in Midnapore and 24-Parganas, a comprehensive plan was drawn up not only for giving immediate relief to the distressed but also for restoring them to normal condition within a short space of time. All these measures were called relief measures and no distinction was made between the measures necessary for immediate relief and those aiming at ehabilitation. Mr........... 's Demi-official letter may be taken as reflecting some anxiety on the part of Government lest Midnapore expenditure, in view of the ambitious plans previously drawn up, might be excessive in the altered circumstances in comparison with the needs of other parts of the province—but the figures do not show that it caused any slowing down of relief operations proper. To demonstrate this a statement is enclosed showing the quarterly expenditure incurred on relief measures in Midnapore and 24-Parganas from October 1942 to December 1943. Both these districts suffered severely from the cyclone of 1942 though devastation was far more widespread and intense in Midnapore than in 24-Parganas. It will be seen from the figures that between October 1942 and June 1943 expenditure on Agricultural Loans and Gratuitous Relief in Midnapore was of the order of Rs. 1 crore and Rs. 1 crore 14 lakhs respectively; the corresponding expenditure in 24-Parganas during this period was Rs. 15 lakhs and 9 lakhs respectively. Therefore expenditure in Midnapore was about 9 times more on Agricultural Loans and 12 times more on Gratuitous Relief. In the following six months *i.e.* between July and December 1943, 23 lakhs were spent on Agricultural Loans in Midnapore and 1 crore on Gratuitous Relief while the figures for 24-Parganas for the corresponding period were Rs. 2 lakhs and 9½ lakhs respectively. There was thus no noticeable decline in relief operations in Midnapore as compared to 24-Parganas.

VI

A Statement showing the Expenditure on Relief Measures in Midnapore and 24-Parganas between October 1942 and December 1943.

Midnapore

(Area affected by the cyclone—3600 Sq. miles with a population of 2·3 millions.)

	Agricultural loans.	Gratuitous Relief.	Test works.
October to December 1942	19,00,000	24,28,000	5,05,000
January to March 1943	37,25,000	19,30,000	5,25,000
April to June 1943	44,00,000	69,80,000	62,48,900
July to September 1943	21,63,000	64,15,000	..
October to December 1943	1,50,000	38,28,000	..

24-Parganas.

(Area affected by the cyclone—400 Sq. miles with a population of 2 lakhs.)

	Agricultural loans.	Gratuitous Relief.	Test works.
October to December 1942	..	82,000	50,000
January to March 1943	4,60,000	3,03,500	50,000
April to June 1943	10,05,500	5,00,000	3,00,000
July to September 1943	1,05,000	2,95,000	..
October to December 1943	1,10,000	6,60,000	..